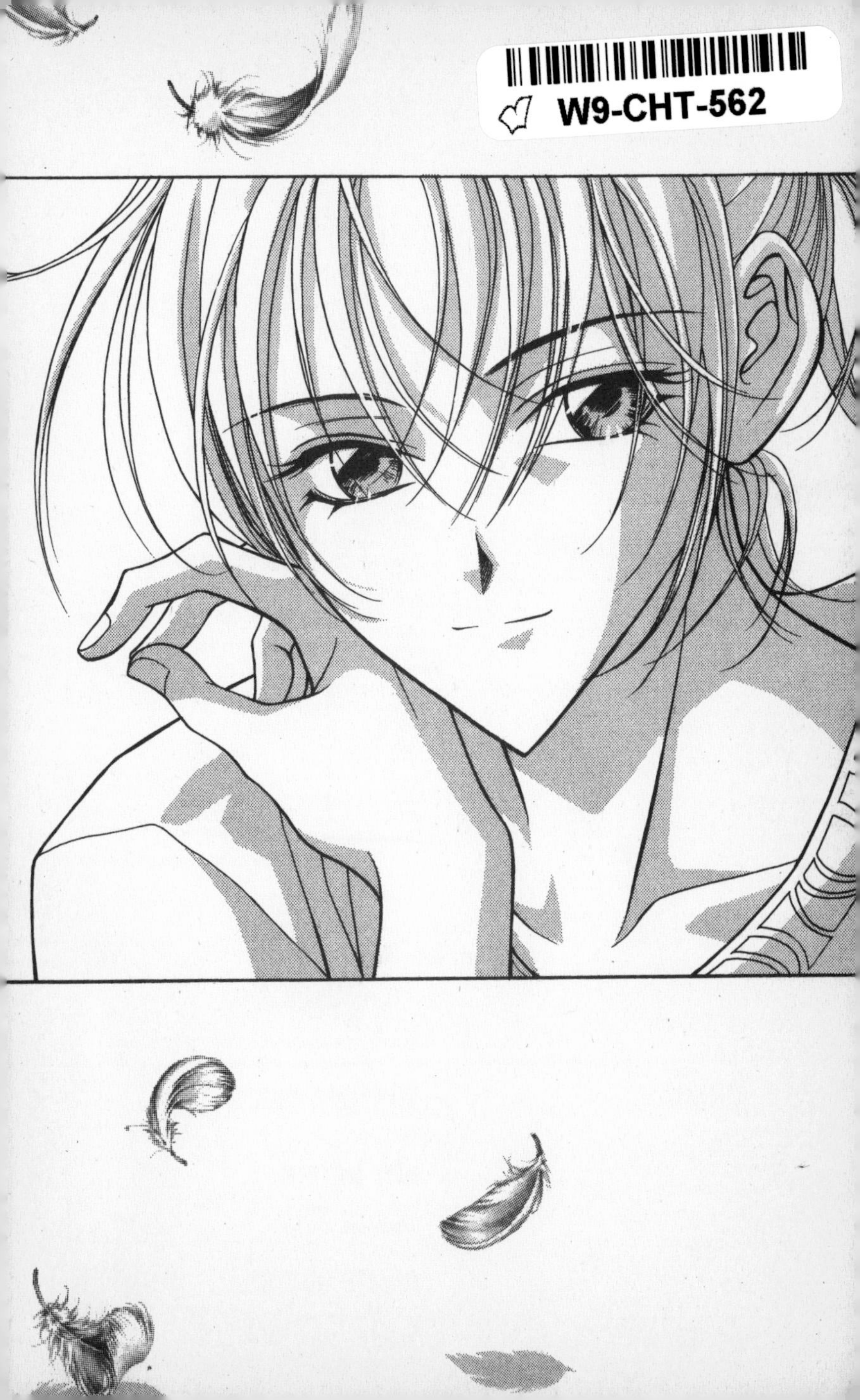

ALSO AVAILABLE FROM 🎬TOKYOPOP®

MANGA

.HACK//LEGEND OF THE TWILIGHT*
@LARGE (December 2003)
ANGELIC LAYER*
BABY BIRTH*
BATTLE ROYALE*
BRAIN POWERED*
BRIGADOON*
CARDCAPTOR SAKURA
CARDCAPTOR SAKURA: MASTER OF THE CLOW*
CHOBITS*
CHRONICLES OF THE CURSED SWORD
CLAMP SCHOOL DETECTIVES*
CLOVER
CONFIDENTIAL CONFESSIONS*
CORRECTOR YUI
COWBOY BEBOP*
COWBOY BEBOP: SHOOTING STAR*
CYBORG 009*
DEMON DIARY
DIGIMON*
DRAGON HUNTER
DRAGON KNIGHTS*
DUKLYON: CLAMP SCHOOL DEFENDERS*
ERICA SAKURAZAWA*
FAKE*
FLCL*
FORBIDDEN DANCE*
GATE KEEPERS*
G GUNDAM*
GRAVITATION*
GTO*
GUNDAM WING
GUNDAM WING: BATTLEFIELD OF PACIFISTS
GUNDAM WING: ENDLESS WALTZ*
GUNDAM WING: THE LAST OUTPOST*
HAPPY MANIA*
HARLEM BEAT
I.N.V.U.
INITIAL D*
ISLAND
JING: KING OF BANDITS*
JULINE
KARE KANO*
KINDAICHI CASE FILES, THE*
KING OF HELL
KODOCHA: SANA'S STAGE*
LOVE HINA*
LUPIN III*
MAGIC KNIGHT RAYEARTH*

MAGIC KNIGHT RAYEARTH II* (COMING SOON)
MAN OF MANY FACES*
MARMALADE BOY*
MARS*
MIRACLE GIRLS
MIYUKI-CHAN IN WONDERLAND*
MONSTERS, INC.
PARADISE KISS*
PARASYTE
PEACH GIRL
PEACH GIRL: CHANGE OF HEART*
PET SHOP OF HORRORS*
PLANET LADDER*
PLANETES*
PRIEST
RAGNAROK
RAVE MASTER*
REALITY CHECK
REBIRTH
REBOUND*
RISING STARS OF MANGA
SABER MARIONETTE J*
SAILOR MOON
SAINT TAIL
SAMURAI DEEPER KYO*
SAMURAI GIRL: REAL BOUT HIGH SCHOOL*
SCRYED*
SHAOLIN SISTERS*
SHIRAHIME-SYO: SNOW GODDESS TALES* (Dec. 2003)
SHUTTERBOX
SORCERER HUNTERS
THE SKULL MAN*
THE VISION OF ESCAFLOWNE*
TOKYO MEW MEW*
UNDER THE GLASS MOON
VAMPIRE GAME*
WILD ACT*
WISH*
WORLD OF HARTZ (November 2003)
X-DAY*
ZODIAC P.I. *

For more information visit www.TOKYOPOP.com

*INDICATES 100% AUTHENTIC MANGA (RIGHT-TO-LEFT FORMAT)

CINE-MANGA™

CARDCAPTORS
JACKIE CHAN ADVENTURES (November 2003)
JIMMY NEUTRON
KIM POSSIBLE
LIZZIE MCGUIRE
POWER RANGERS: NINJA STORM
SPONGEBOB SQUAREPANTS
SPY KIDS 2

NOVELS

KARMA CLUB (April 2004)
SAILOR MOON

TOKYOPOP KIDS

STRAY SHEEP

ART BOOKS

CARDCAPTOR SAKURA*
MAGIC KNIGHT RAYEARTH*

ANIME GUIDES

COWBOY BEBOP ANIME GUIDES
GUNDAM TECHNICAL MANUALS
SAILOR MOON SCOUT GUIDES

080503

DEMON DIARY

Translator - Lauren Na
English Adaptation - Kelly Sue DeConnick
Retouch and Lettering - Christina R. Siri
Cover Layout - Aaron Suhr
Graphic Designer - Deron Bennett

Editor - Rob Tokar
Managing Editor - Jill Freshney
Production Coordinator - Antonio DePietro
Production Managers - Jennifer Miller & Mutsumi Miyazaki
Art Director - Matt Alford
Editorial Director - Jeremy Ross
VP of Production - Ron Klamert
President & C.O.O. - John Parker
Publisher & C.E.O. - Stuart Levy

Email: editor@TOKYOPOP.com
Come visit us online at www.TOKYOPOP.com

A  **TOKYOPOP** Manga

TOKYOPOP Inc.
5900 Wilshire Blvd. Suite 2000
Los Angeles, CA 90036

Demon Diary Volume 4

MAWAN-ILGI 1 ©2000 by KARA. All rights reserved.
First published in KOREA in 2000 by SIGONGSA Co., Ltd.
English translation rights arranged by SIGONGSA Co., Ltd.

English text copyright ©2003 TOKYOPOP Inc.

ISBN: 1-59182-157-6

First TOKYOPOP printing: November 2003

10 9 8 7 6 5 4 3 2 1
Printed in the USA

DEMON DIARY

Art by Kara
Story by Lee Yun Hee

VOLUME 4

Los Angeles • Tokyo • London

Who's Who In Demon Diary

An orphan, Raenef had to join thieves at an early age in order to survive. Among the thieves, Raenef's kind, gentle, and somewhat ditzy nature made him stand out. Approached by Eclipse, Raenef was eager for a change from his life of stealing to eat. Unfortunately, Raenef's cheerful and kind-hearted qualities are even less desirable in a demon lord than they are in a thief. Though a poor student and a regular source of embarrassment for Eclipse, Raenef desperately wants to become the greatest demon lord ever.

Raenef

Eclipse

Eclipse is a demon of the highest order with an impressive resume. When the fourth Demon Lord Raenef died without designating an heir, Eclipse was charged with finding and mentoring Raenef the Fifth. Tall, dark, and mysterious, Eclipse is a wise and noble demon and his new pupil's ineptitude is a blow to Eclipse's prestige in the Demon Courts. Despite their differences, Eclipse finds himself strangely drawn to Raenef.

SENSING POWERFUL MAGIC COMING FROM RAENEF'S CASTLE, THE HUMAN KNIGHT ERUTIS INTENDED TO BUILD HER REPUTATION BY SLAYING THE DEMON LORD WITHIN. AT FIRST, SHE FOUND IT HARD TO TAKE RAENEF SERIOUSLY BUT, AFTER THE DEMON LORD-IN-TRAINING SHATTERED HER SWORD, ERUTIS SOON FOUND HERSELF OUTMATCHED. TO SAVE HER OWN LIFE, SHE CONVINCED RAENEF TO TAKE HER ON AS HIS HENCHMAN RATHER THAN KILLING HER. SINCE THEN, THEY HAVE BECOME CLOSE FRIENDS.

ERUTIS

THE SOLE SURVIVOR OF A DEMONIC ATTACK ON HIS HOMETOWN, CHRIS WAS RESCUED AND ADOPTED BY HEJEM, HIGH CLERIC OF THE NEARBY TEMPLE OF RASED. AS HEJEM'S DISCIPLE, CHRIS IS DESTINED TO BE THE TEMPLE'S NEXT HIGH CLERIC. THOUGH THE GOD RASED SUPPRESSED CHRIS' MEMORIES OF THE TRAUMATIC ATTACK, CHRIS HAS RETAINED AN INTENSE HATRED OF DEMONS. AGAINST HEJEM'S WISHES, CHRIS CREATED A DEMON SUMMONING SIGN AND CAPTURED RAENEF. THE SCUFFLE BETWEEN THE DEMON LORD-IN-TRAINING AND THE FUTURE HIGH CLERIC WAS BRIEF AND, AS AN APOLOGY (AND TO TEACH CHRIS HUMILITY), HEJEM SENT CHRIS TO LIVE WITH RAENEF FOR A SHORT TIME. DESPITE HIMSELF, CHRIS HAS DEVELOPED A FRIENDSHIP WITH RAENEF.

CHRIS

A FEMALE DEMON, MERUHESAE IS ALSO A POWERFUL SEER. WHEN ECLIPSE WAS ASSIGNED TO LOCATE RAENEF THE FIFTH, IT WAS MERUHESAE WHO POINTED THE DEMON IN THE RIGHT DIRECTION.

MERUHESAE

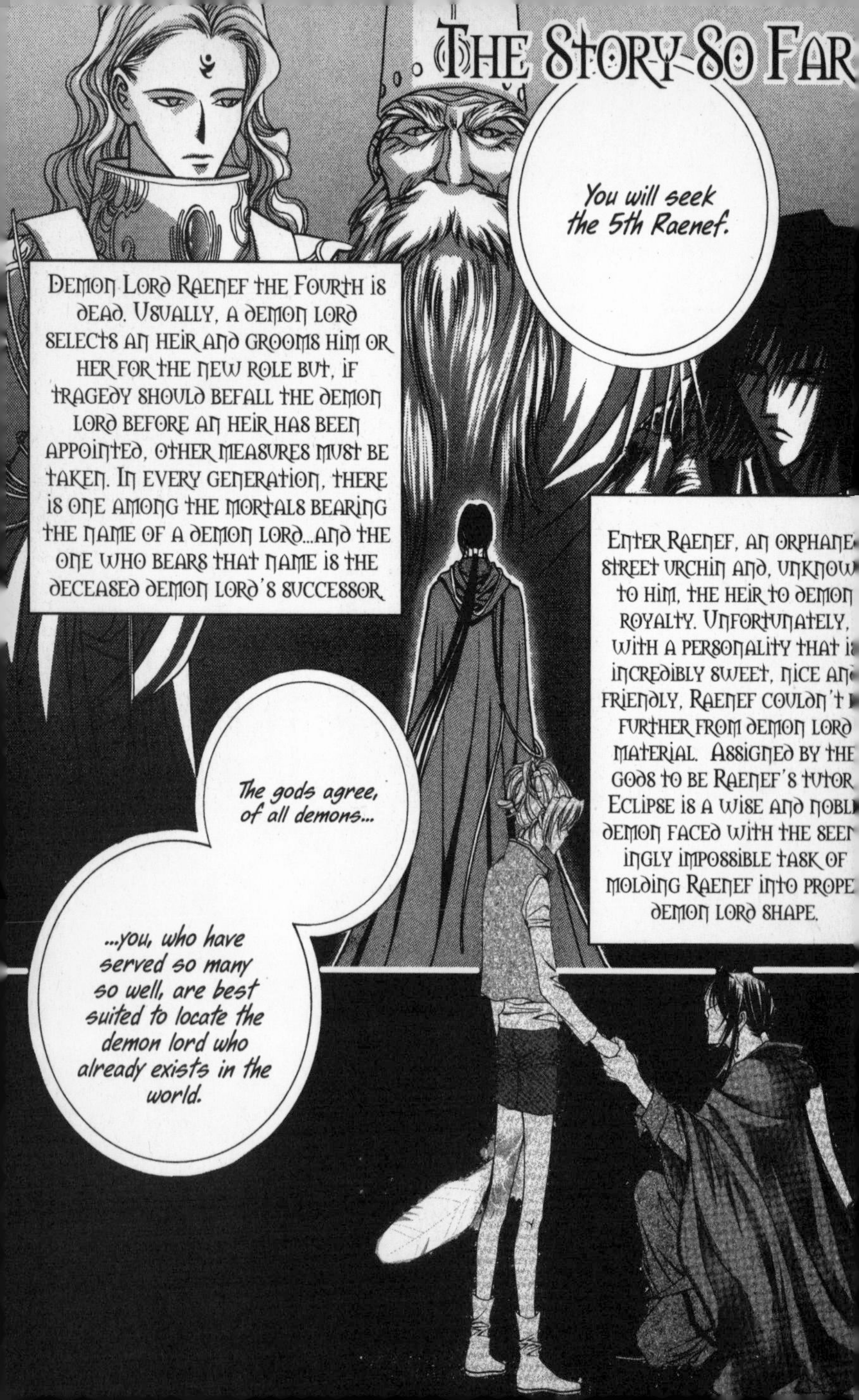
The Story So Far
You will seek the 5th Raenef.
Demon Lord Raenef the Fourth is dead. Usually, a demon lord selects an heir and grooms him or her for the new role but, if tragedy should befall the demon lord before an heir has been appointed, other measures must be taken. In every generation, there is one among the mortals bearing the name of a demon lord...and the one who bears that name is the deceased demon lord's successor.
Enter Raenef, an orphane street urchin and, unknow to him, the heir to demon royalty. Unfortunately, with a personality that i incredibly sweet, nice an friendly, Raenef couldn't further from demon lord material. Assigned by the gods to be Raenef's tutor Eclipse is a wise and nobl demon faced with the seem ingly impossible task of molding Raenef into prope demon lord shape.
The gods agree, of all demons...
...you, who have served so many so well, are best suited to locate the demon lord who already exists in the world.

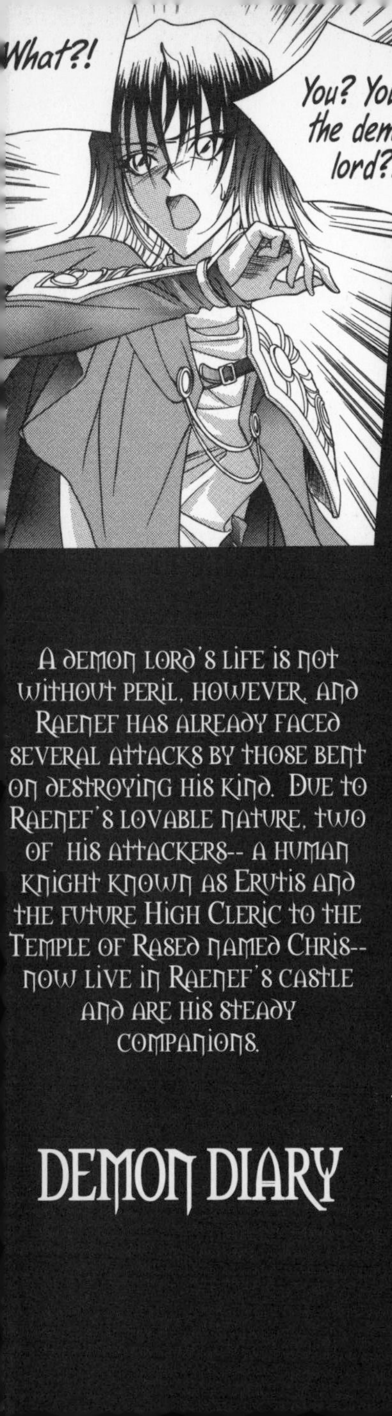
What?!
You? You're the demon lord?!

A demon lord's life is not without peril, however, and Raenef has already faced several attacks by those bent on destroying his kind. Due to Raenef's lovable nature, two of his attackers-- a human knight known as Erutis and the future High Cleric to the Temple of Rased named Chris-- now live in Raenef's castle and are his steady companions.

DEMON DIARY

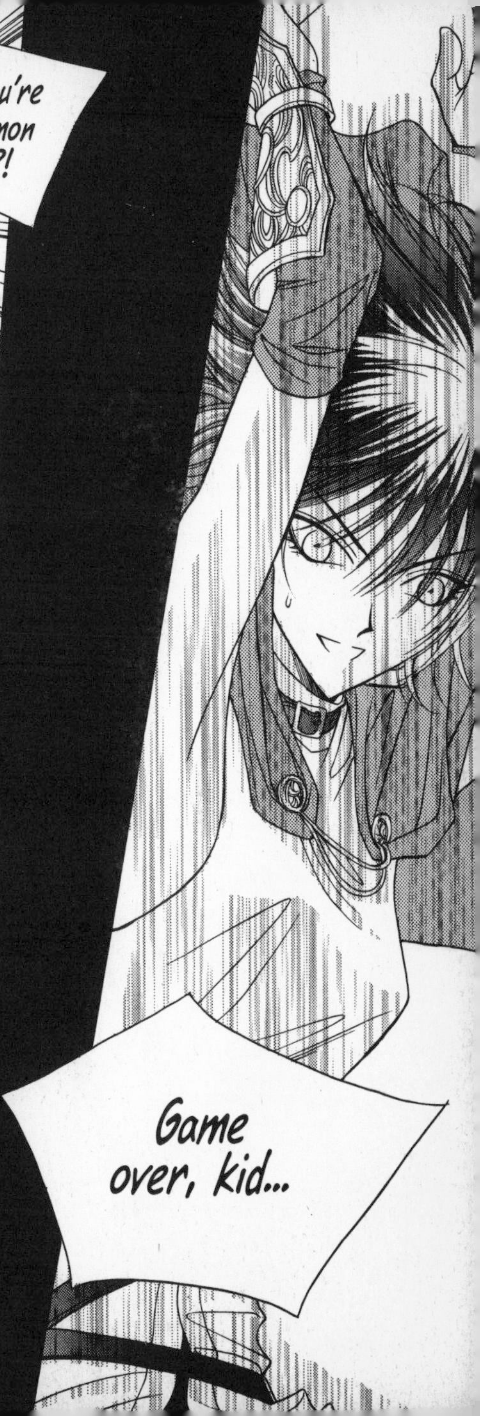
Game over, kid...

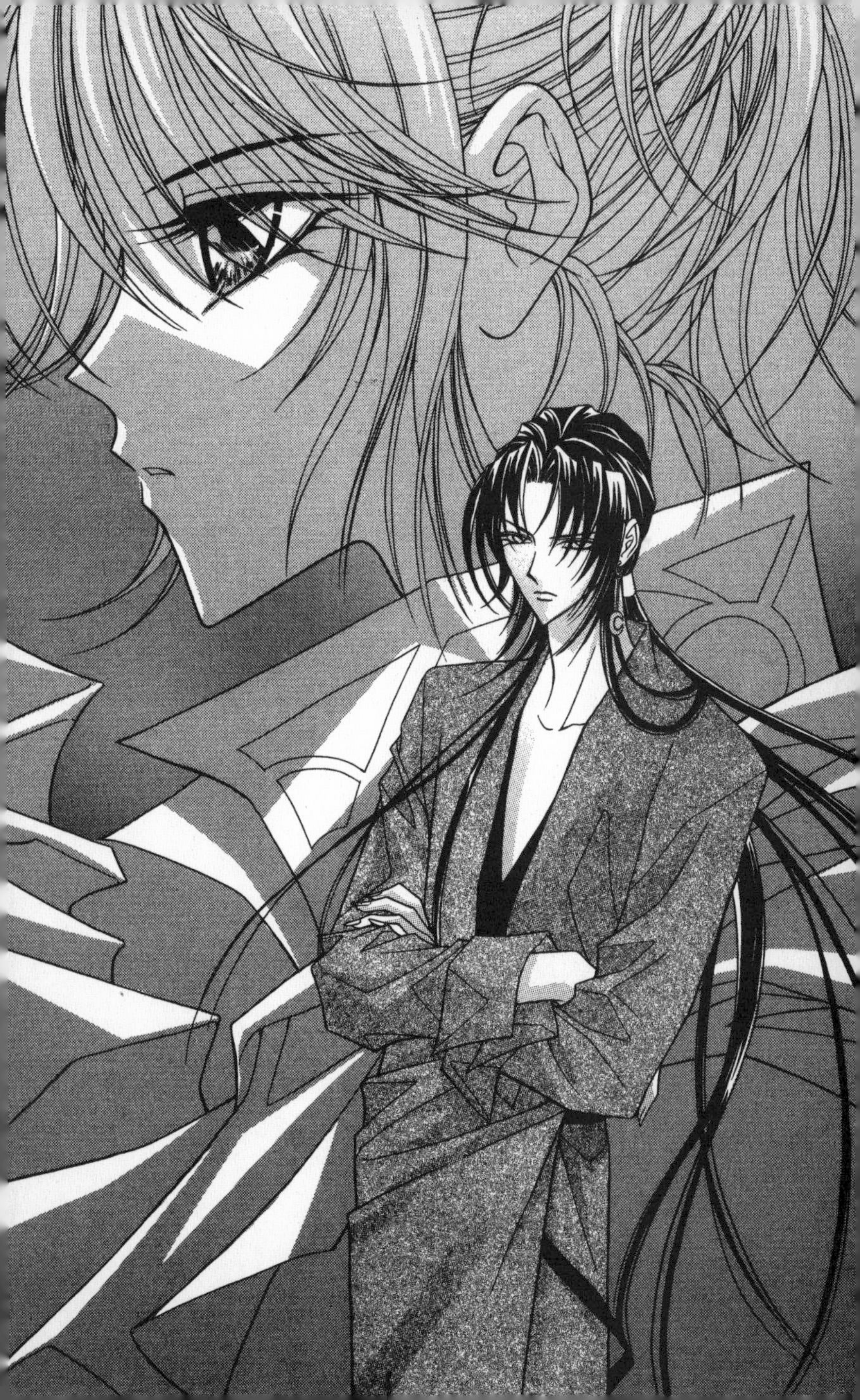

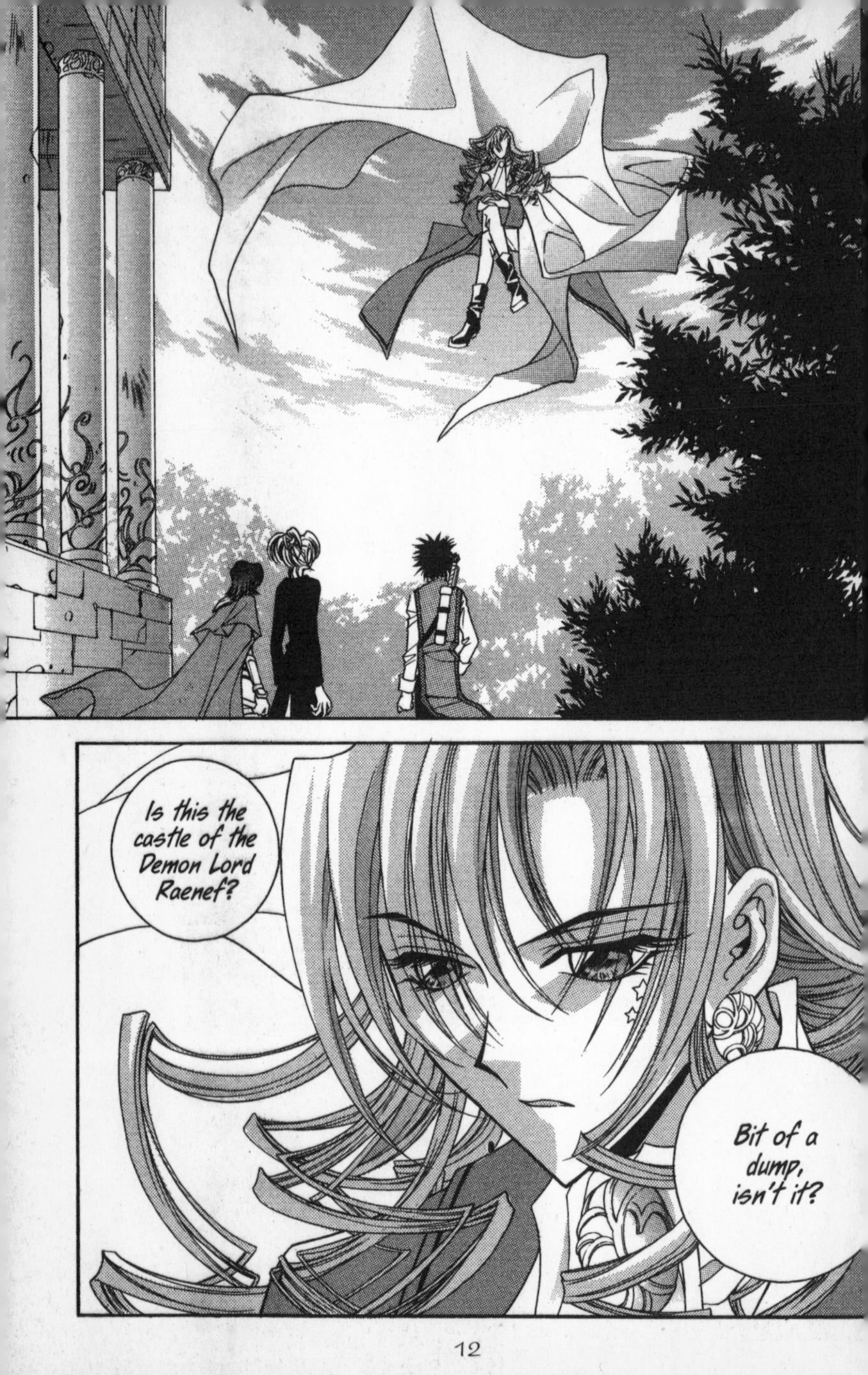
Is this the castle of the Demon Lord Raenef?
Bit of a dump, isn't it?

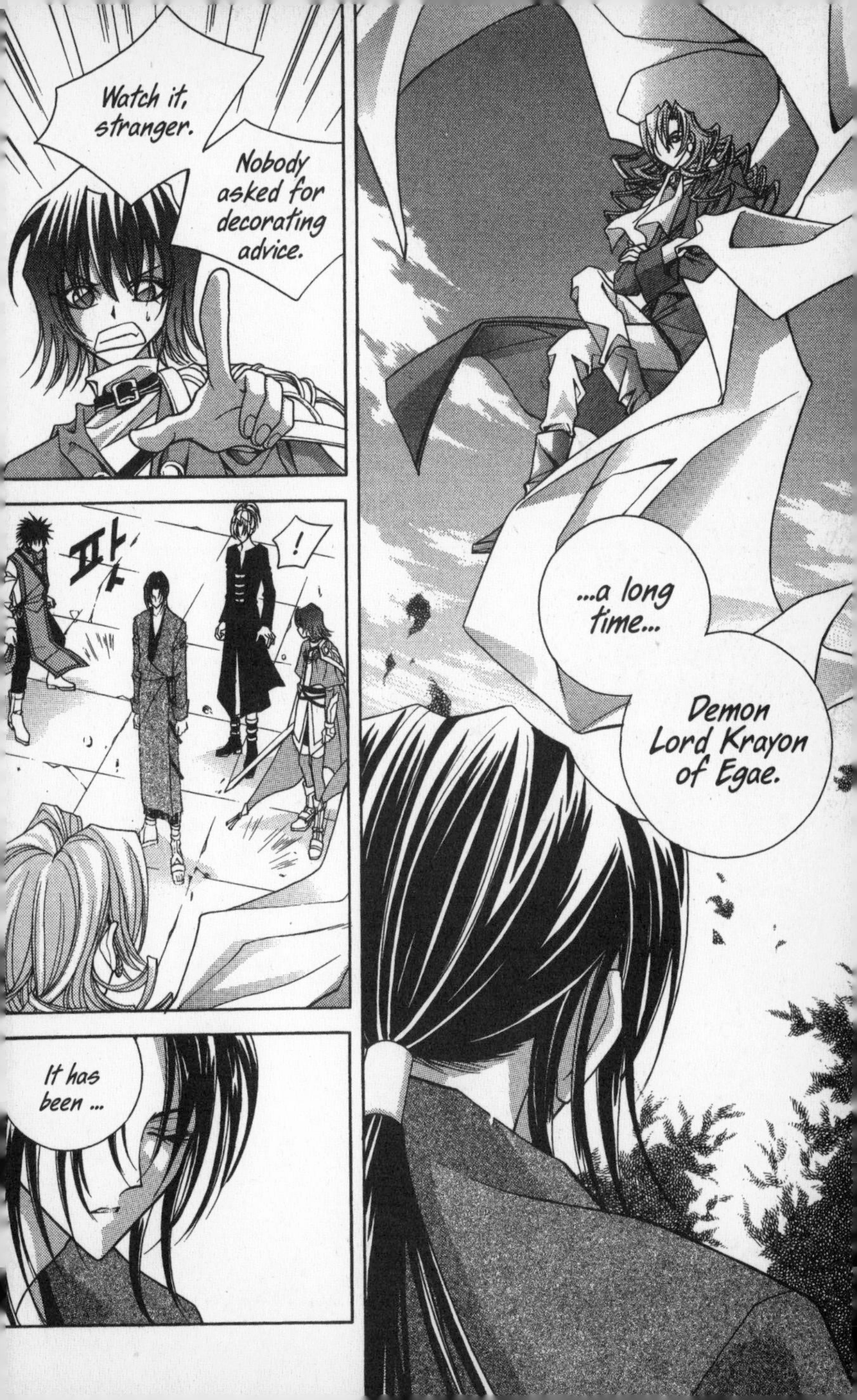
Watch it, stranger.
Nobody asked for decorating advice.
파
!
It has been ...
...a long time...
Demon Lord Krayon of Egae.

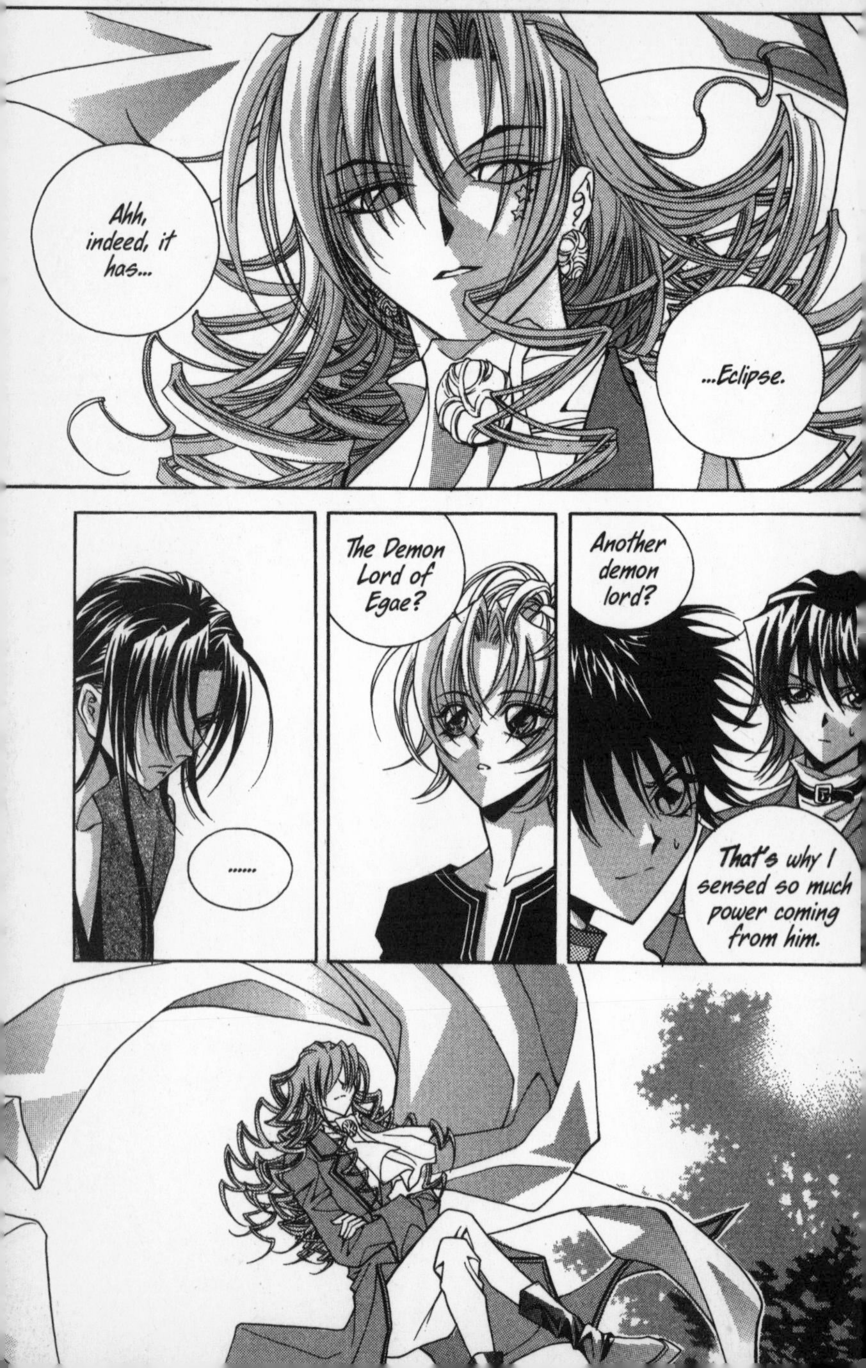
Ahh, indeed, it has...
...Eclipse.
Another demon lord?
That's why I sensed so much power coming from him.
The Demon Lord of Egae?
......

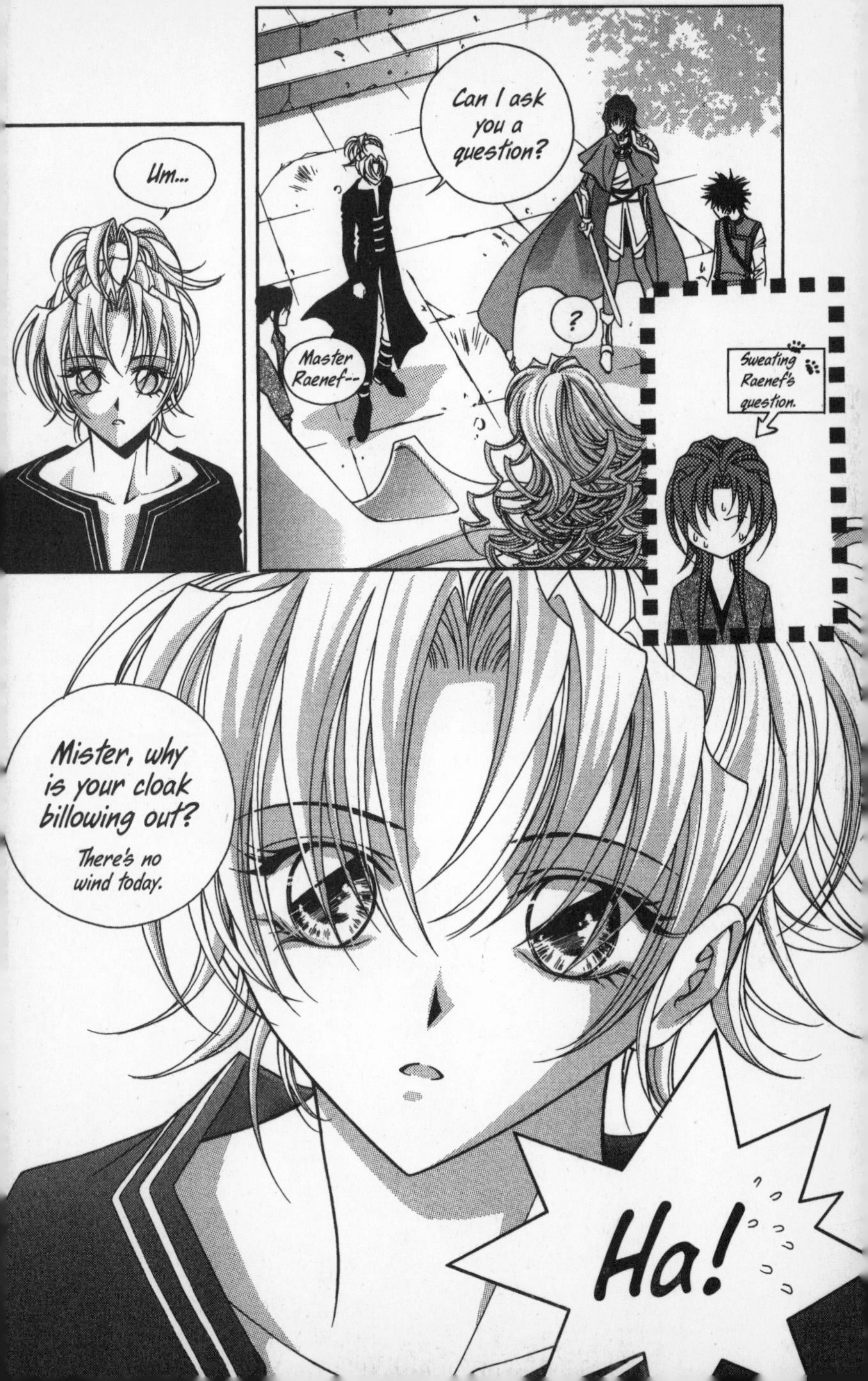
Um...
Can I ask you a question?
Master Raenef--
?
Sweating Raenef's question.
Mister, why is your cloak billowing out?
There's no wind today.
Ha!

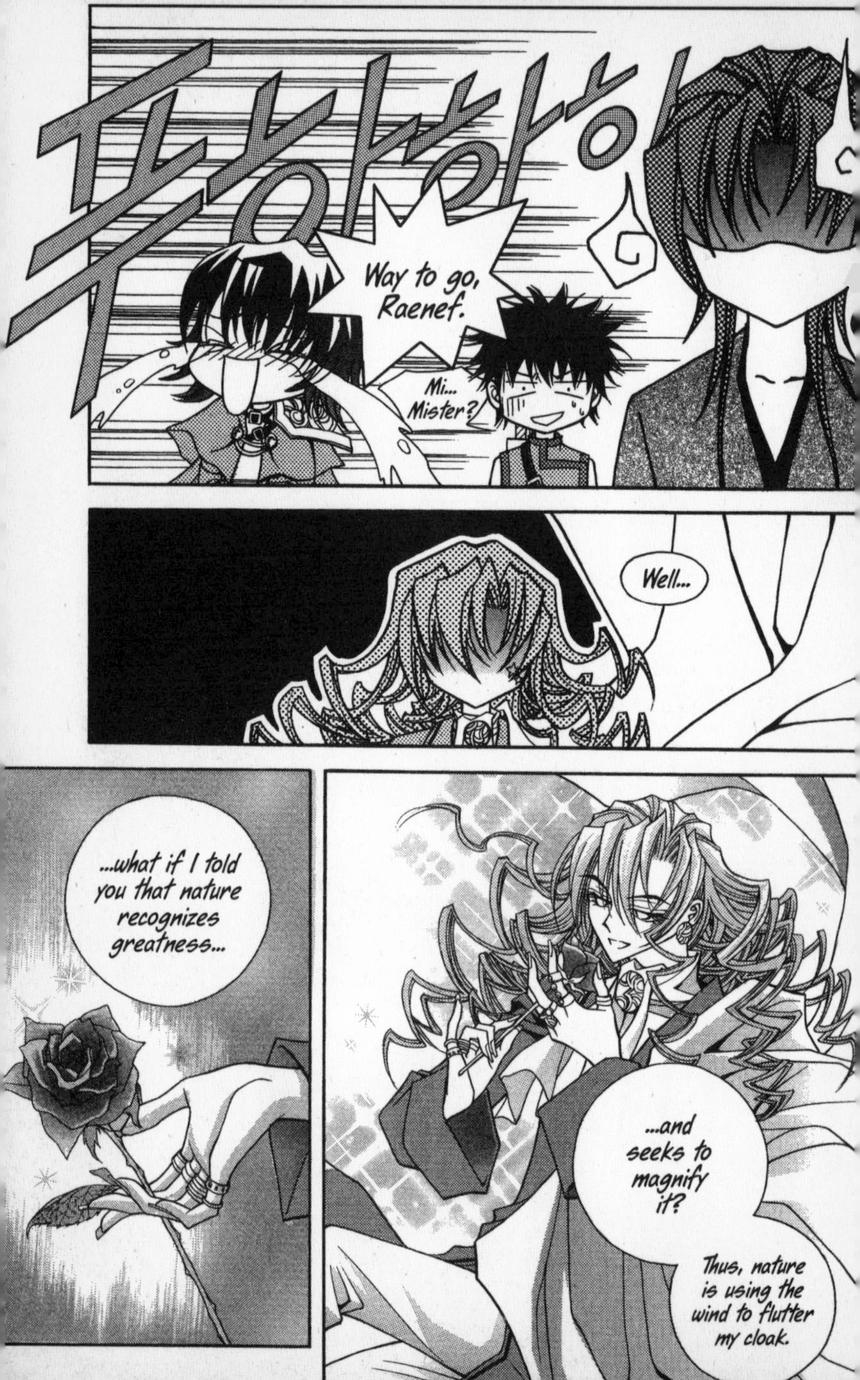
Way to go, Raenef.
Mi... Mister?
Well...
...what if I told you that nature recognizes greatness...
...and seeks to magnify it?
Thus, nature is using the wind to flutter my cloak.

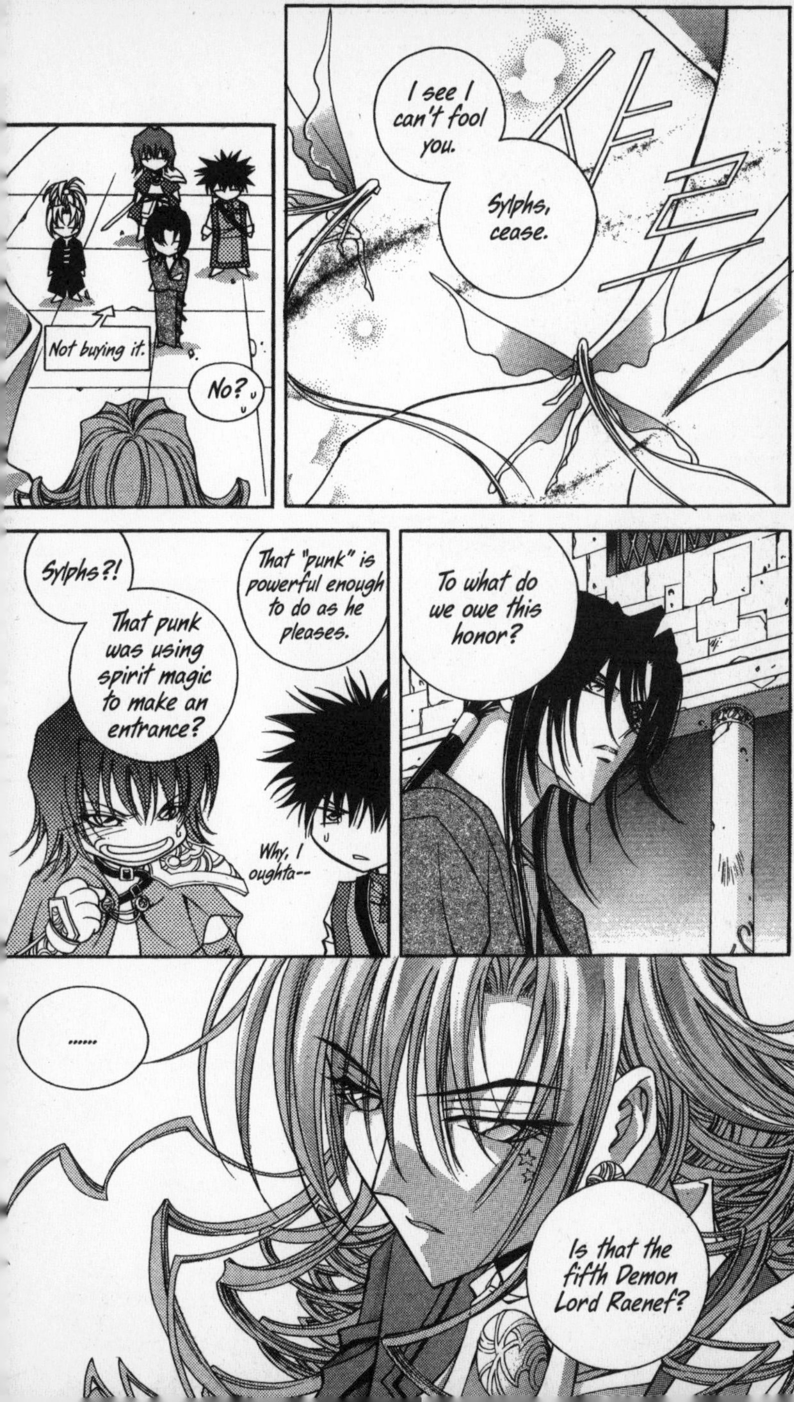
I see I can't fool you.
Sylphs, cease.
Not buying it.
No?
To what do we owe this honor?
Sylphs?!
That punk was using spirit magic to make an entrance?
That "punk" is powerful enough to do as he pleases.
Why, I oughta--
......
Is that the fifth Demon Lord Raenef?

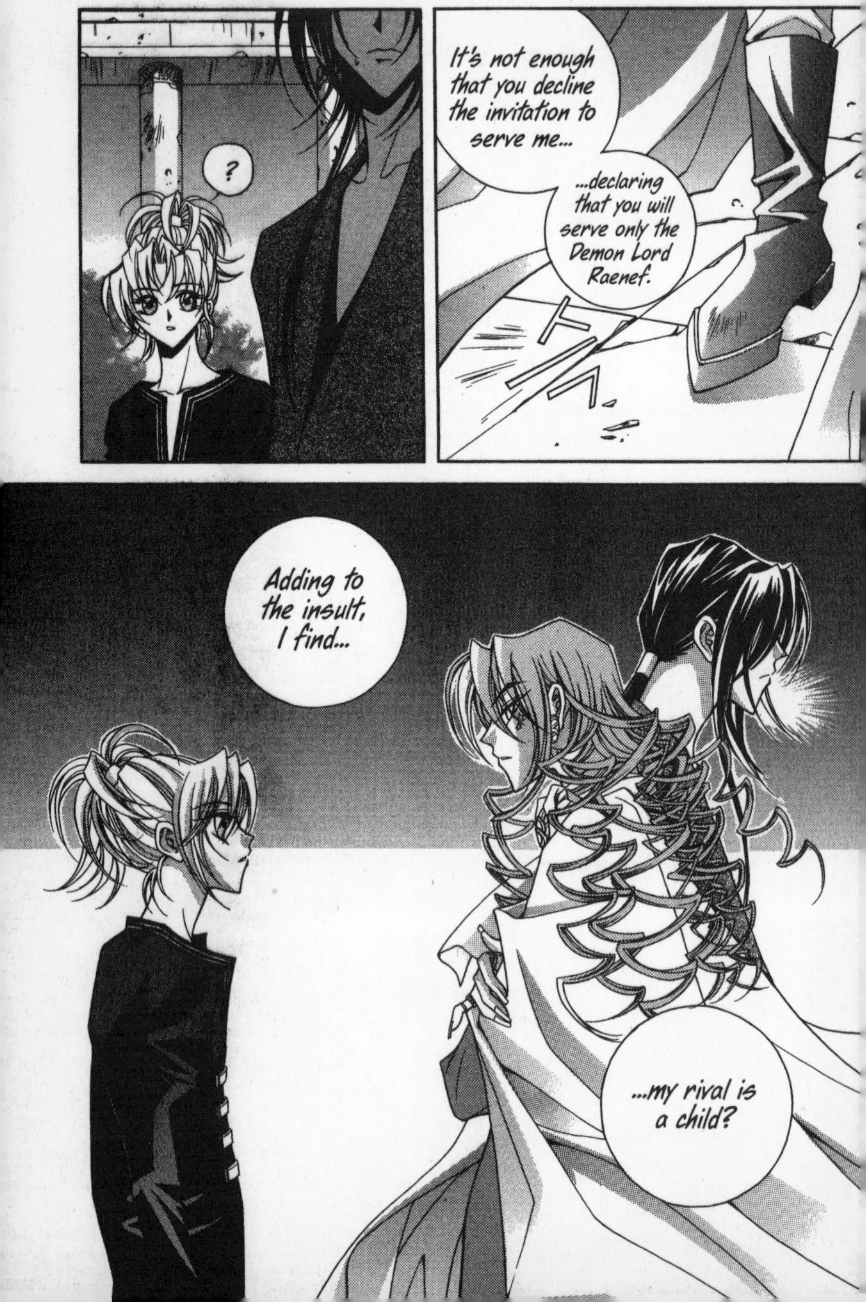
It's not enough that you decline the invitation to serve me...
...declaring that you will serve only the Demon Lord Raenef.
?
Adding to the insult, I find...
...my rival is a child?

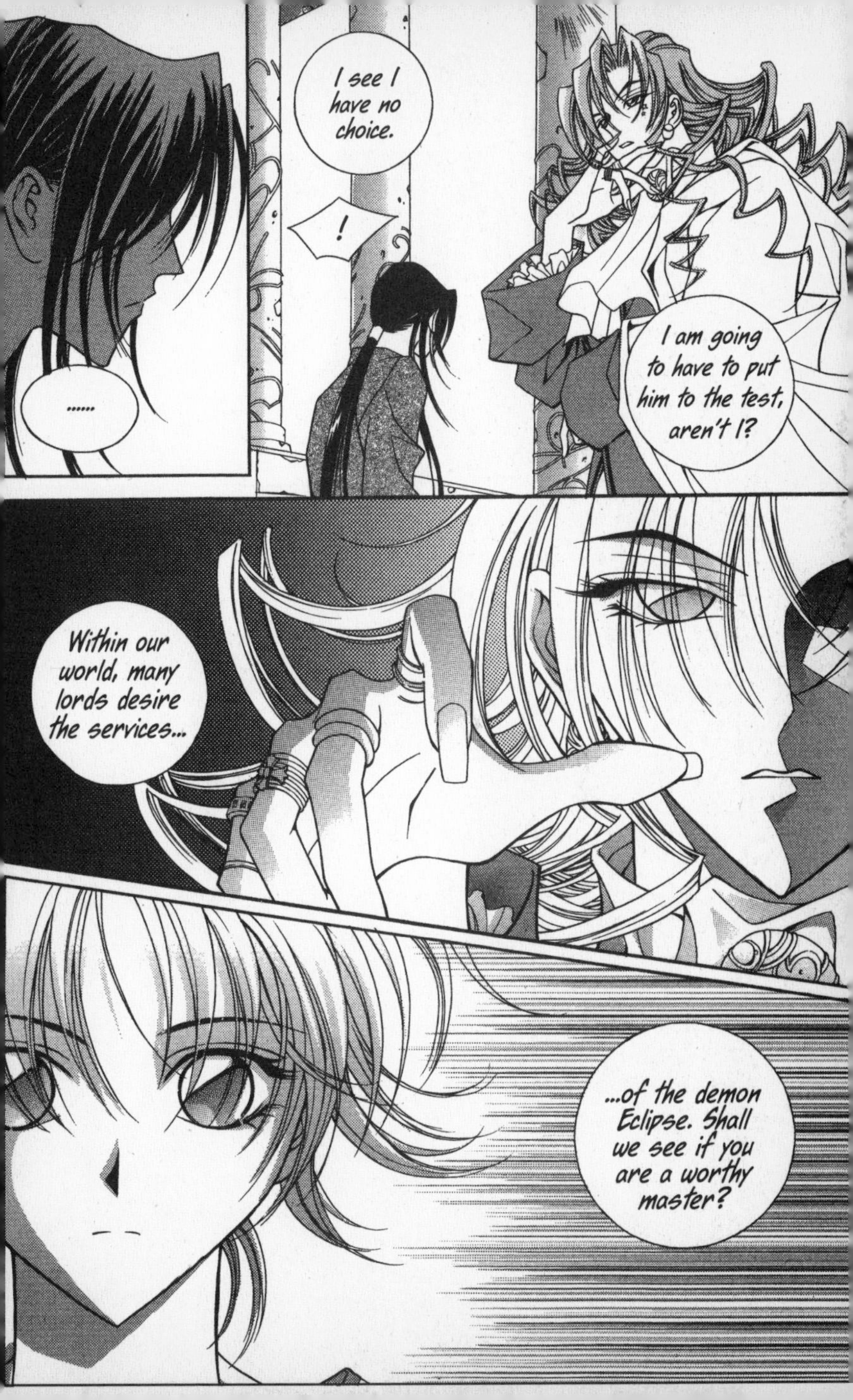
I am going to have to put him to the test, aren't I?
I see I have no choice.
!
......
Within our world, many lords desire the services...
...of the demon Eclipse. Shall we see if you are a worthy master?

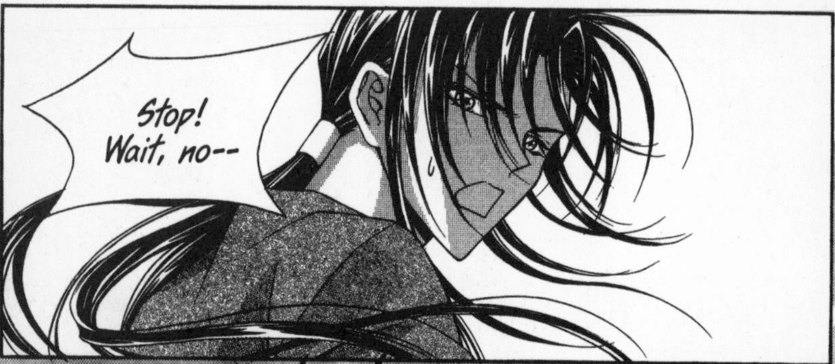
Stop!
Wait, no--

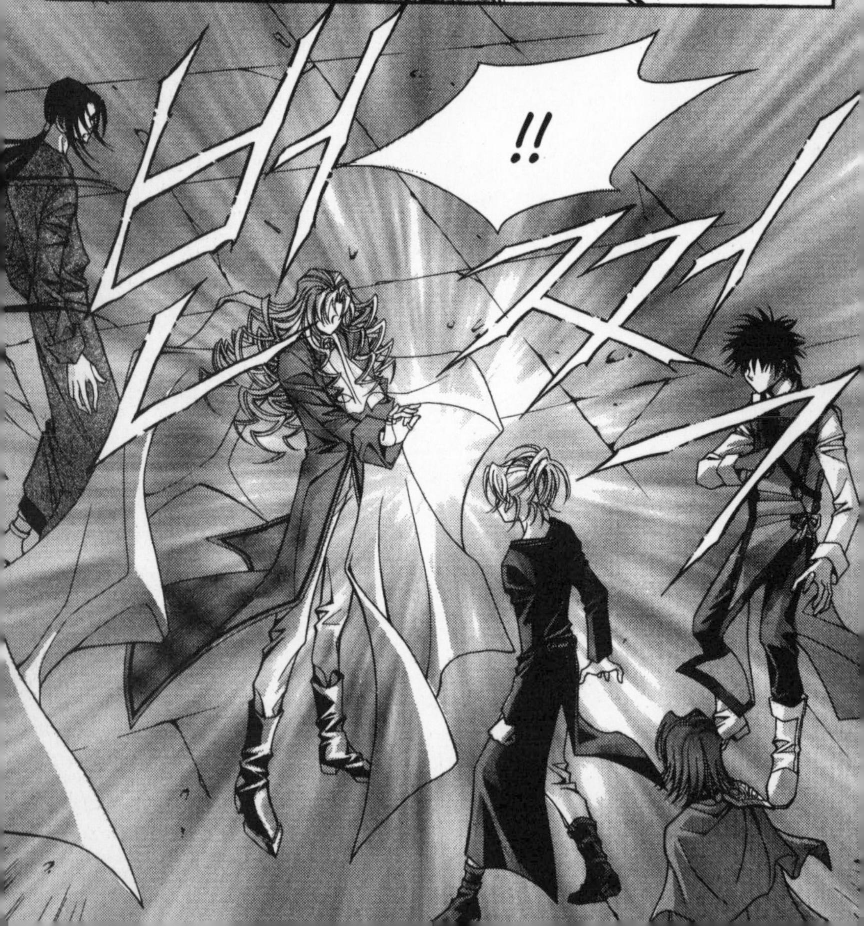
!!

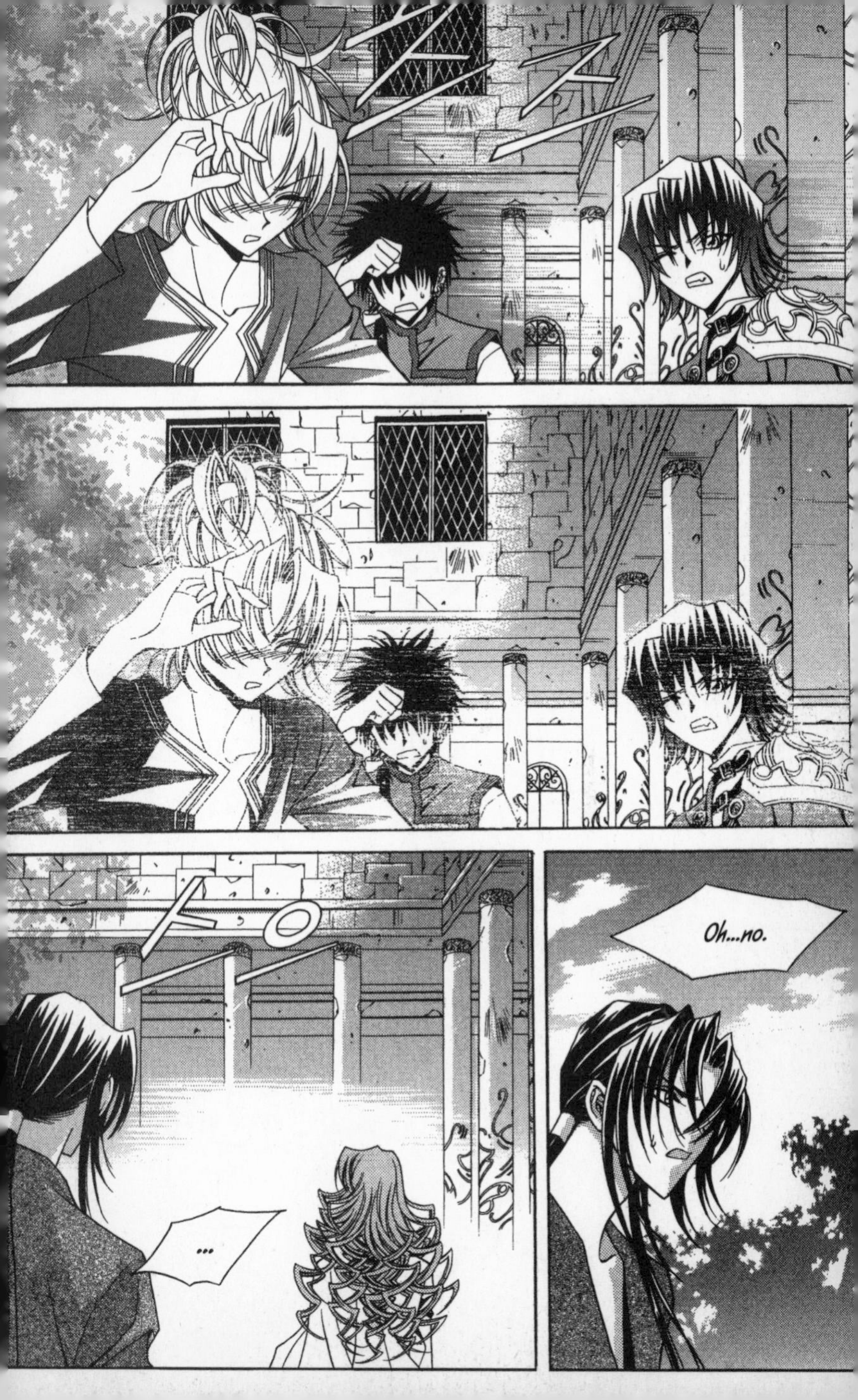
Oh...no.
...

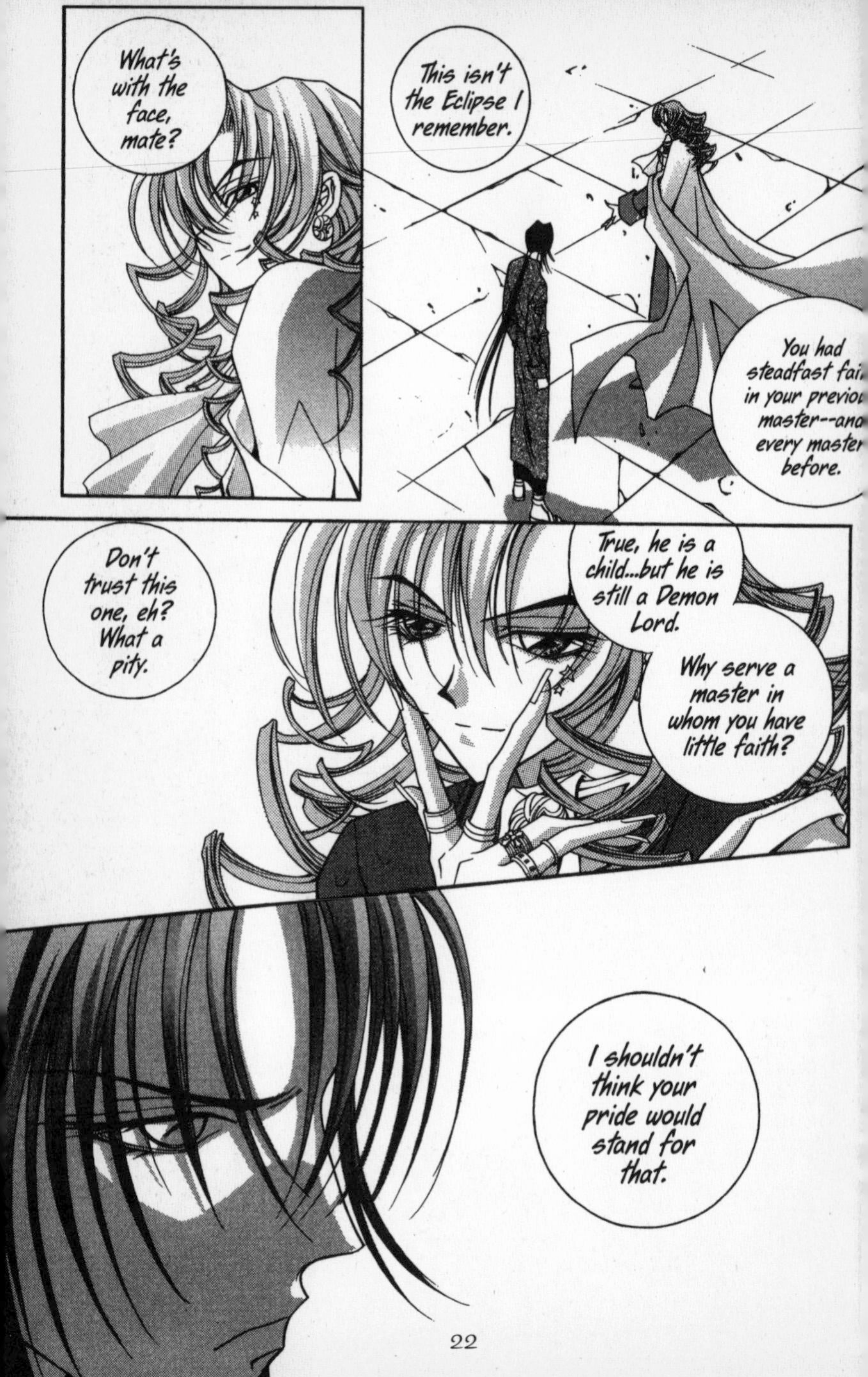
This isn't the Eclipse I remember.
You had steadfast fai in your previo master--and every master before.
What's with the face, mate?
True, he is a child...but he is still a Demon Lord.
Why serve a master in whom you have little faith?
Don't trust this one, eh? What a pity.
I shouldn't think your pride would stand for that.

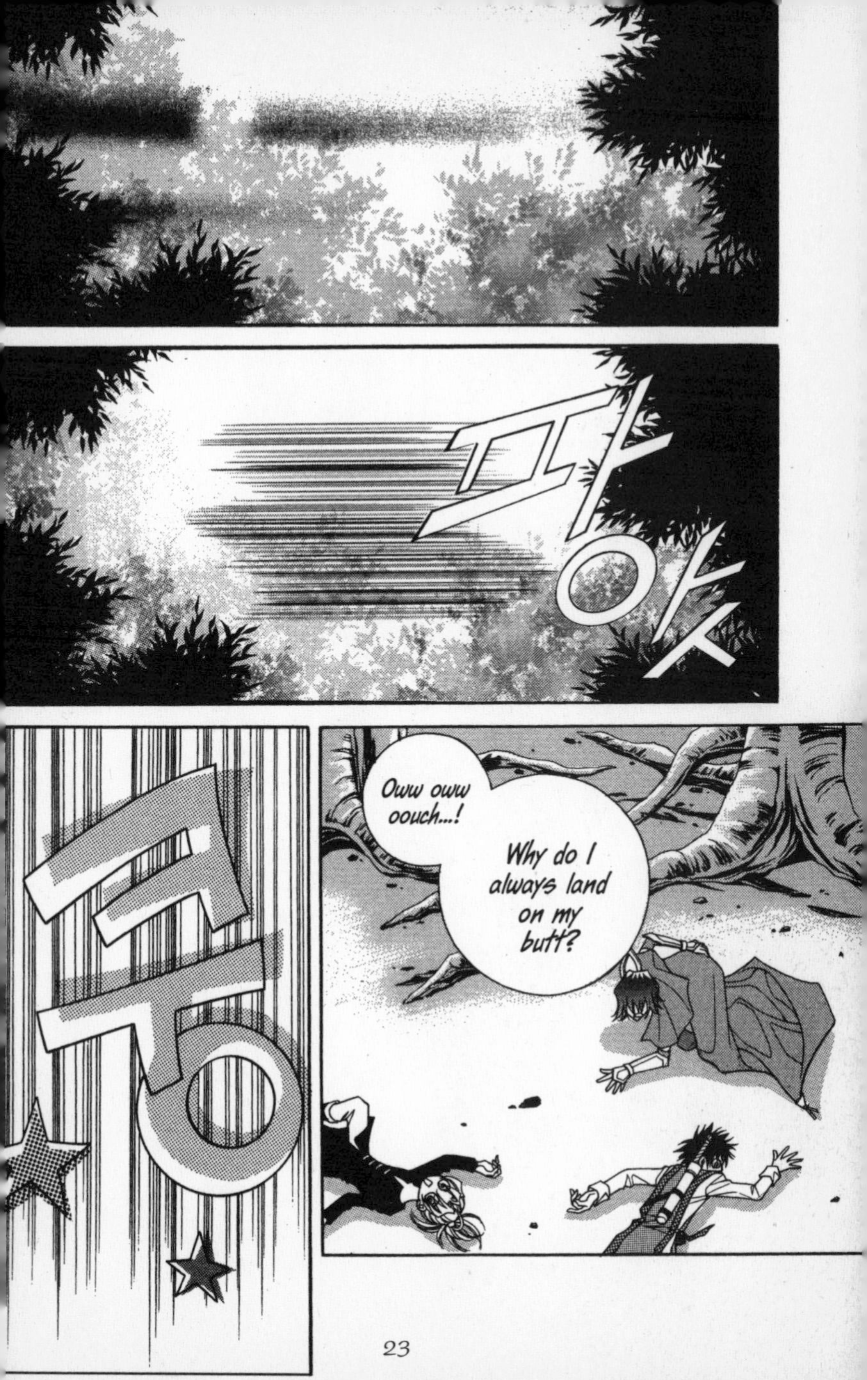
Oww oww oouch...!
Why do I always land on my butt?

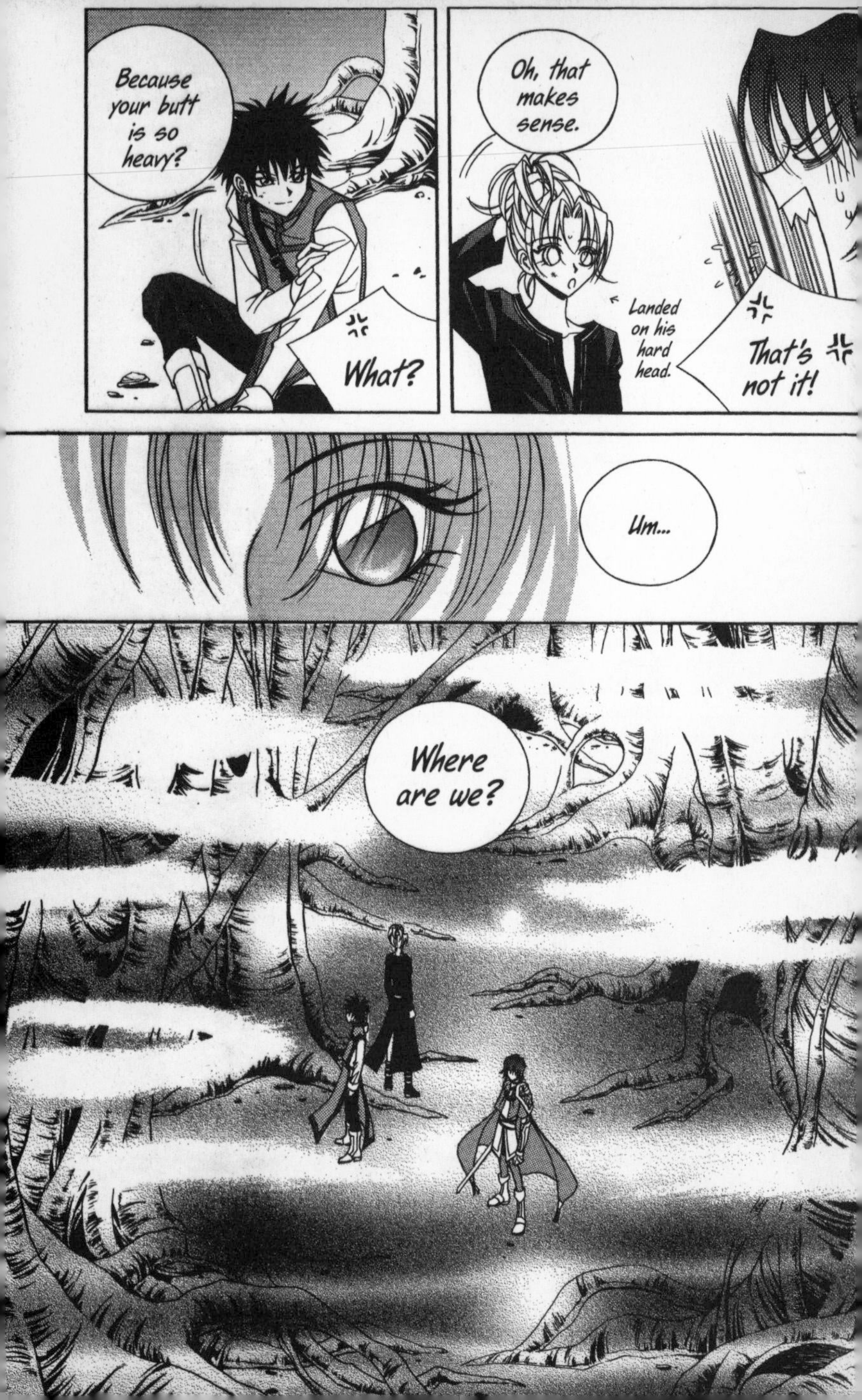

Because your butt is so heavy?
What?
Oh, that makes sense.
Landed on his hard head.
That's not it!
Um...
Where are we?

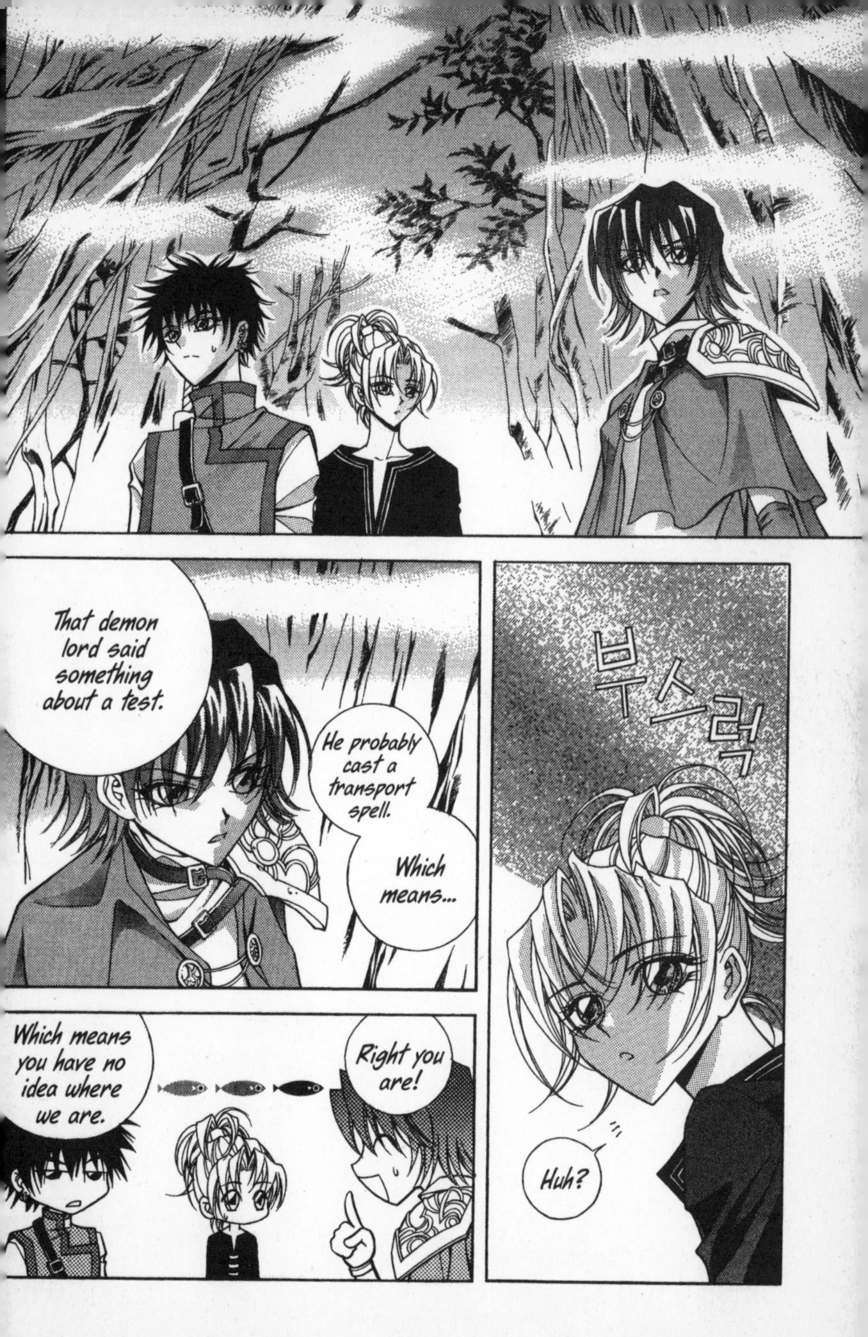
That demon lord said something about a test.
He probably cast a transport spell.
Which means...
Which means you have no idea where we are.
Right you are!
부스럭
Huh?

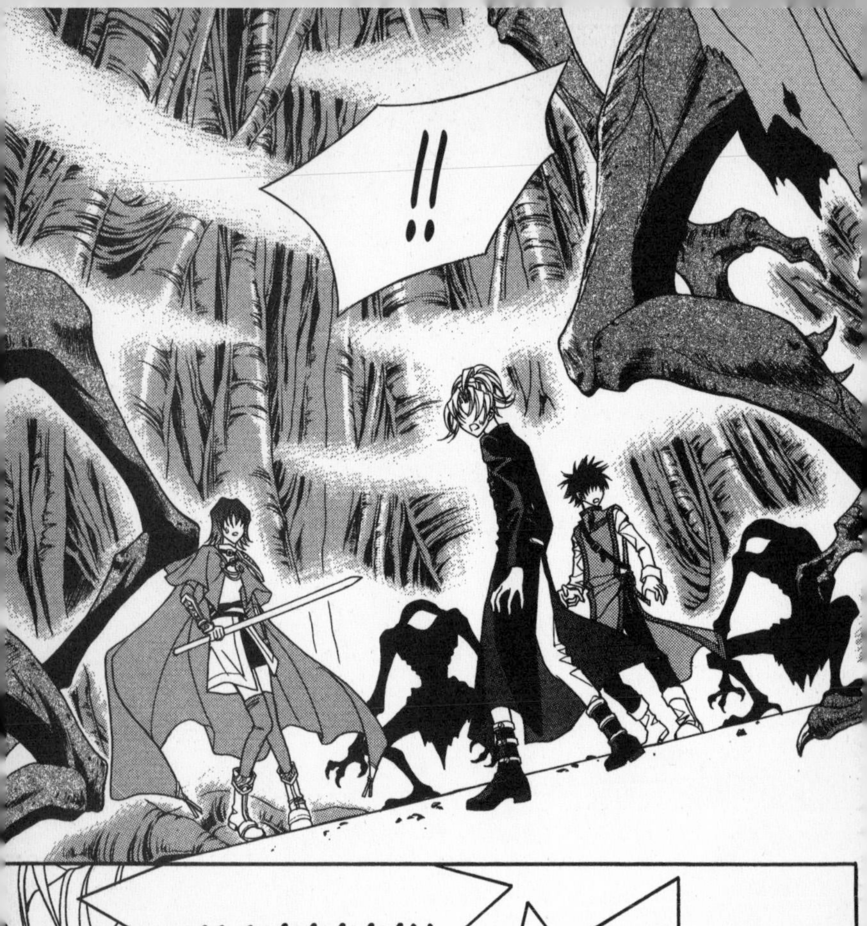
!!
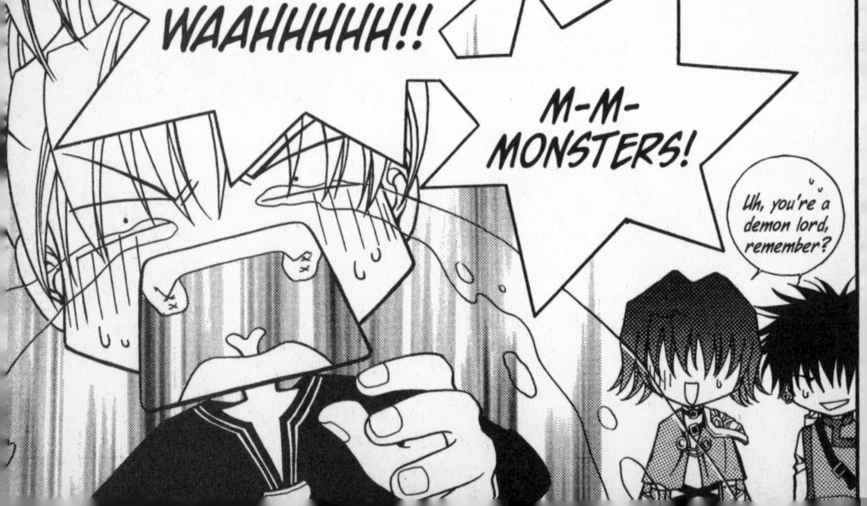
WAAHHHHH!!
M-M-MONSTERS!
Uh, you're a demon lord, remember?

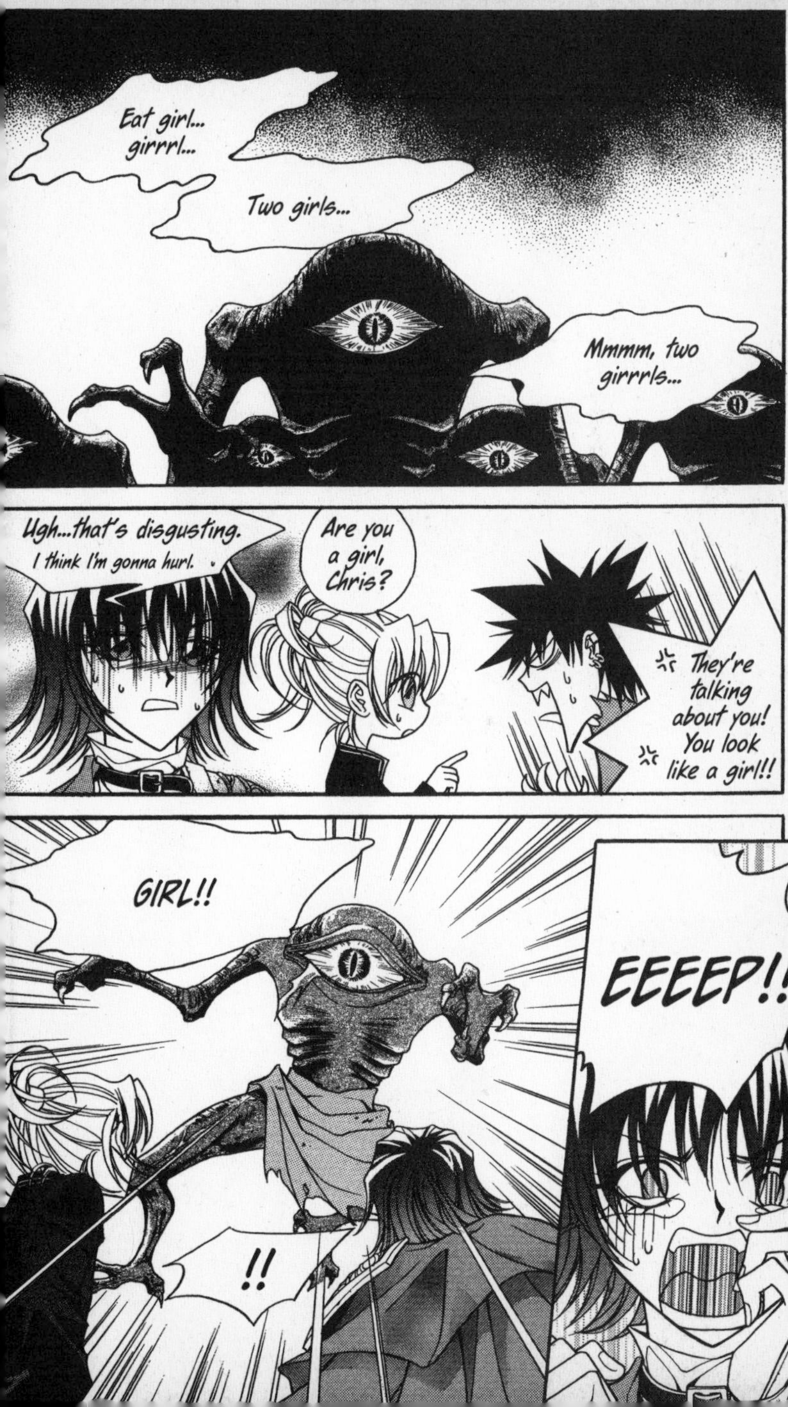
Eat girl... girrrl...
Two girls...
Mmmm, two girrrls...
Ugh...that's disgusting. I think I'm gonna hurl.
Are you a girl, Chris?
They're talking about you! You look like a girl!!
GIRL!!
!!
EEEEP!!

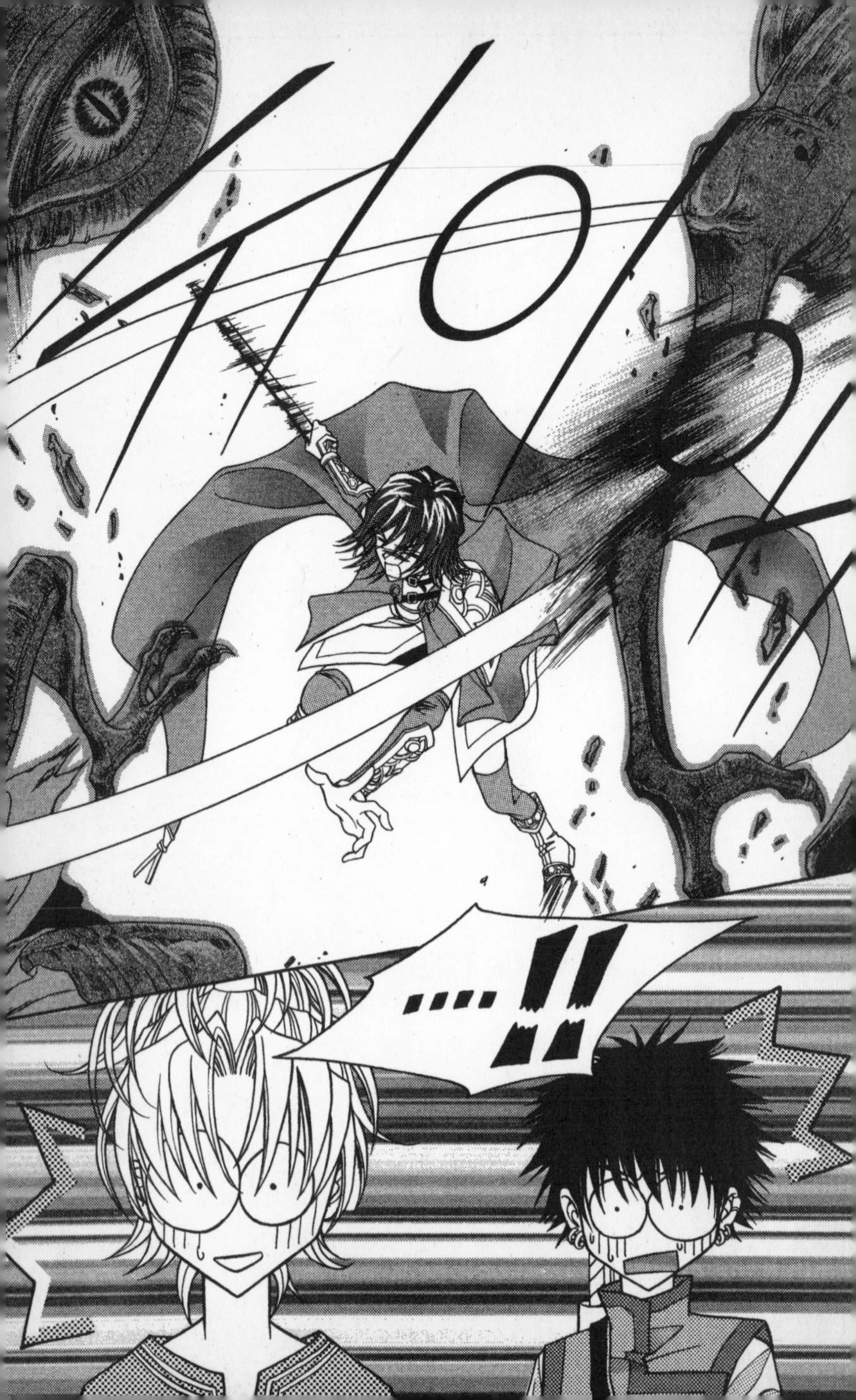
....!!

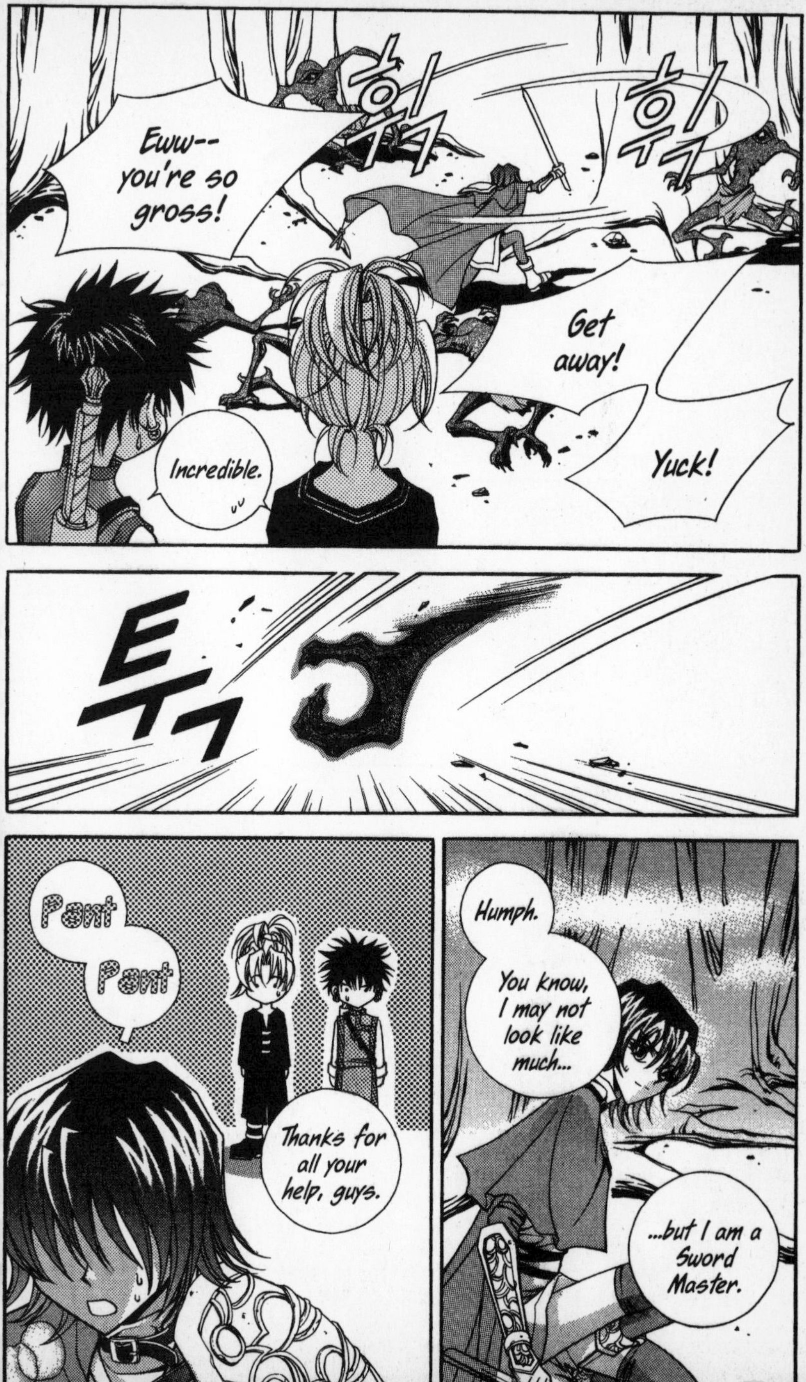
Eww-- you're so gross!
Incredible.
Get away!
Yuck!
Pant
Pant
Thanks for all your help, guys.
Humph.
You know, I may not look like much...
...but I am a Sword Master.

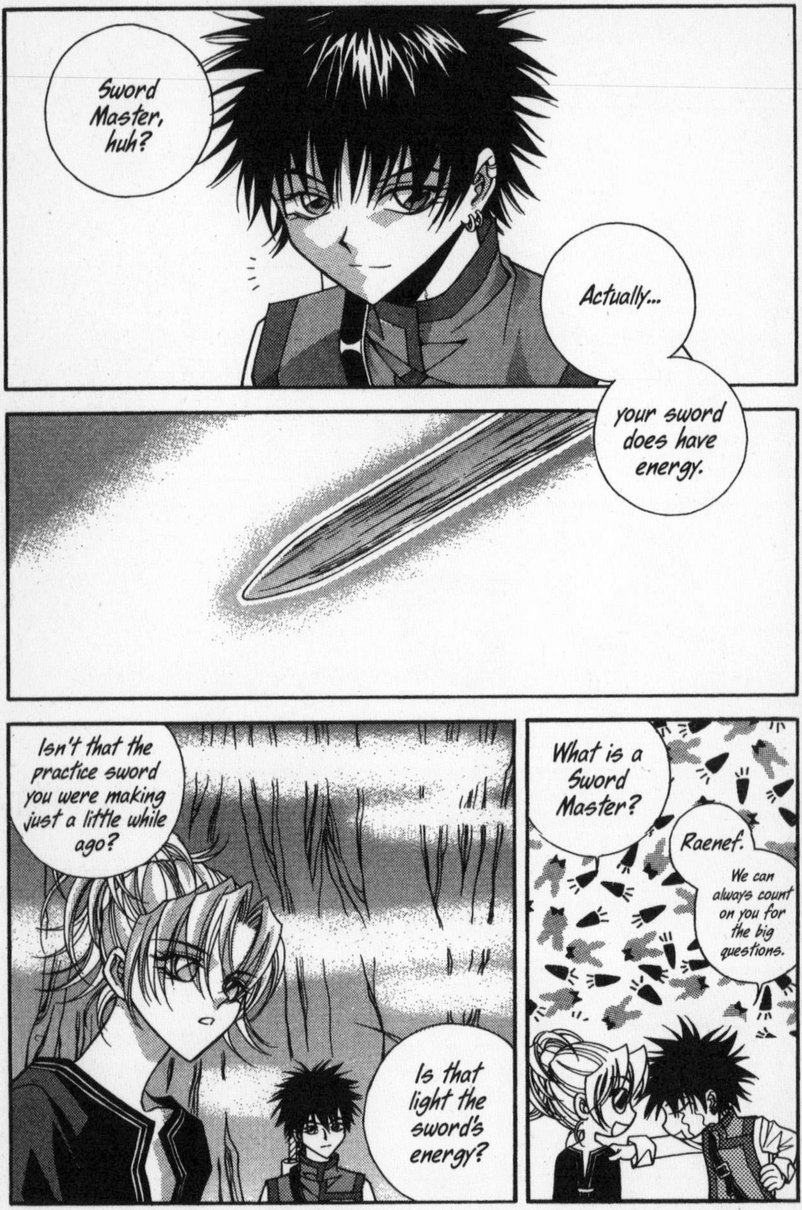
Sword Master, huh?
Actually...
your sword does have energy.
Isn't that the practice sword you were making just a little while ago?
Is that light the sword's energy?
What is a Sword Master?
Raenef.
We can always count on you for the big questions.

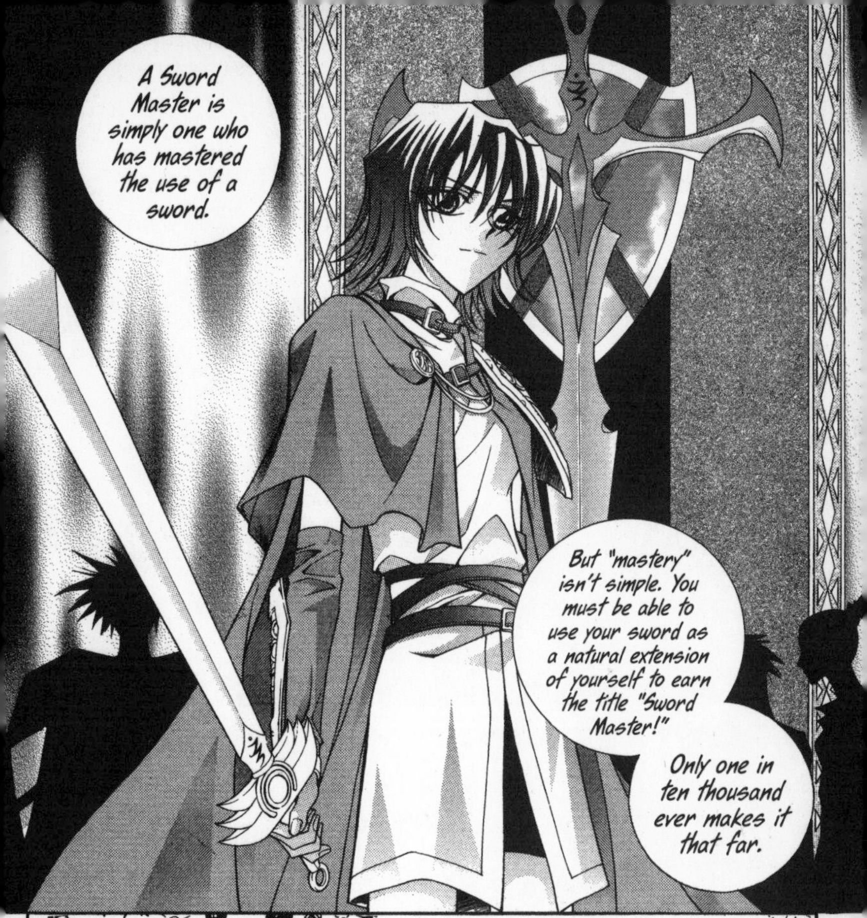
A Sword Master is simply one who has mastered the use of a sword.
But "mastery" isn't simple. You must be able to use your sword as a natural extension of yourself to earn the title "Sword Master!"
Only one in ten thousand ever makes it that far.

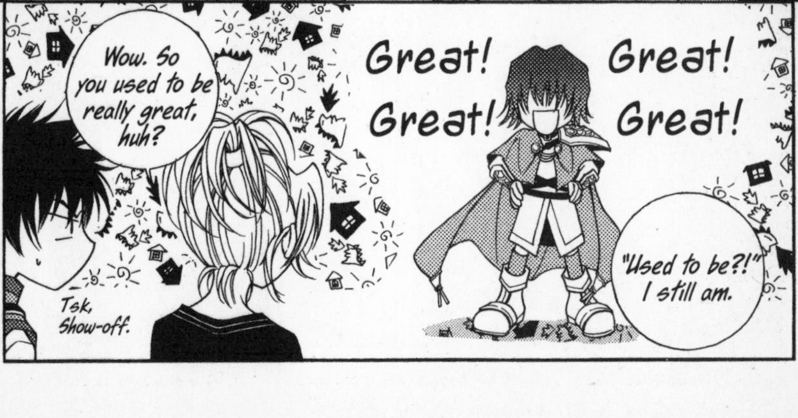
Wow. So you used to be really great, huh?
Great! Great!
Great! Great!
"Used to be?!" I still am.
Tsk, Show-off.

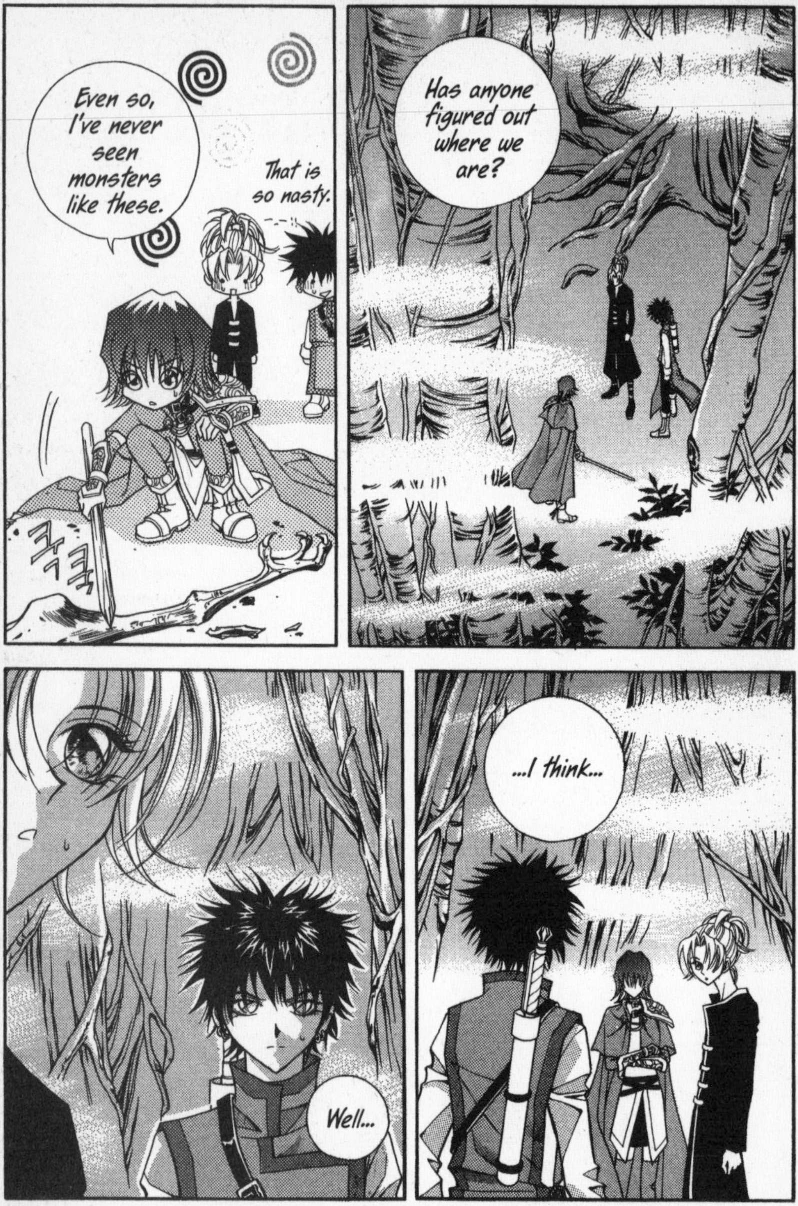
Even so, I've never seen monsters like these.
That is so nasty.
Has anyone figured out where we are?
Well...
...I think...

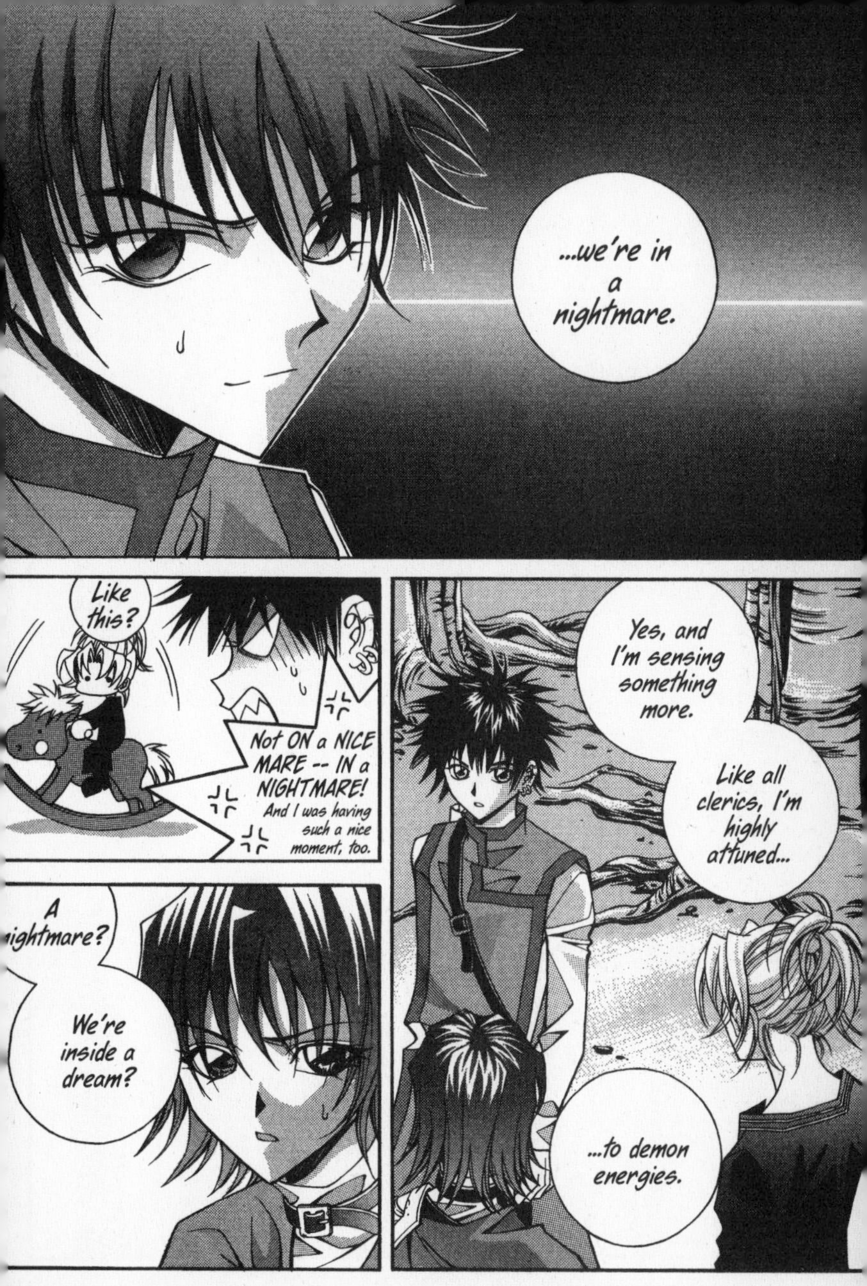
...we're in a nightmare.
Like this?
Not ON a NICE MARE -- IN a NIGHTMARE! And I was having such a nice moment, too.
A nightmare?
We're inside a dream?
Yes, and I'm sensing something more.
Like all clerics, I'm highly attuned...
...to demon energies.

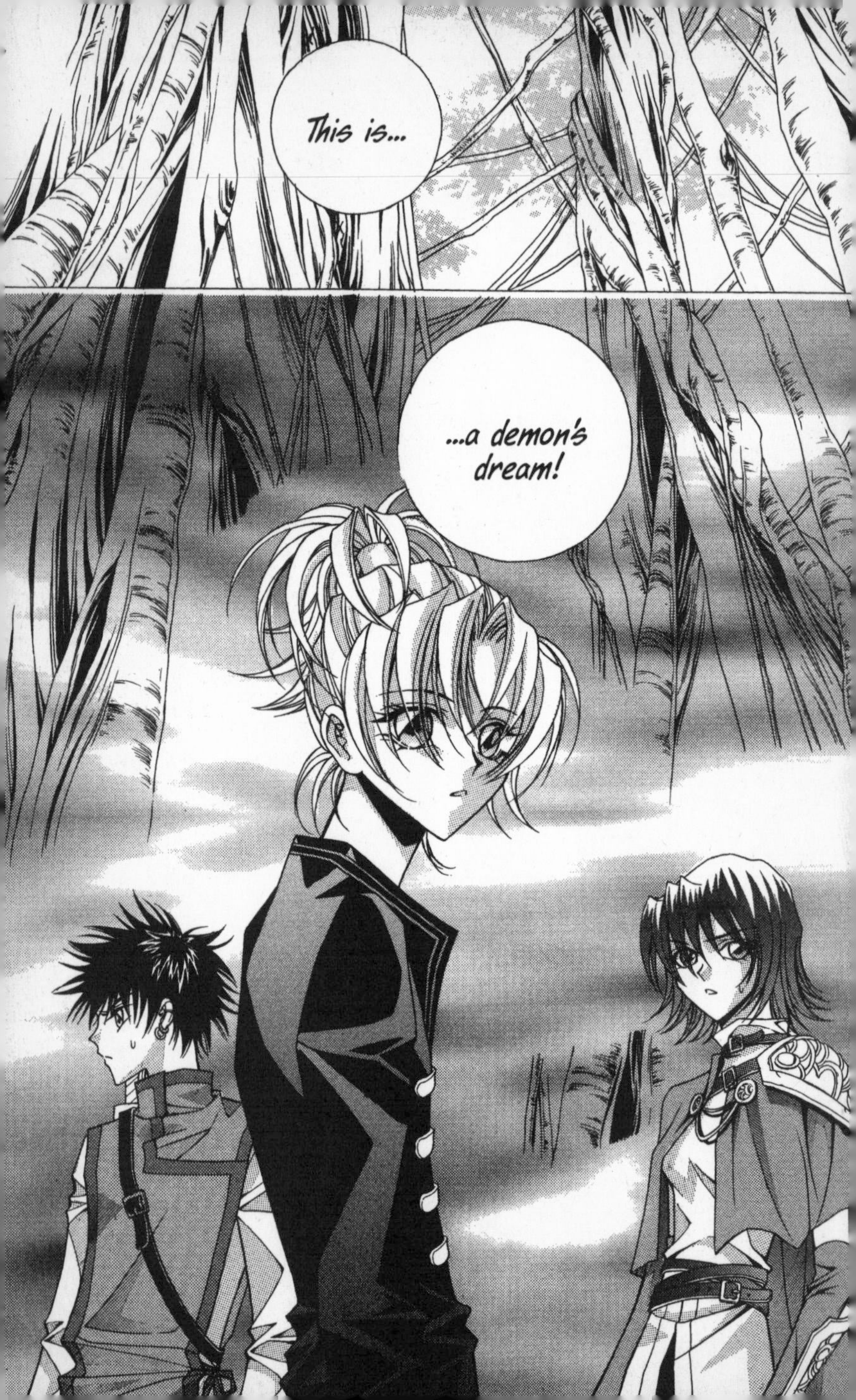
This is...
...a demon's dream!

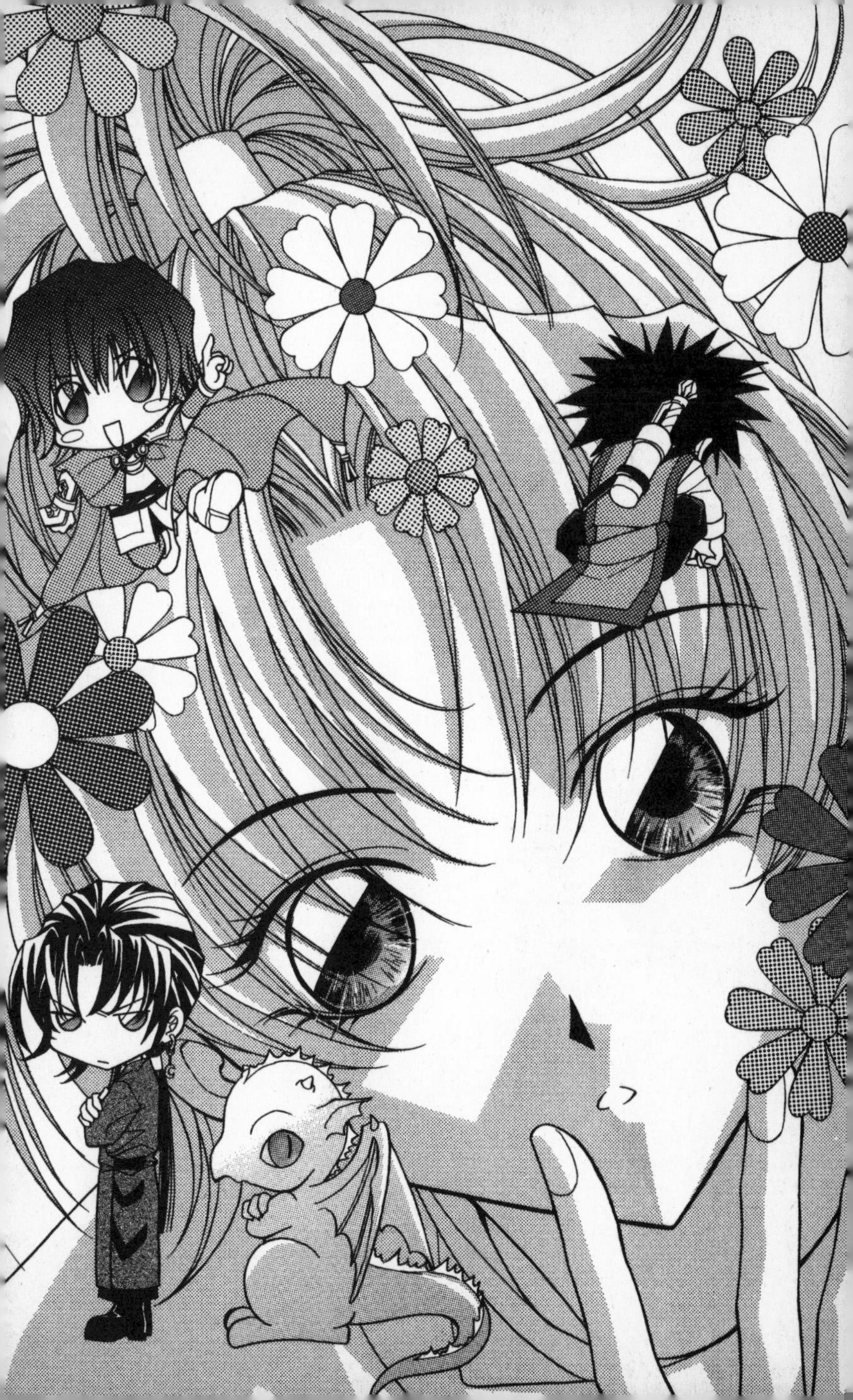

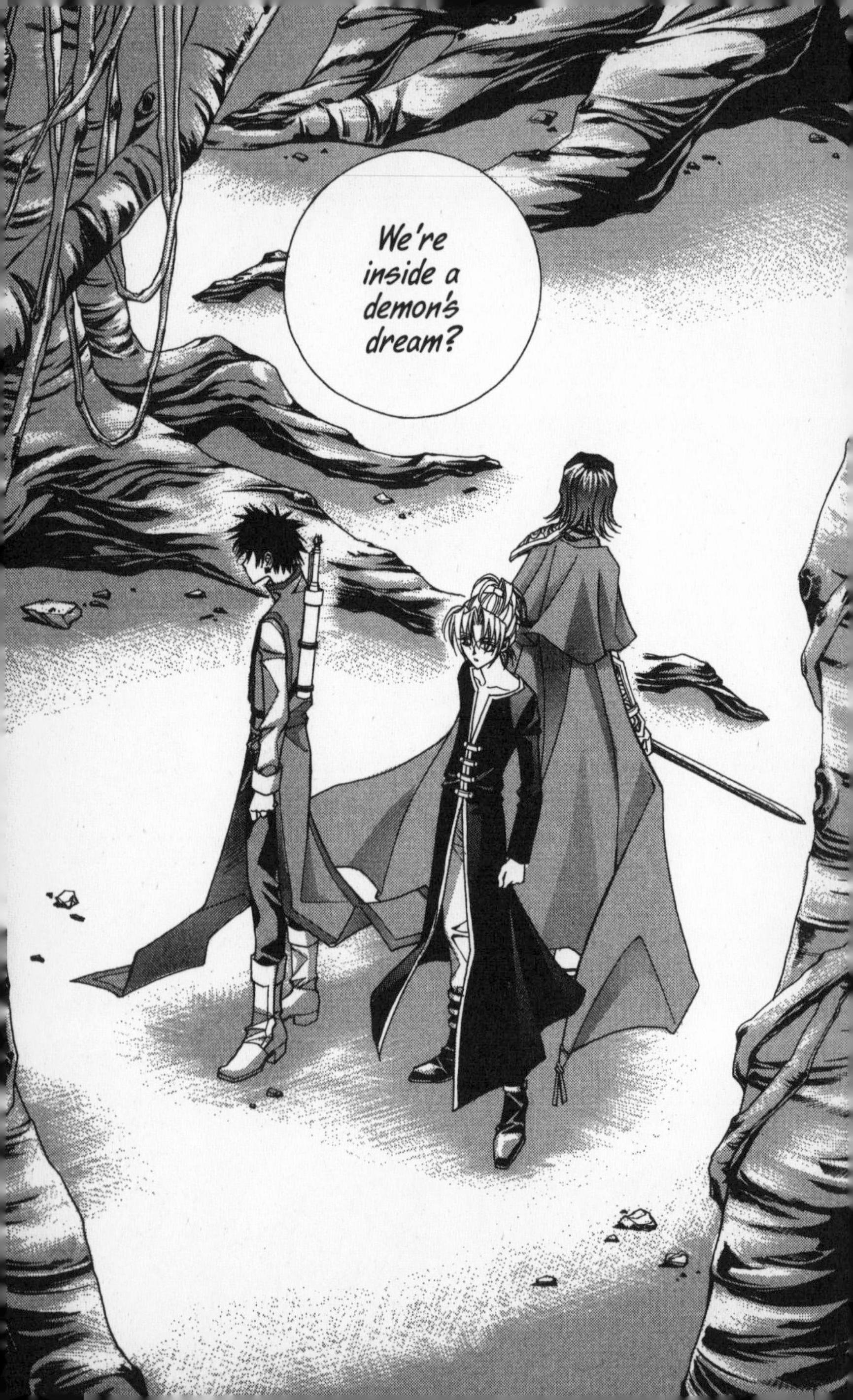
We're inside a demon's dream?

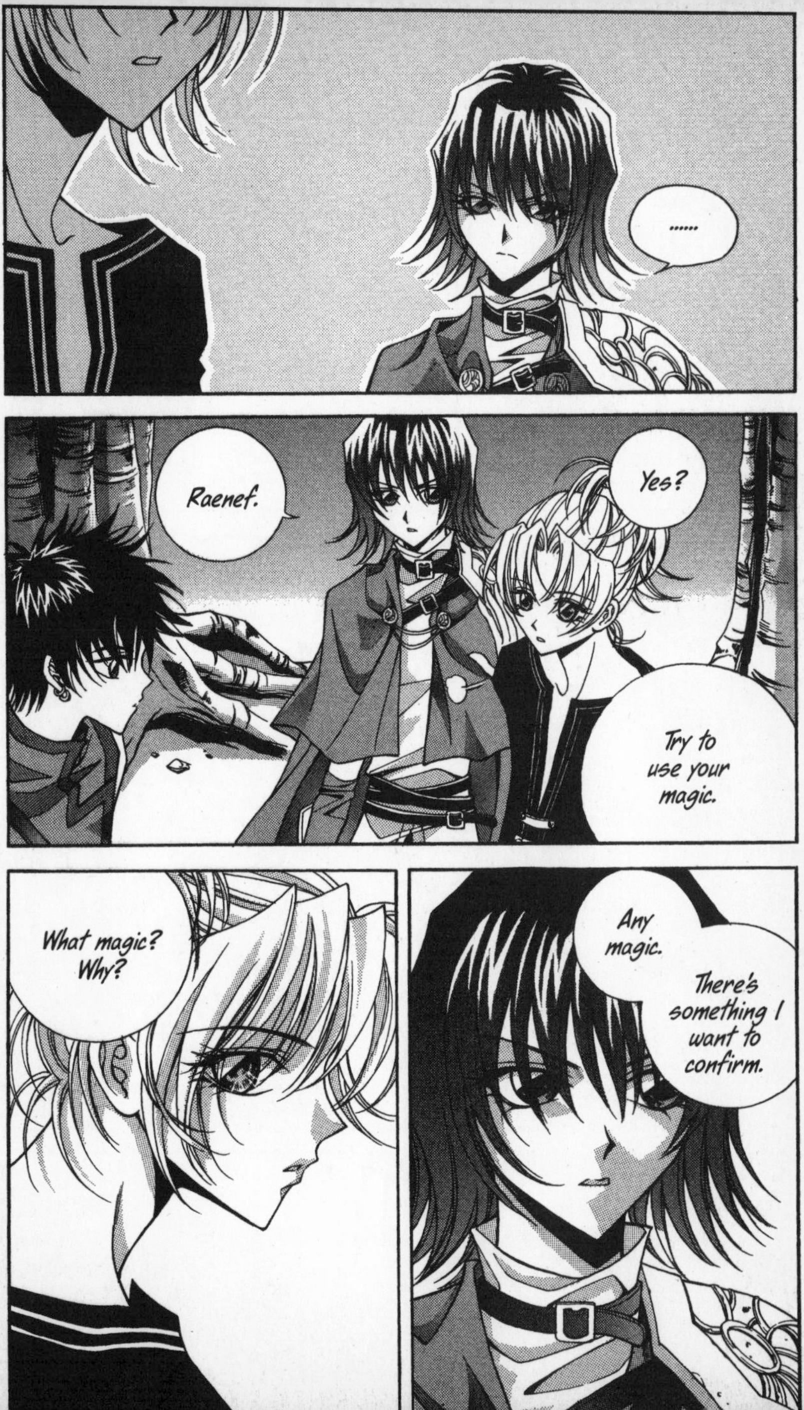
......
Raenef.
Yes?
Try to use your magic.
What magic? Why?
Any magic.
There's something I want to confirm.

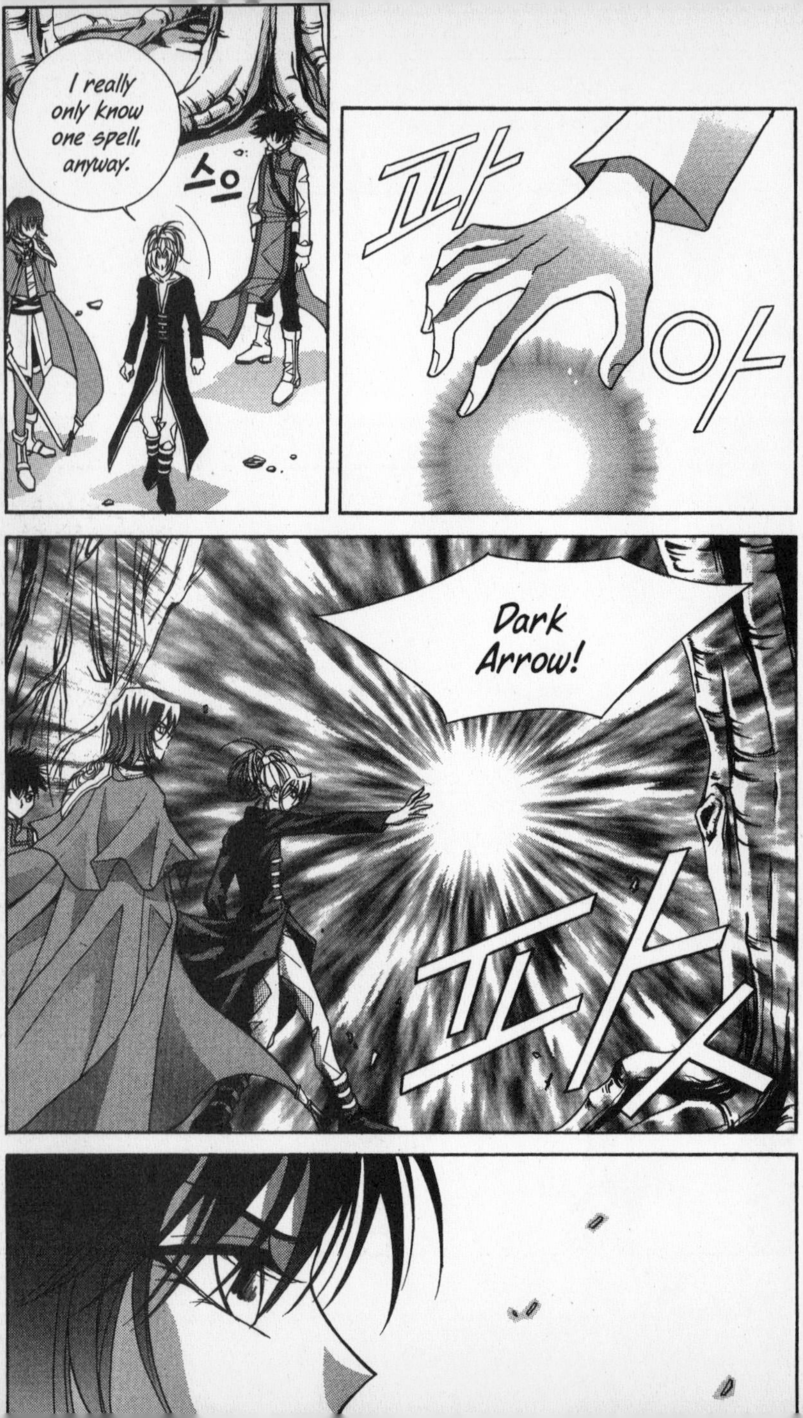
I really only know one spell, anyway.
스으
파아
Dark Arrow!
팟

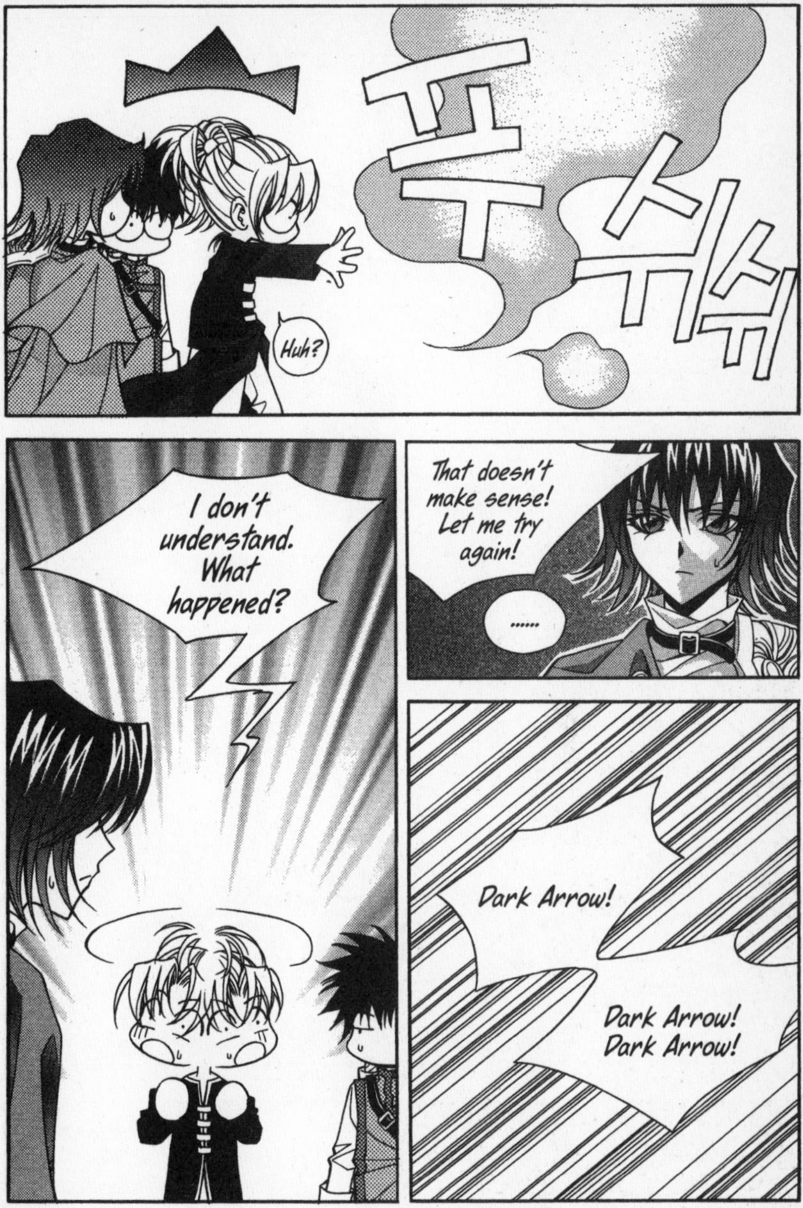
Huh?
I don't understand. What happened?
That doesn't make sense! Let me try again!
......
Dark Arrow!
Dark Arrow! Dark Arrow!

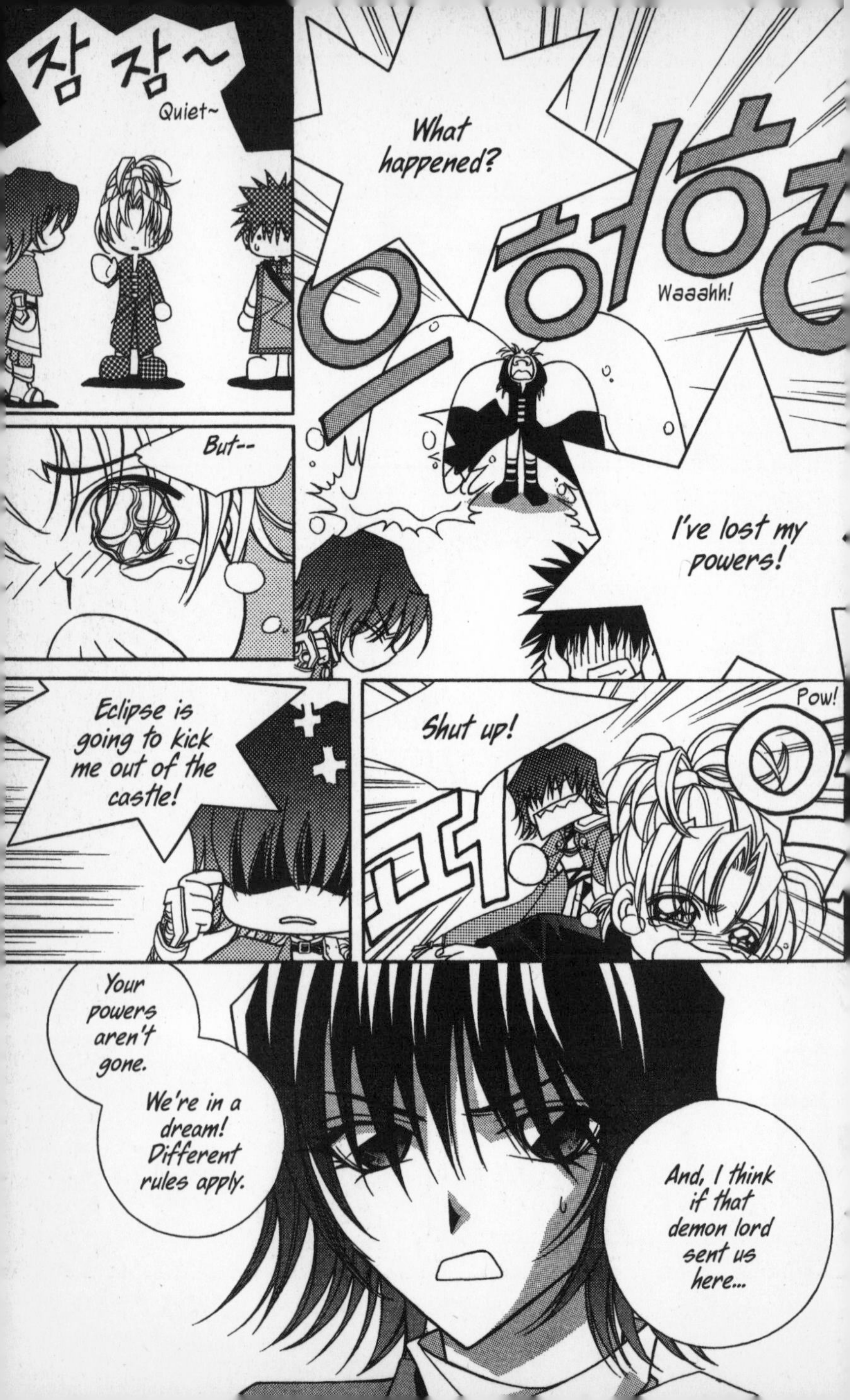
잠 잠~
Quiet~
But--
What happened?
Waaahh!
I've lost my powers!
Eclipse is going to kick me out of the castle!
Shut up!
Pow!
Your powers aren't gone.
We're in a dream! Different rules apply.
And, I think if that demon lord sent us here...

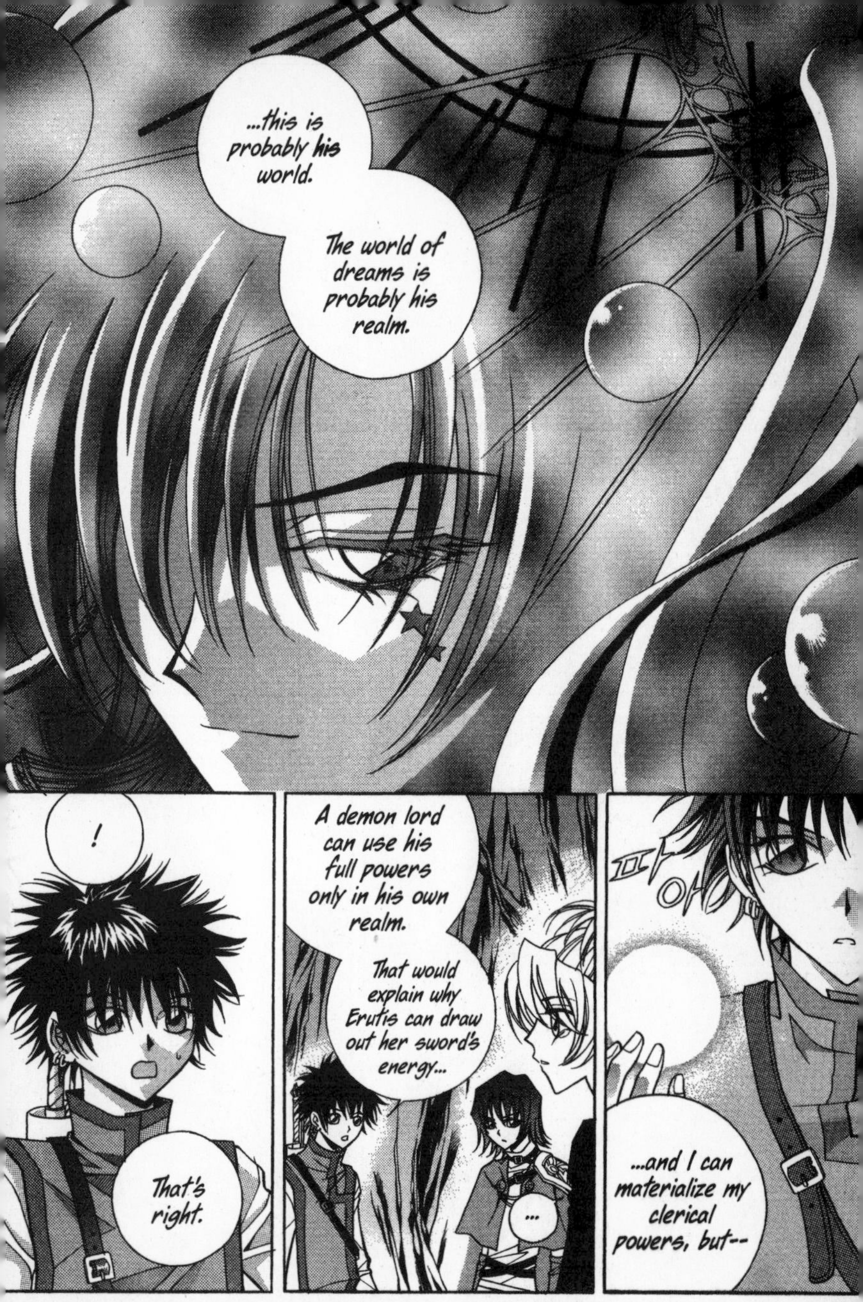
...this is probably his world.
The world of dreams is probably his realm.
!
That's right.
A demon lord can use his full powers only in his own realm.
That would explain why Erutis can draw out her sword's energy...
...
...and I can materialize my clerical powers, but--

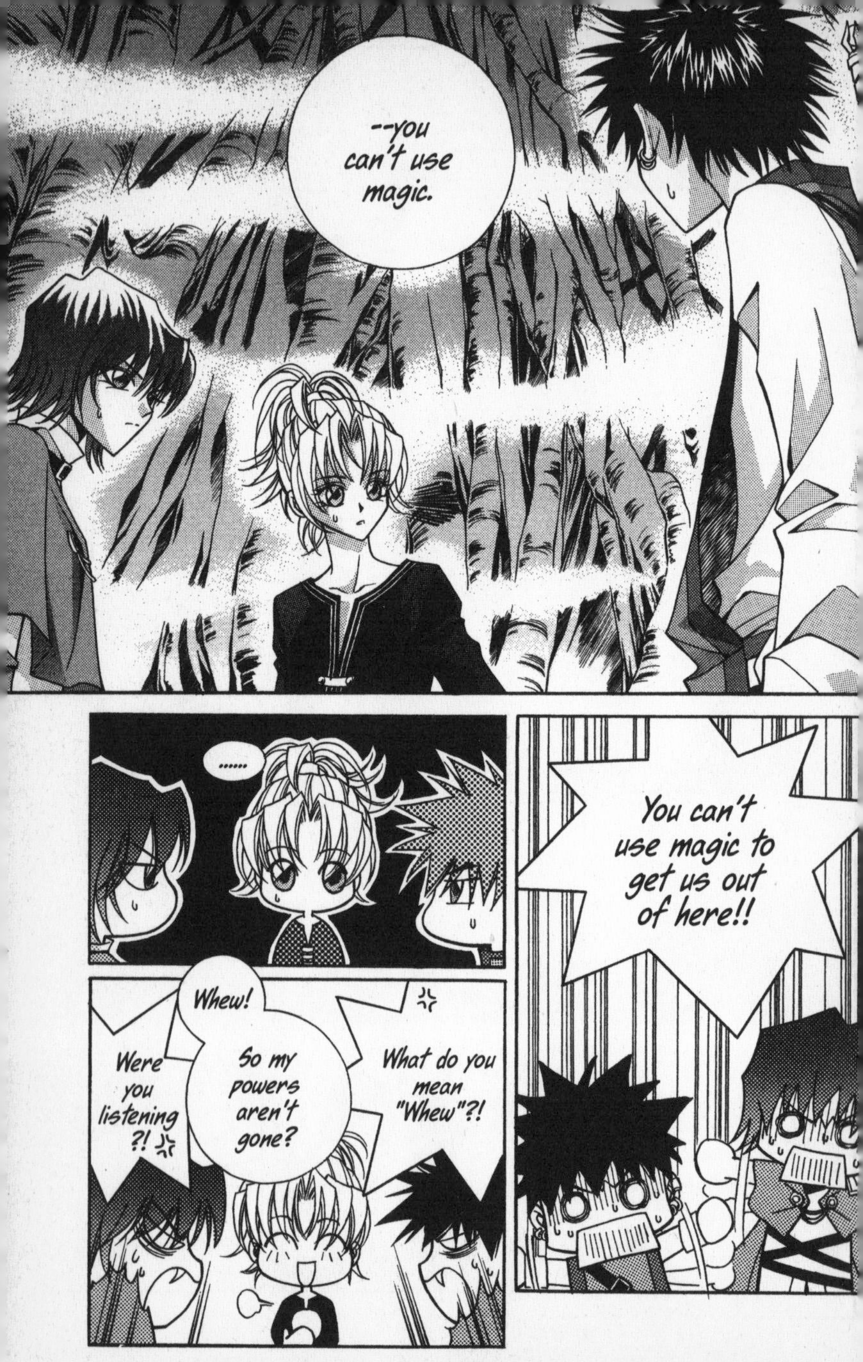
--you can't use magic.
......
You can't use magic to get us out of here!!
Whew!
So my powers aren't gone?
What do you mean "Whew"?!
Were you listening ?!

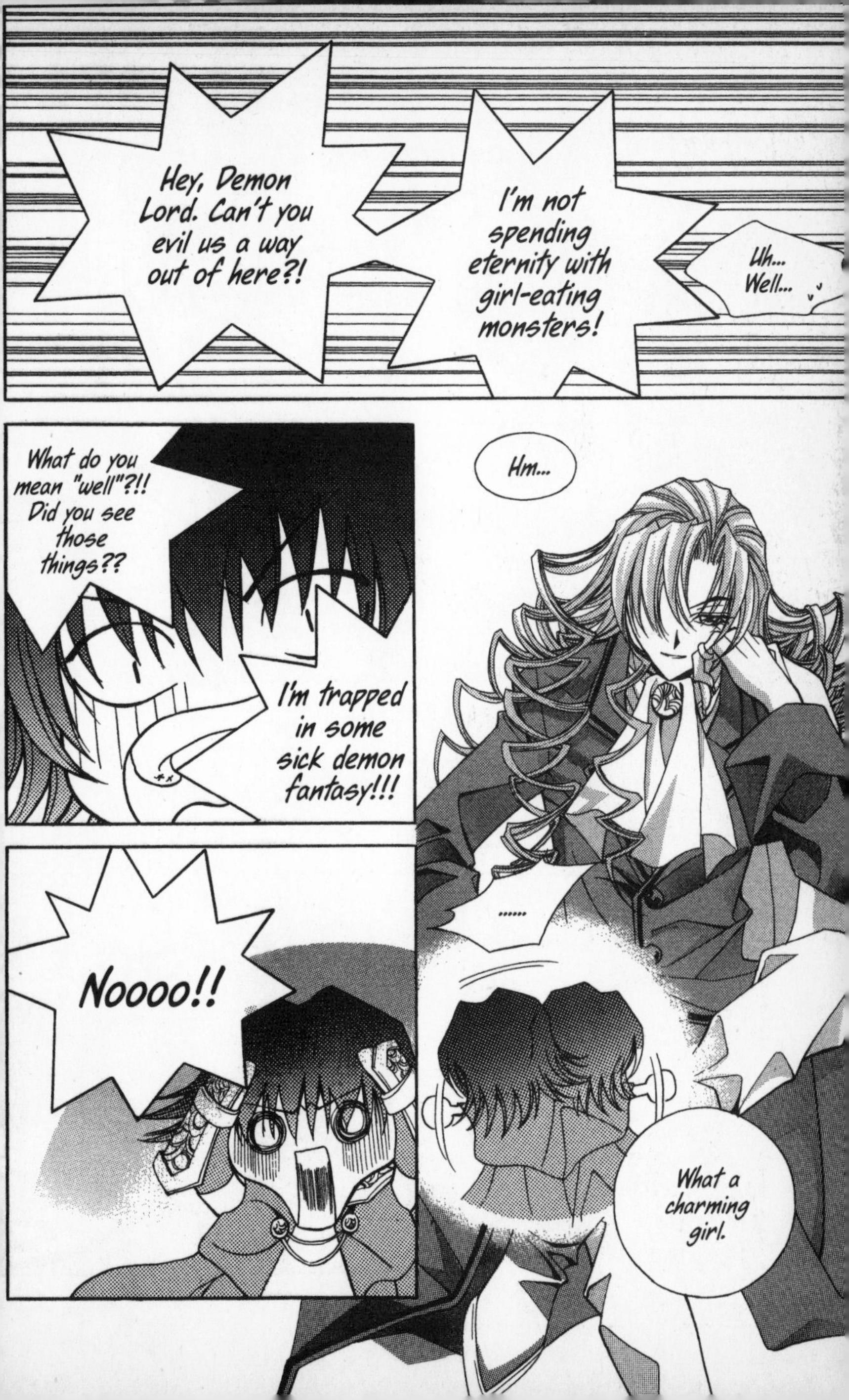
Hey, Demon Lord. Can't you evil us a way out of here?!
I'm not spending eternity with girl-eating monsters!
Uh... Well...
What do you mean "well"?!! Did you see those things??
I'm trapped in some sick demon fantasy!!!
Noooo!!
Hm...
......
What a charming girl.

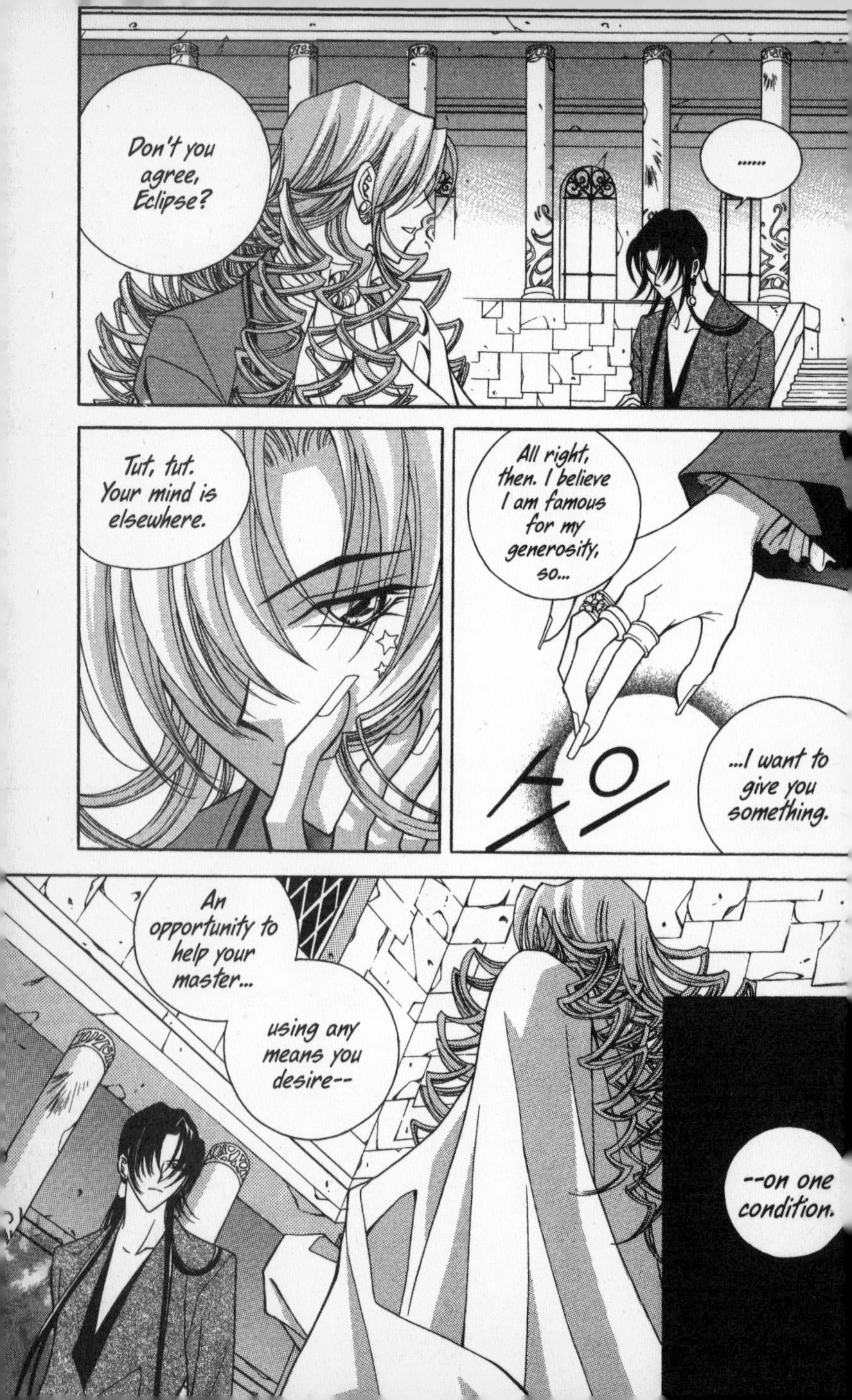
Don't you agree, Eclipse?
......
Tut, tut. Your mind is elsewhere.
All right, then. I believe I am famous for my generosity, so...
...I want to give you something.
An opportunity to help your master...
using any means you desire--
--on one condition.

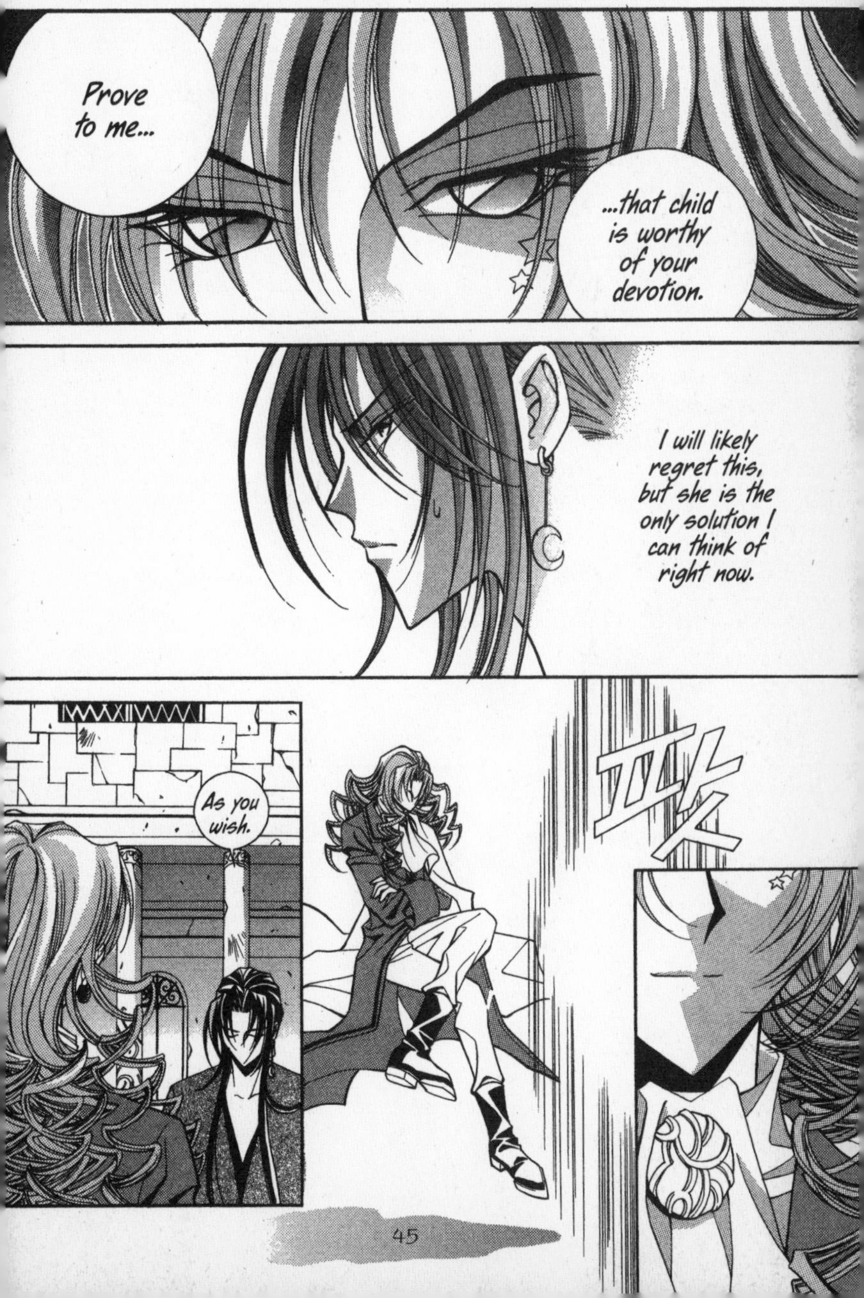
Prove to me...
...that child is worthy of your devotion.
I will likely regret this, but she is the only solution I can think of right now.
As you wish.

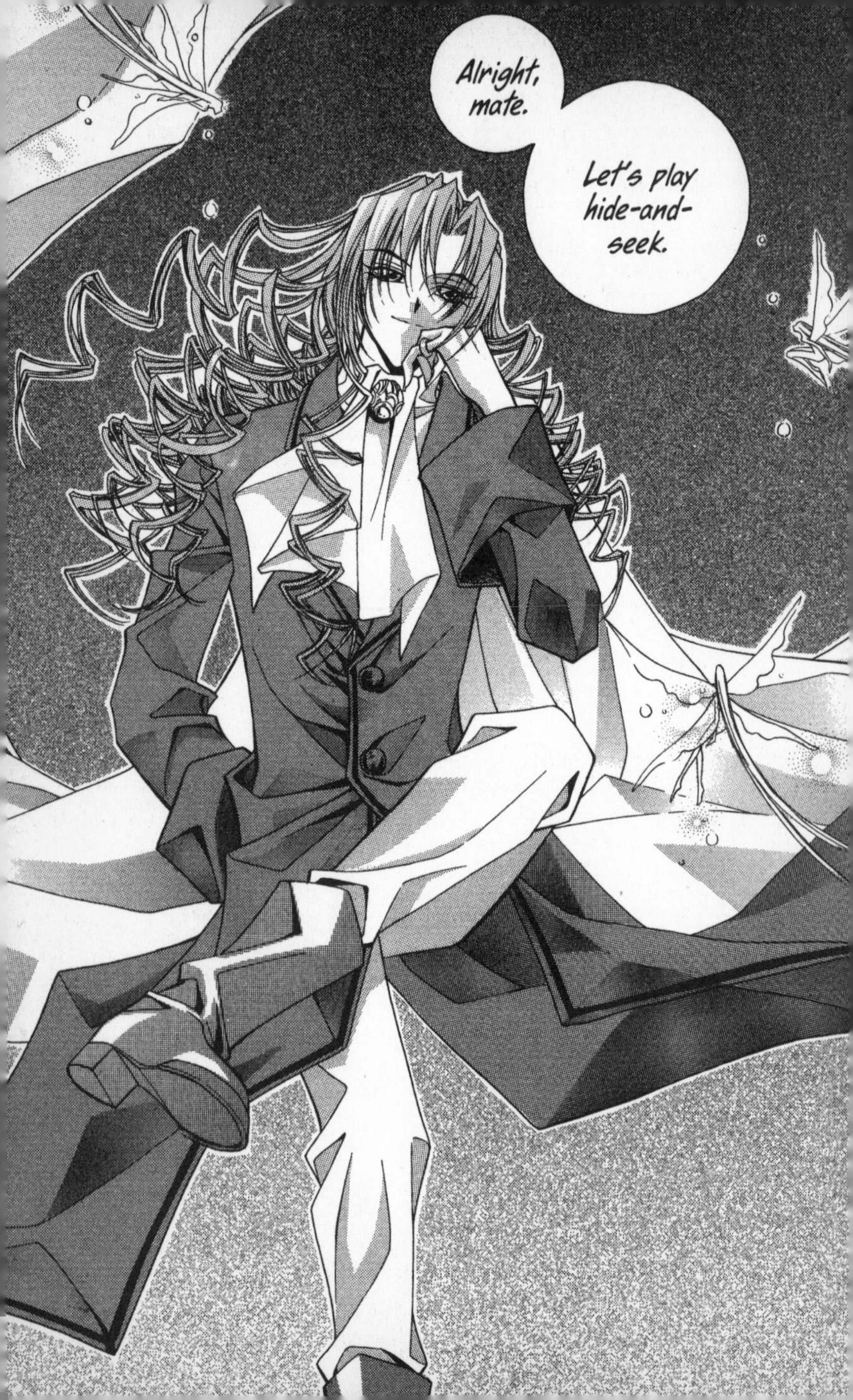
Alright, mate.
Let's play hide-and-seek.

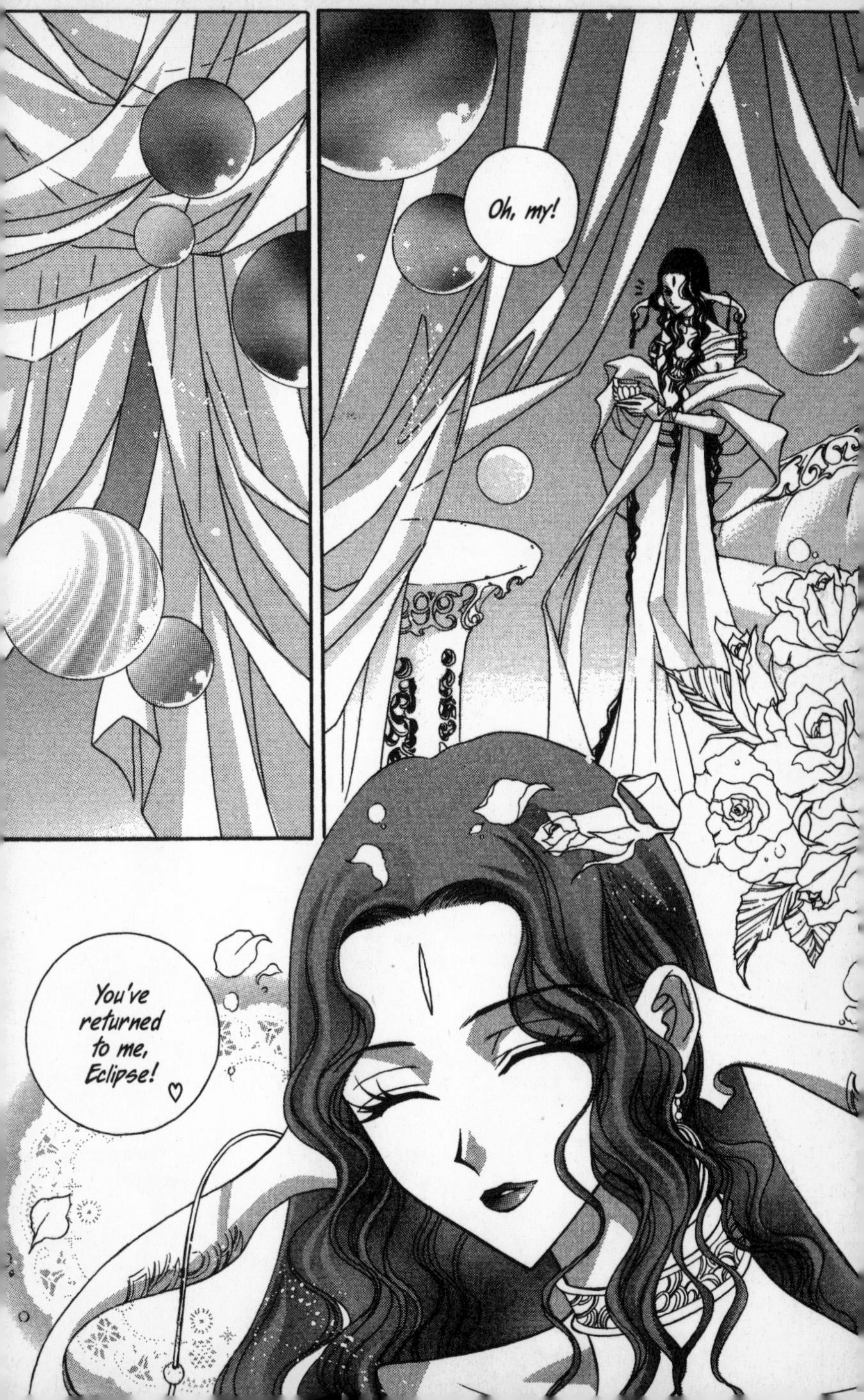
Oh, my!
You've returned to me, Eclipse! ♡

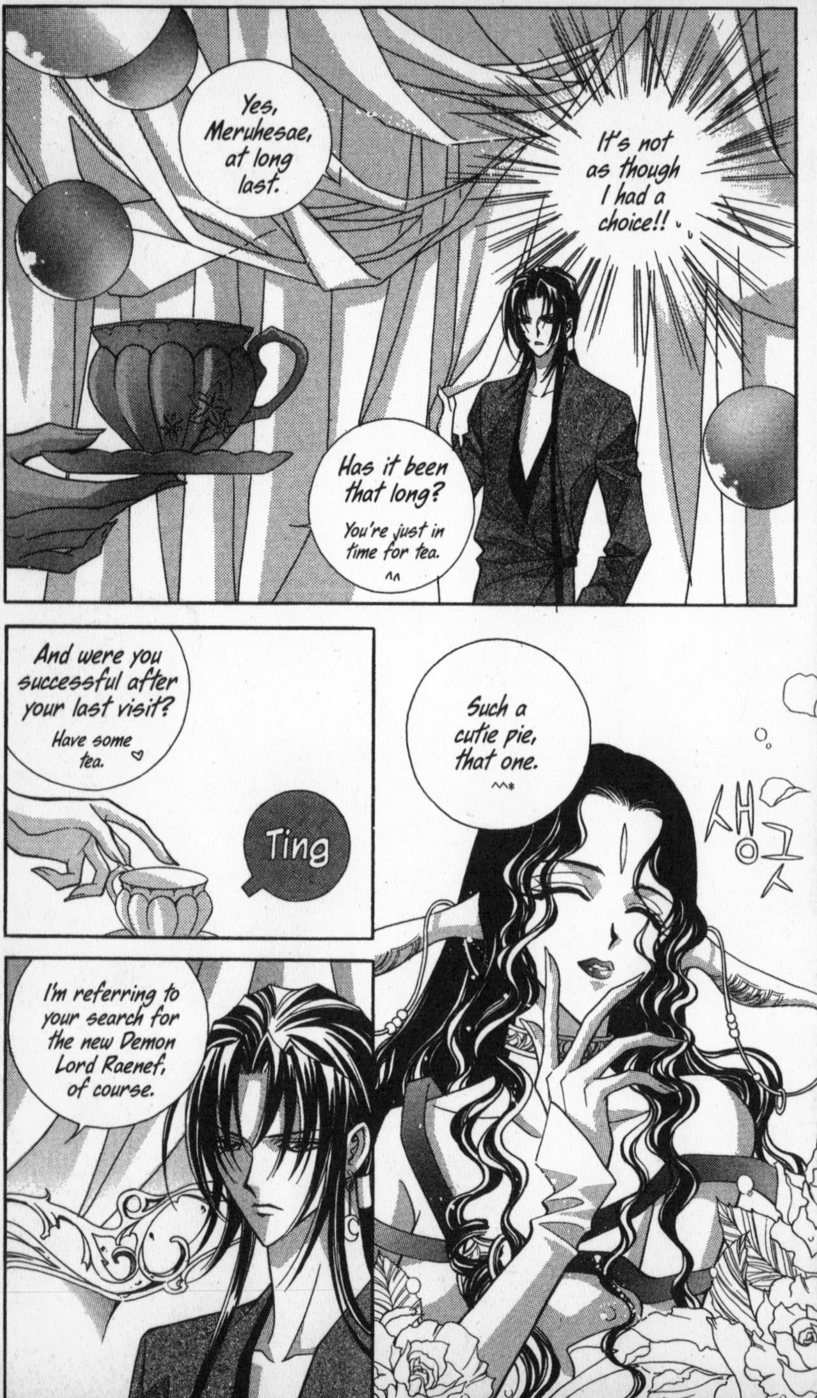
Yes, Meruhesae, at long last.
It's not as though I had a choice!!
Has it been that long?
You're just in time for tea. ^^
And were you successful after your last visit?
Have some tea. ♡
Ting
I'm referring to your search for the new Demon Lord Raenef, of course.
Such a cutie pie, that one. ^^*

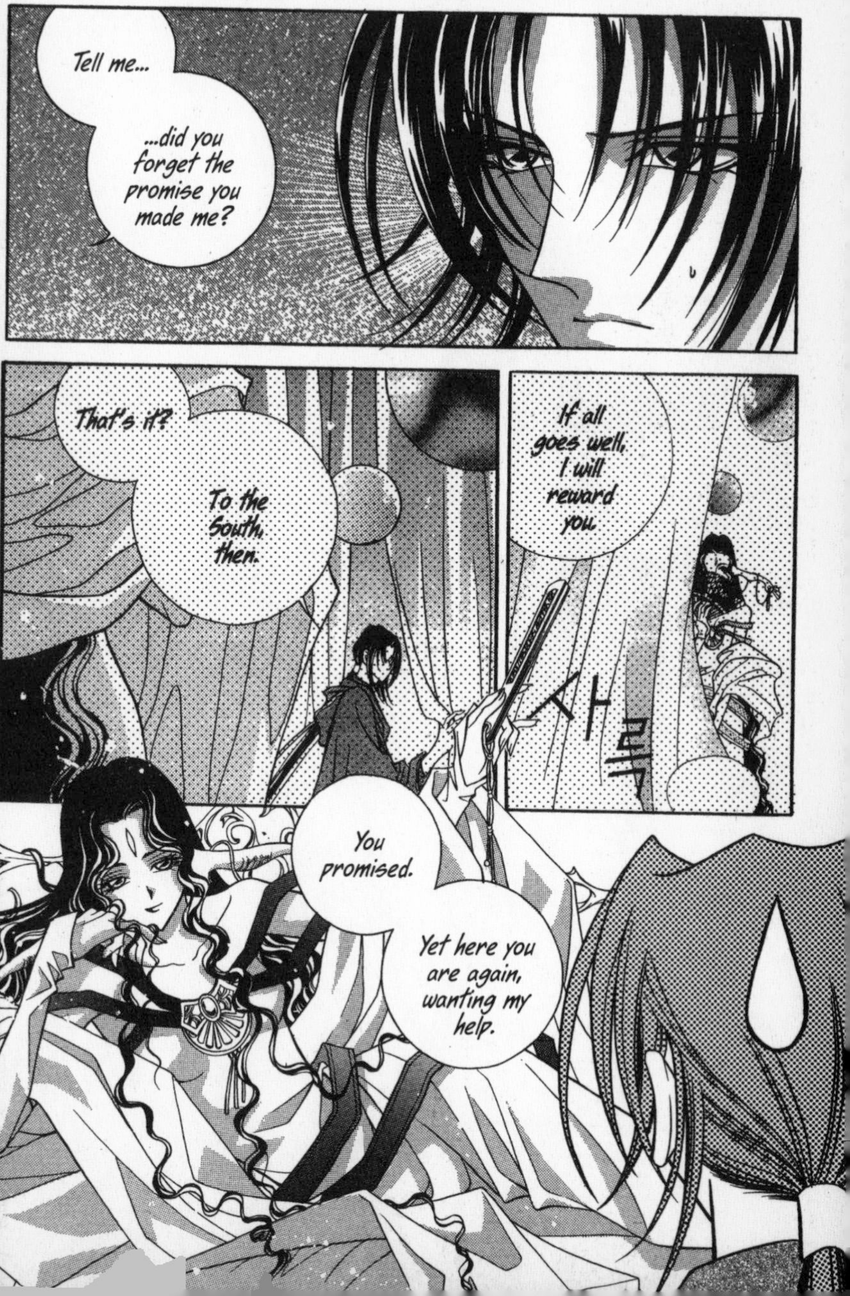

Tell me...
...did you forget the promise you made me?
If all goes well, I will reward you.
That's it?
To the South, then.
You promised.
Yet here you are again, wanting my help.

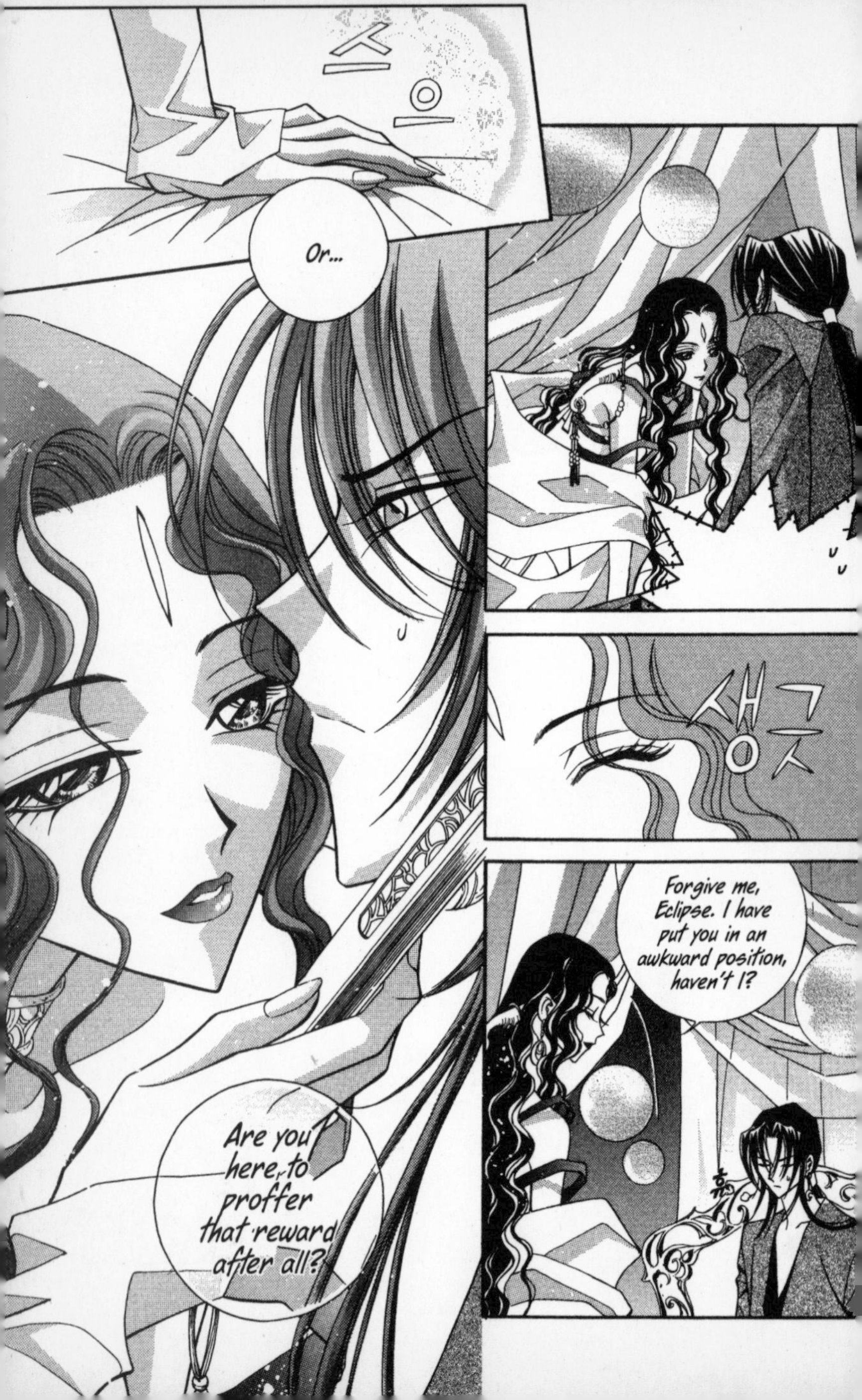
스으
Or...
Are you here to proffer that reward after all?
Forgive me, Eclipse. I have put you in an awkward position, haven't I?

I do intend to reward you, Meruhesae--

Give us a kiss, then. ♡

—Mwah

Who does she think she's talking to?! -_-+

Now, you're not trying to charm a free reading out of me, are you?

No.

I can't vouch for my readings without an offering, you know.

Come on now, for this reading and the last...

Give me a real kiss, and I'll tell you what I see.

새글
새글
Smile

51

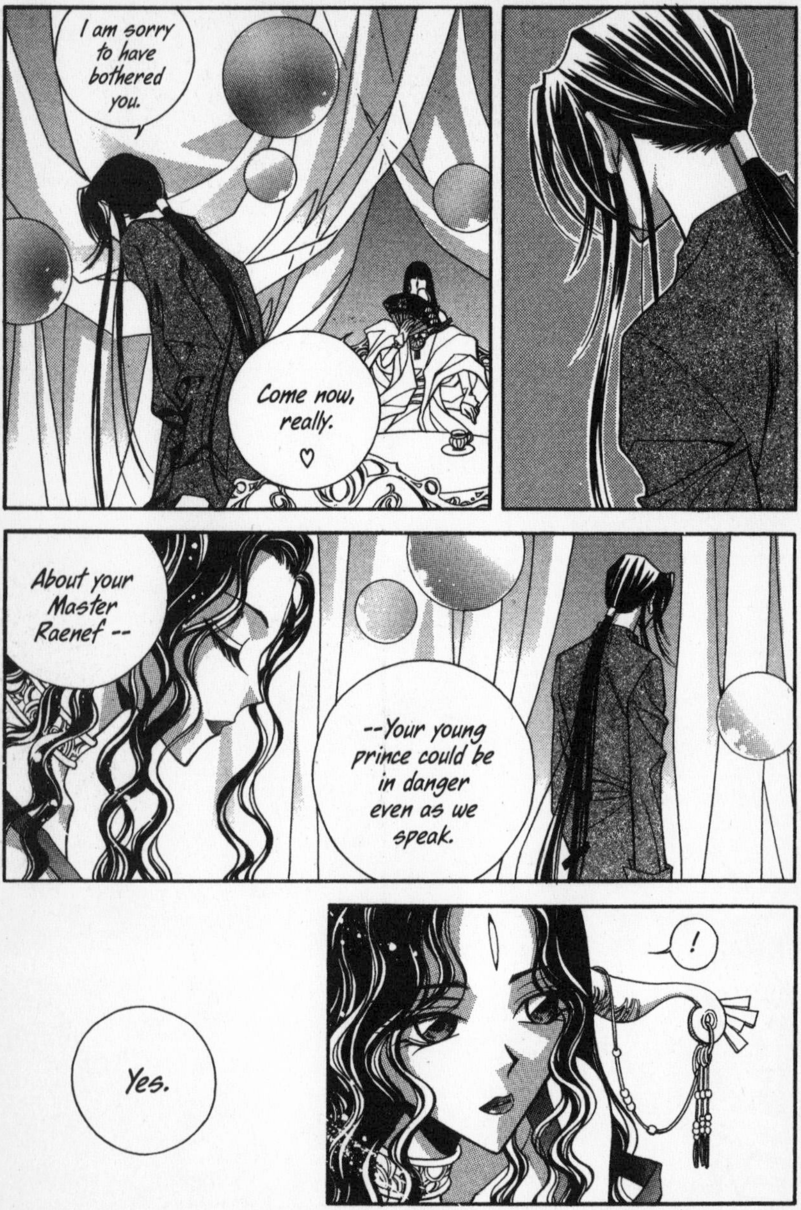
I am sorry to have bothered you.
Come now, really. ♡
About your Master Raenef --
--Your young prince could be in danger even as we speak.
!
Yes.

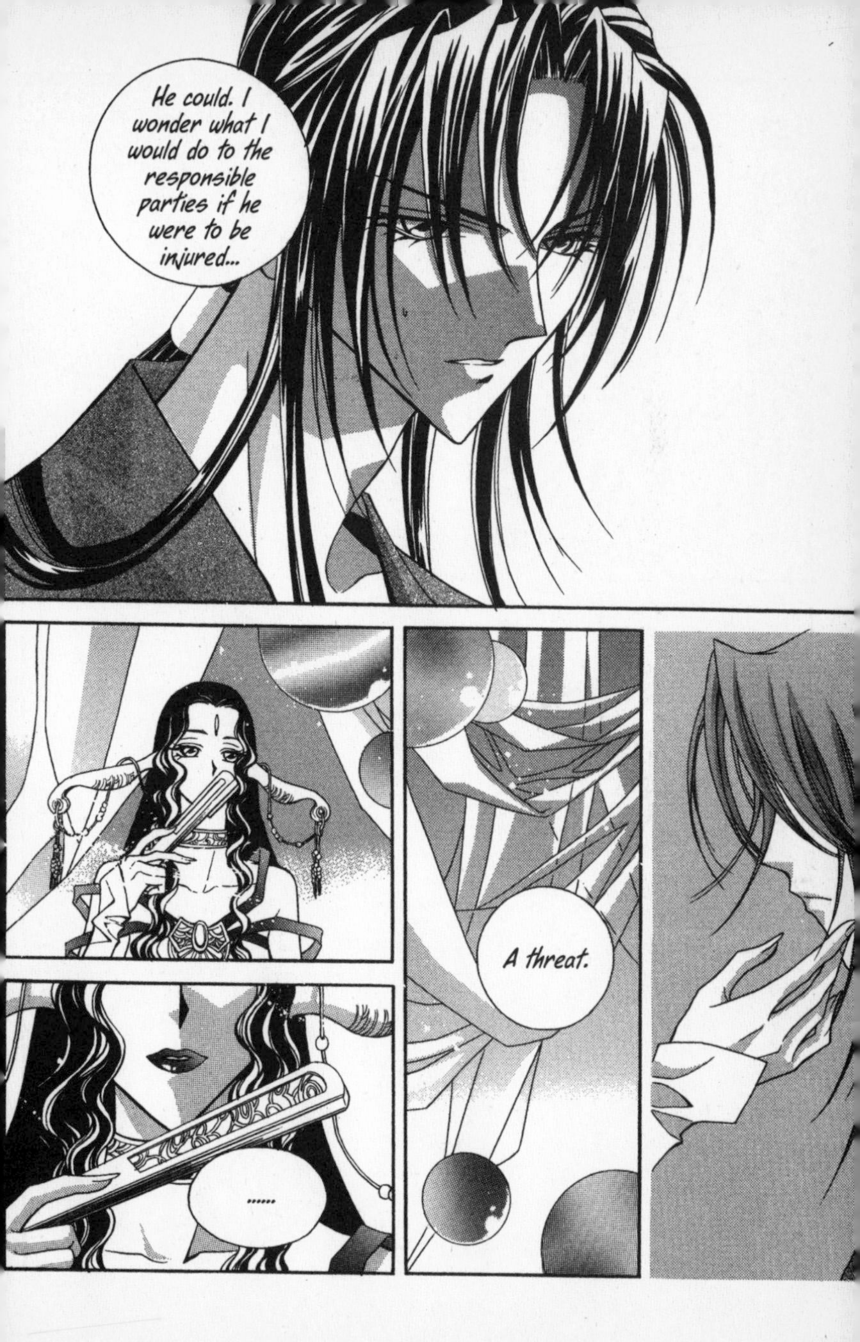
He could. I wonder what I would do to the responsible parties if he were to be injured...
A threat.
......

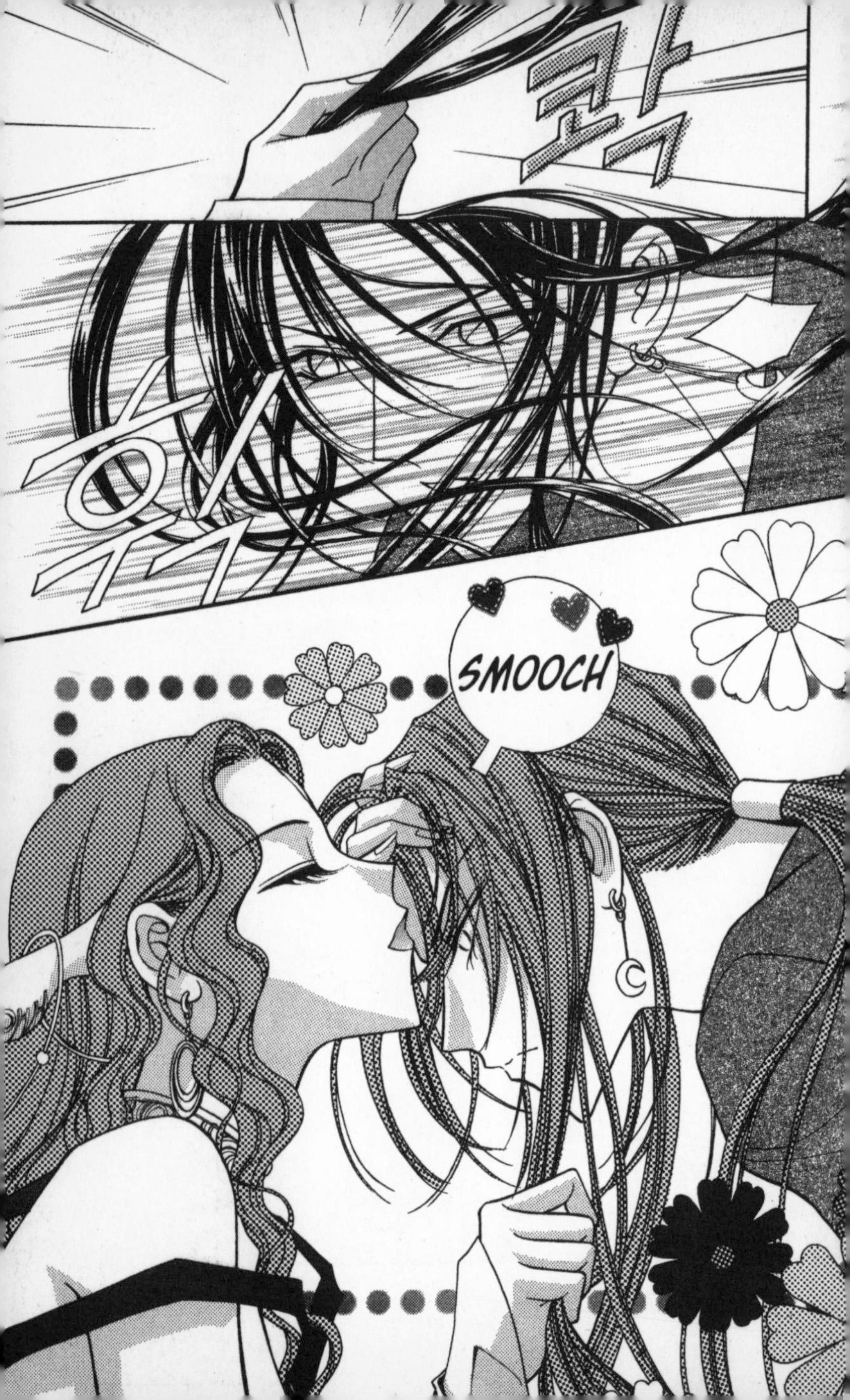
SMOOCH

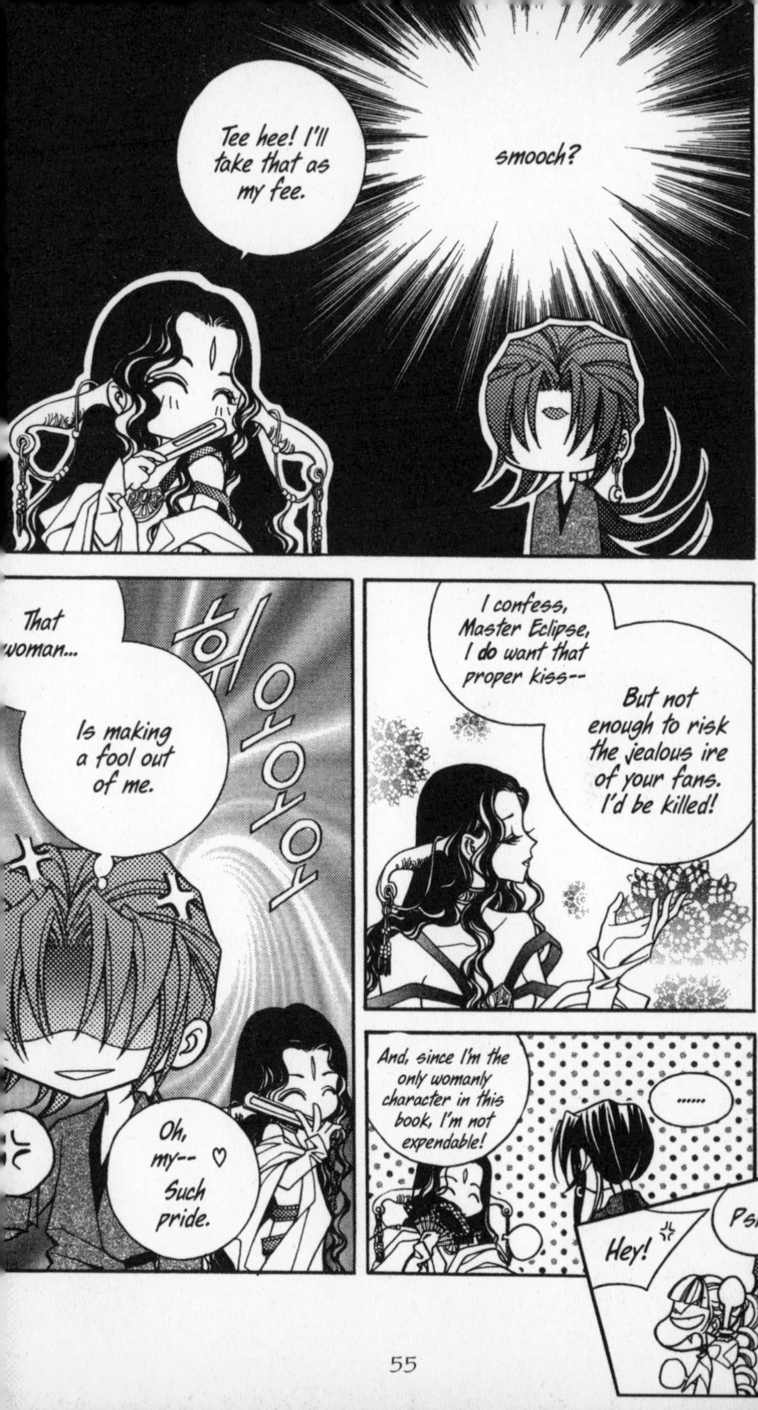
Tee hee! I'll take that as my fee.
smooch?
That woman...
Is making a fool out of me.
Oh, my-- ♡
Such pride.
I confess, Master Eclipse, I do want that proper kiss--
But not enough to risk the jealous ire of your fans. I'd be killed!
And, since I'm the only womanly character in this book, I'm not expendable!
......
Hey!
Pshaw.

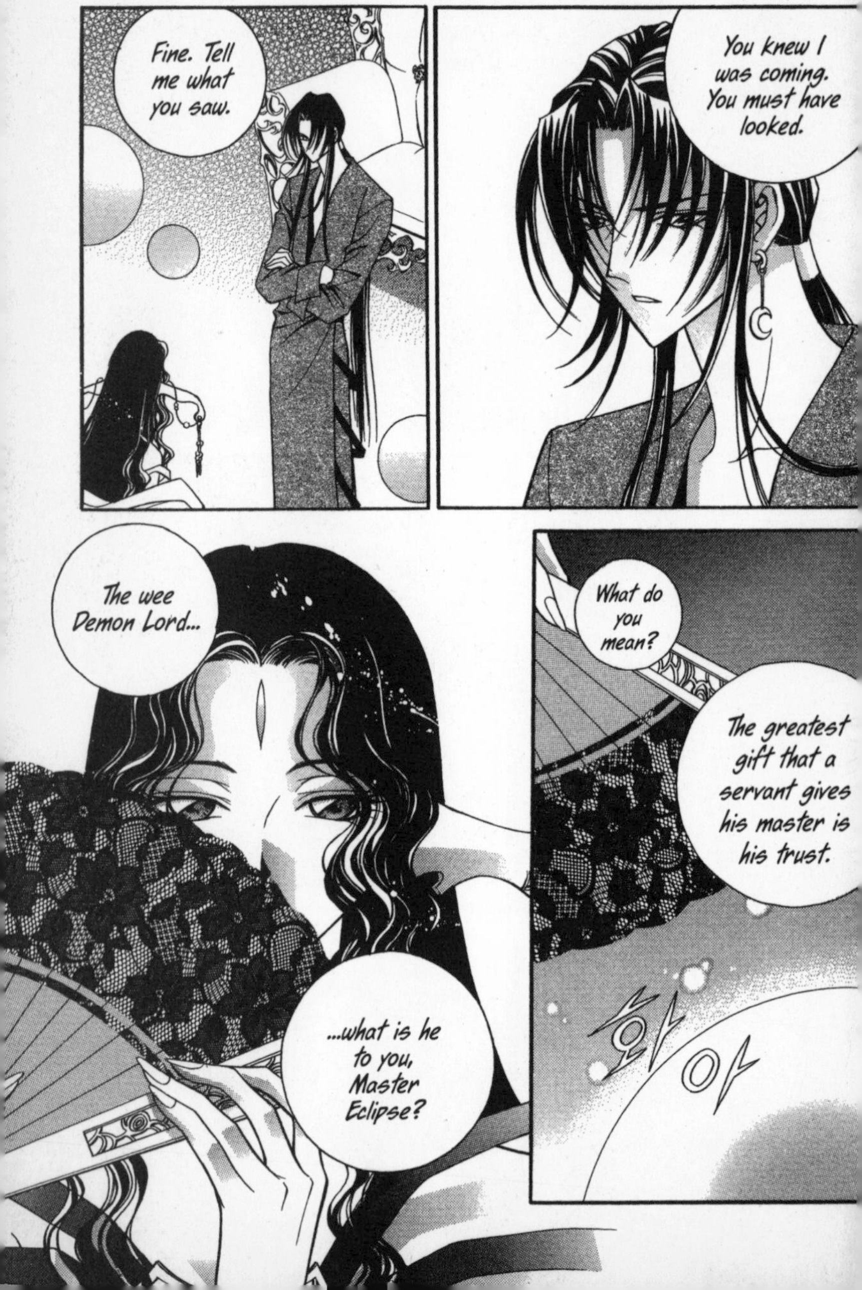
Fine. Tell me what you saw.
You knew I was coming. You must have looked.
The wee Demon Lord...
...what is he to you, Master Eclipse?
What do you mean?
The greatest gift that a servant gives his master is his trust.

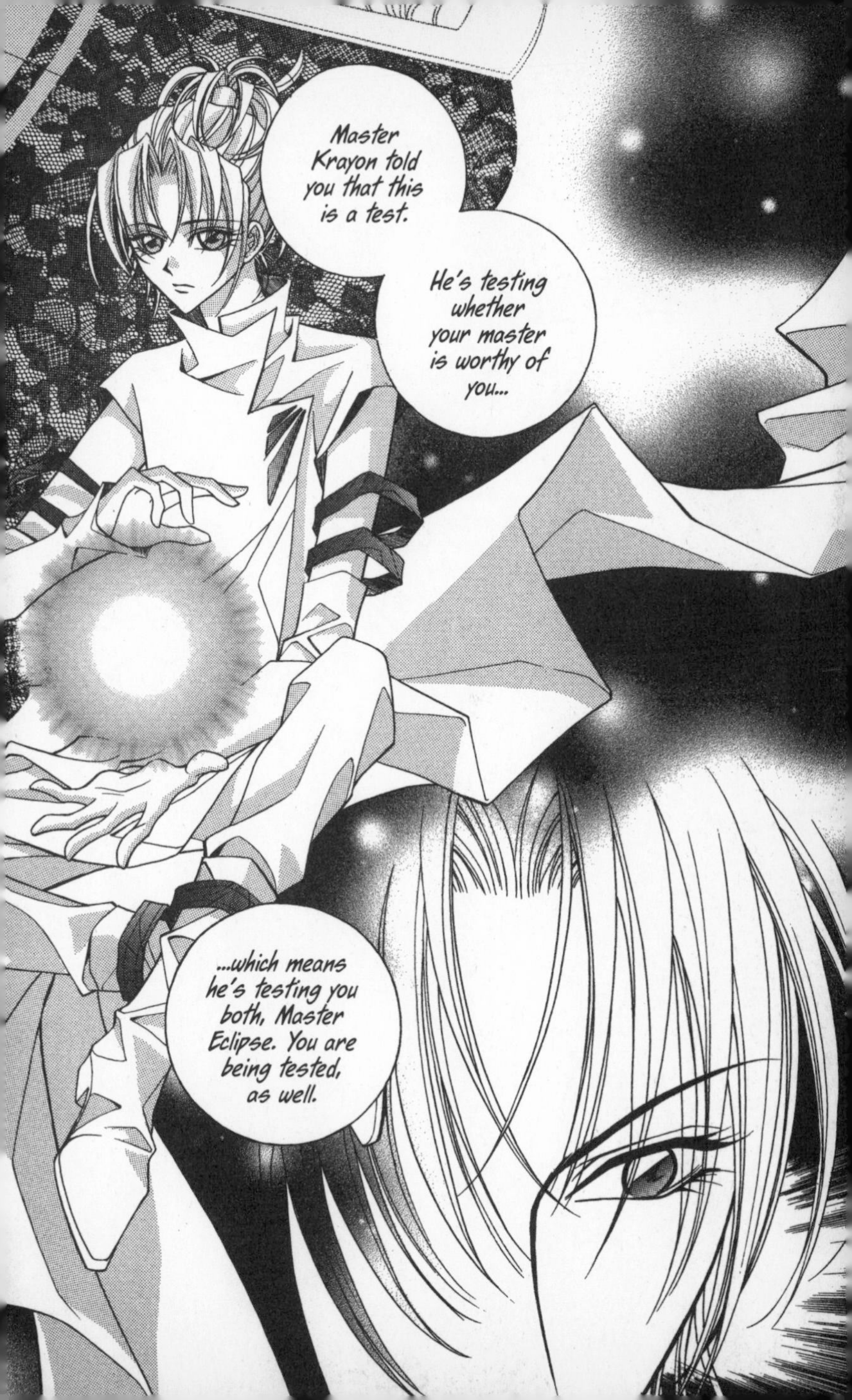
Master Krayon told you that this is a test.
He's testing whether your master is worthy of you...
...which means he's testing you both, Master Eclipse. You are being tested, as well.

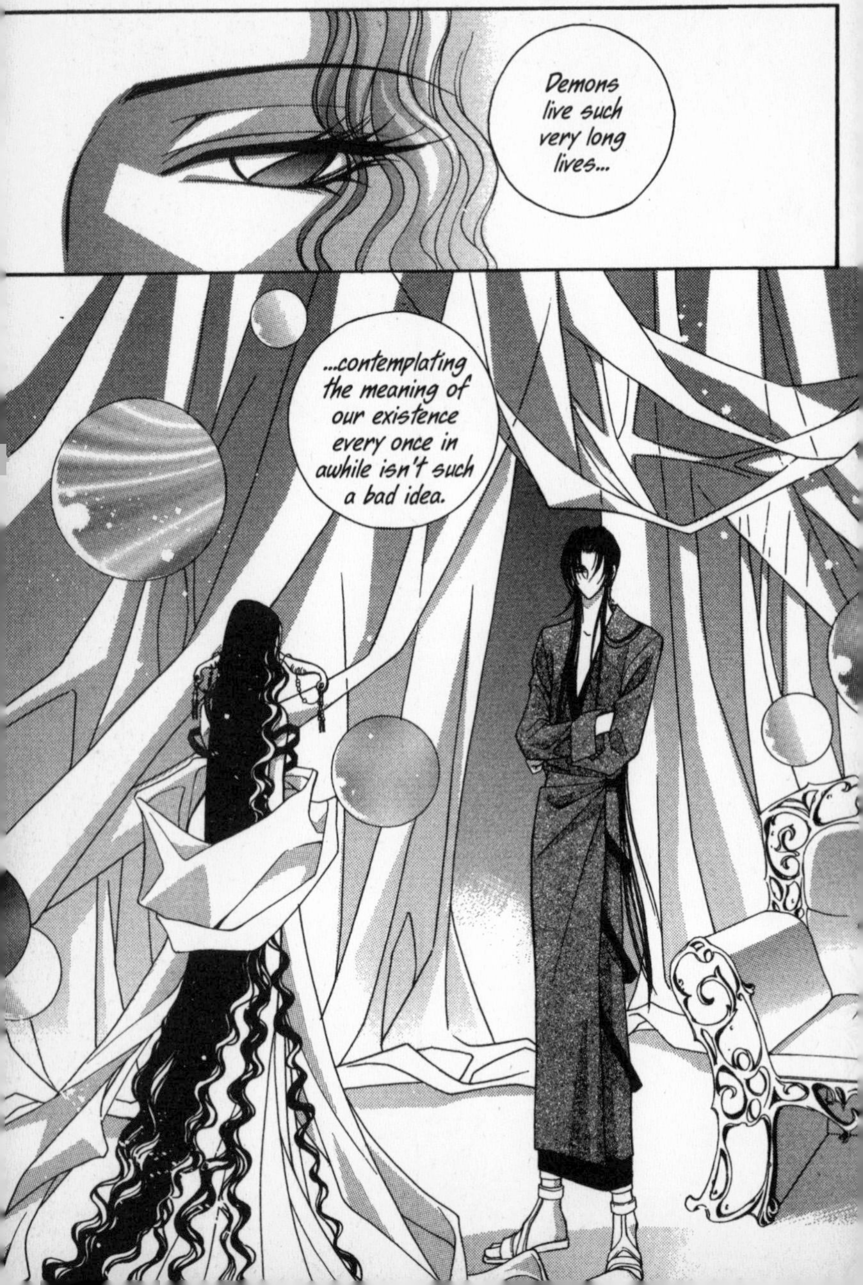
Demons live such very long lives...
...contemplating the meaning of our existence every once in awhile isn't such a bad idea.

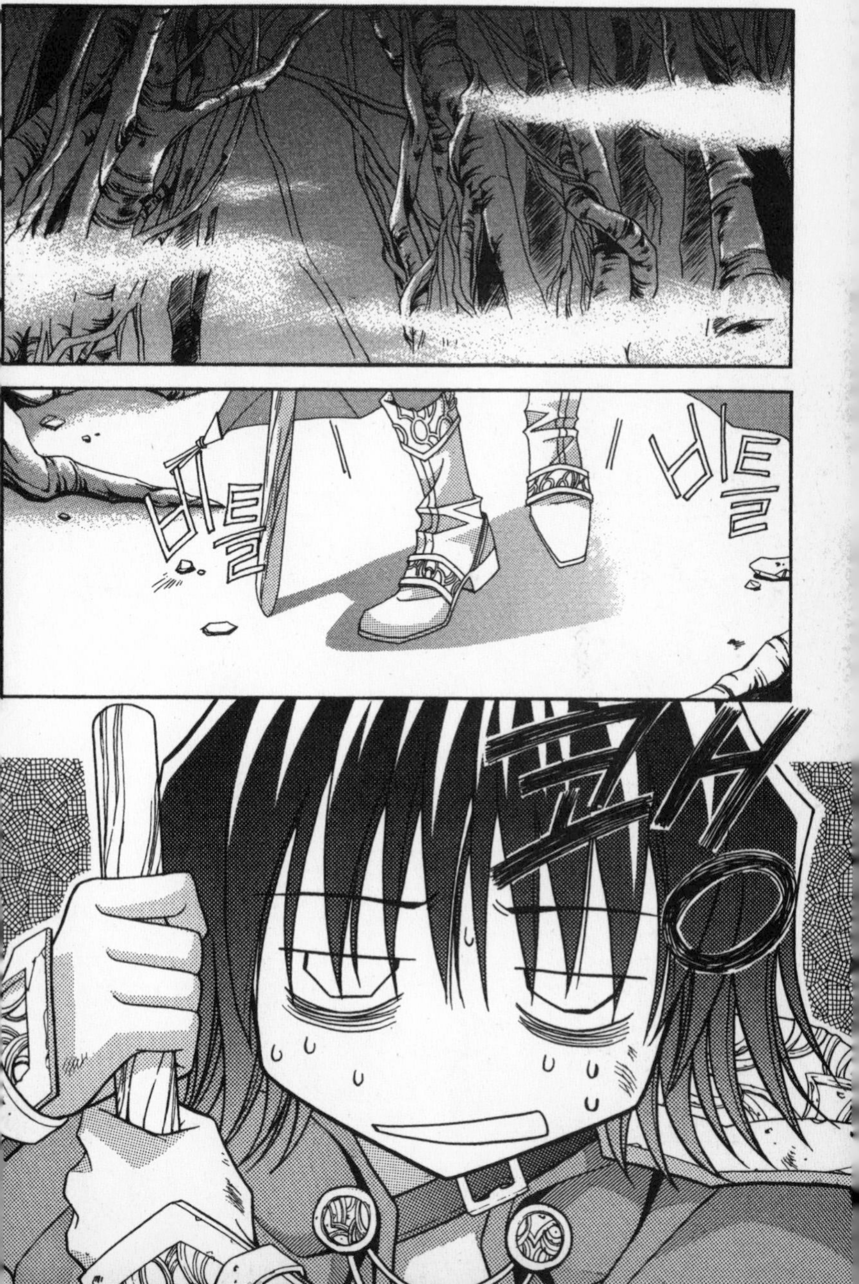

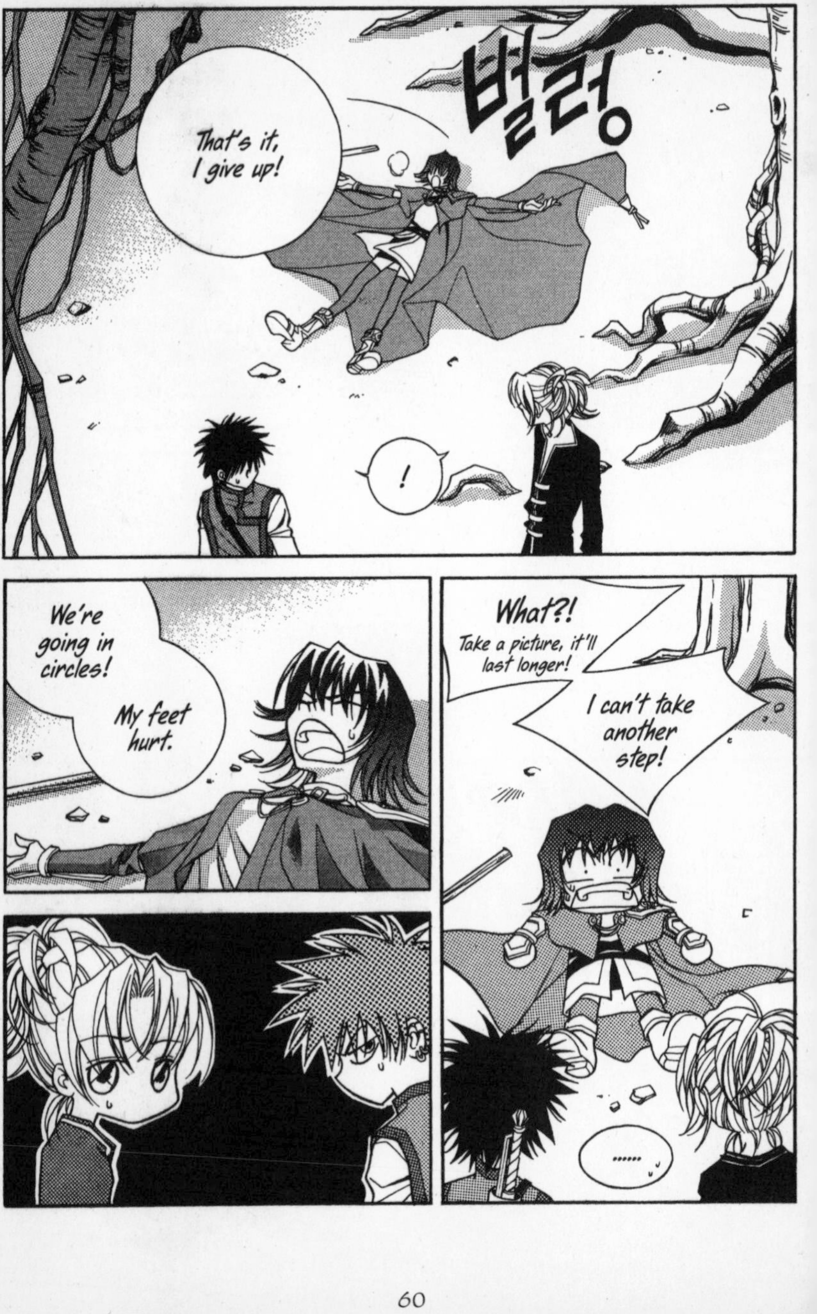
벌렁
That's it, I give up!
!
We're going in circles!
My feet hurt.
What?! Take a picture, it'll last longer!
I can't take another step!
......

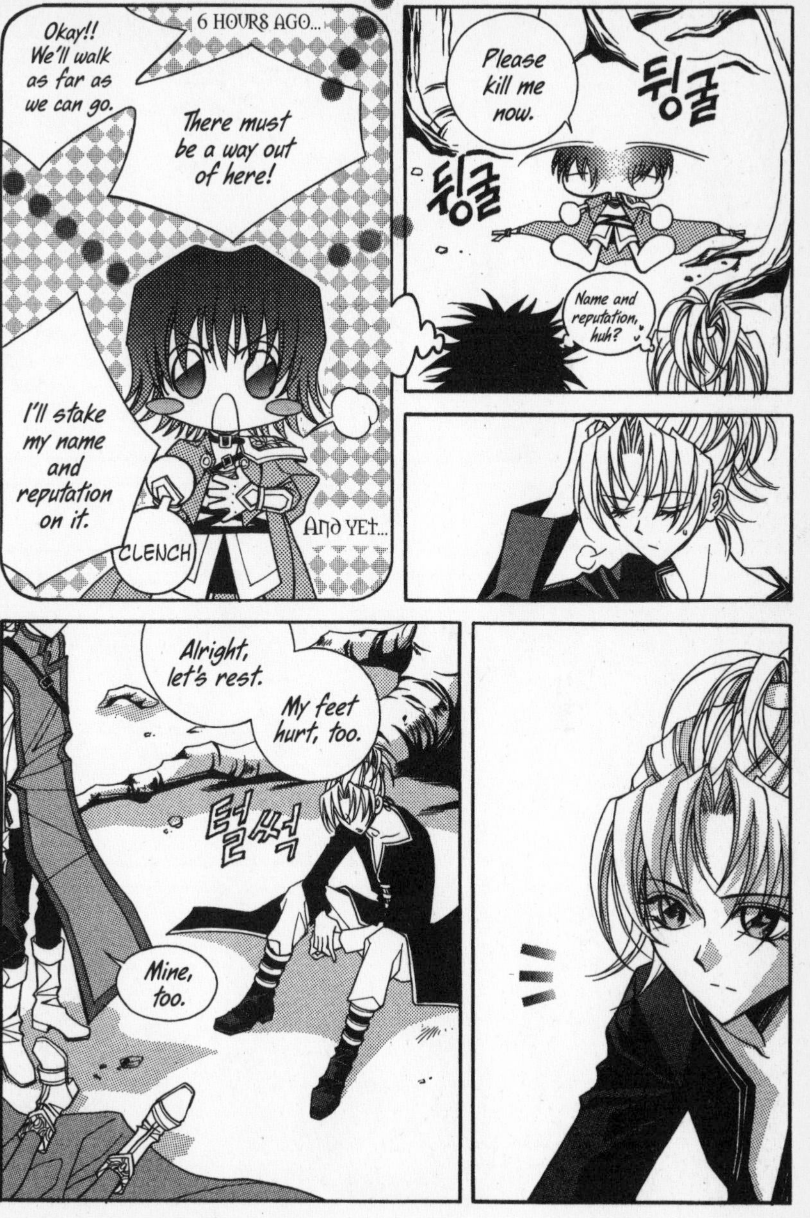
6 HOURS AGO...
Okay!! We'll walk as far as we can go.
There must be a way out of here!
I'll stake my name and reputation on it.
CLENCH
And yet...
Please kill me now.
뒹굴
뒹굴
Name and reputation, huh?
Alright, let's rest.
My feet hurt, too.
털썩
Mine, too.

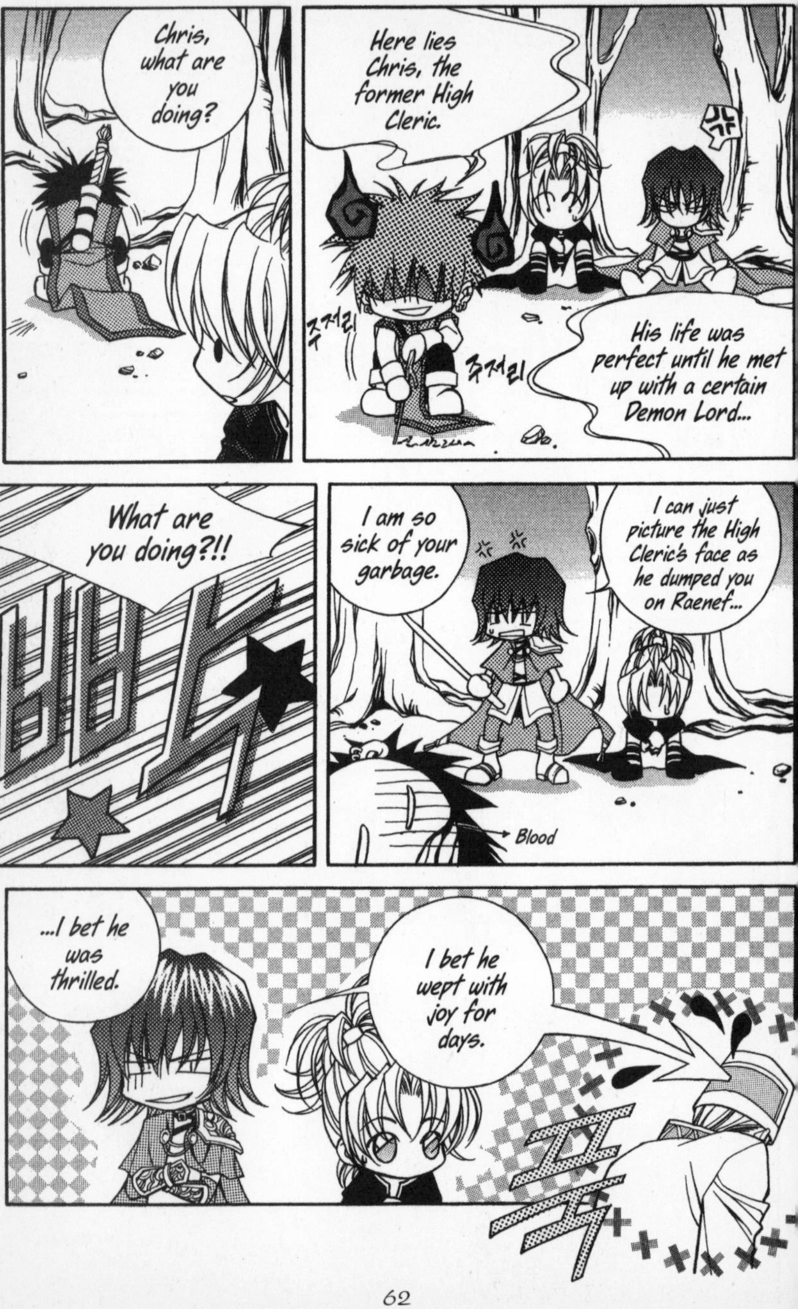
Chris, what are you doing?
Here lies Chris, the former High Cleric.
주저리
주저리
His life was perfect until he met up with a certain Demon Lord...
What are you doing?!!
I am so sick of your garbage.
I can just picture the High Cleric's face as he dumped you on Raenef...
Blood
...I bet he was thrilled.
I bet he wept with joy for days.

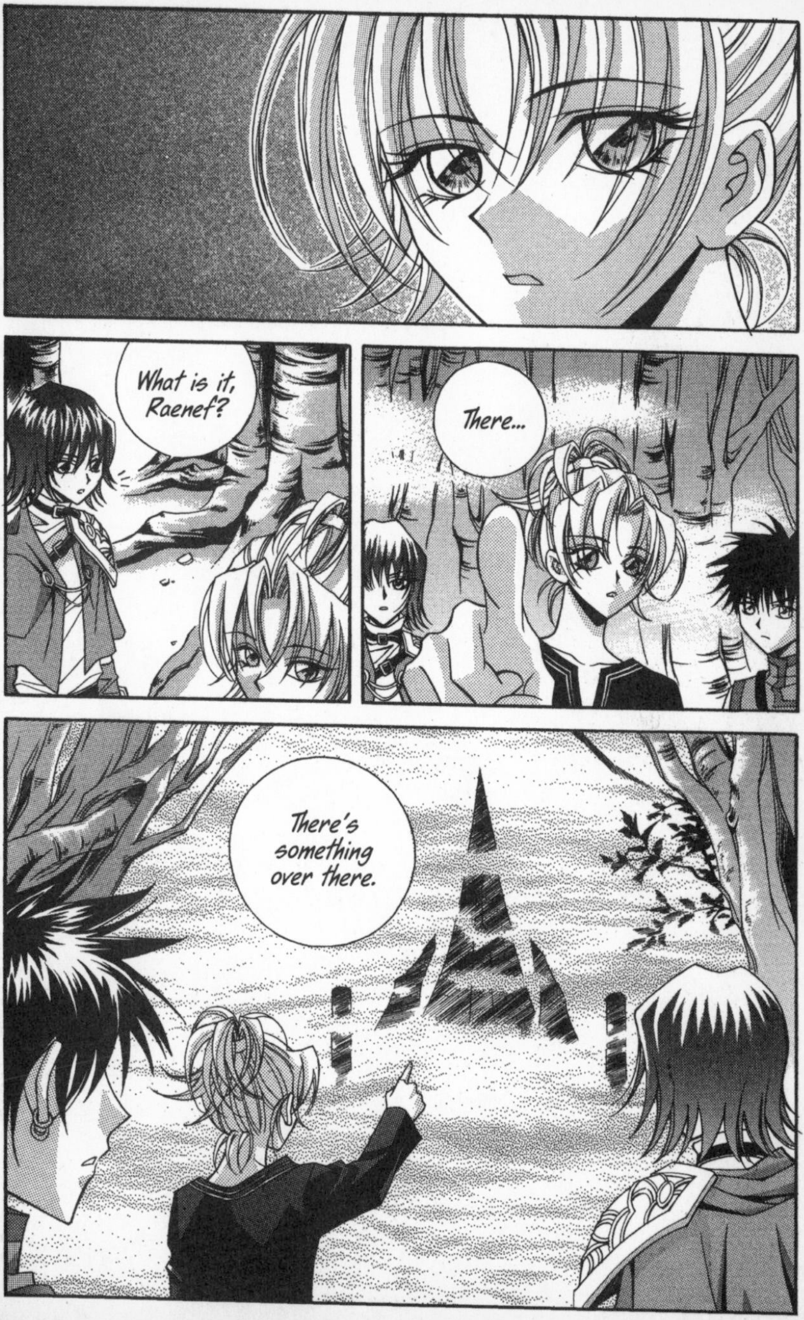
What is it, Raenef?
There...
There's something over there.

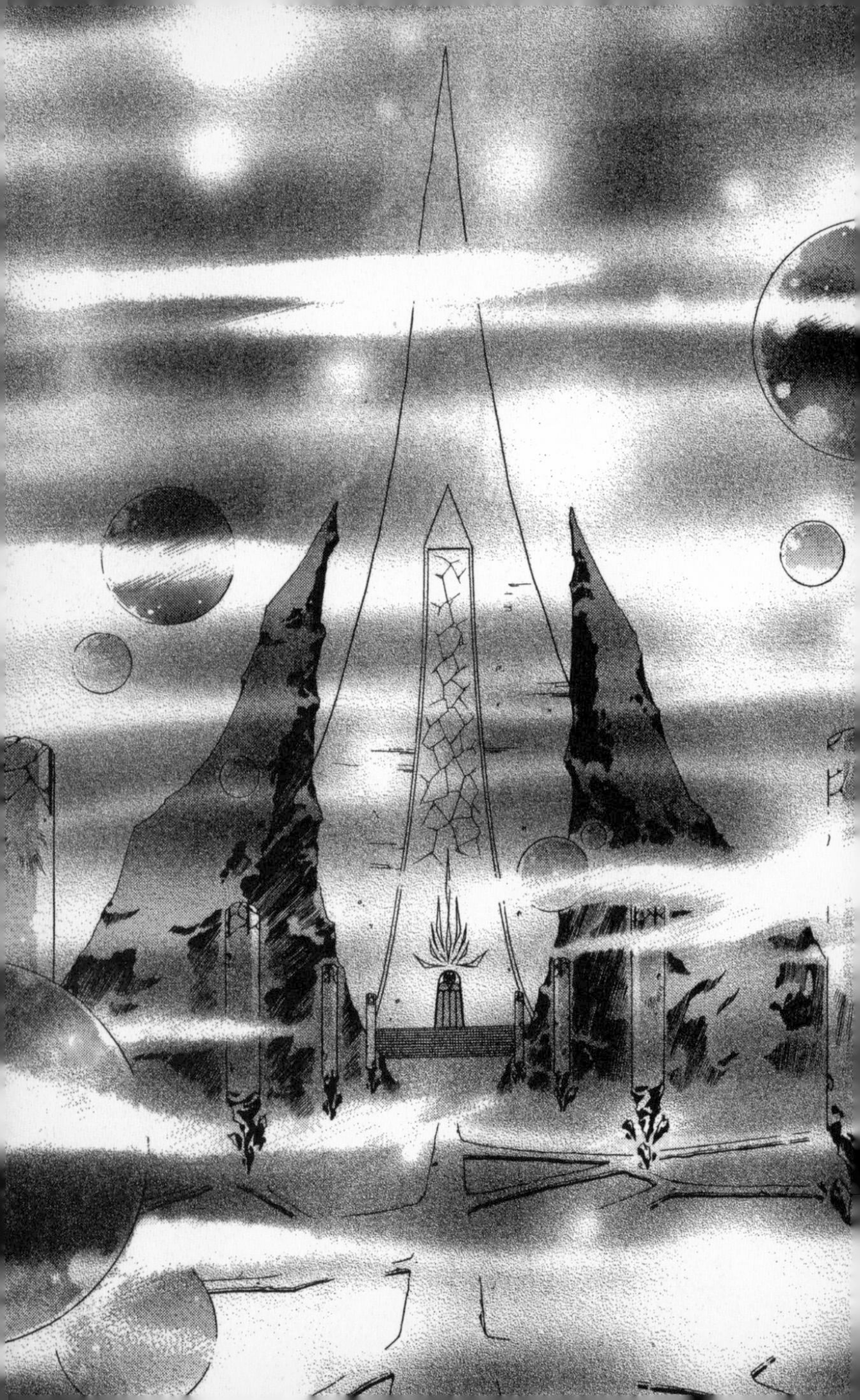

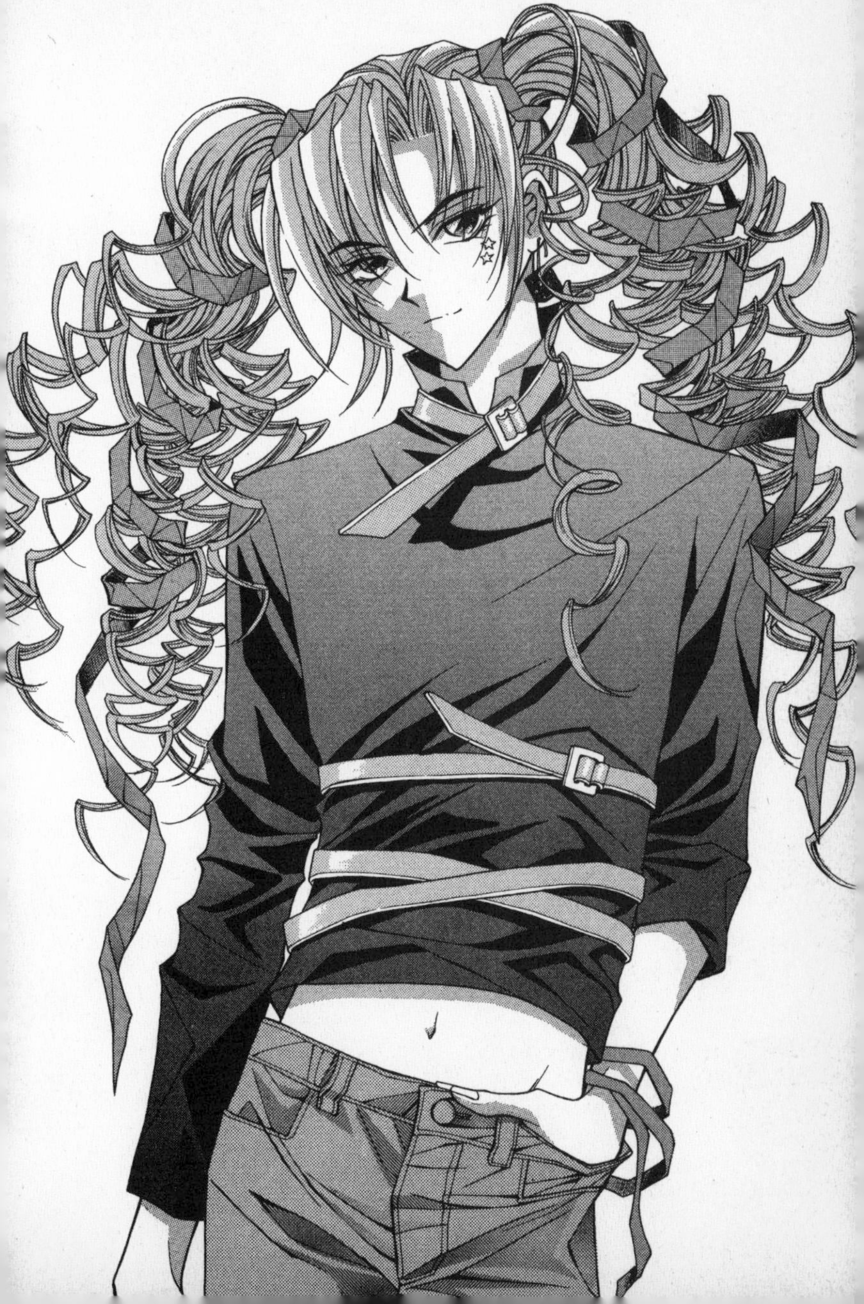

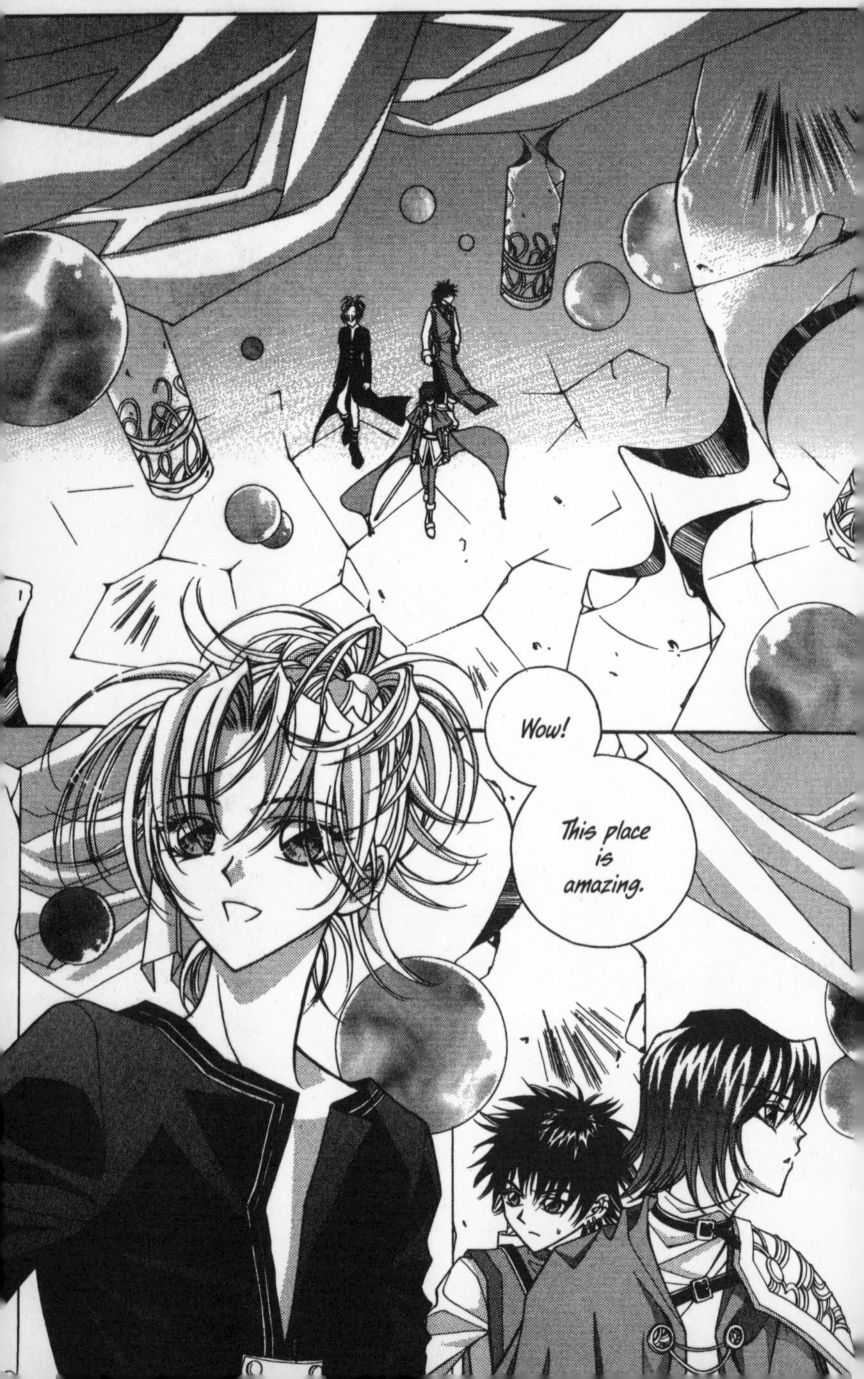
Wow!
This place is amazing.

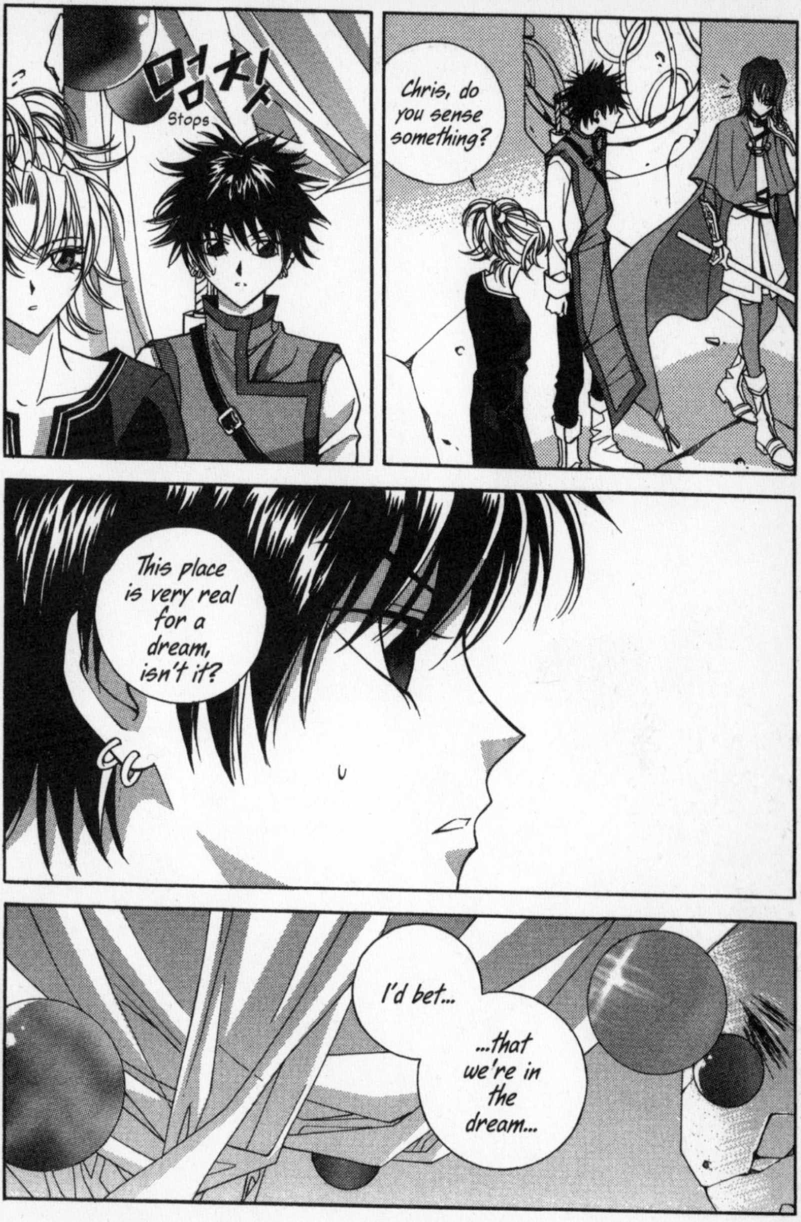
멈칫!
Stops
Chris, do you sense something?
This place is very real for a dream, isn't it?
I'd bet...
...that we're in the dream...

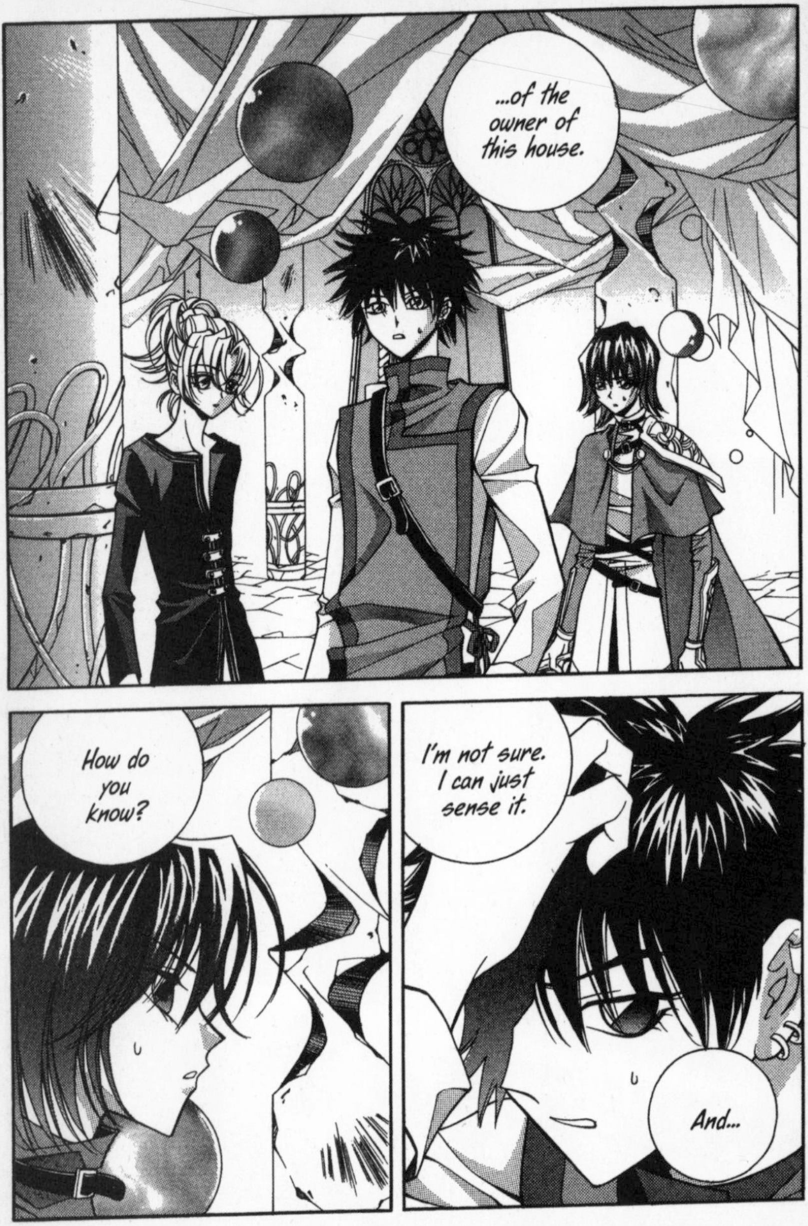
...of the owner of this house.
How do you know?
I'm not sure. I can just sense it.
And...

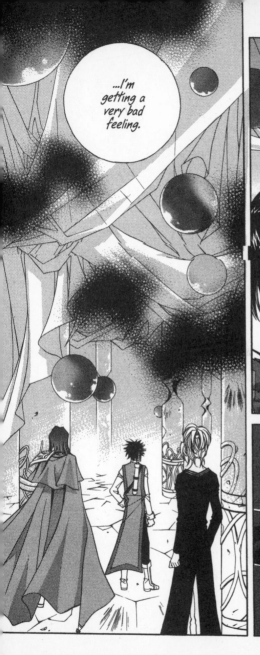

...I'm getting a very bad feeling.

A bad feeling? I don't feel anything.

Lean

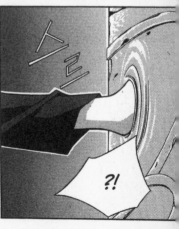

?!

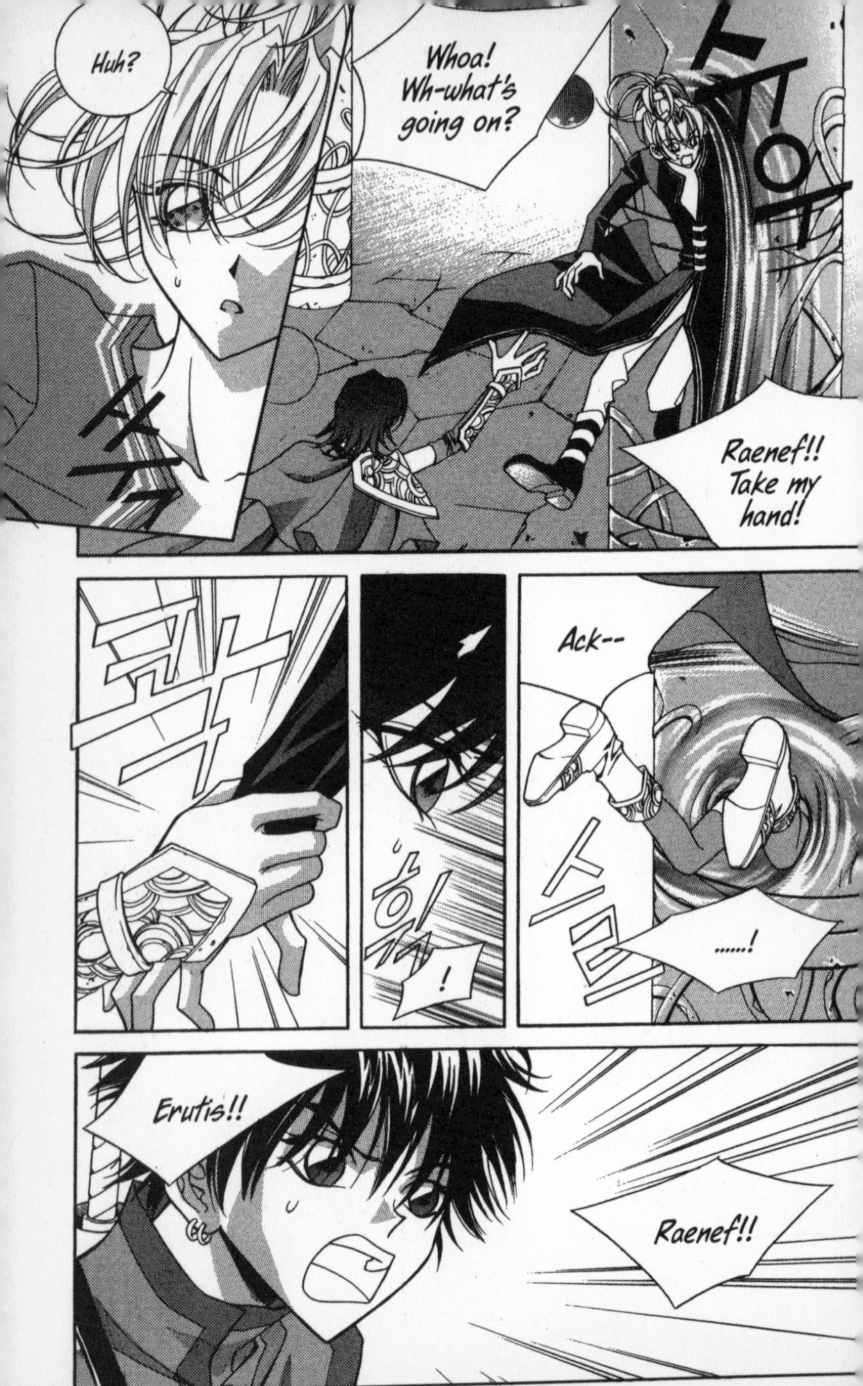
Huh?
Whoa! Wh-what's going on?
Raenef!! Take my hand!
!
Ack--
......!
Erutis!!
Raenef!!

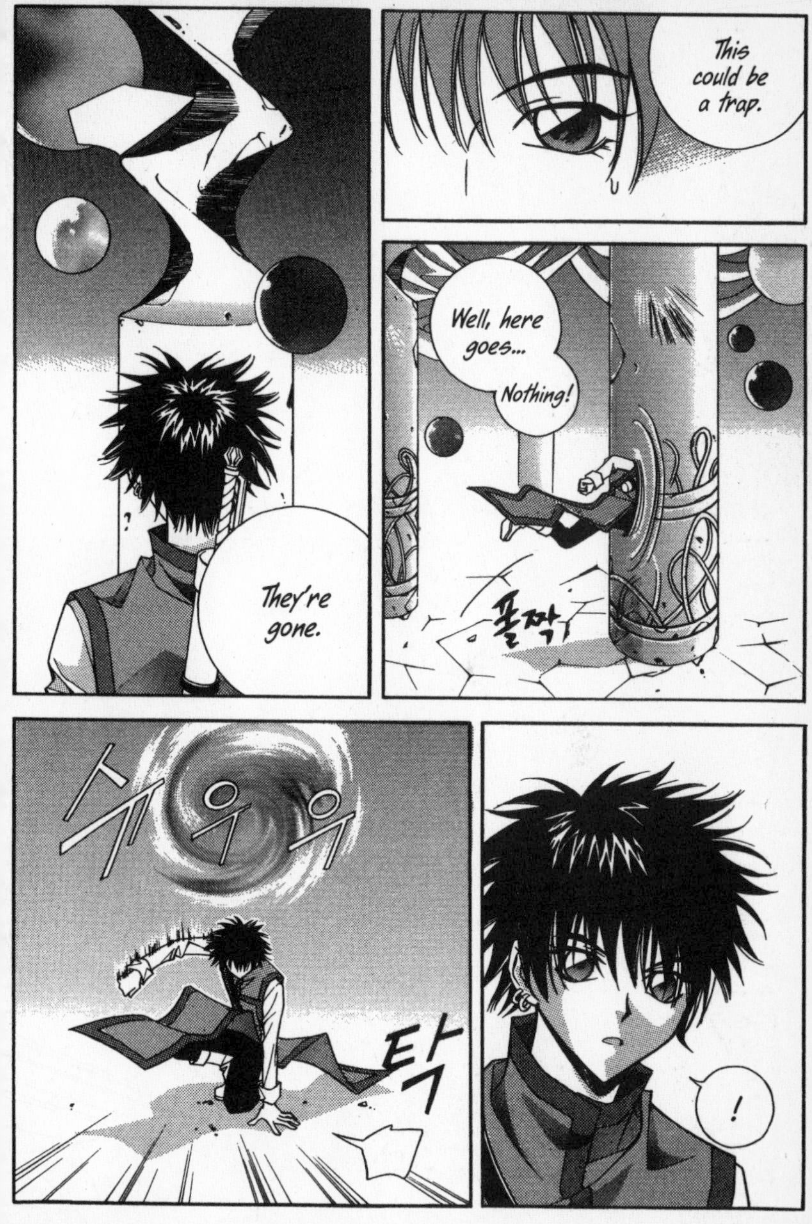
They're gone.
This could be a trap.
Well, here goes...
Nothing!
폴짝
탁
!

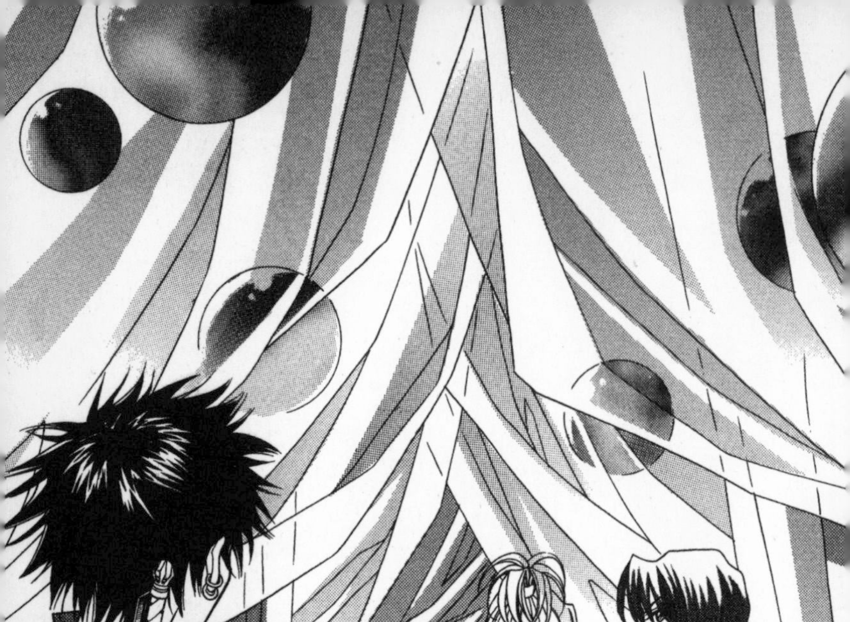

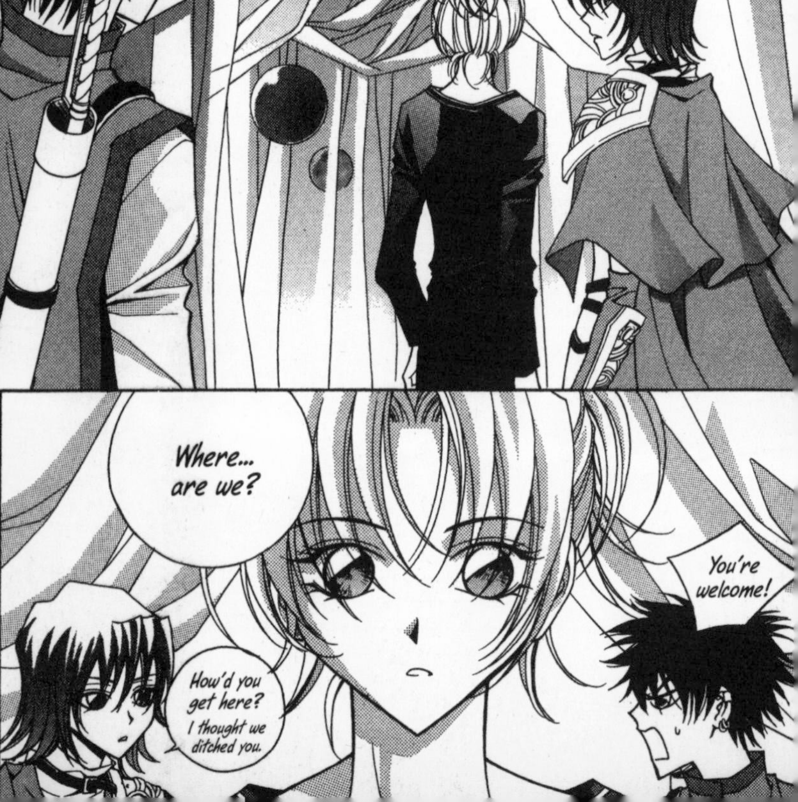
You're welcome!
Where... are we?
How'd you get here? I thought we ditched you.

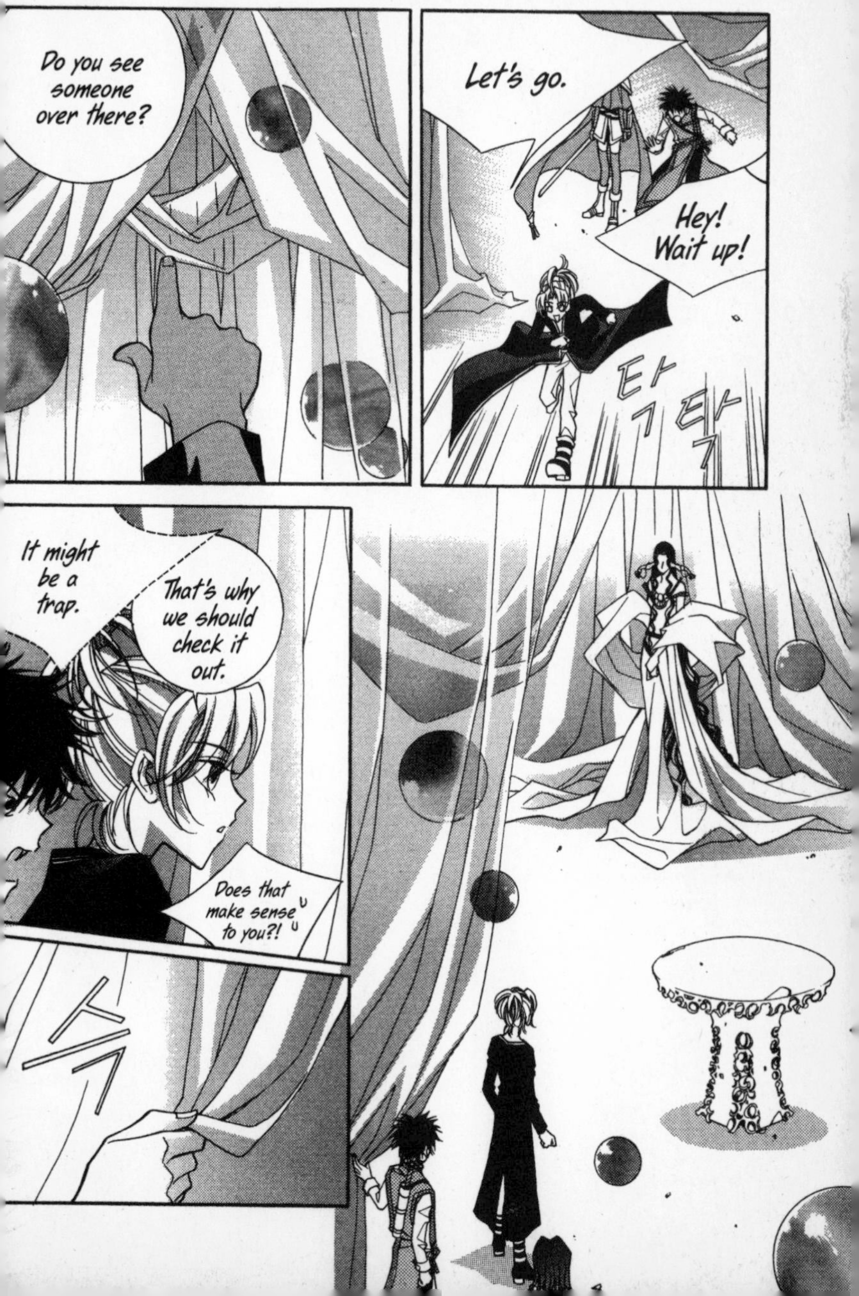
Do you see someone over there?
Let's go.
Hey! Wait up!
탁탁
It might be a trap.
That's why we should check it out.
Does that make sense to you?!

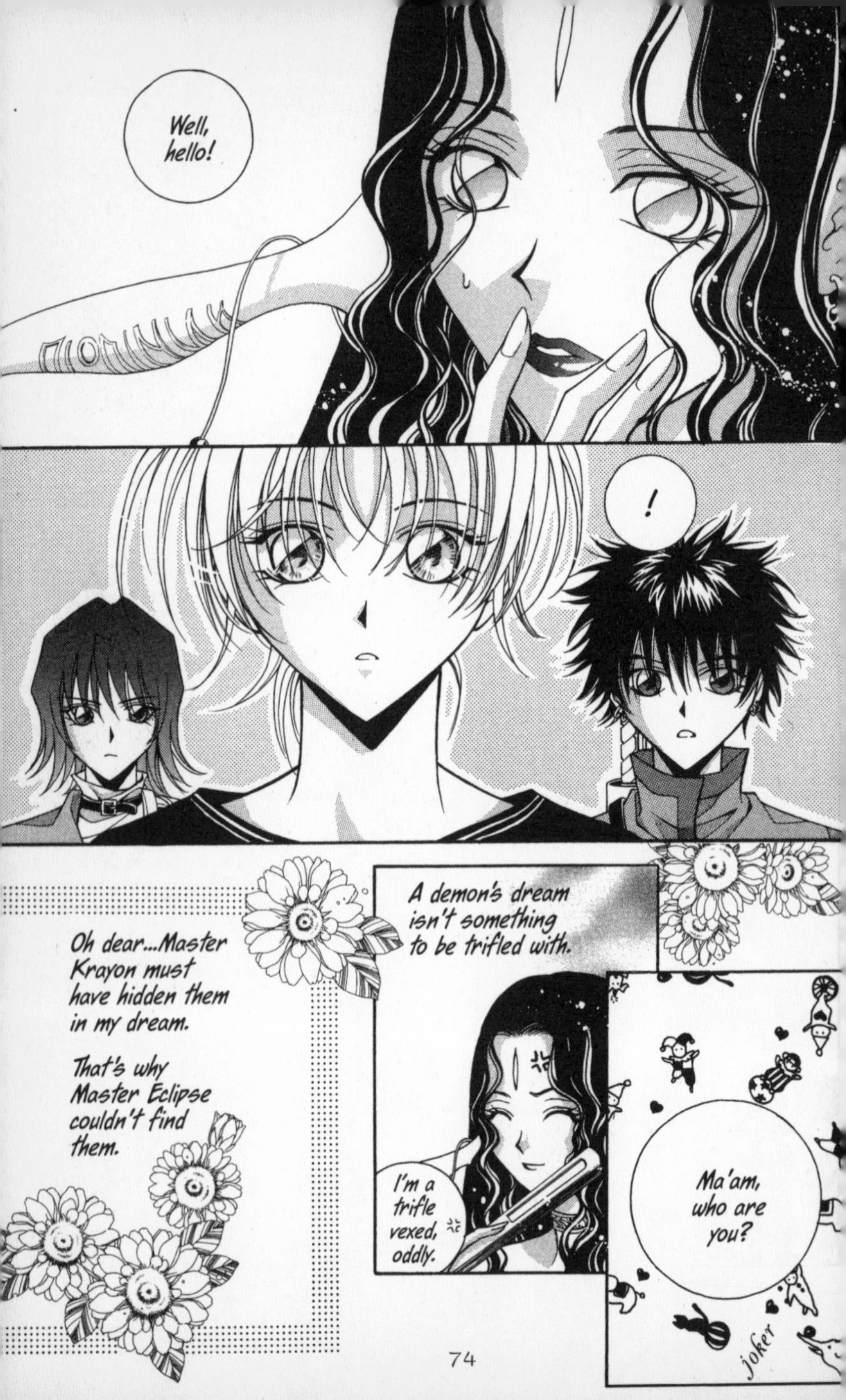
Well, hello!
!
Ma'am, who are you?
joker
A demon's dream isn't something to be trifled with.
I'm a trifle vexed, oddly.
Oh dear...Master Krayon must have hidden them in my dream.
That's why Master Eclipse couldn't find them.

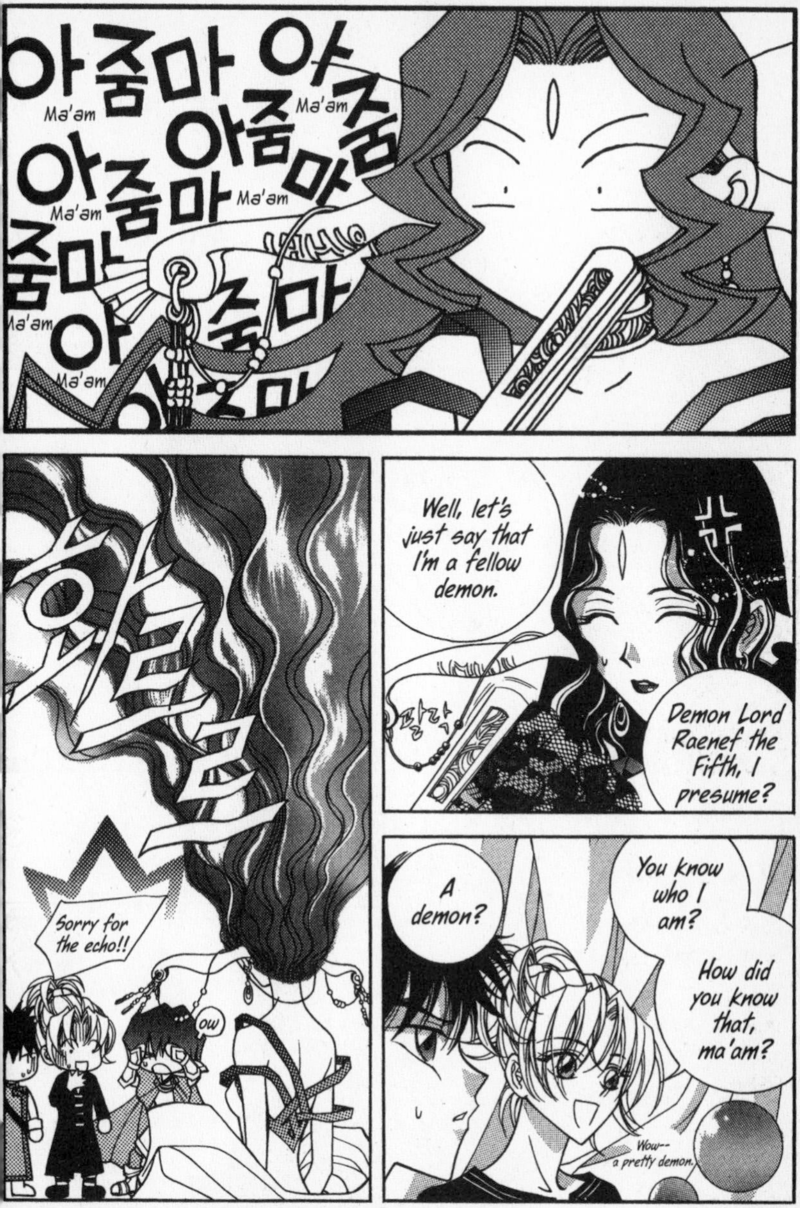
아줌마
Ma'am
Ma'am
아줌마
Ma'am
Ma'am
Ma'am
Ma'am
Sorry for the echo!!
ow
Well, let's just say that I'm a fellow demon.
Demon Lord Raenef the Fifth, I presume?
A demon?
You know who I am?
How did you know that, ma'am?
Wow-- a pretty demon.

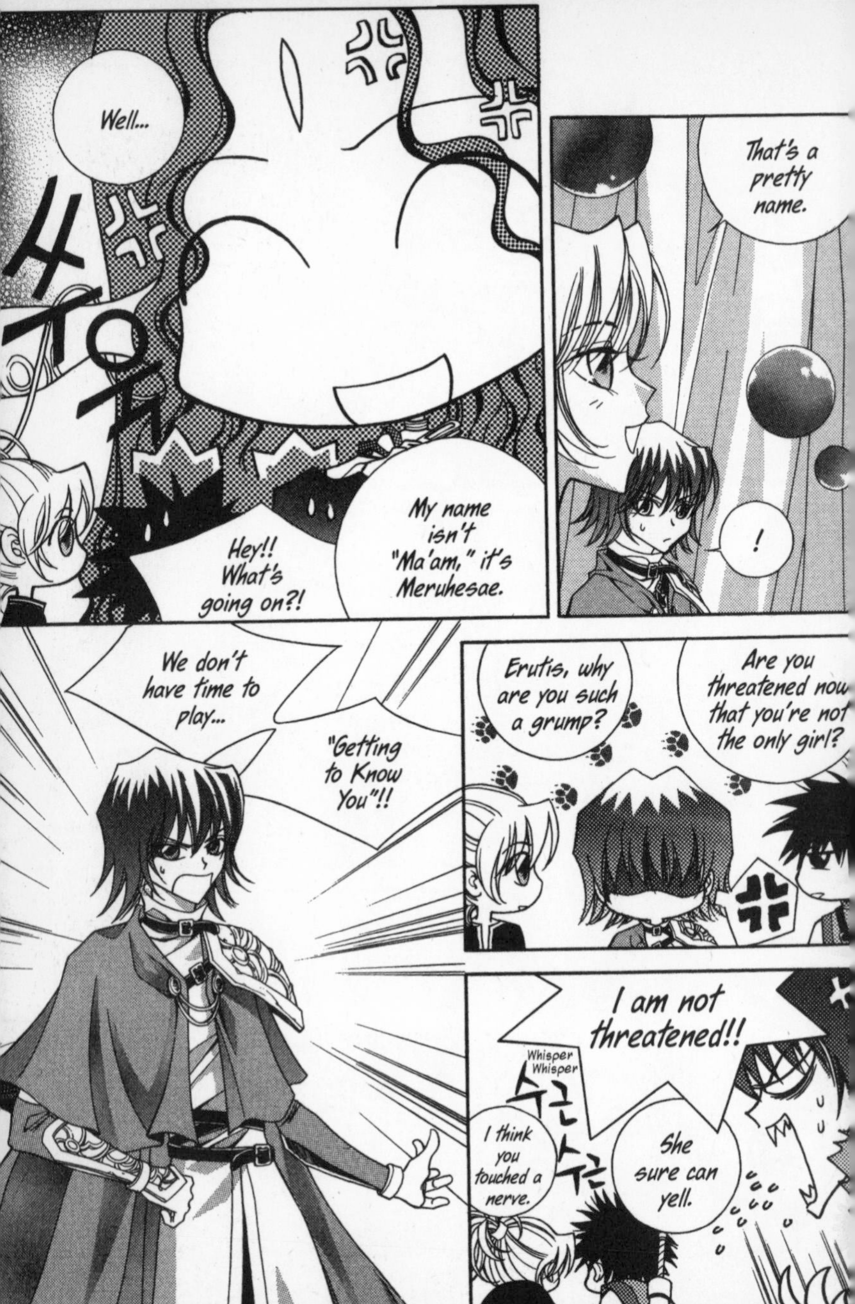
Well...
My name isn't "Ma'am," it's Meruhesae.
Hey!! What's going on?!
That's a pretty name.
!
We don't have time to play...
"Getting to Know You"!!
Erutis, why are you such a grump?
Are you threatened now that you're not the only girl?
I am not threatened!!
Whisper Whisper
수근수근
I think you touched a nerve.
She sure can yell.

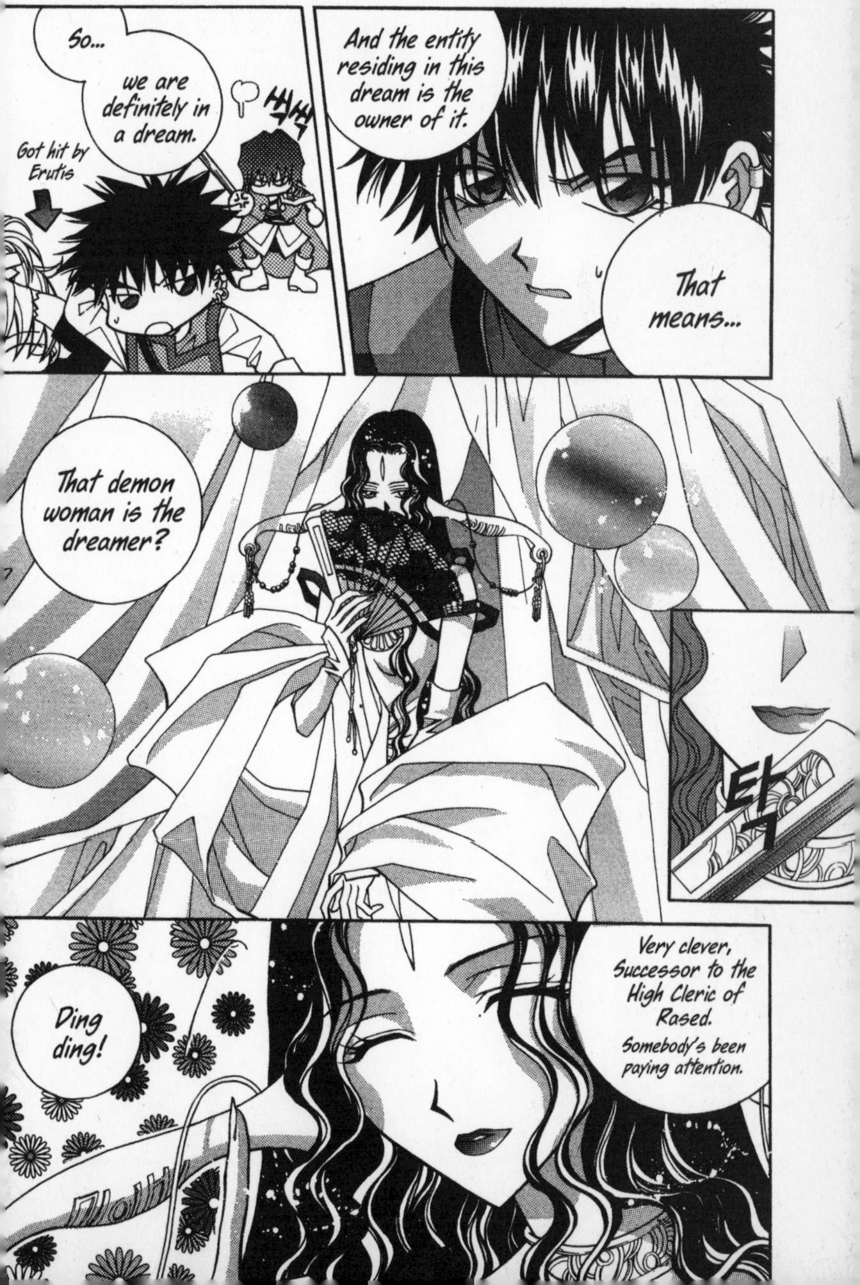
So...
we are definitely in a dream.
Got hit by Erutis
And the entity residing in this dream is the owner of it.
That means...
That demon woman is the dreamer?
탁
Ding ding!
Very clever, Successor to the High Cleric of Rased.
Somebody's been paying attention.

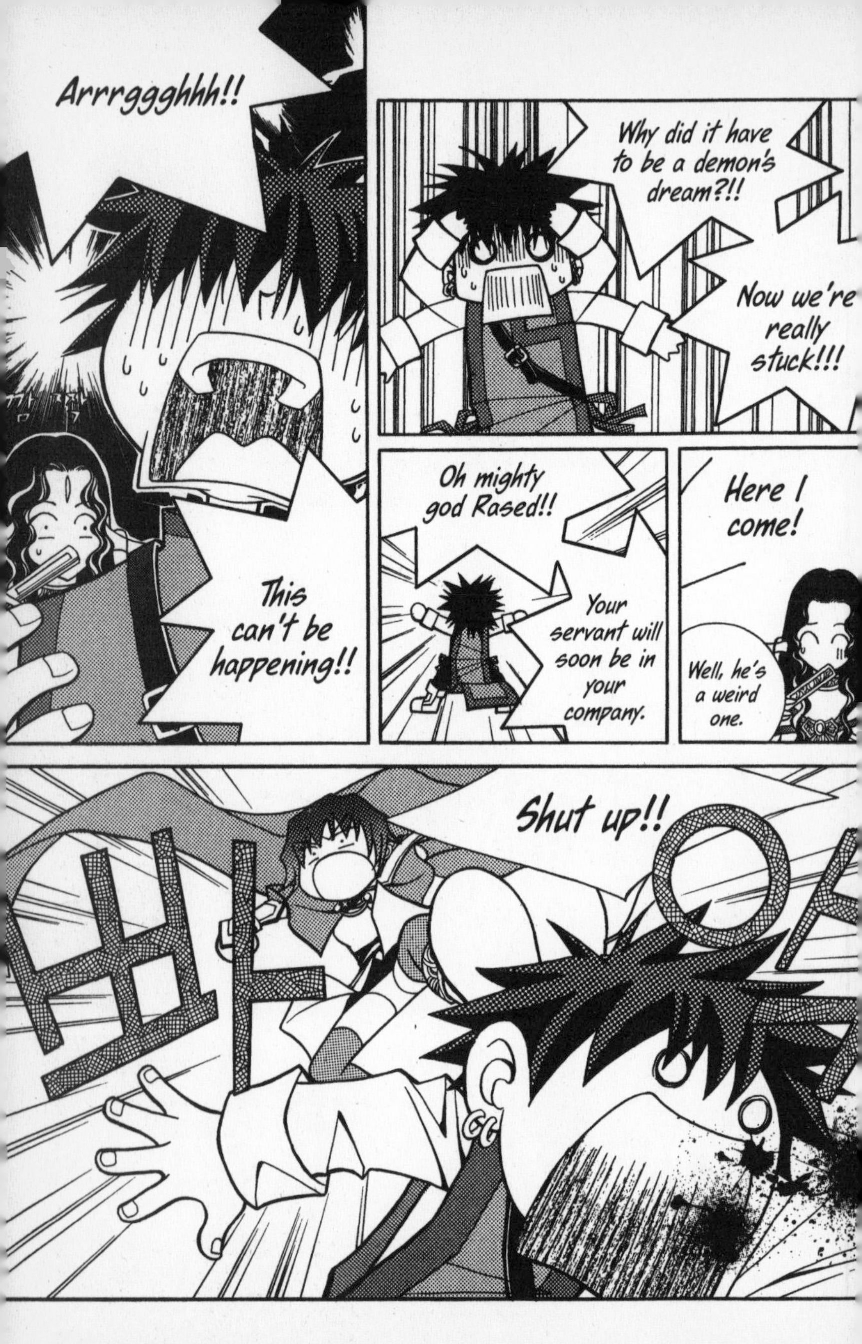
Why did it have to be a demon's dream?!!
Now we're really stuck!!!
Here I come!
Well, he's a weird one.
Oh mighty god Rased!!
Your servant will soon be in your company.
Arrrggghhh!!
This can't be happening!!
Shut up!!

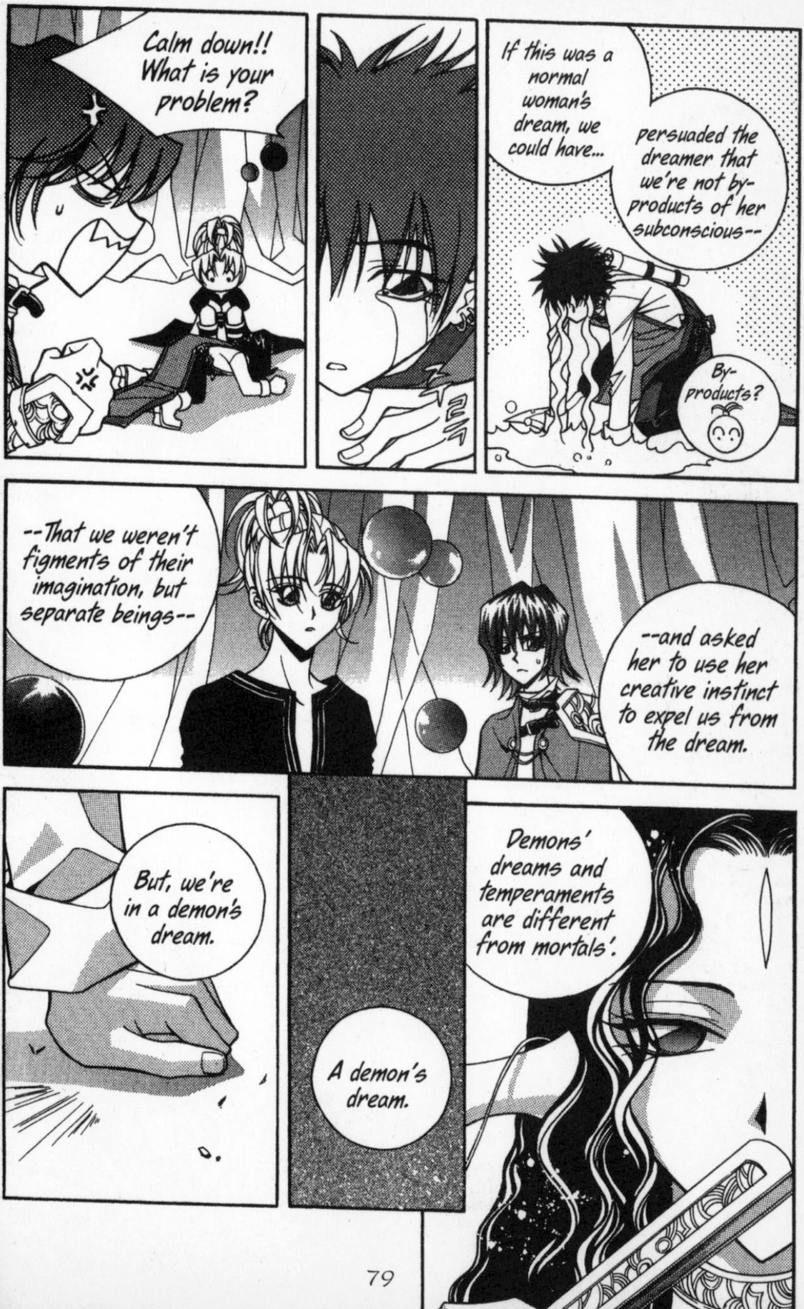
Calm down!! What is your problem?
If this was a normal woman's dream, we could have...
persuaded the dreamer that we're not by-products of her subconscious--
By-products?
--That we weren't figments of their imagination, but separate beings--
--and asked her to use her creative instinct to expel us from the dream.
But, we're in a demon's dream.
A demon's dream.
Demons' dreams and temperaments are different from mortals'.

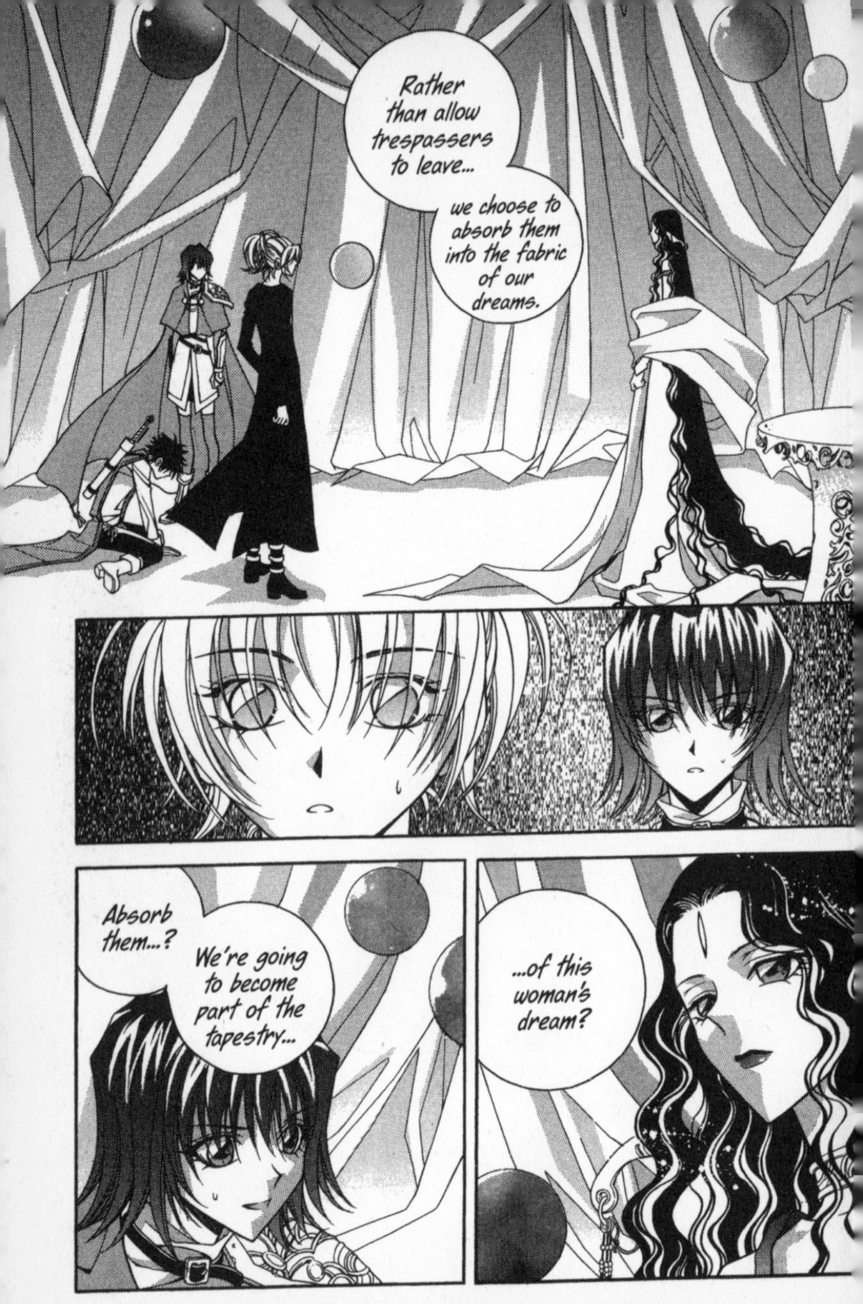
Rather than allow trespassers to leave...
we choose to absorb them into the fabric of our dreams.
...of this woman's dream?
Absorb them...?
We're going to become part of the tapestry...

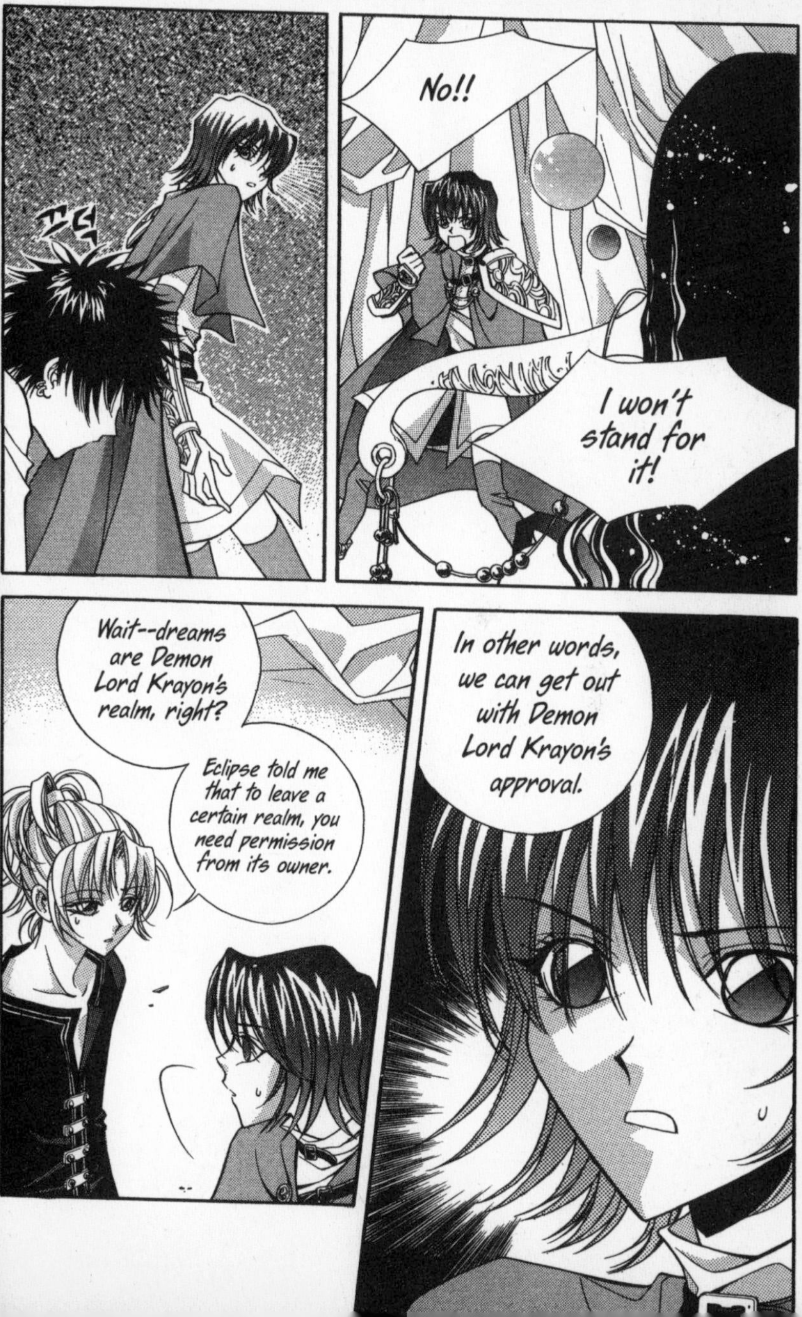
No!!
I won't stand for it!
Wait--dreams are Demon Lord Krayon's realm, right?
Eclipse told me that to leave a certain realm, you need permission from its owner.
In other words, we can get out with Demon Lord Krayon's approval.

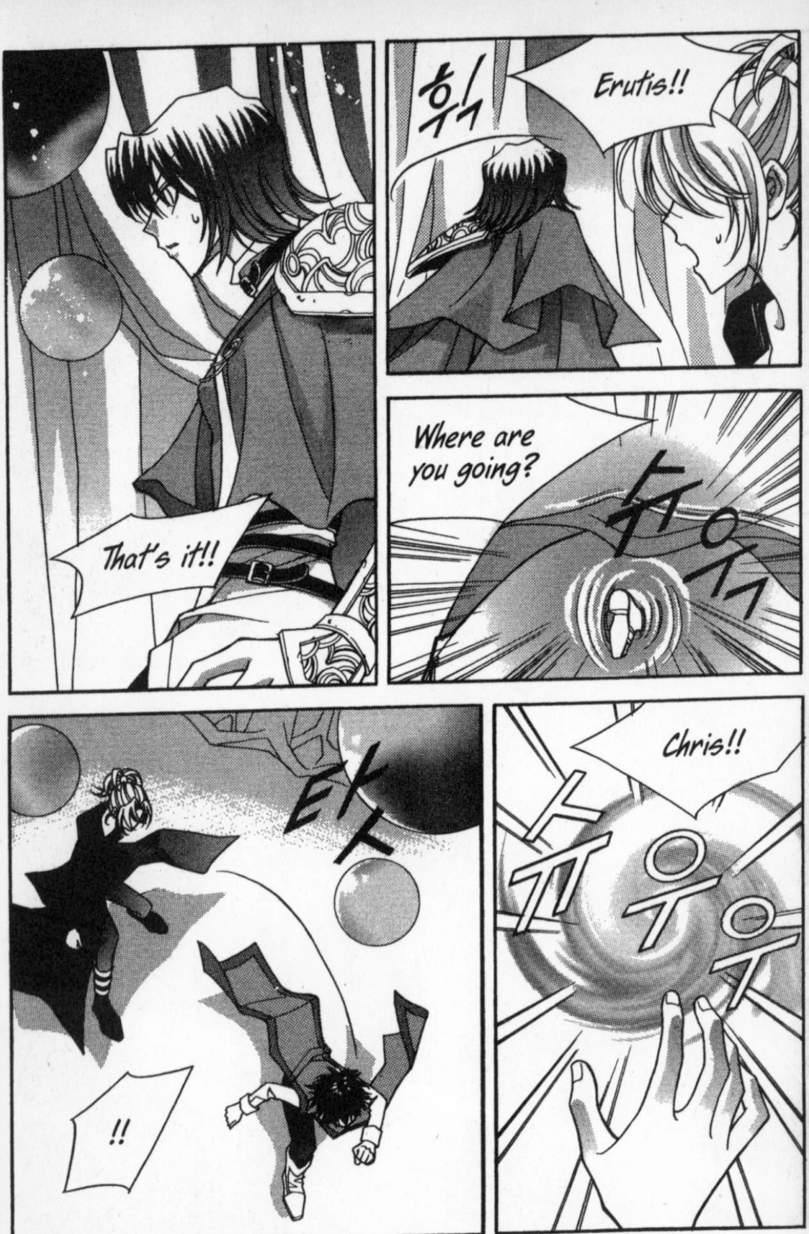
That's it!!
Erutis!!
Where are you going?
!!
Chris!!

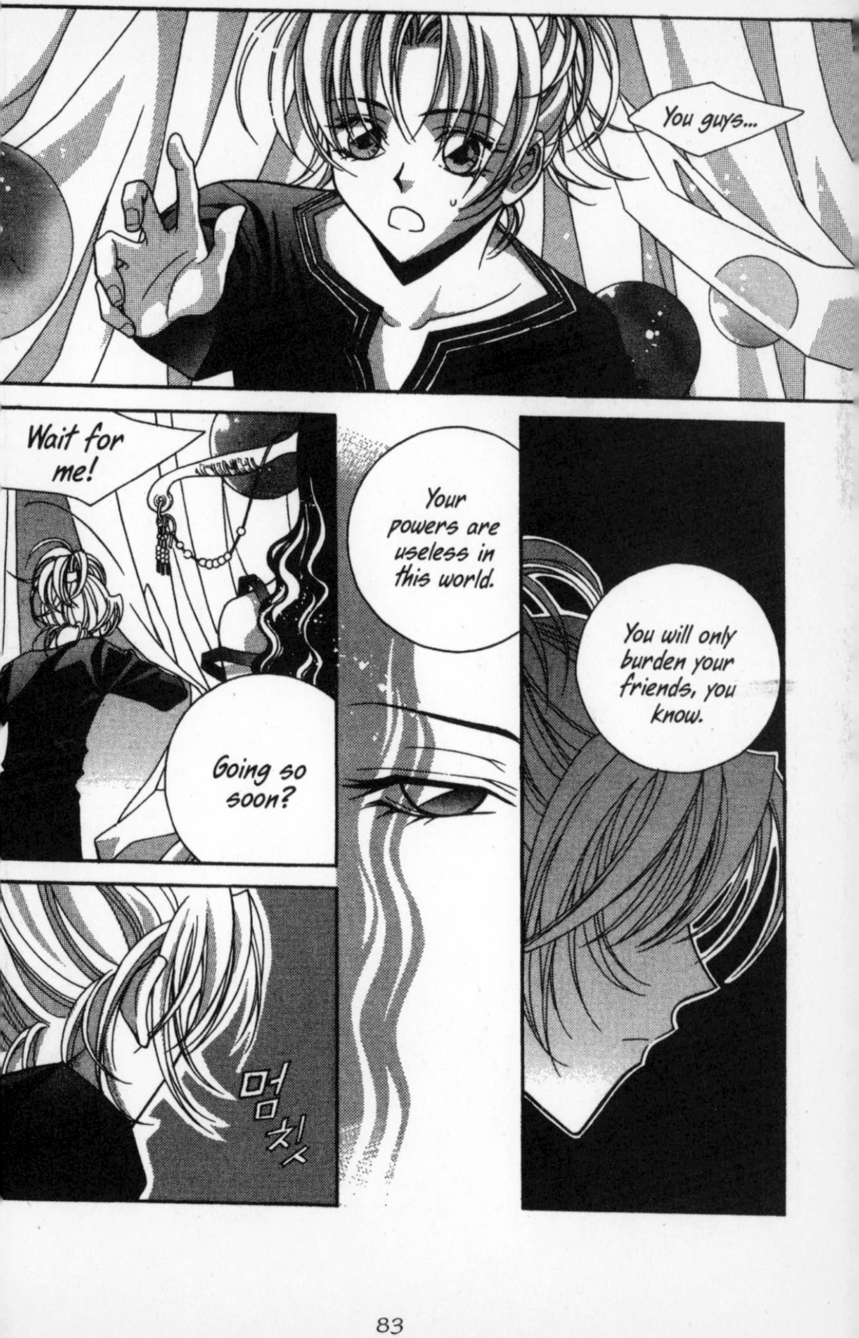
You guys...
Wait for me!
Going so soon?
멈칫
Your powers are useless in this world.
You will only burden your friends, you know.

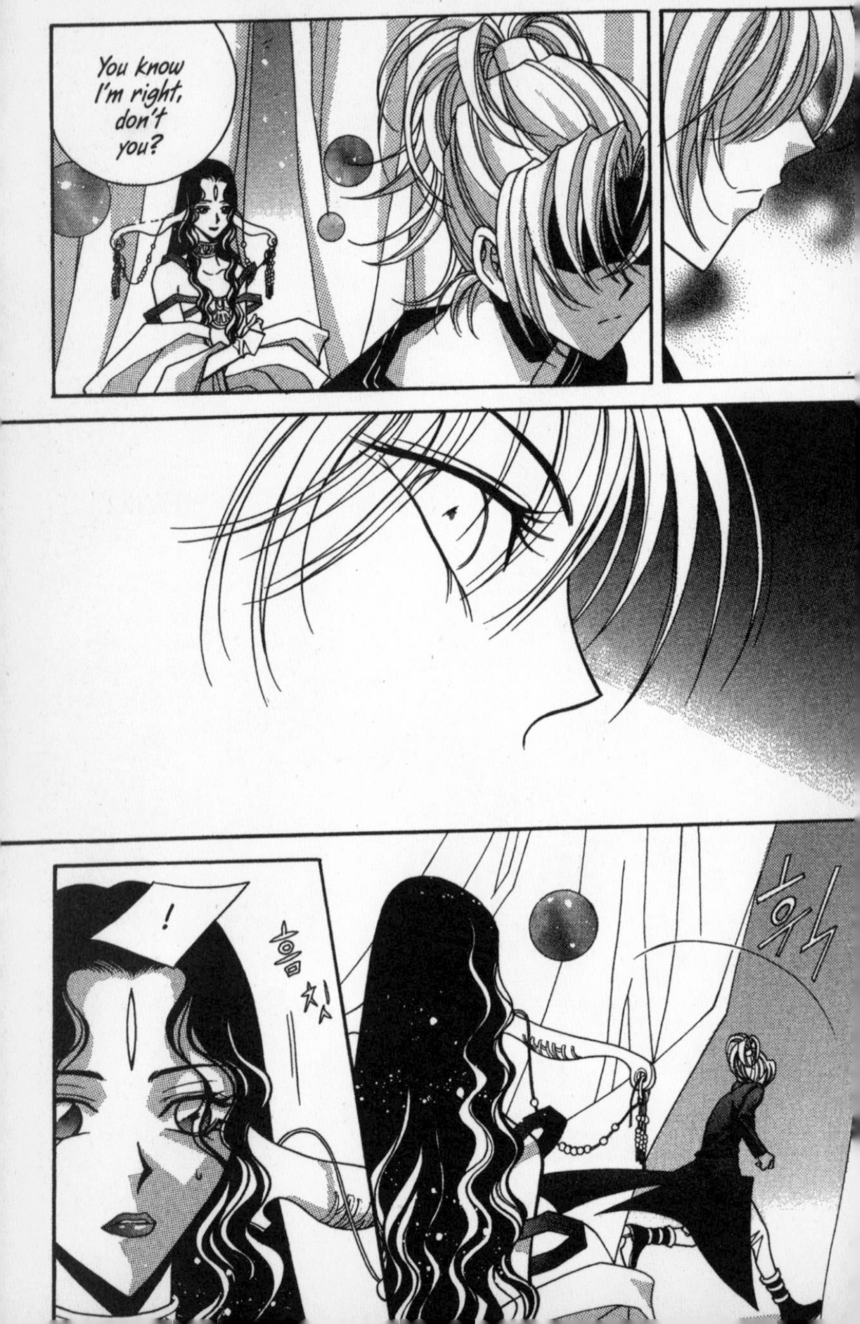
You know I'm right, don't you?
!
흠칫

......

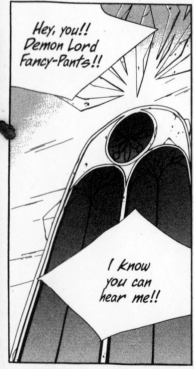

Hey, you!! Demon Lord Fancy-Pants!!

I know you can hear me!!

Show yourself!!

Let's settle this right now!!

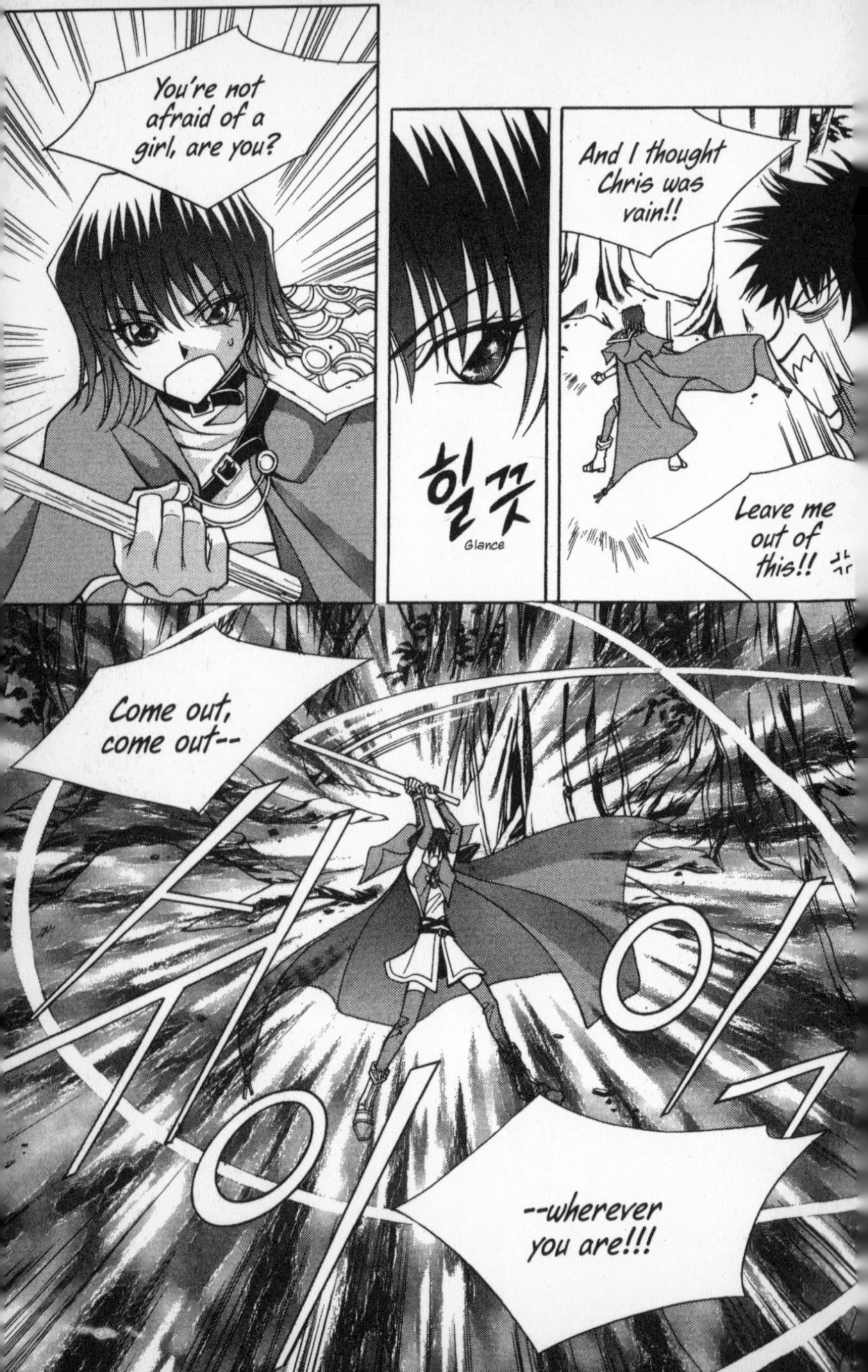
You're not afraid of a girl, are you?
힐끗
Glance
And I thought Chris was vain!!
Leave me out of this!!
Come out, come out--
--wherever you are!!!

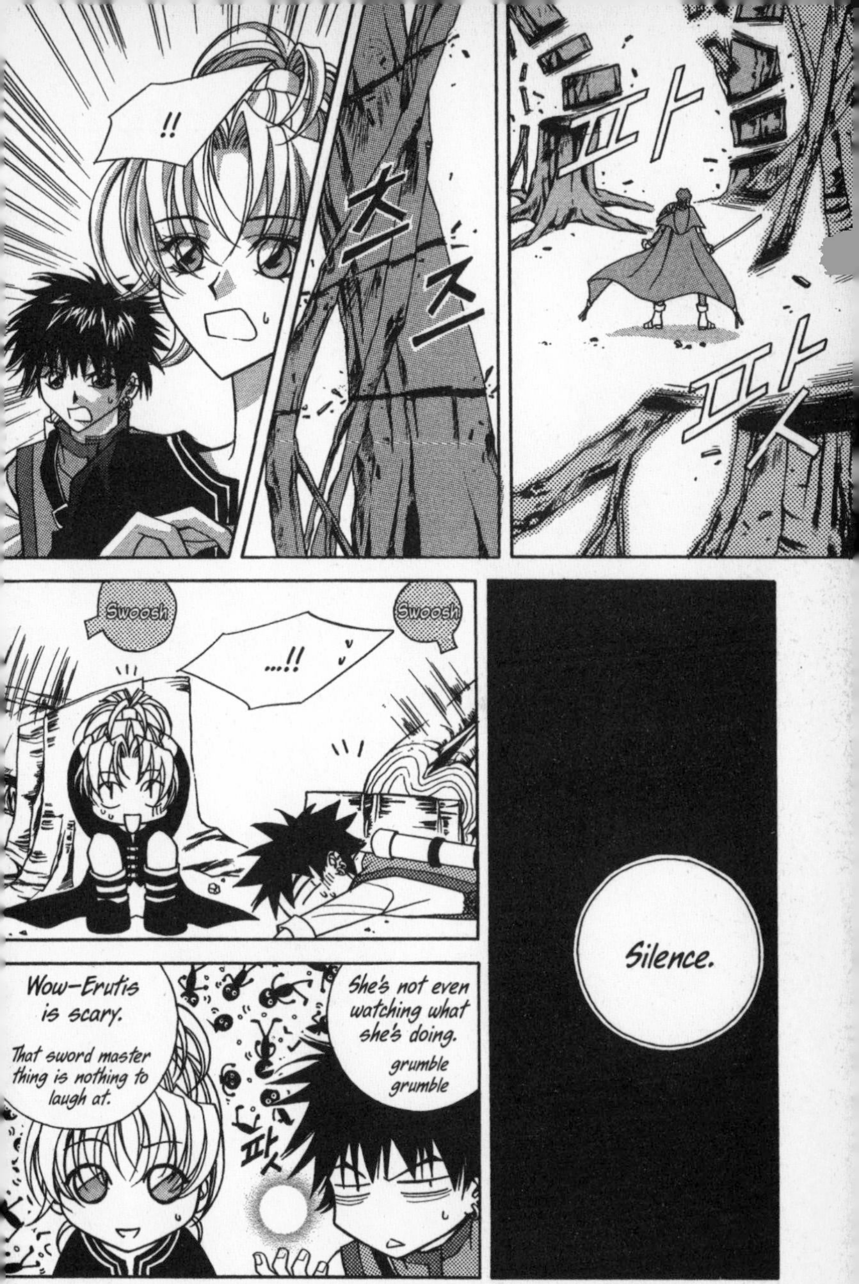
!!
Silence.
Swoosh
Swoosh
...!!
She's not even watching what she's doing.
grumble grumble
Wow—Erutis is scary.
That sword master thing is nothing to laugh at.

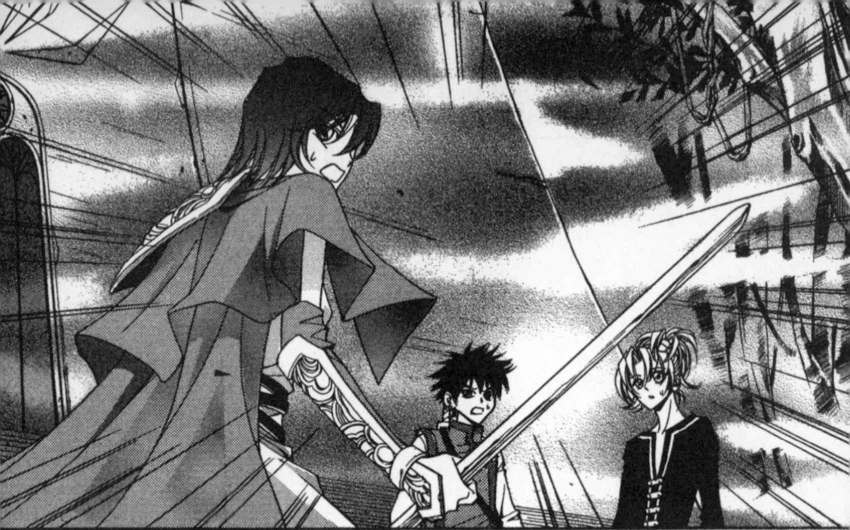

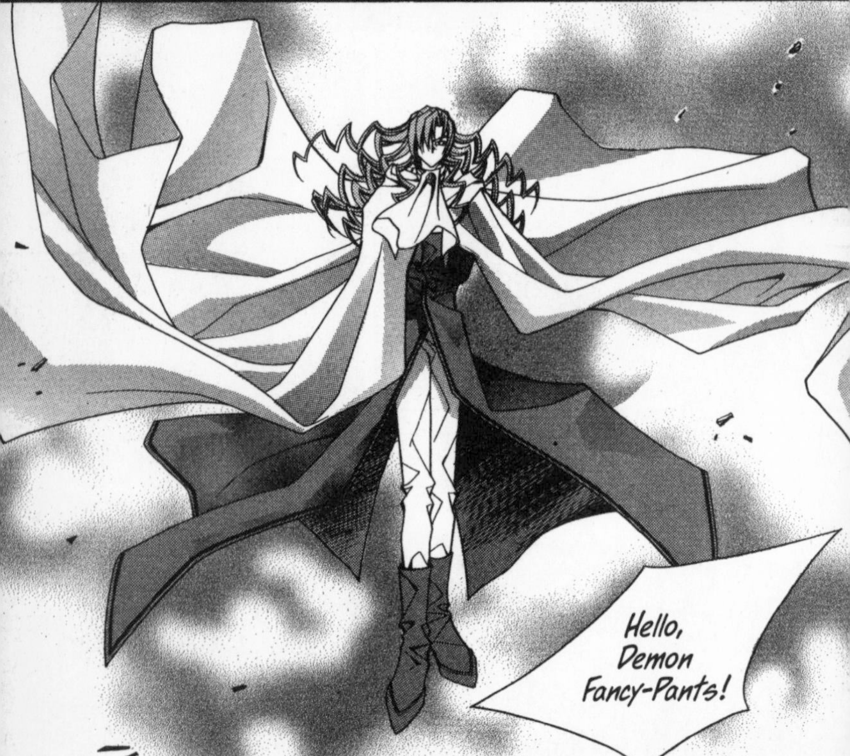
Hello, Demon Fancy-Pants!

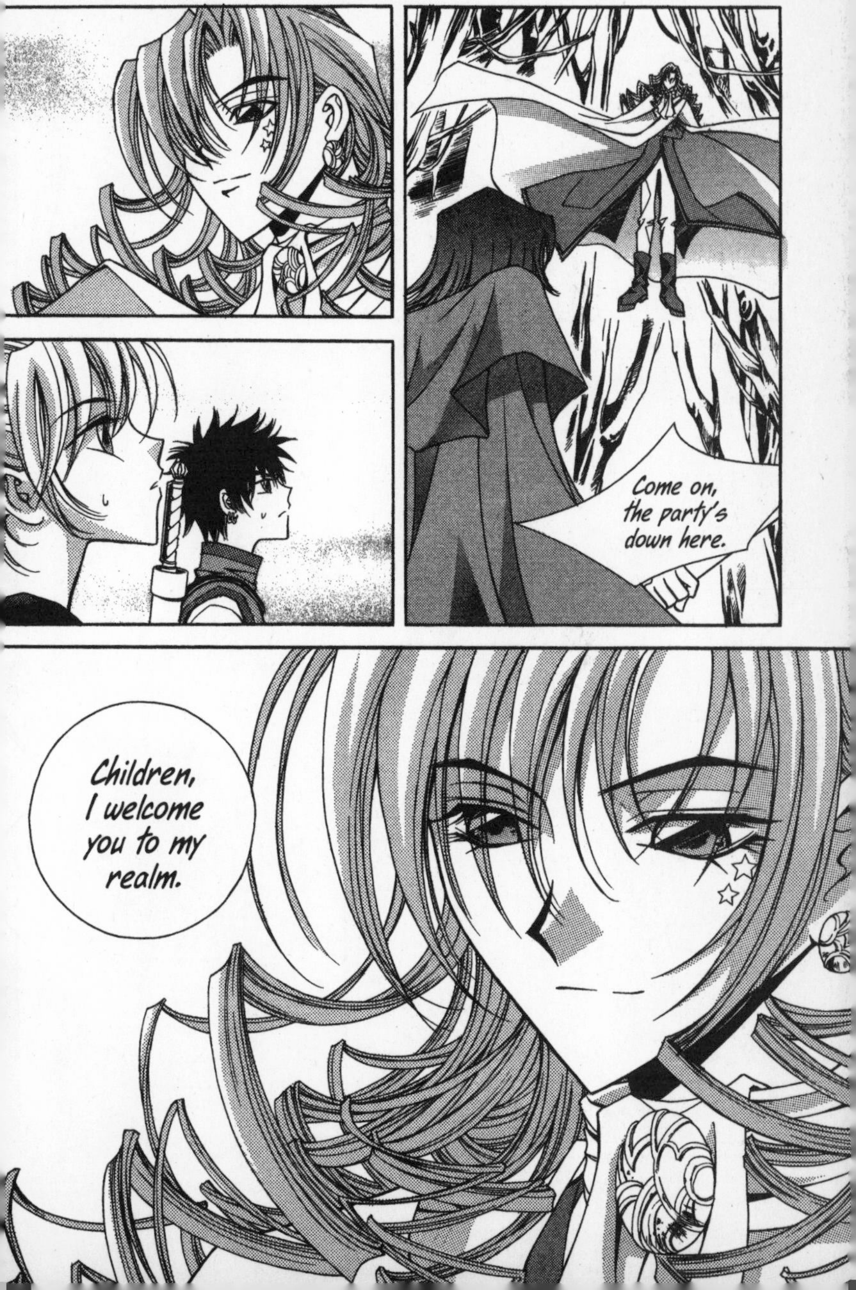
Come on, the party's down here.
Children, I welcome you to my realm.

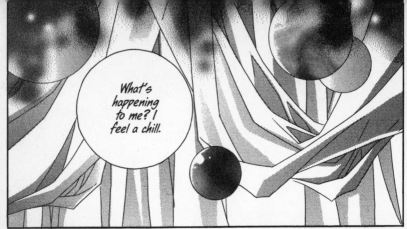

What's happening to me? I feel a chill.

The little one is more powerful than he appears... or knows.

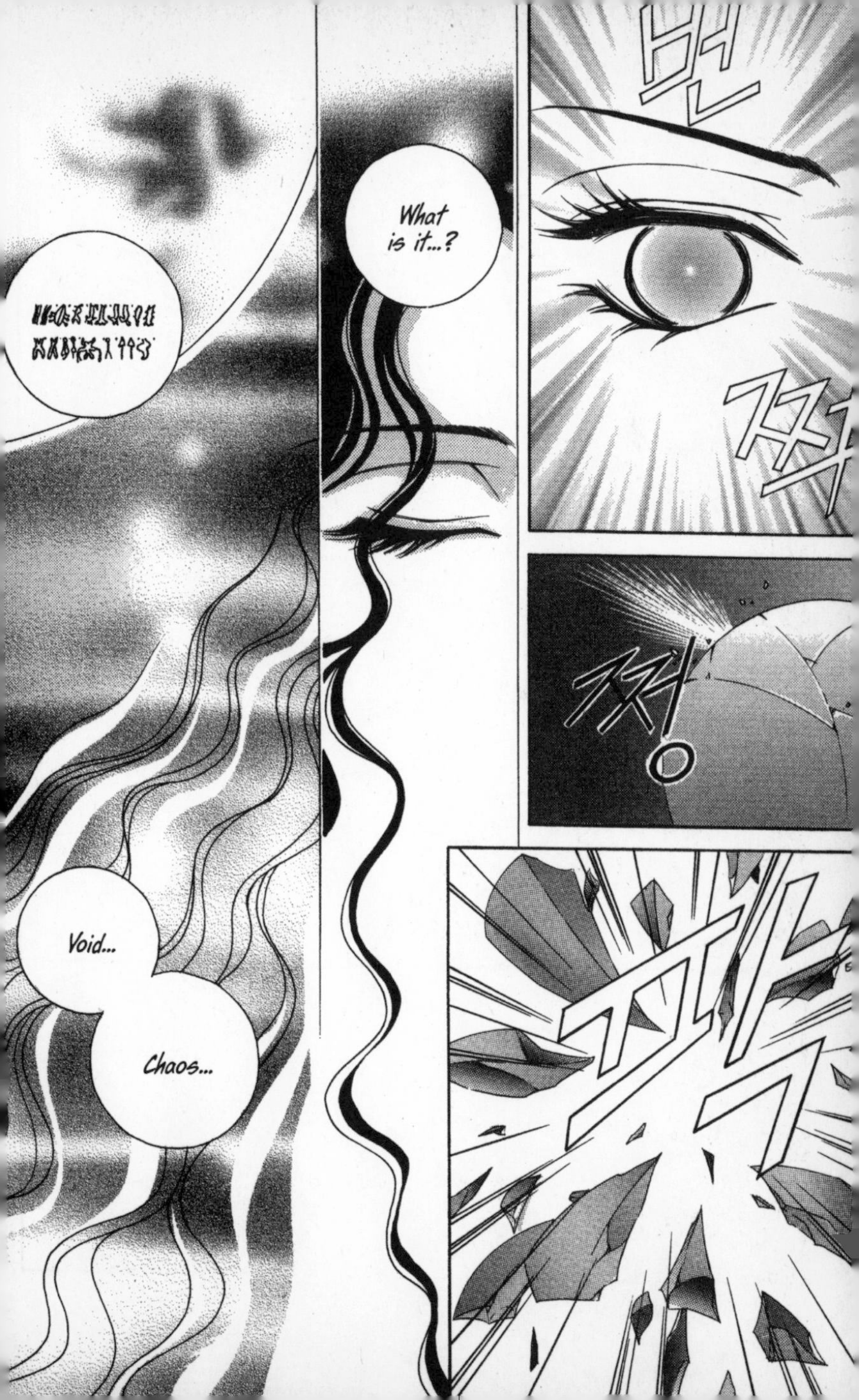
Void...
Chaos...
What is it...?

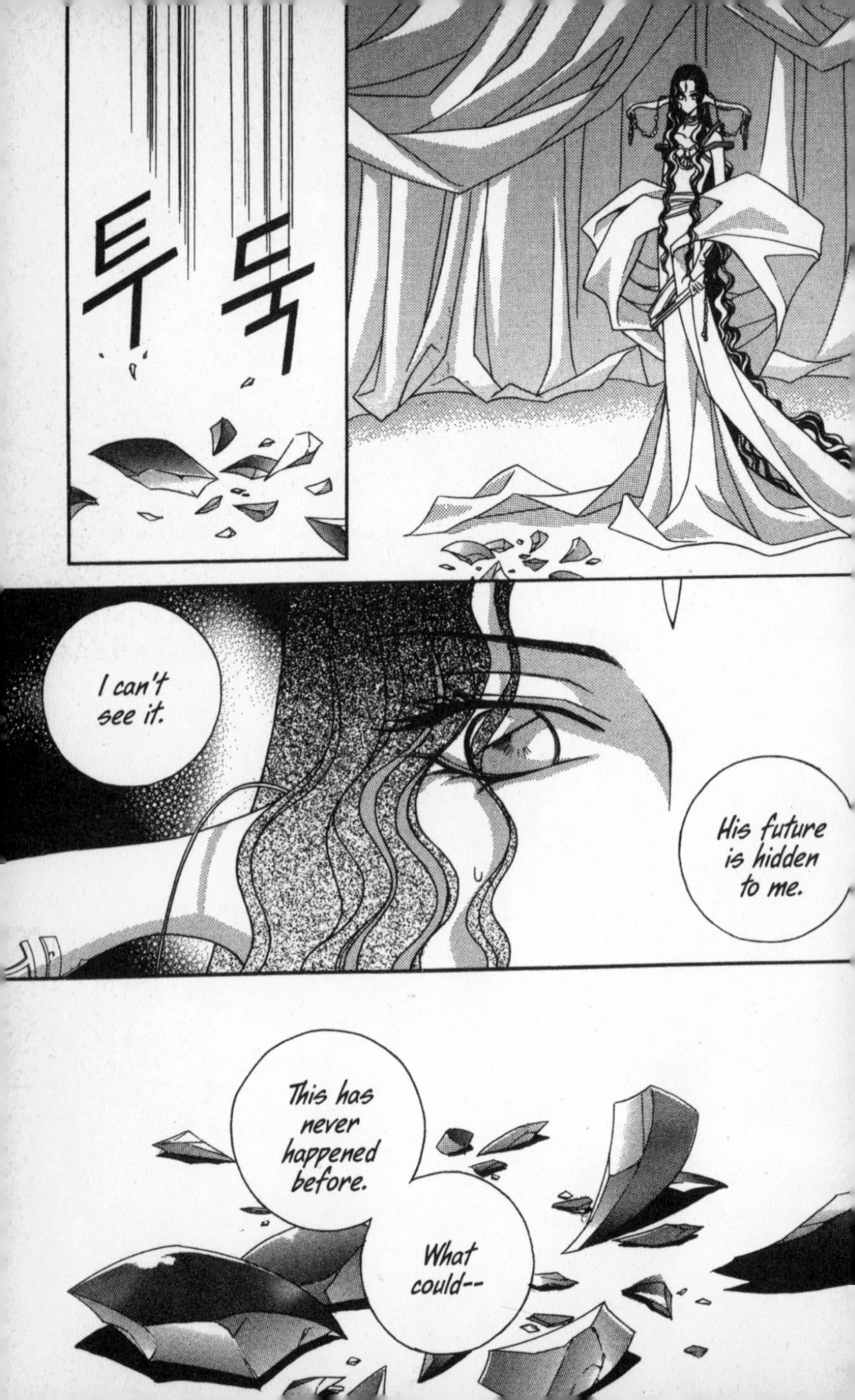

투둑
I can't see it.
His future is hidden to me.
This has never happened before.
What could--

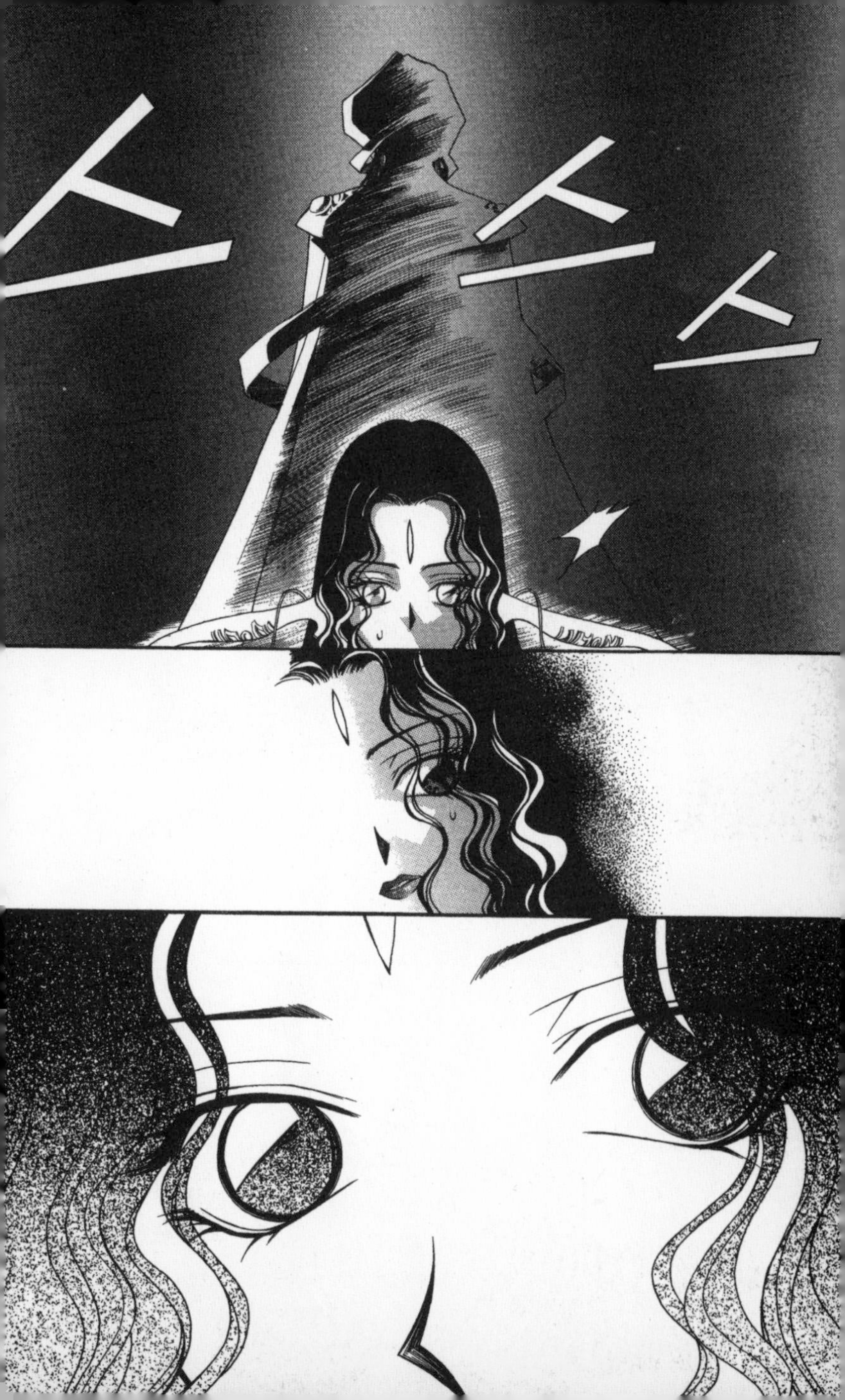

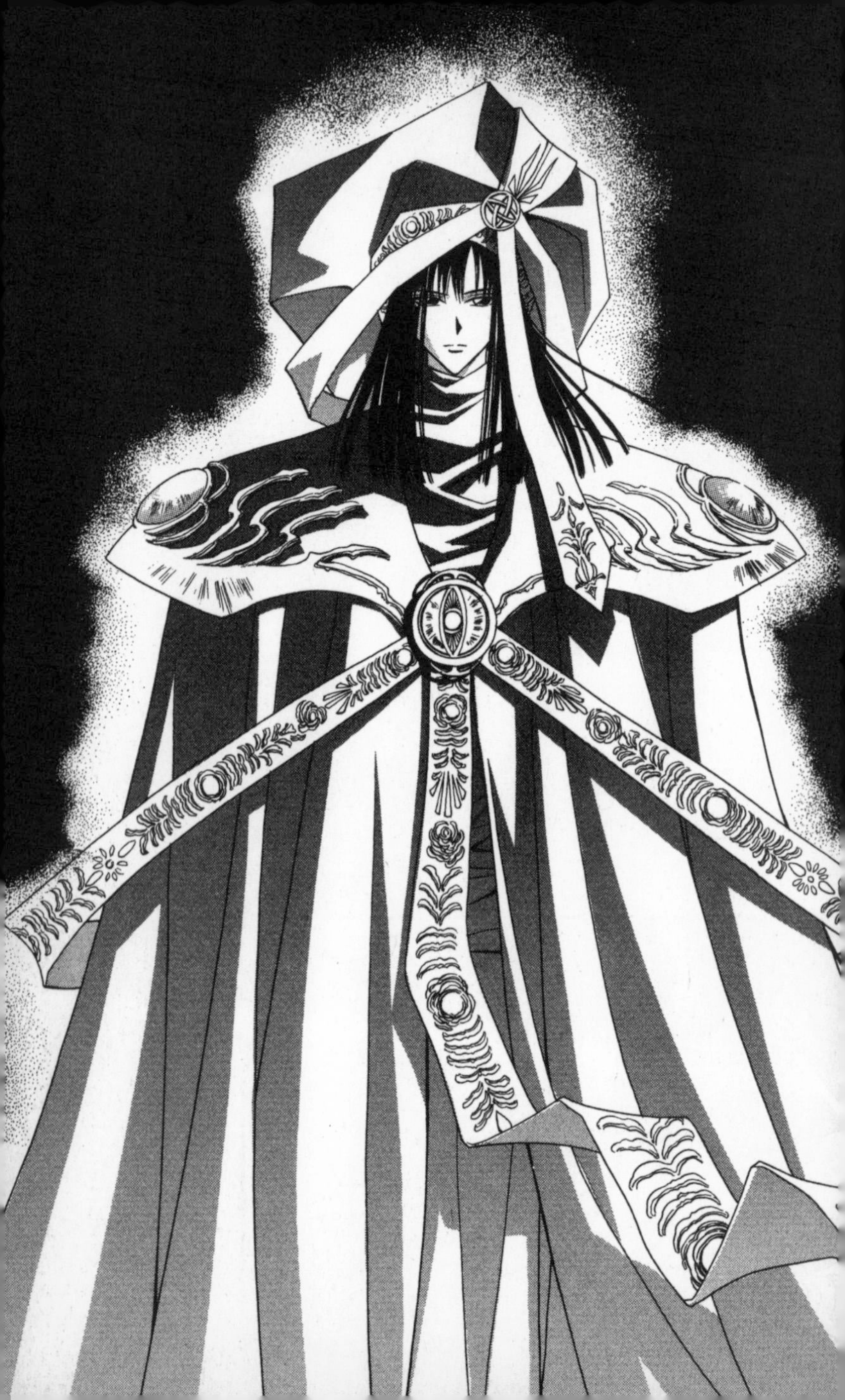

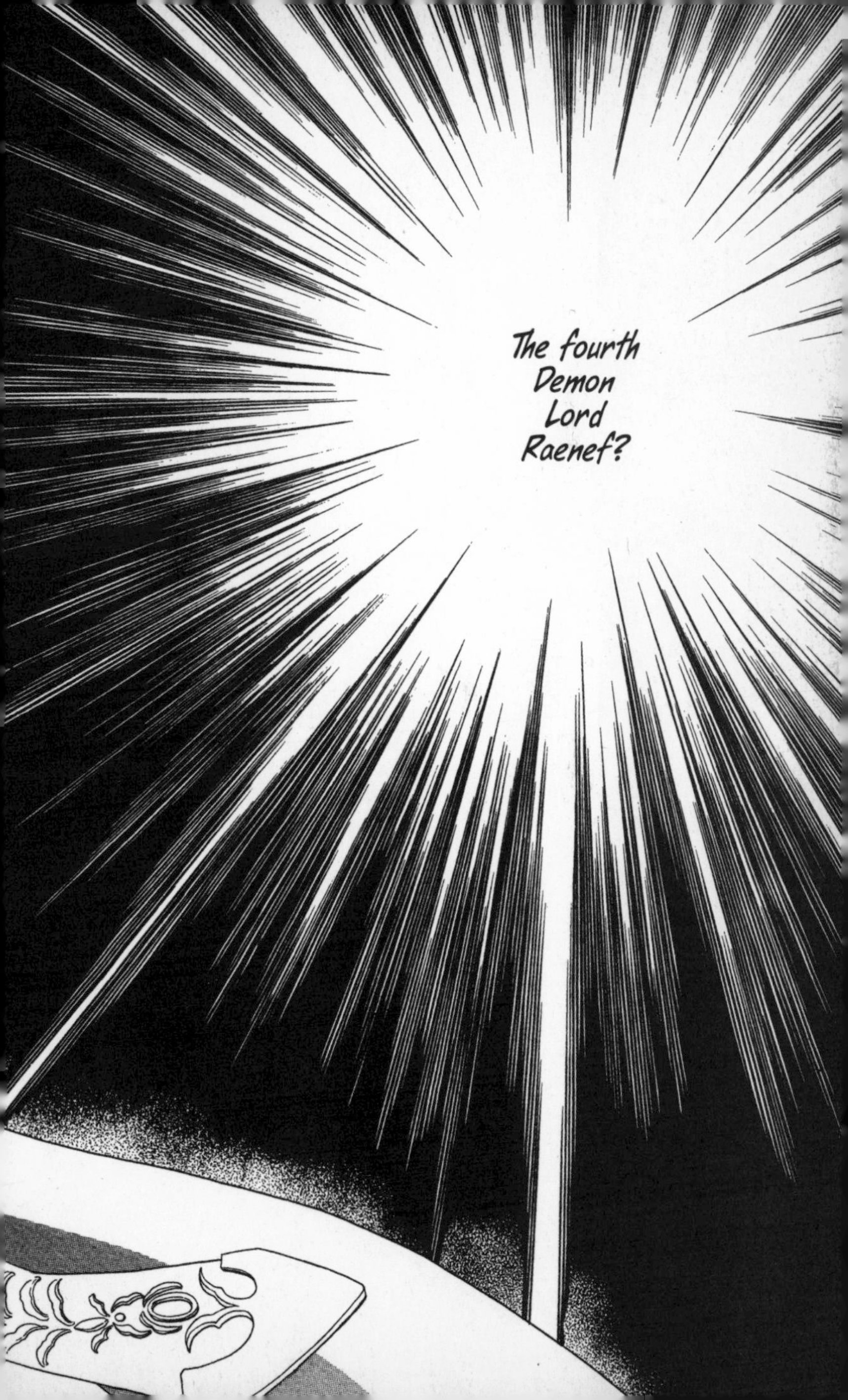
The fourth Demon Lord Raenef?

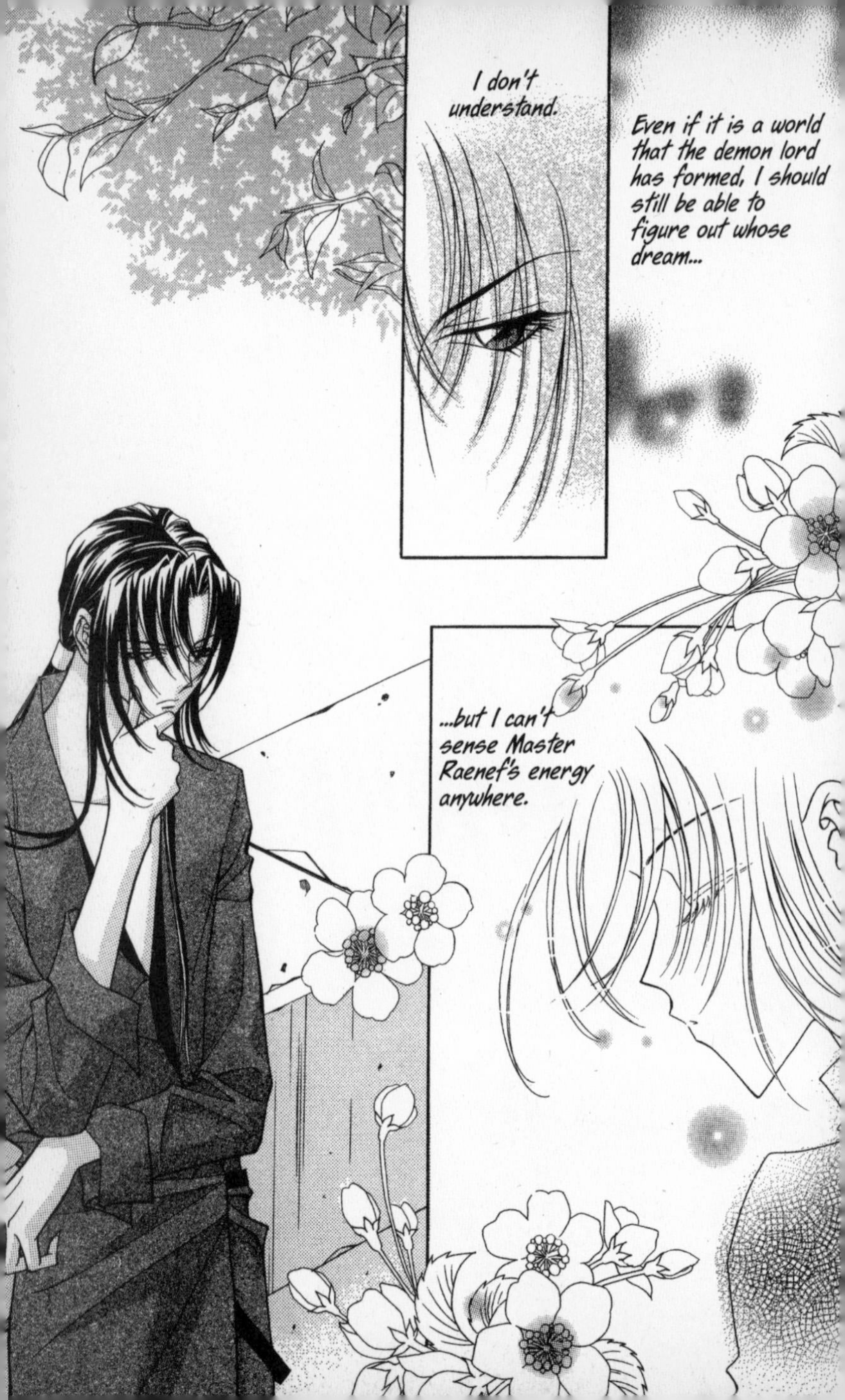
I don't understand.
Even if it is a world that the demon lord has formed, I should still be able to figure out whose dream...
...but I can't sense Master Raenef's energy anywhere.

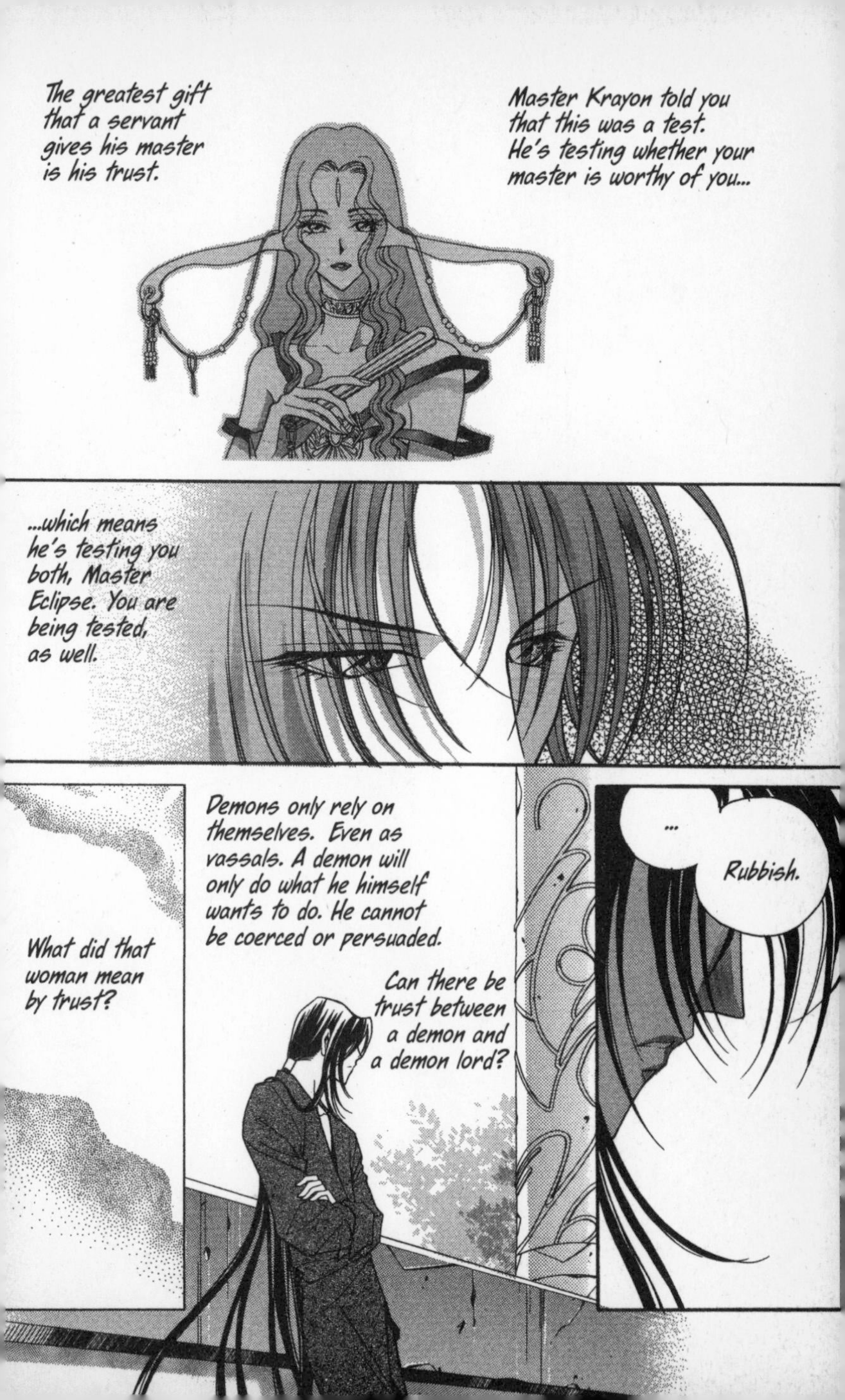
The greatest gift that a servant gives his master is his trust.
Master Krayon told you that this was a test. He's testing whether your master is worthy of you...
...which means he's testing you both, Master Eclipse. You are being tested, as well.
What did that woman mean by trust?
Demons only rely on themselves. Even as vassals. A demon will only do what he himself wants to do. He cannot be coerced or persuaded.
Can there be trust between a demon and a demon lord?
...
Rubbish.

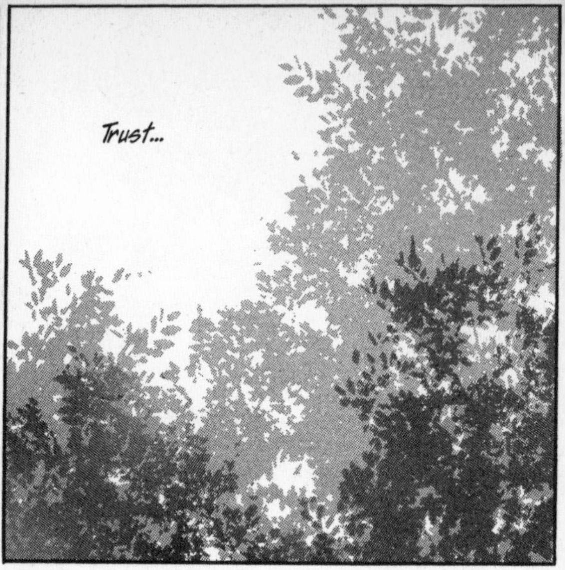
Trust...
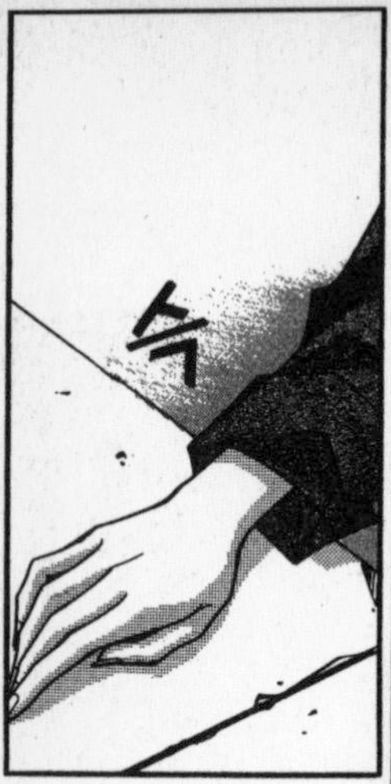
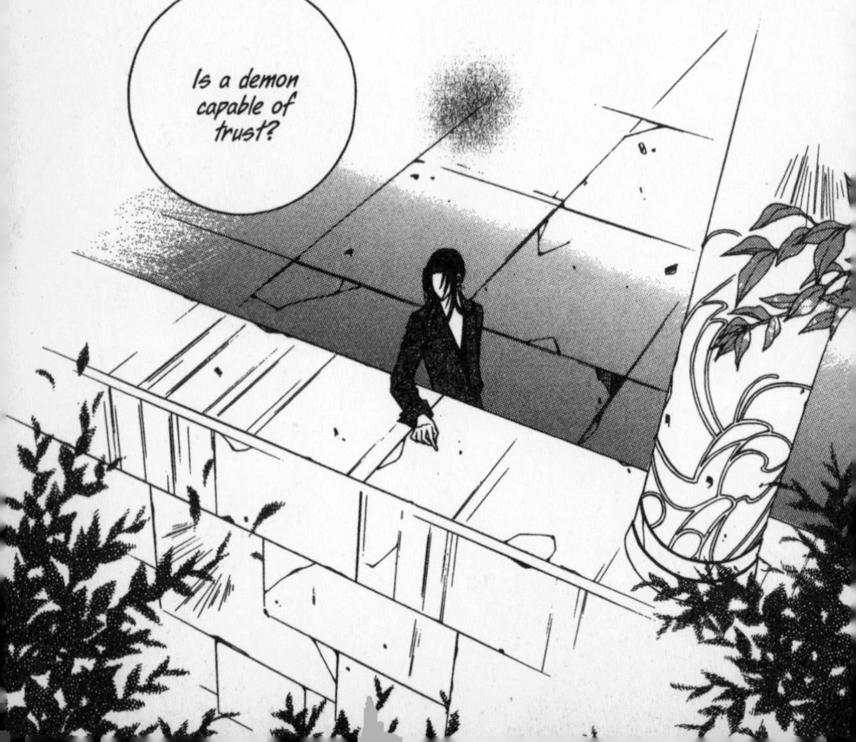
Is a demon capable of trust?

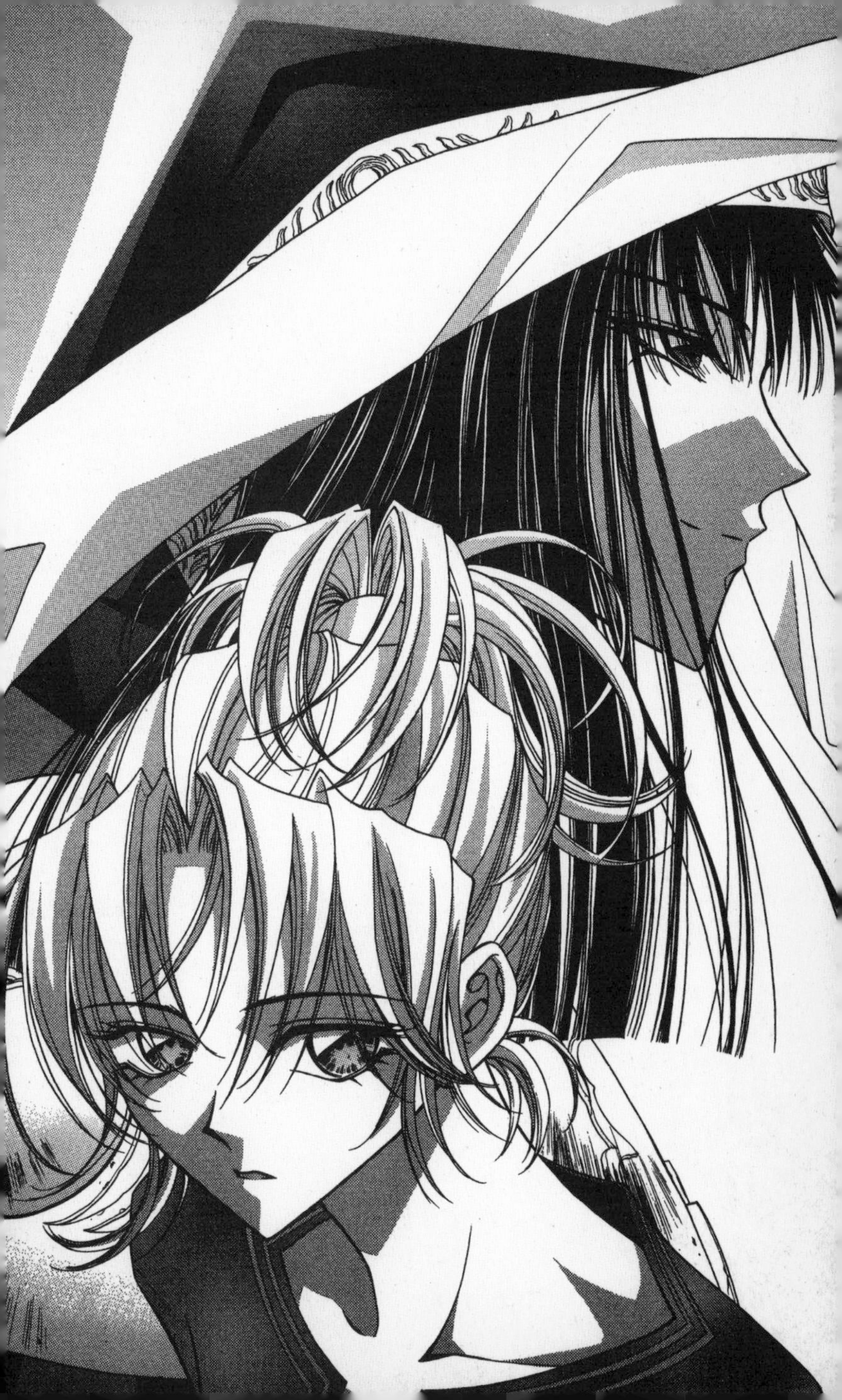

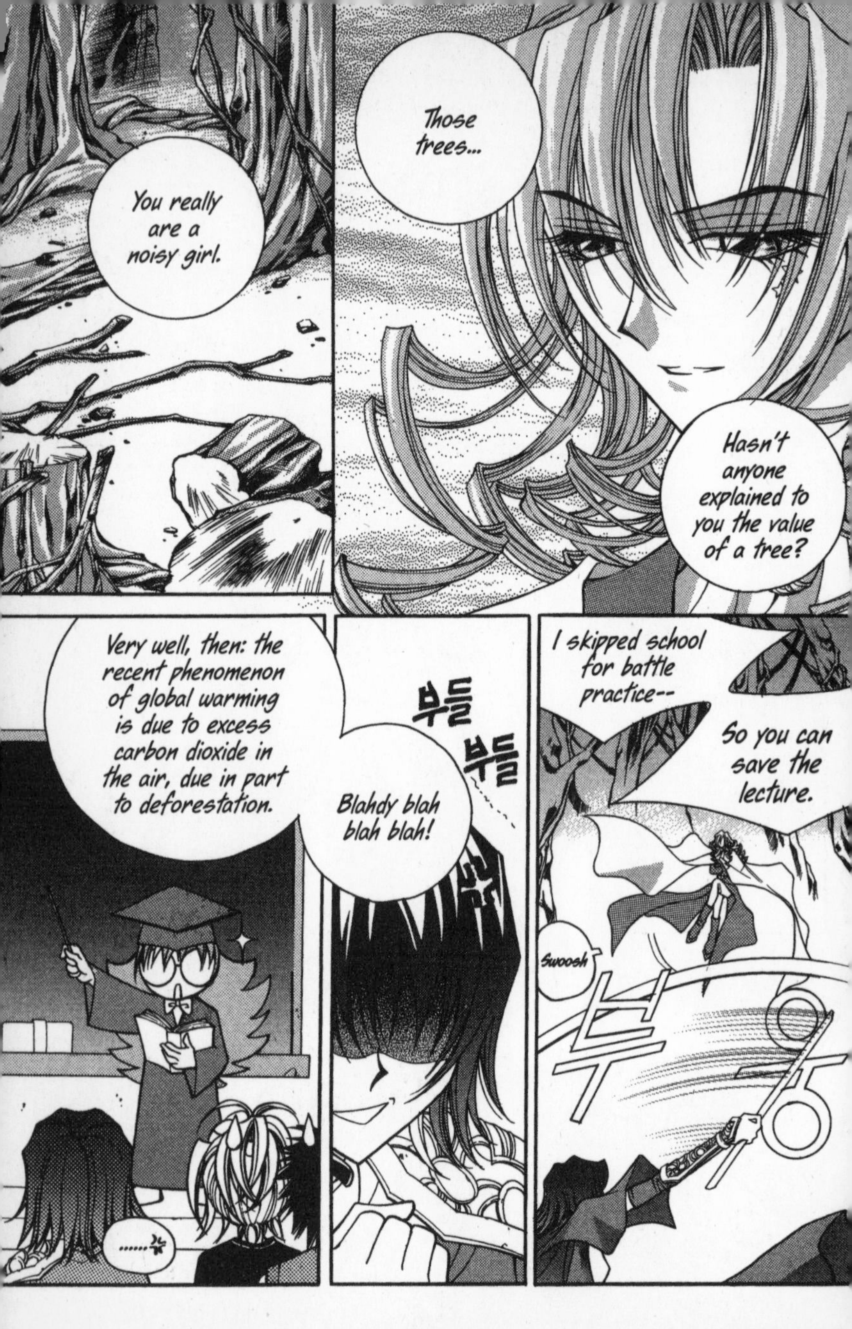
You really are a noisy girl.
Those trees...
Hasn't anyone explained to you the value of a tree?
Very well, then: the recent phenomenon of global warming is due to excess carbon dioxide in the air, due in part to deforestation.
......
부들 부들
Blahdy blah blah blah!
I skipped school for battle practice--
So you can save the lecture.
Swoosh

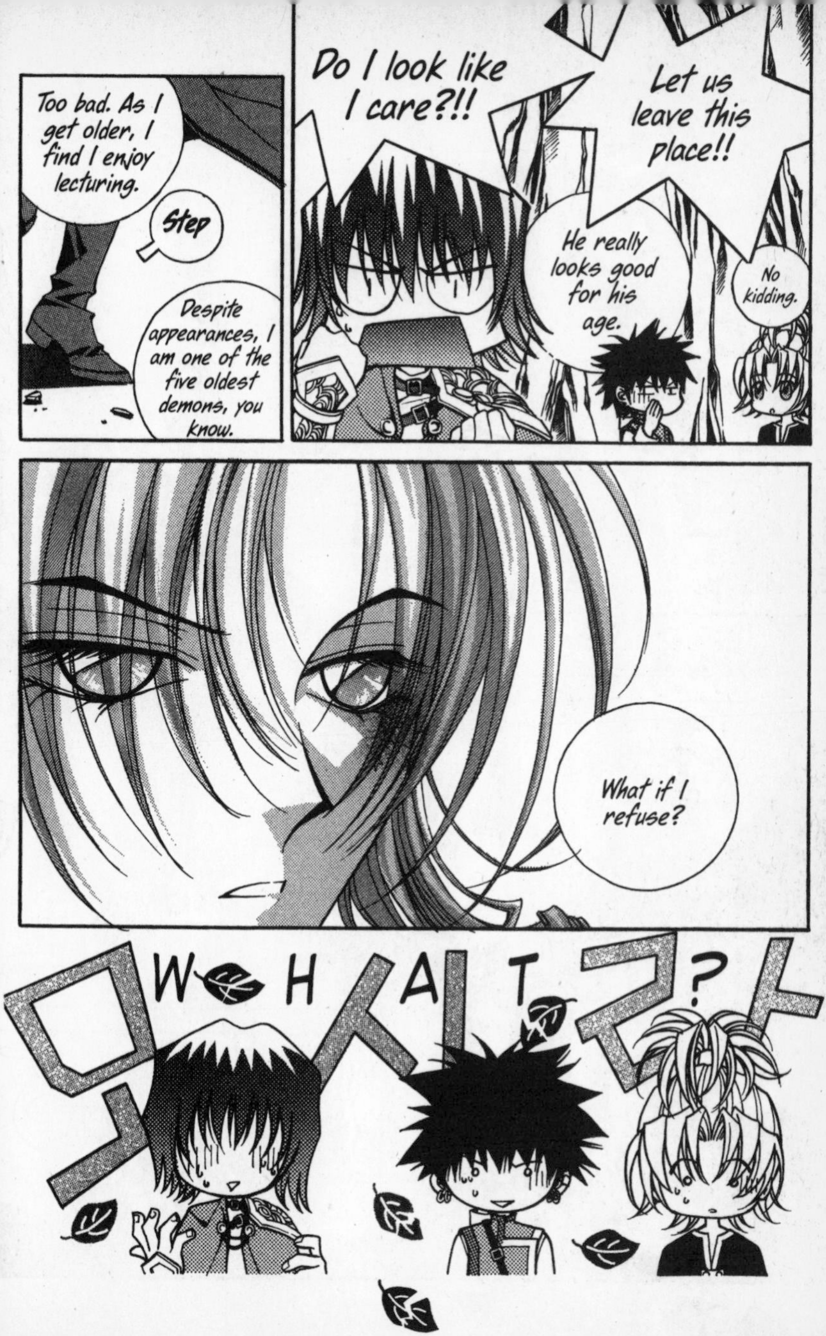
Too bad. As I get older, I find I enjoy lecturing.
Step
Despite appearances, I am one of the five oldest demons, you know.
Do I look like I care?!!
Let us leave this place!!
He really looks good for his age.
No kidding.
What if I refuse?
W H A T ?

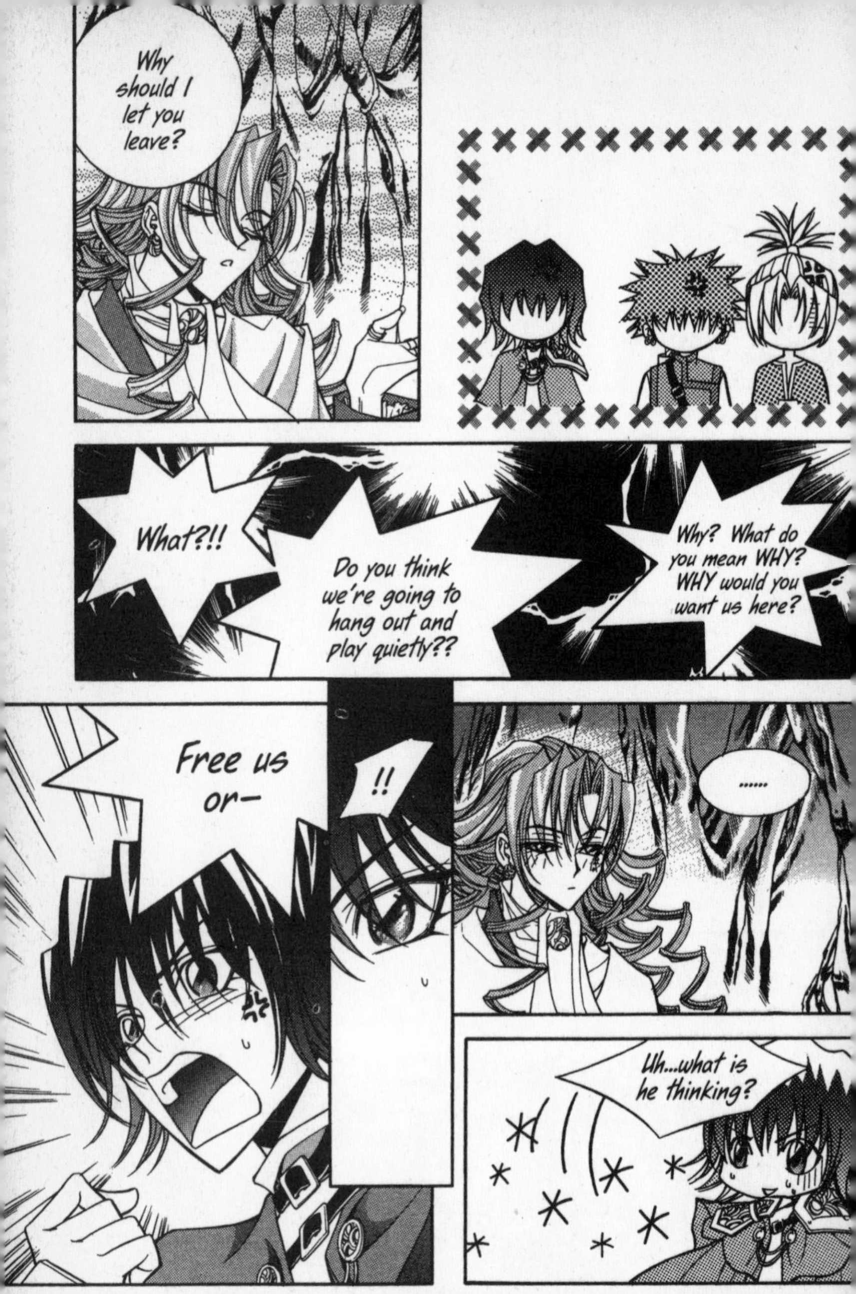
Why should I let you leave?
What?!!
Do you think we're going to hang out and play quietly??
Why? What do you mean WHY? WHY would you want us here?
Free us or–
!!
......
Uh...what is he thinking?

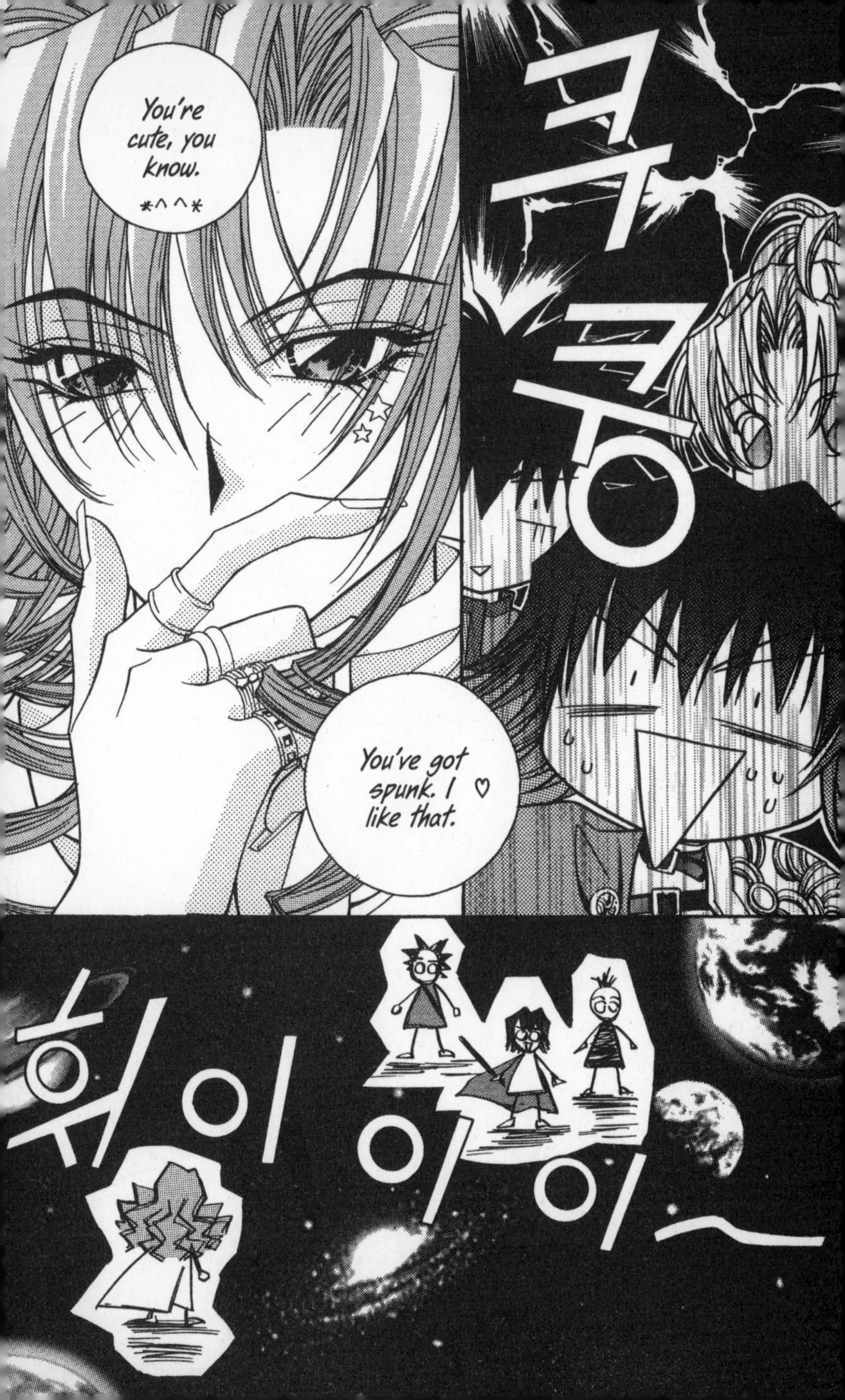
You're cute, you know. *^^*
You've got spunk. I like that. ♡

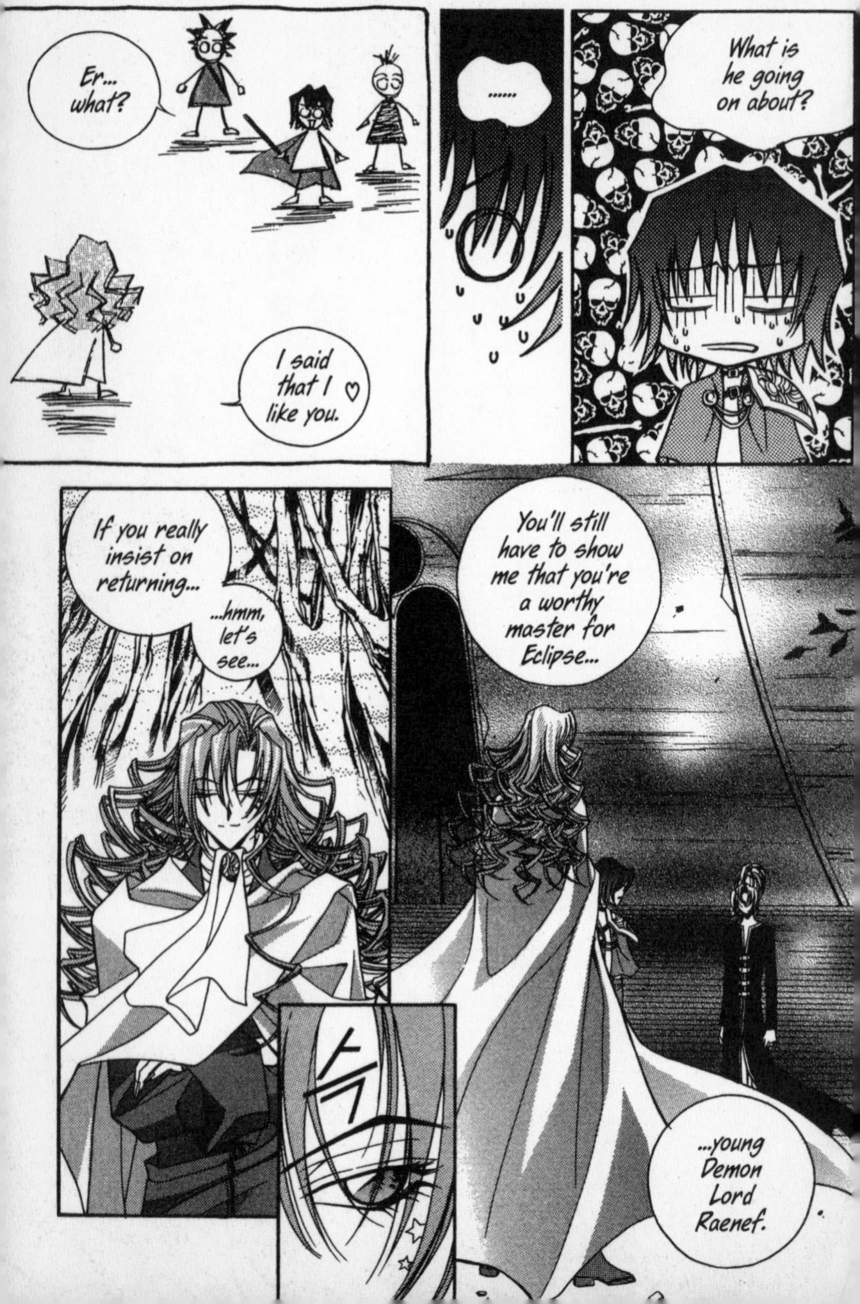
Er... what?
I said that I ♡ like you.
......
What is he going on about?
If you really insist on returning...
...hmm, let's see...
You'll still have to show me that you're a worthy master for Eclipse...
...young Demon Lord Raenef.

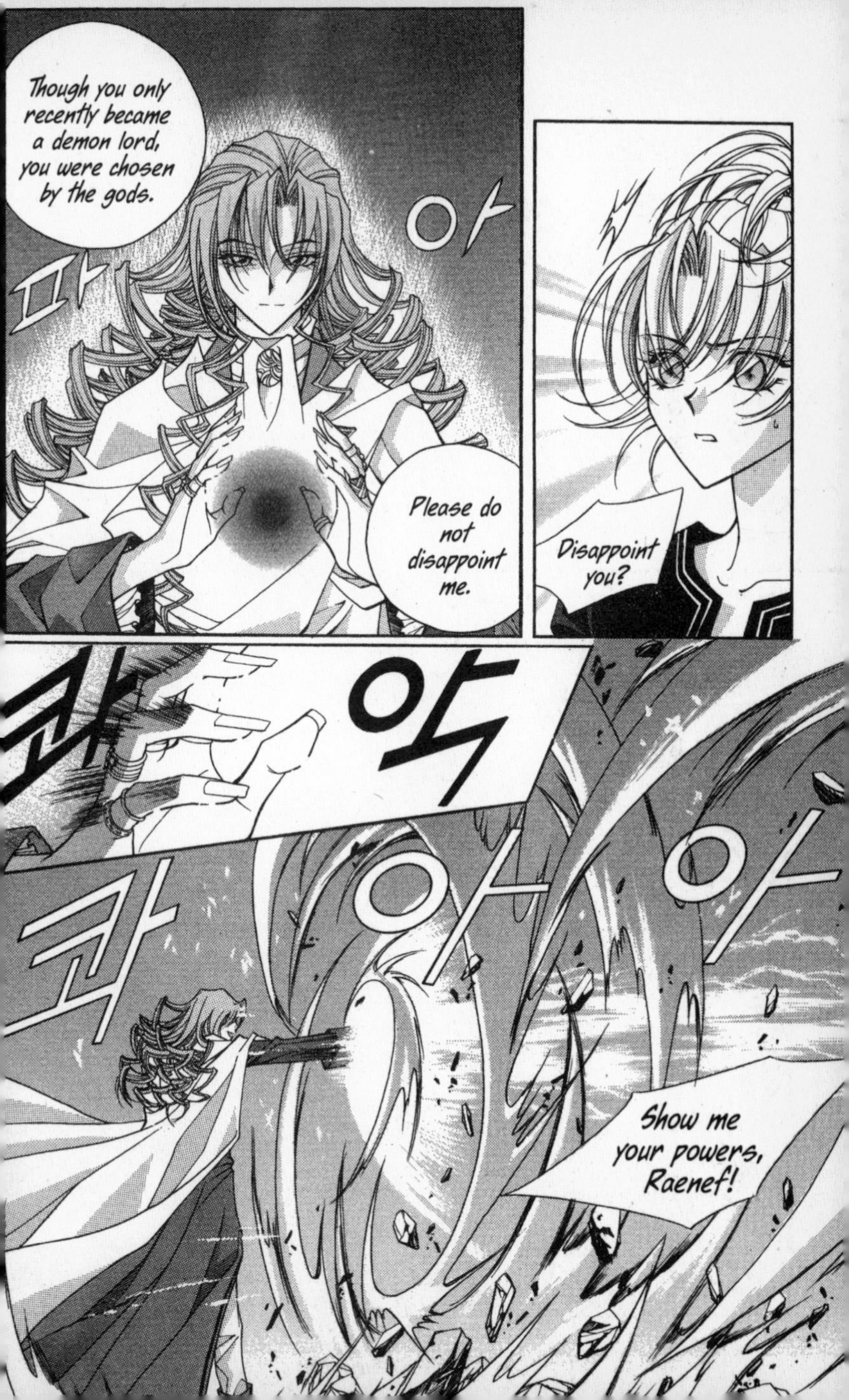
Though you only recently became a demon lord, you were chosen by the gods.
Please do not disappoint me.
Disappoint you?
Show me your powers, Raenef!

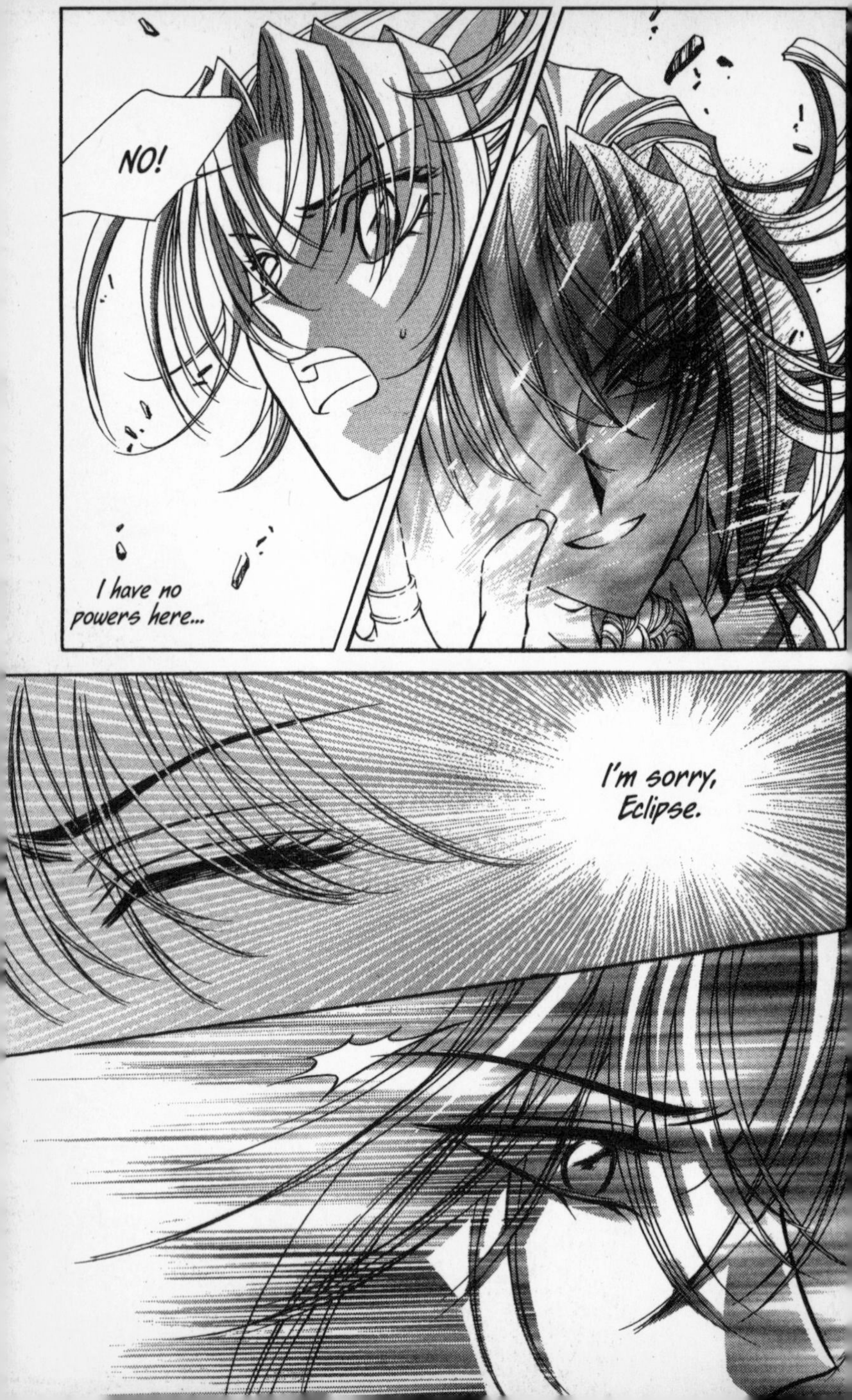
NO!
I have no powers here...
I'm sorry, Eclipse.

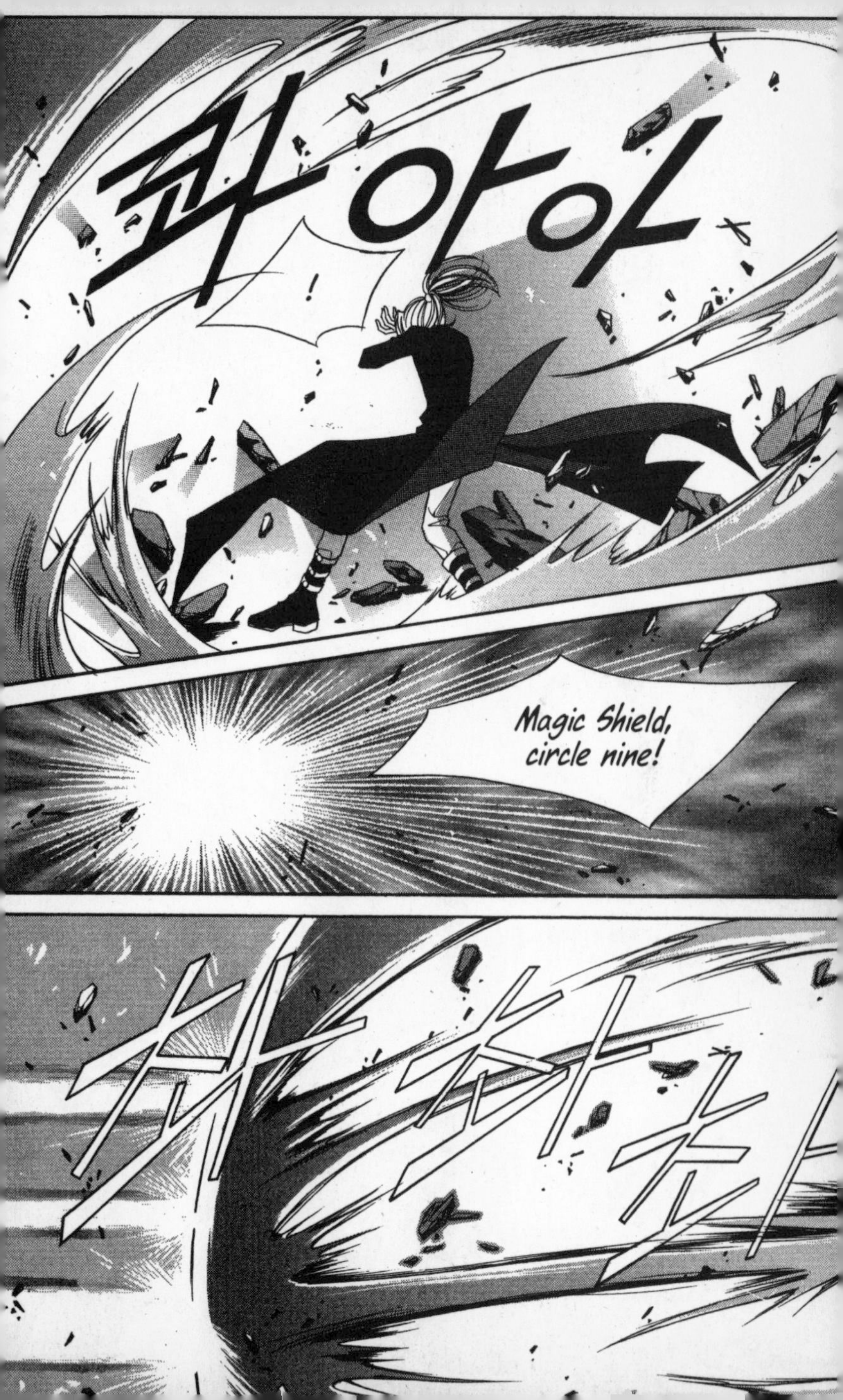
파아아
Magic Shield,
circle nine!

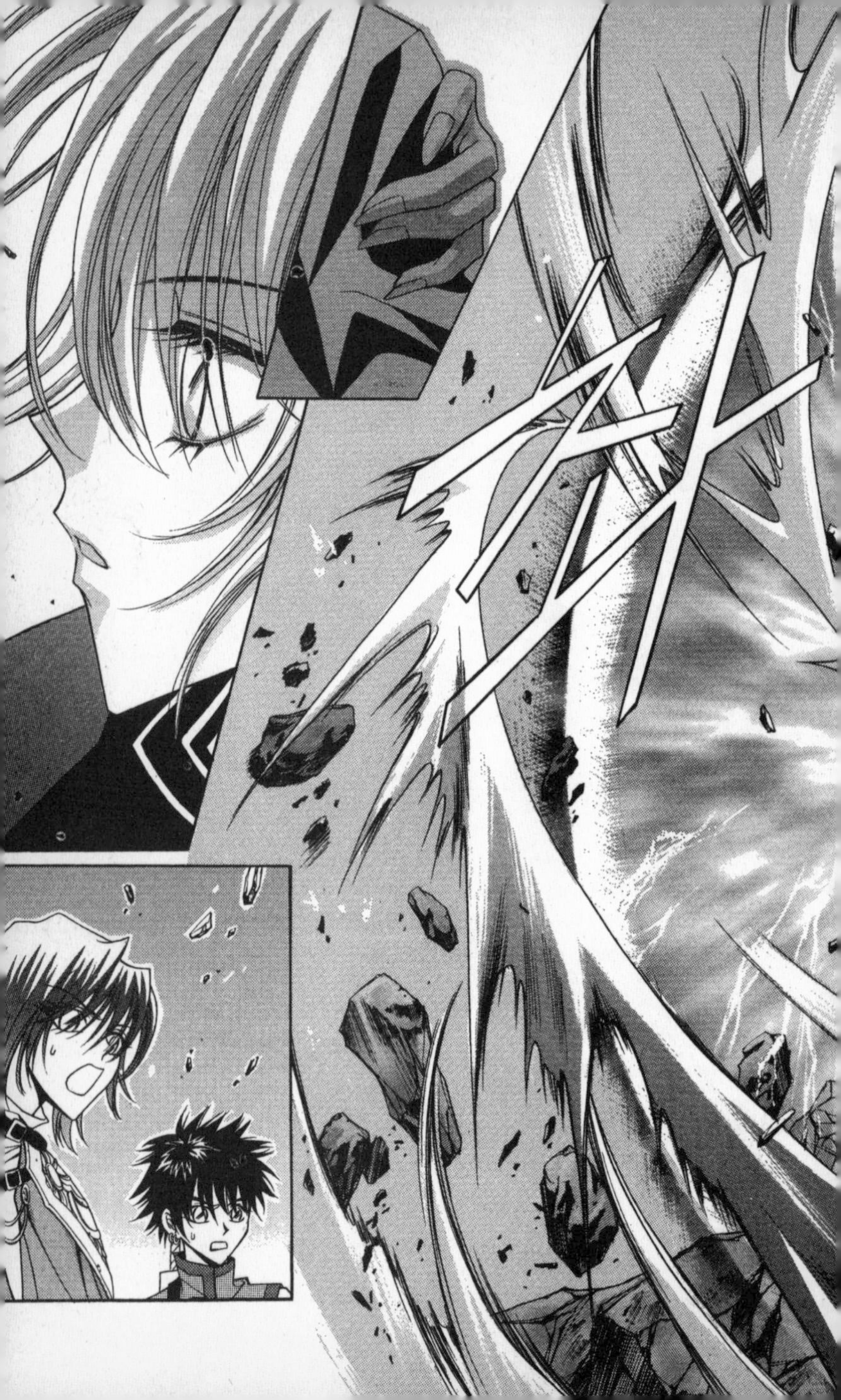

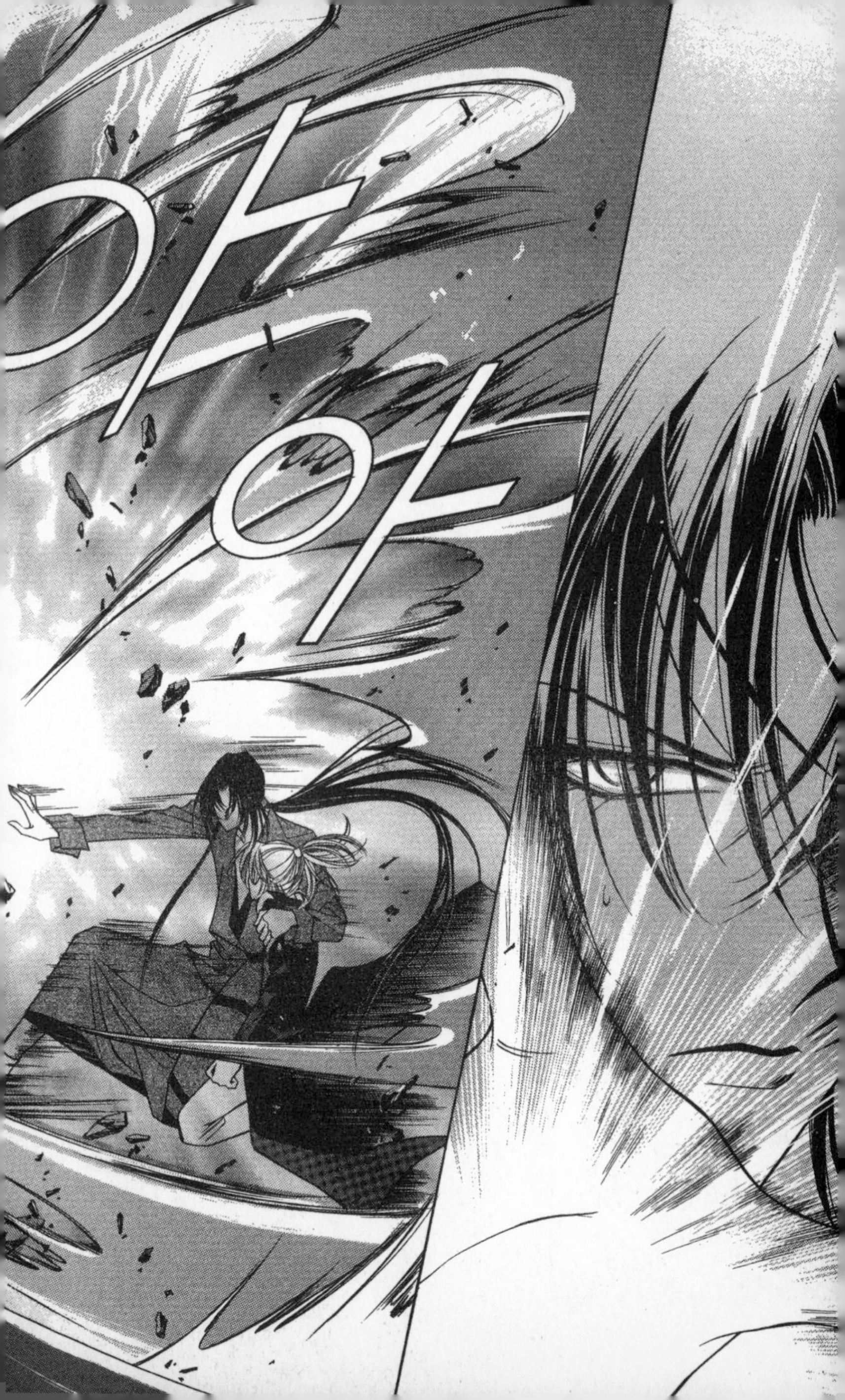
아아

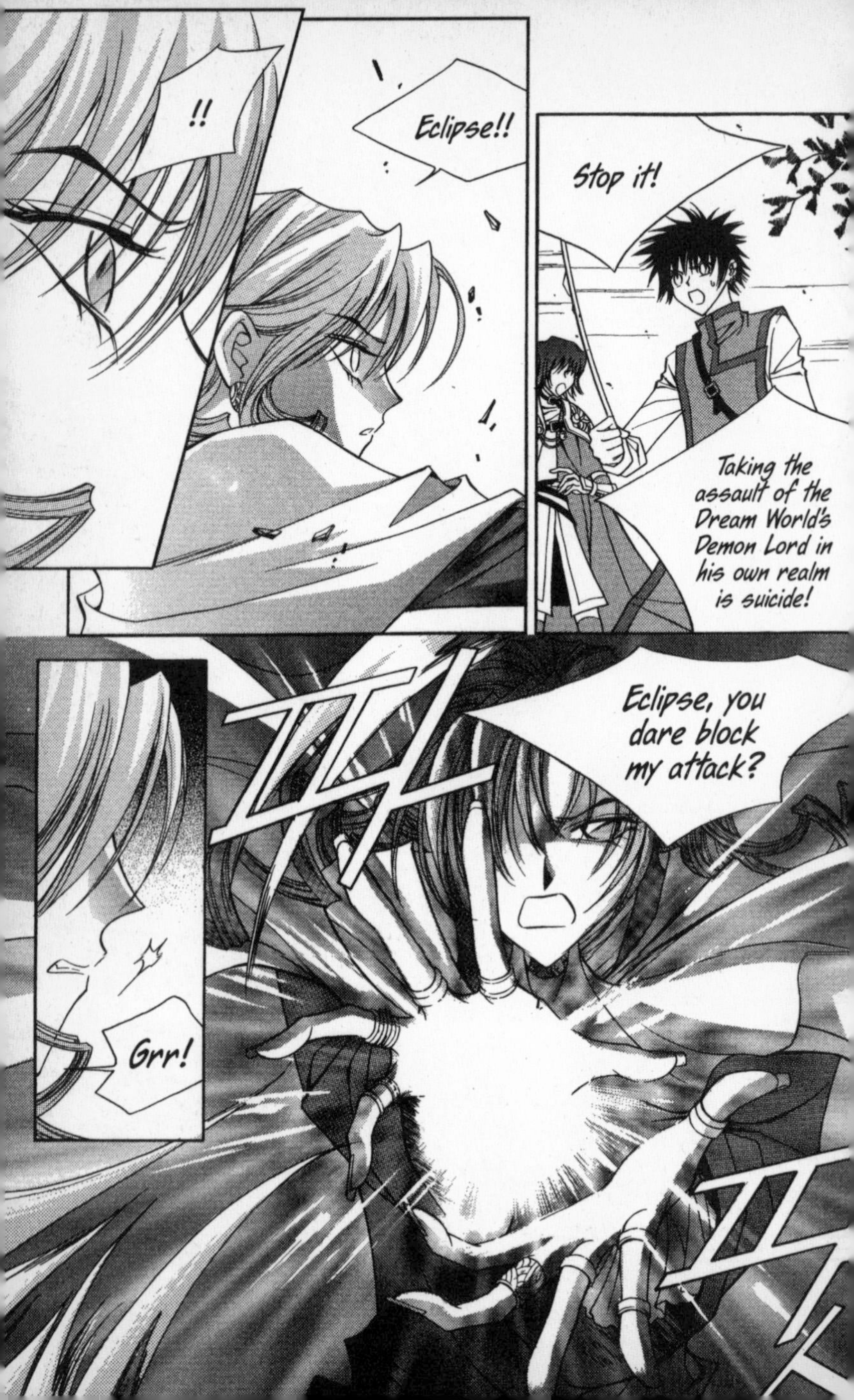
Stop it!
Taking the assault of the Dream World's Demon Lord in his own realm is suicide!
Eclipse!!
!!
Eclipse, you dare block my attack?
Grr!

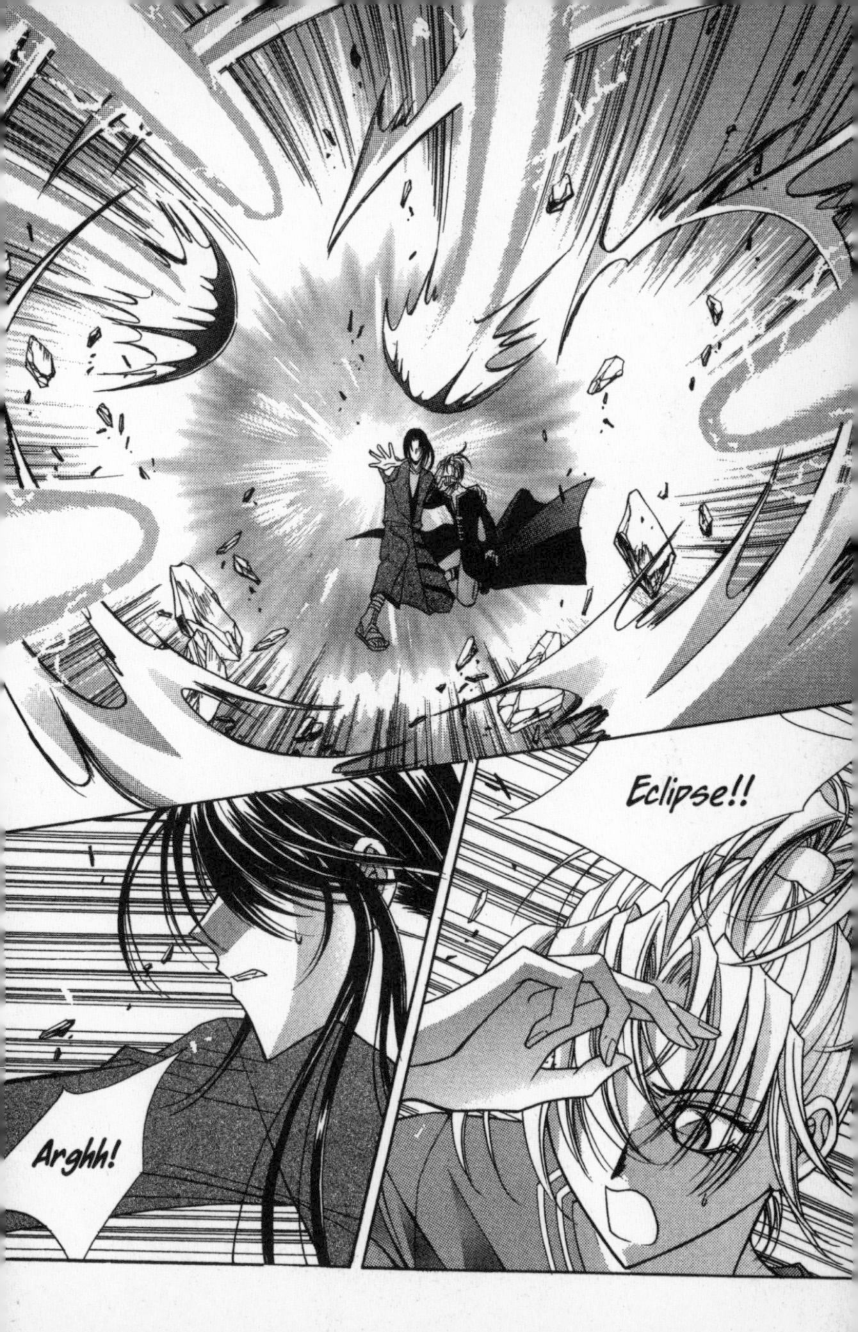
Eclipse!!
Arghh!

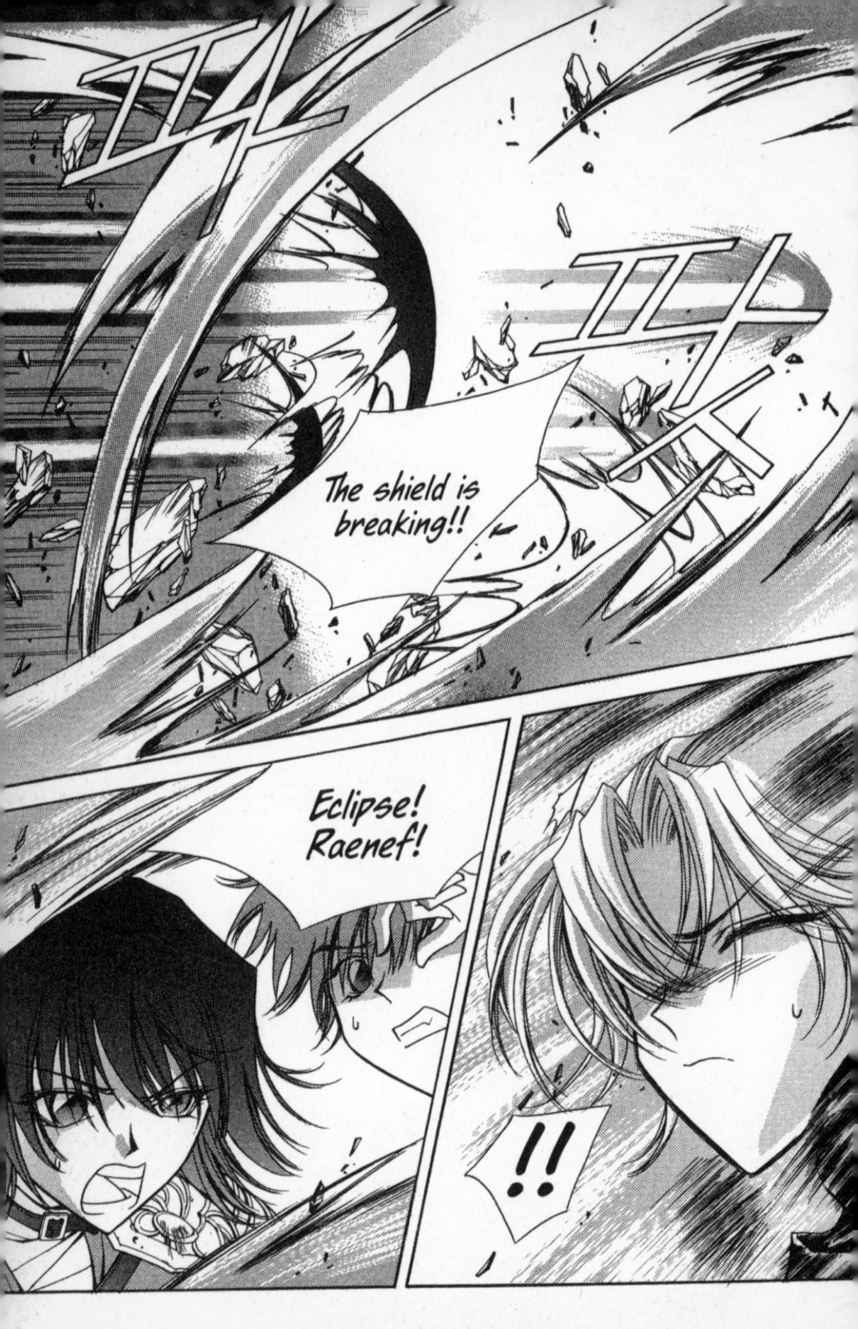
The shield is breaking!!
Eclipse! Raenef!
!!

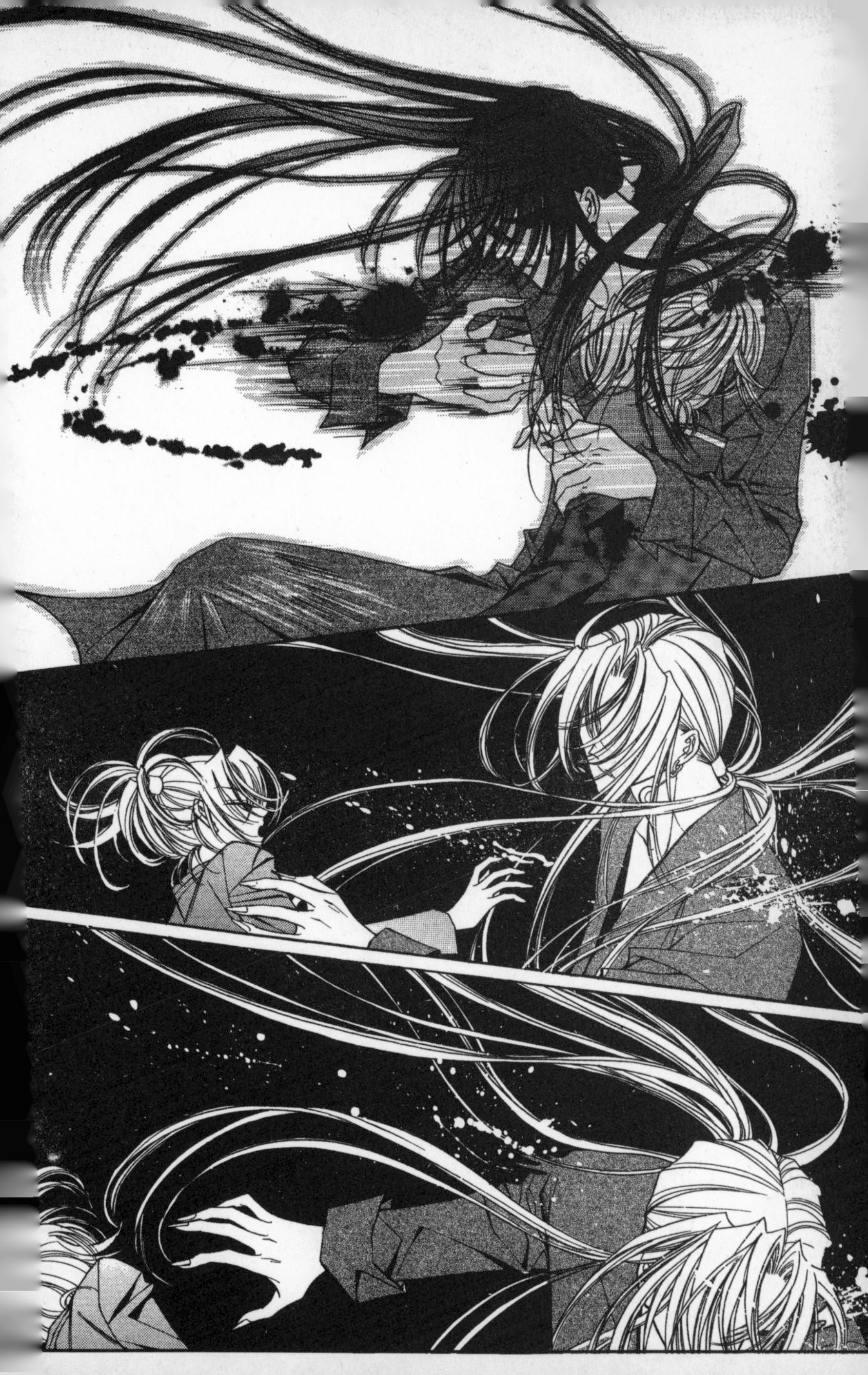

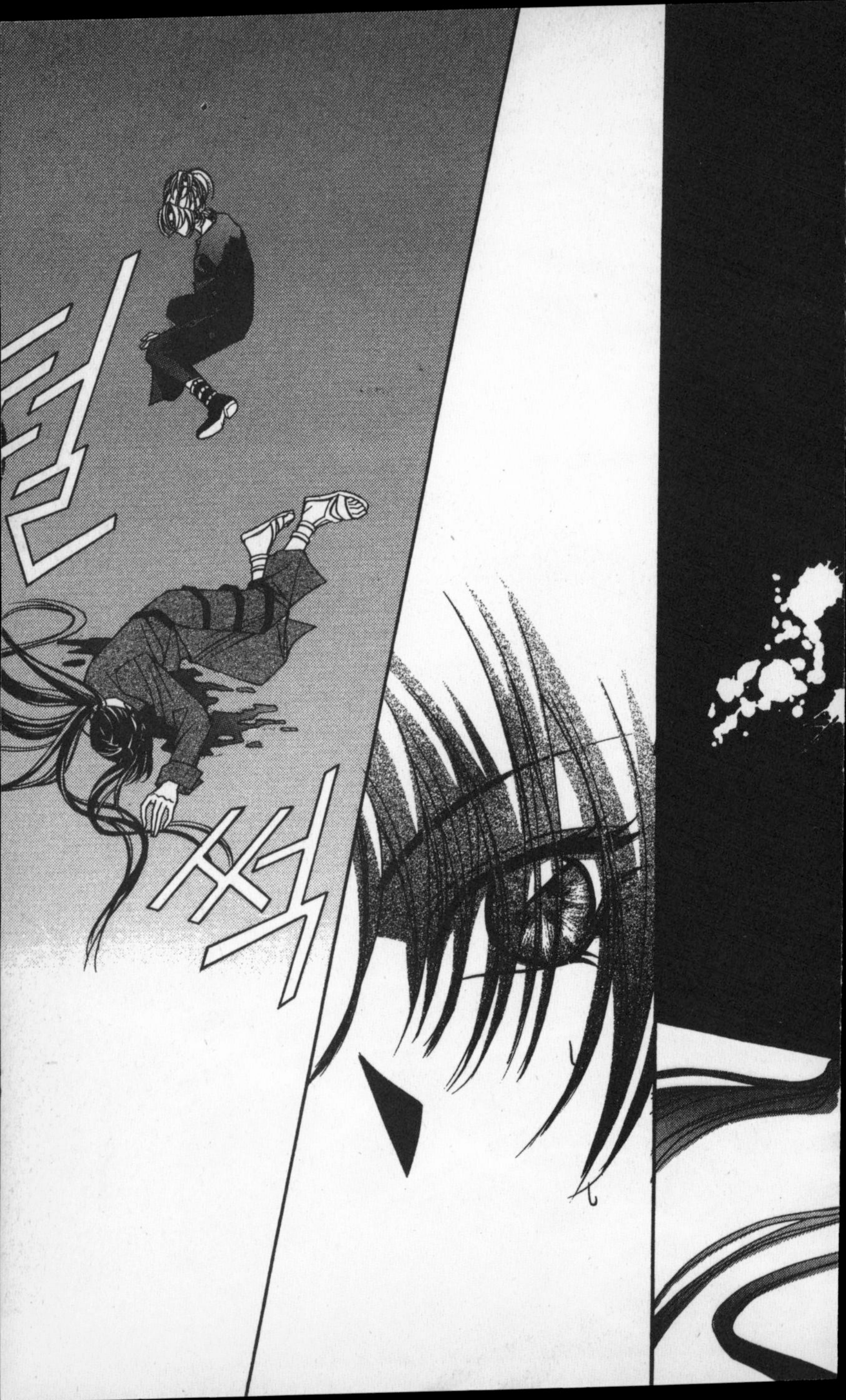

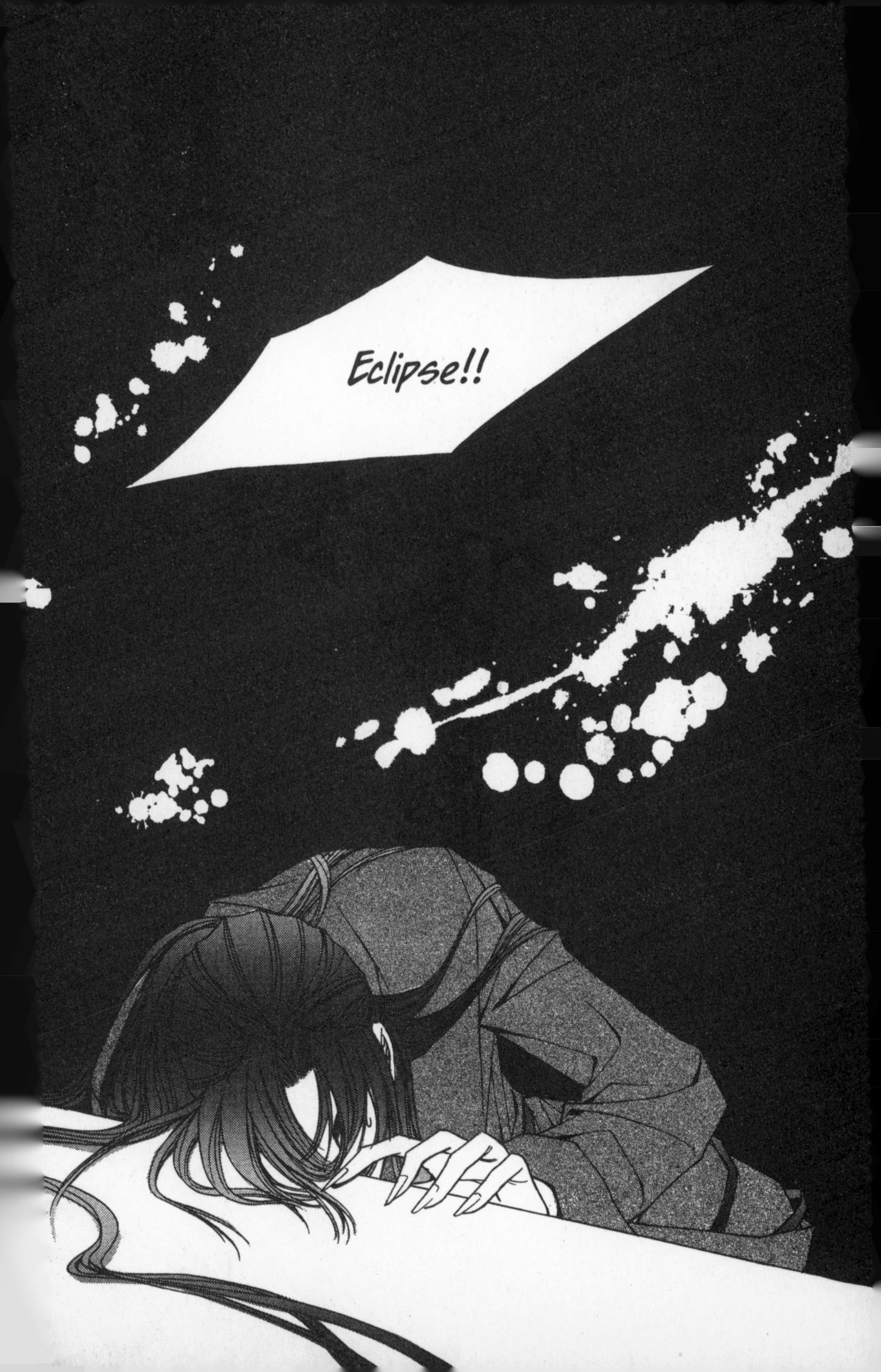
Eclipse!!

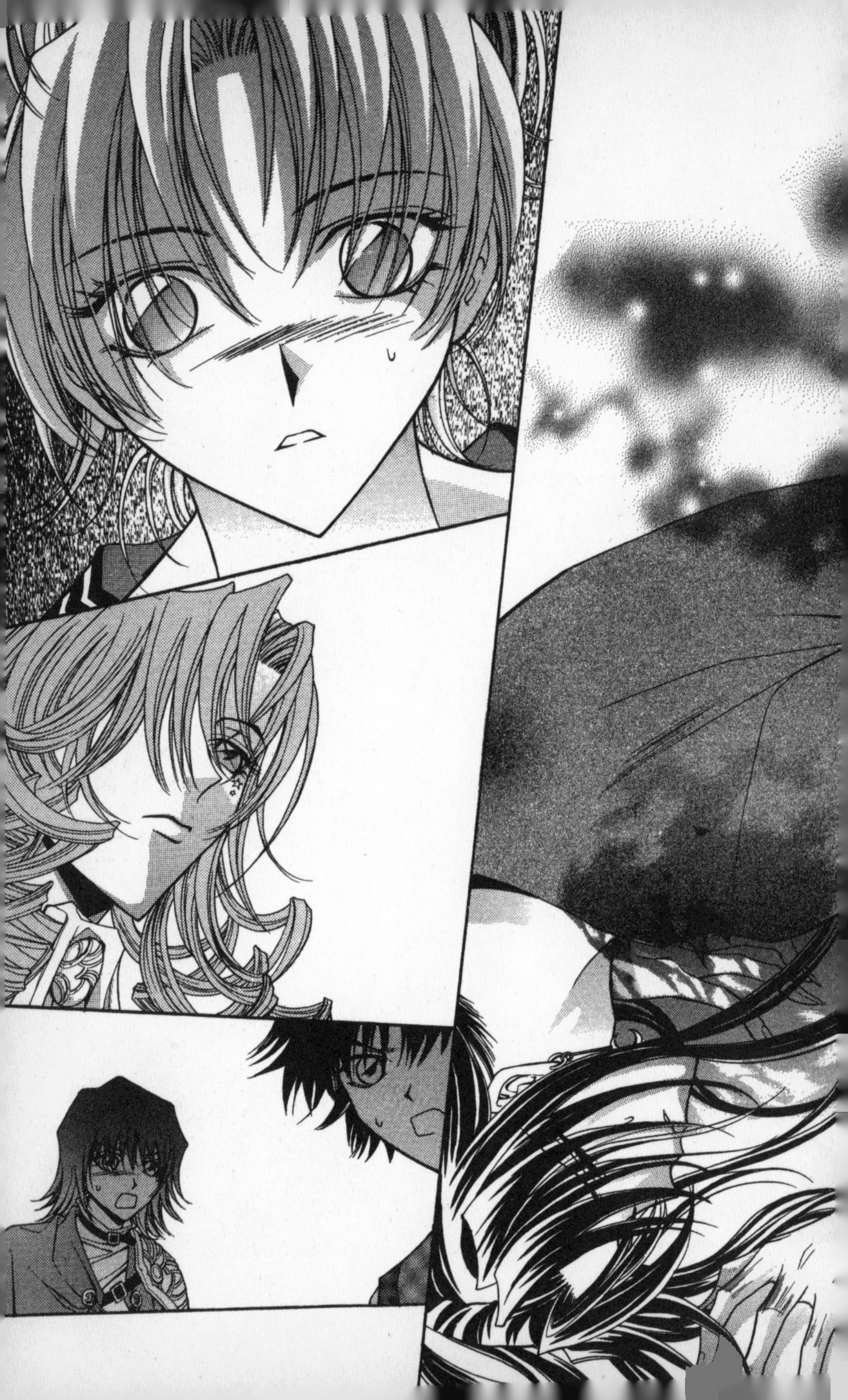

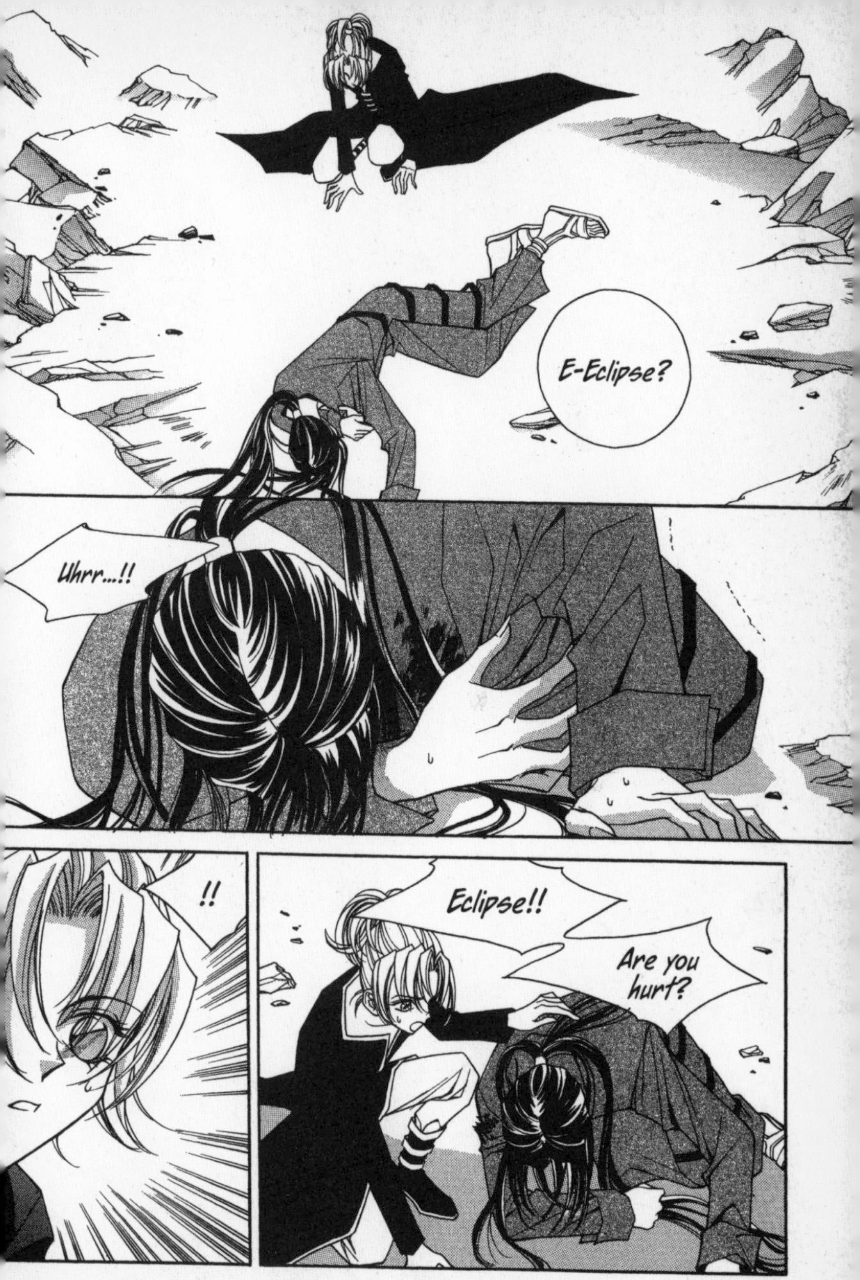
E-Eclipse?
Uhrr...!!
Eclipse!!
Are you hurt?
!!

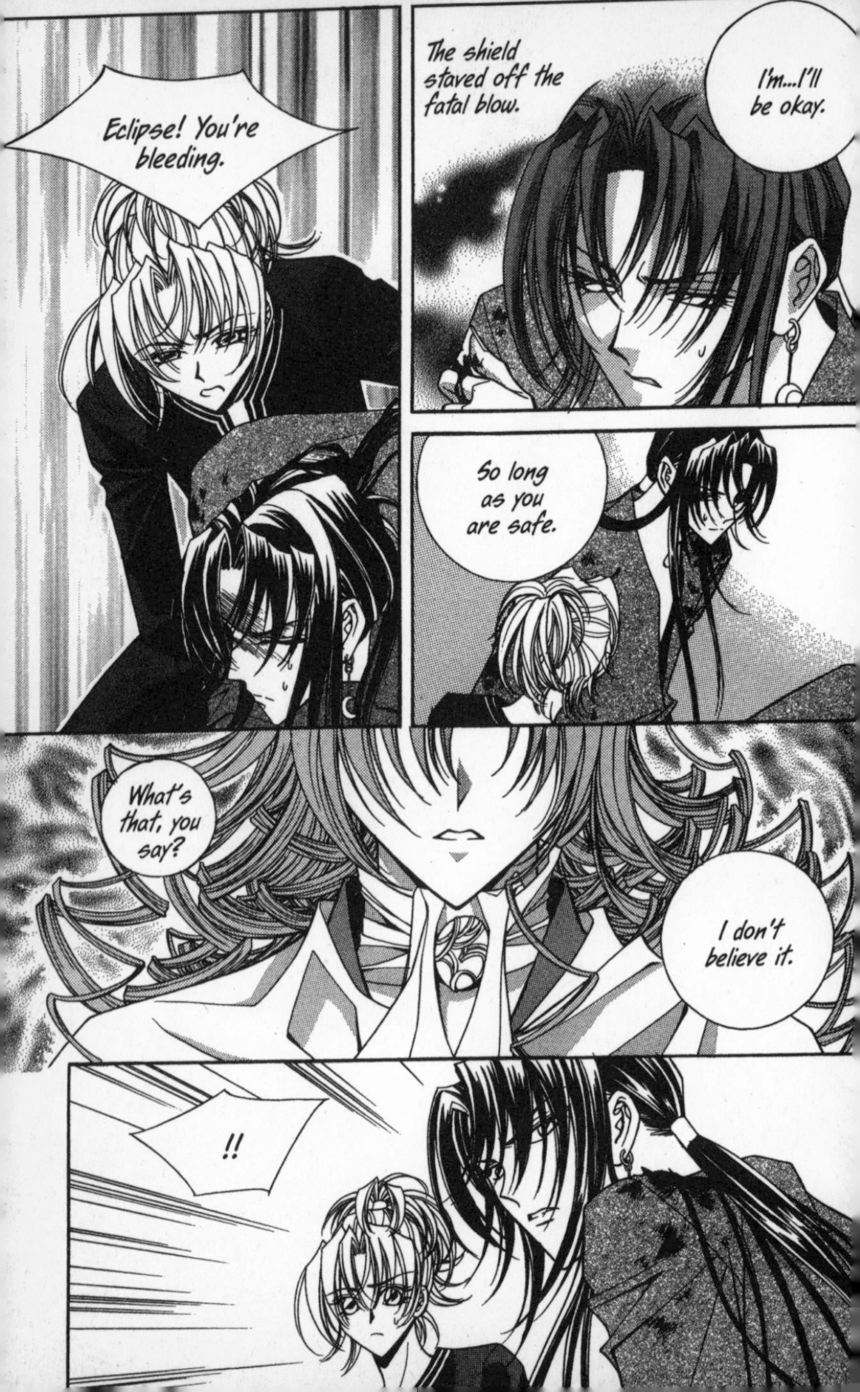

Eclipse! You're bleeding.
The shield staved off the fatal blow.
I'm...I'll be okay.
So long as you are safe.
What's that, you say?
I don't believe it.
!!

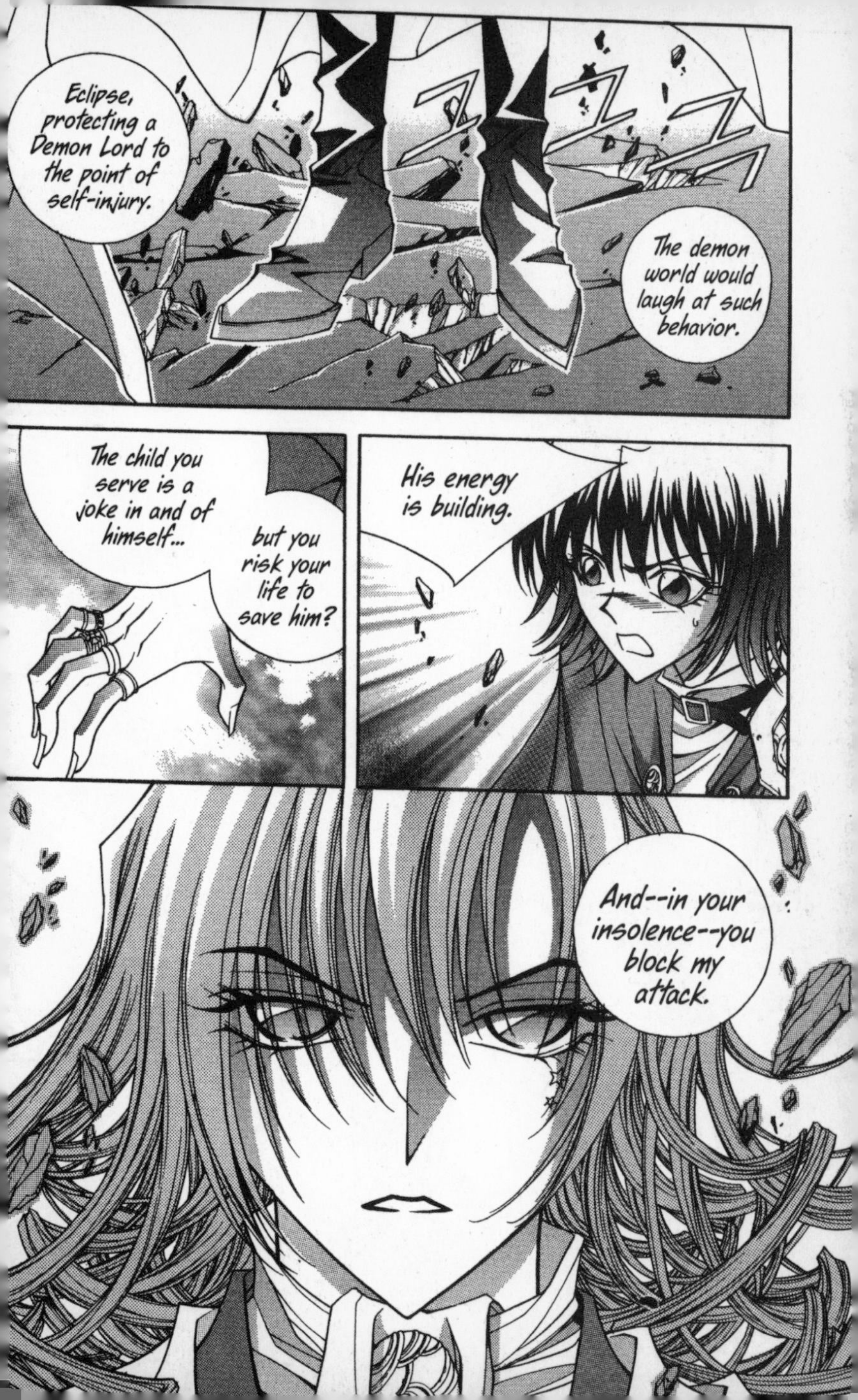
Eclipse, protecting a Demon Lord to the point of self-injury.
The demon world would laugh at such behavior.
His energy is building.
The child you serve is a joke in and of himself...
but you risk your life to save him?
And--in your insolence--you block my attack.

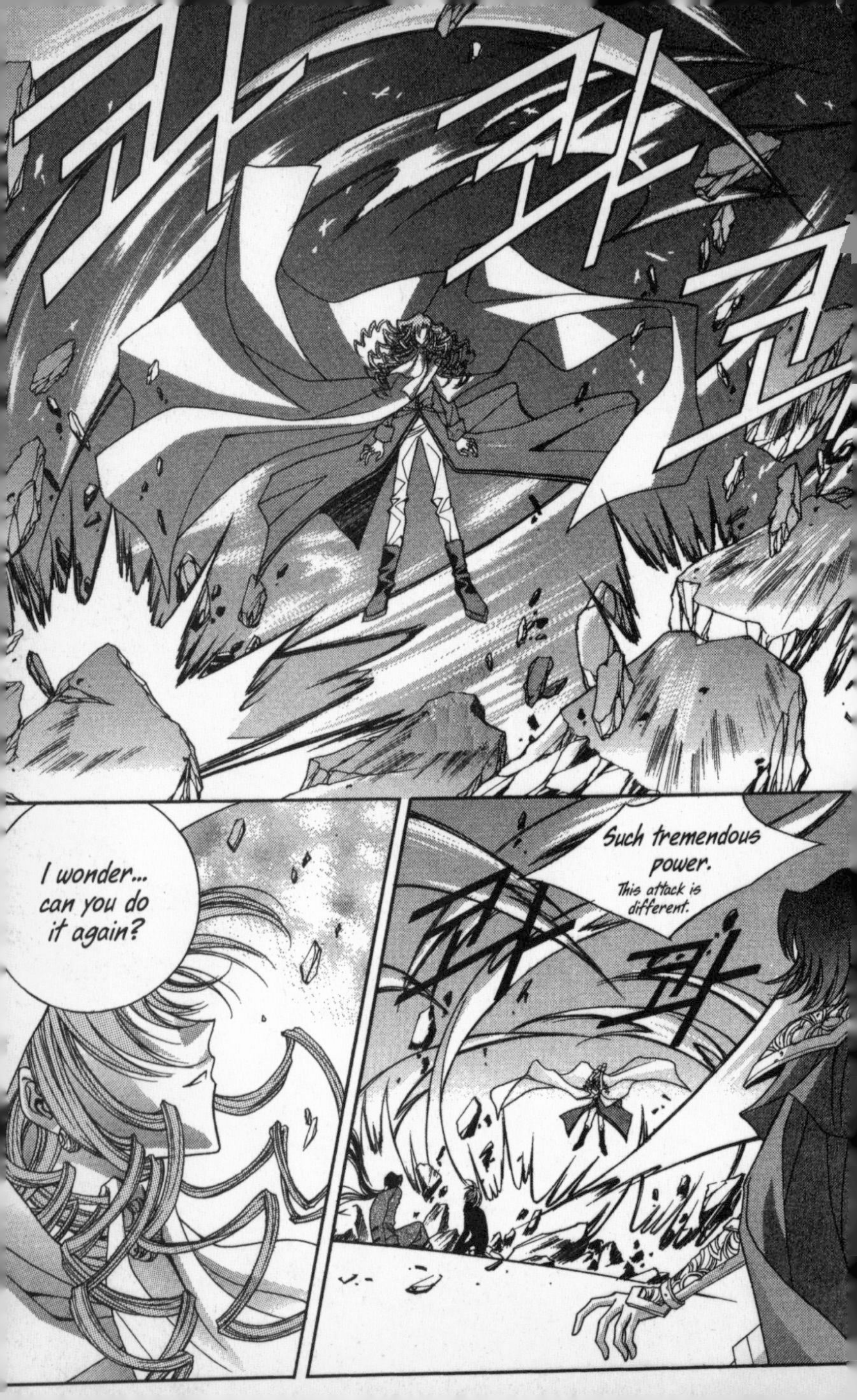
Such tremendous power.
This attack is different.
I wonder... can you do it again?

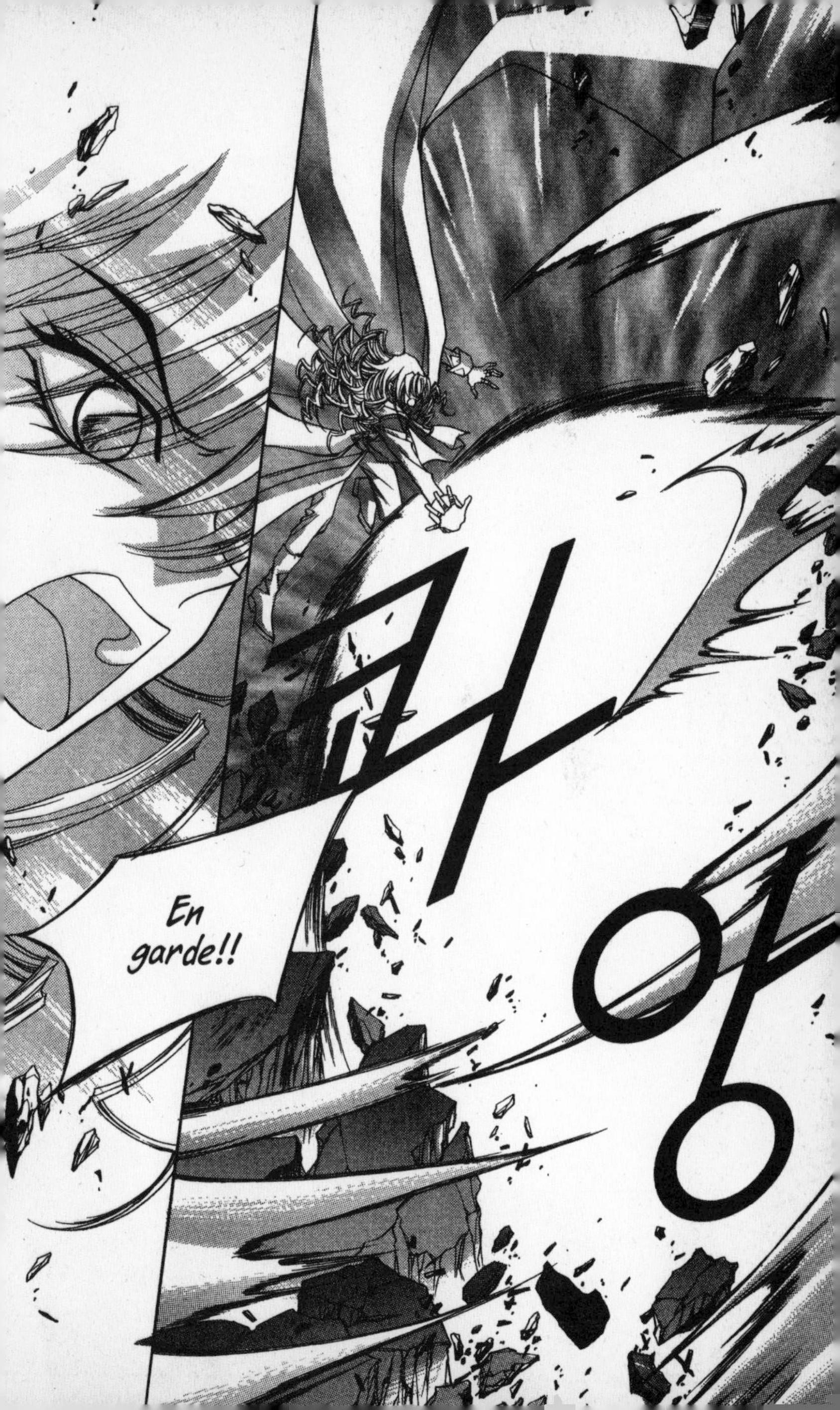
En garde!!

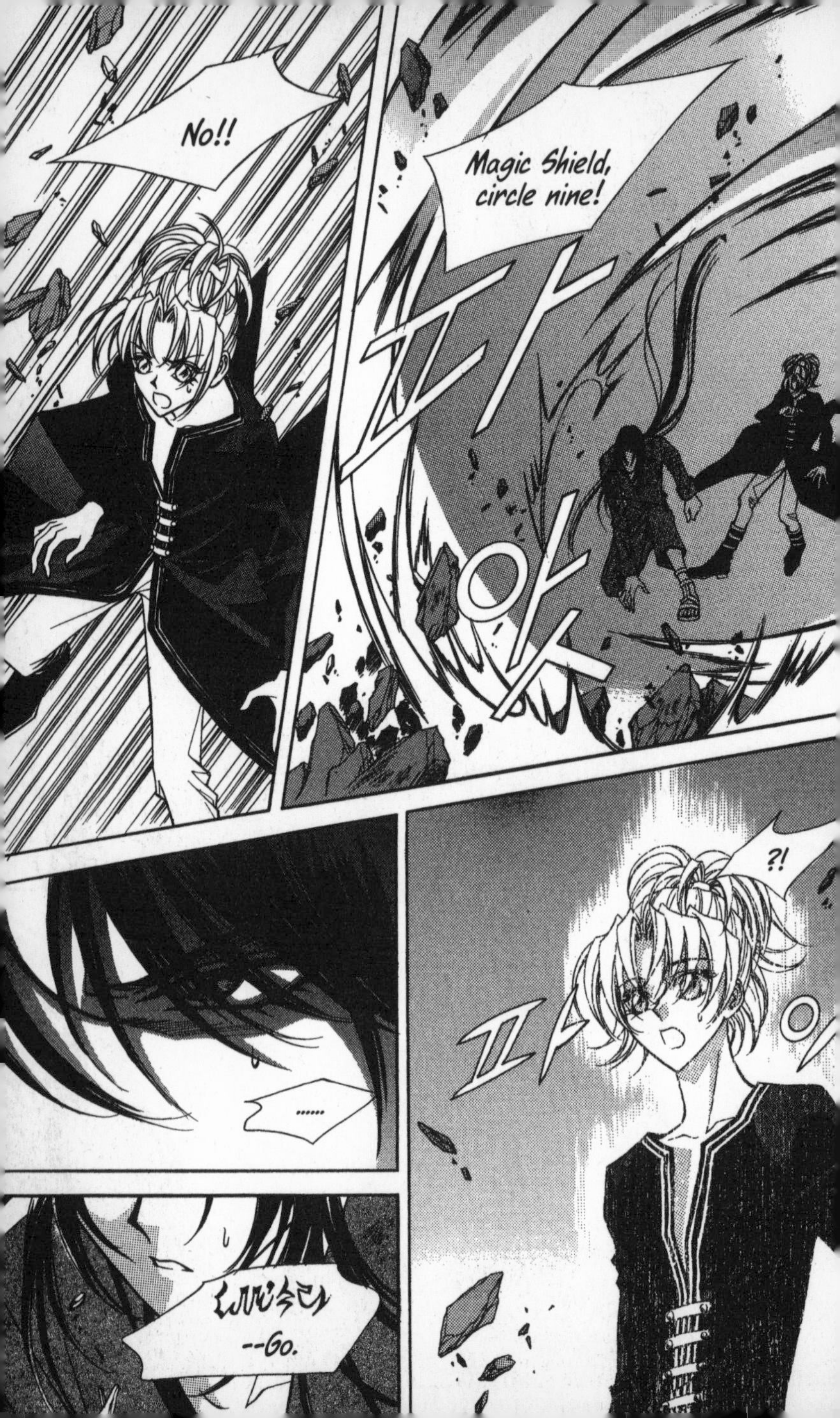
Magic Shield, circle nine!
No!!
?!
......
--Go.

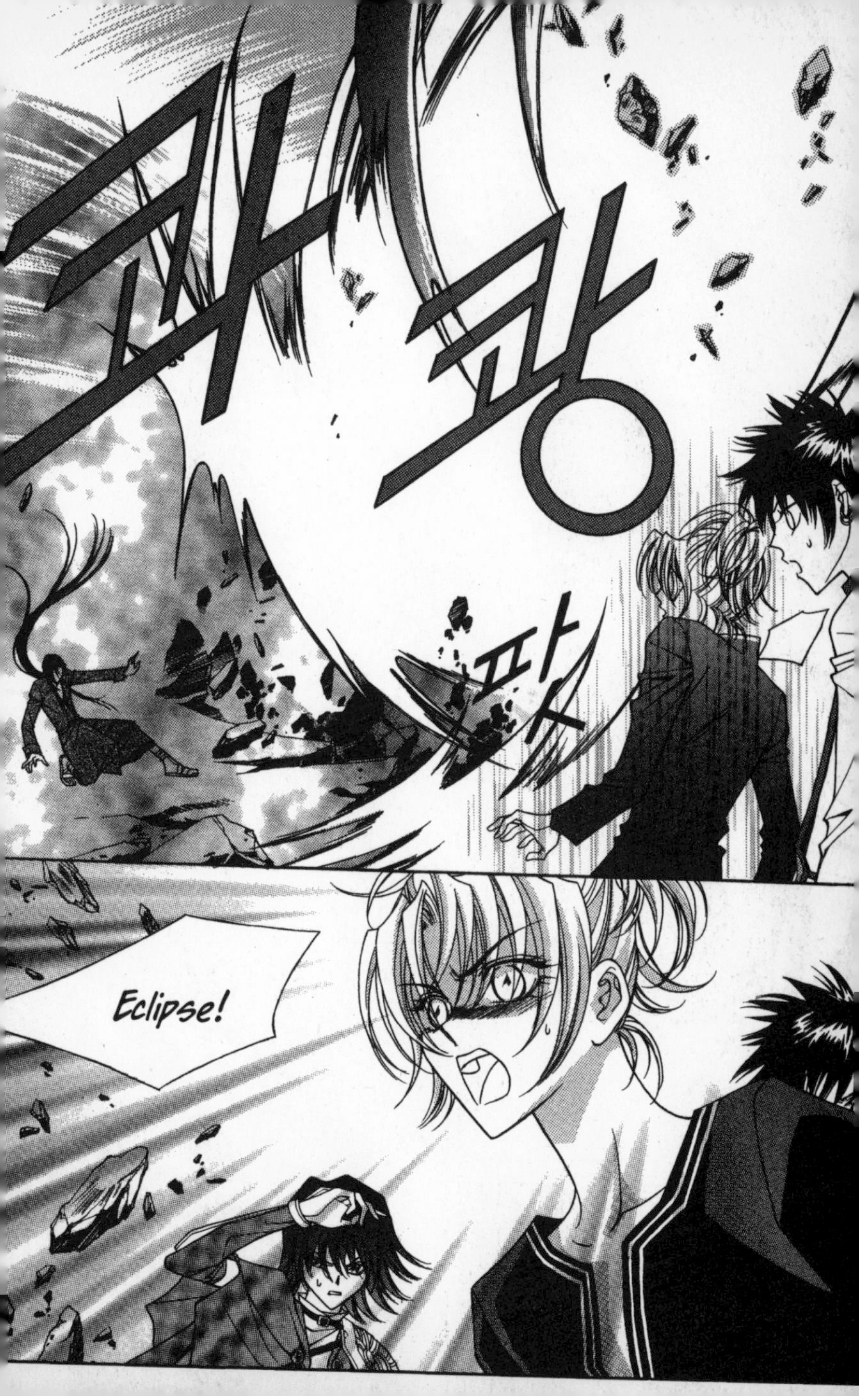
콰광
팟
Eclipse!

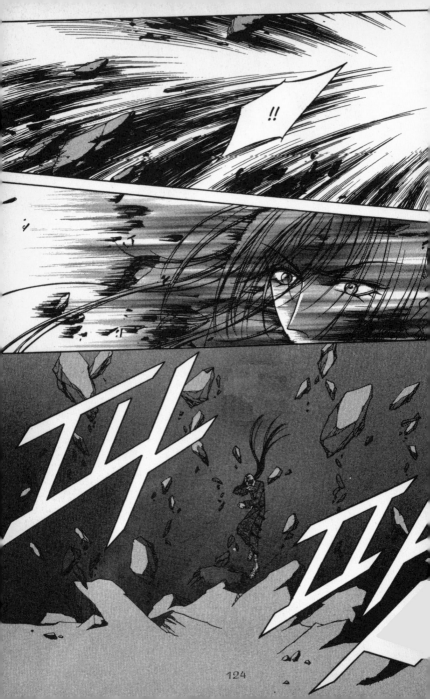

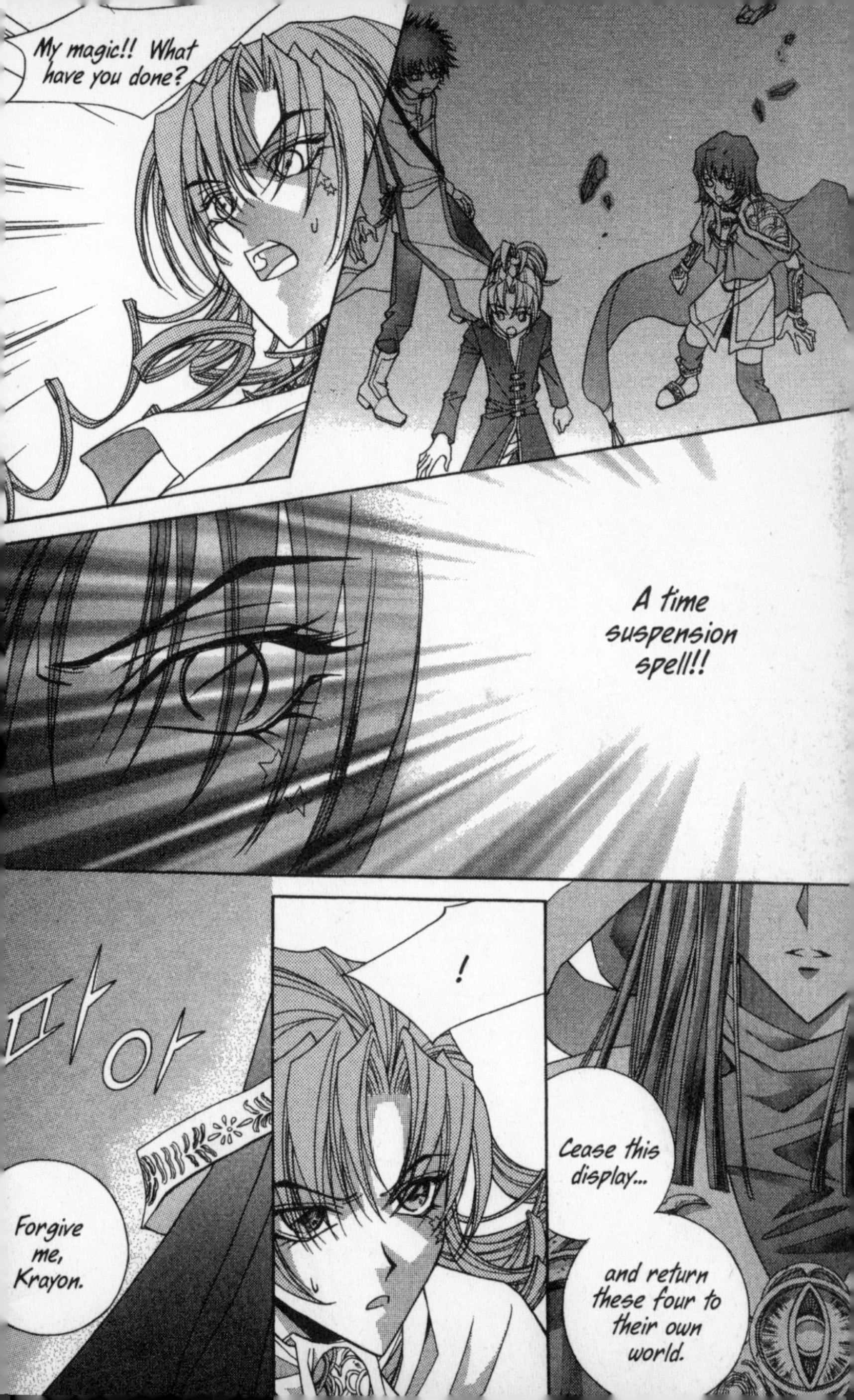

My magic!! What have you done?
A time suspension spell!!
파아
Forgive me, Krayon.
!
Cease this display...
and return these four to their own world.

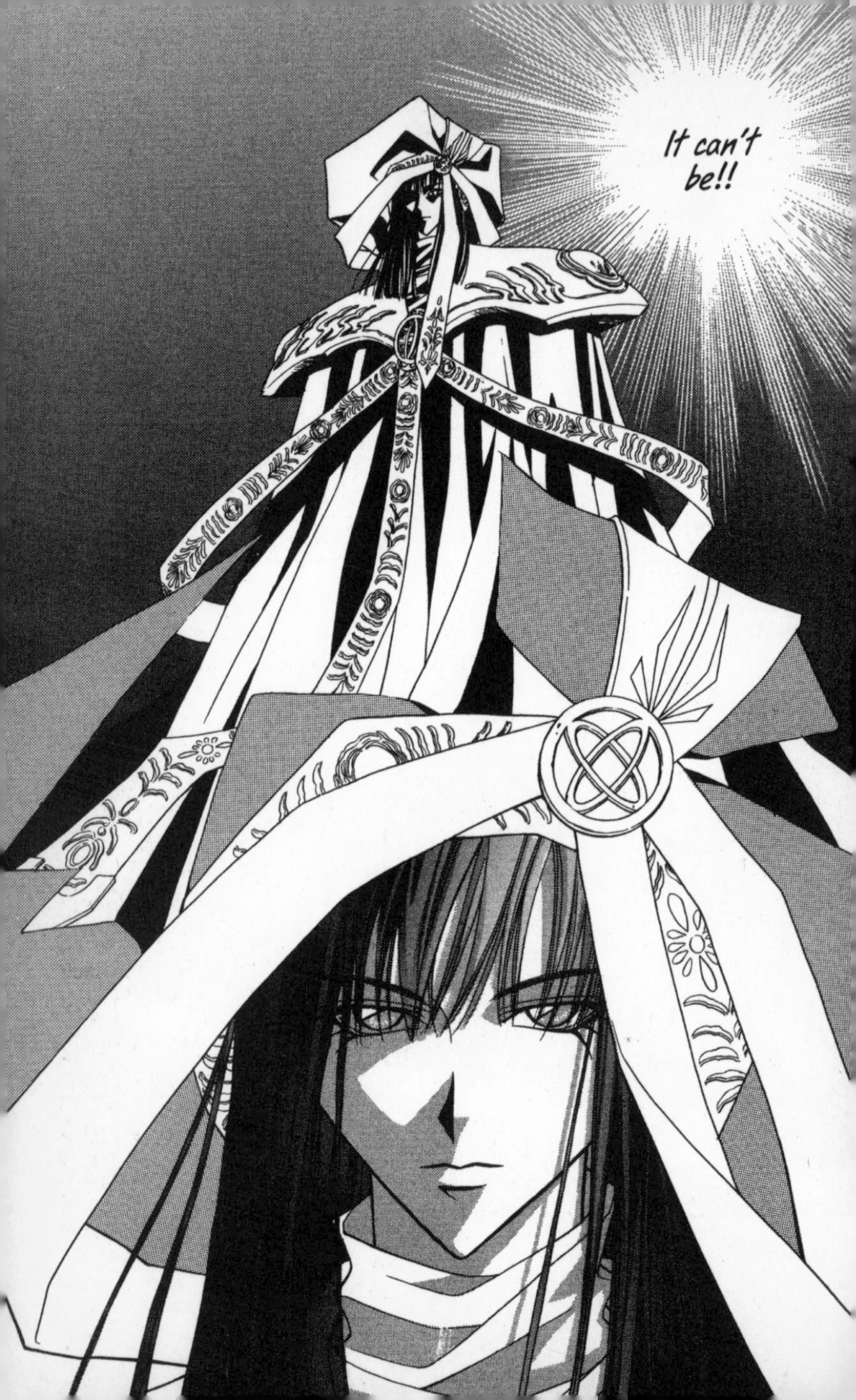
It can't be!!

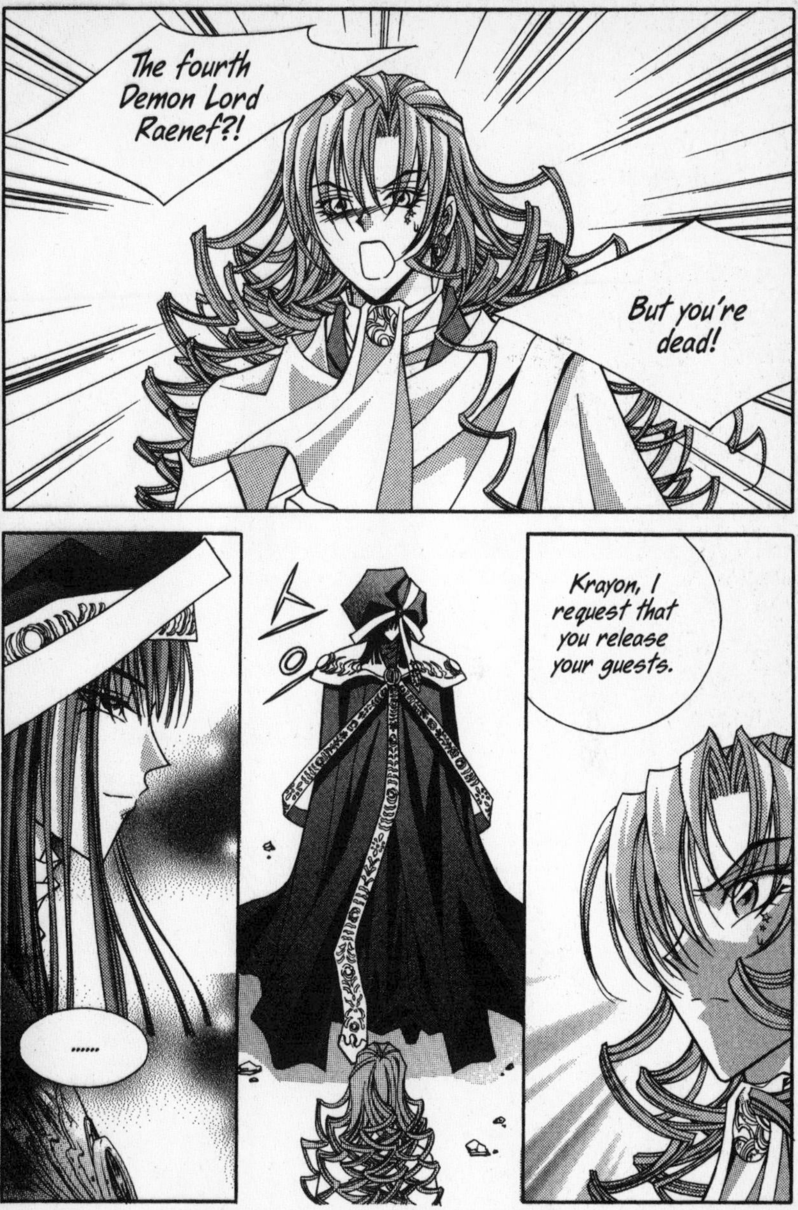
The fourth Demon Lord Raenef?!
But you're dead!
Krayon, I request that you release your guests.
......

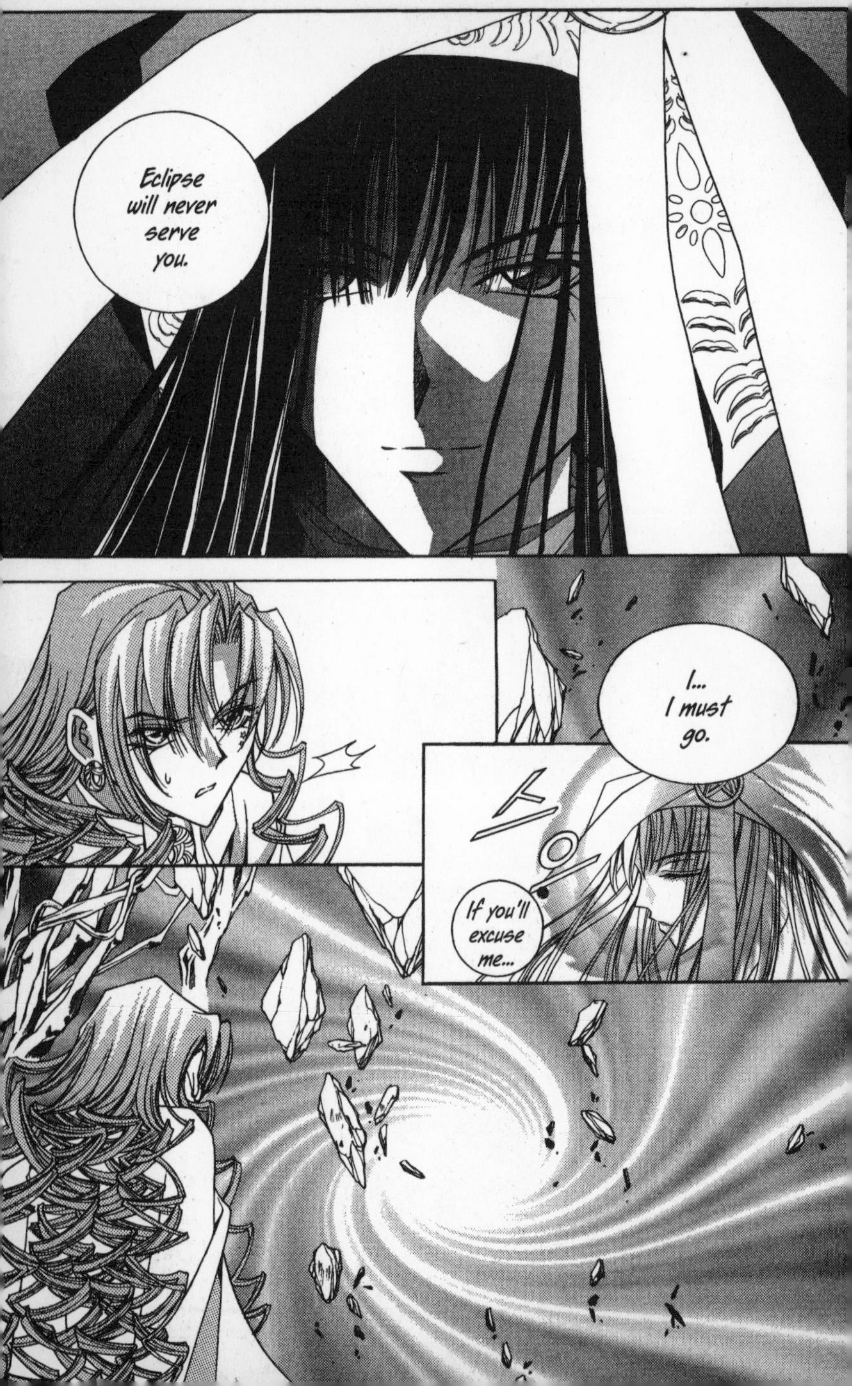
Eclipse will never serve you.
I... I must go.
If you'll excuse me...

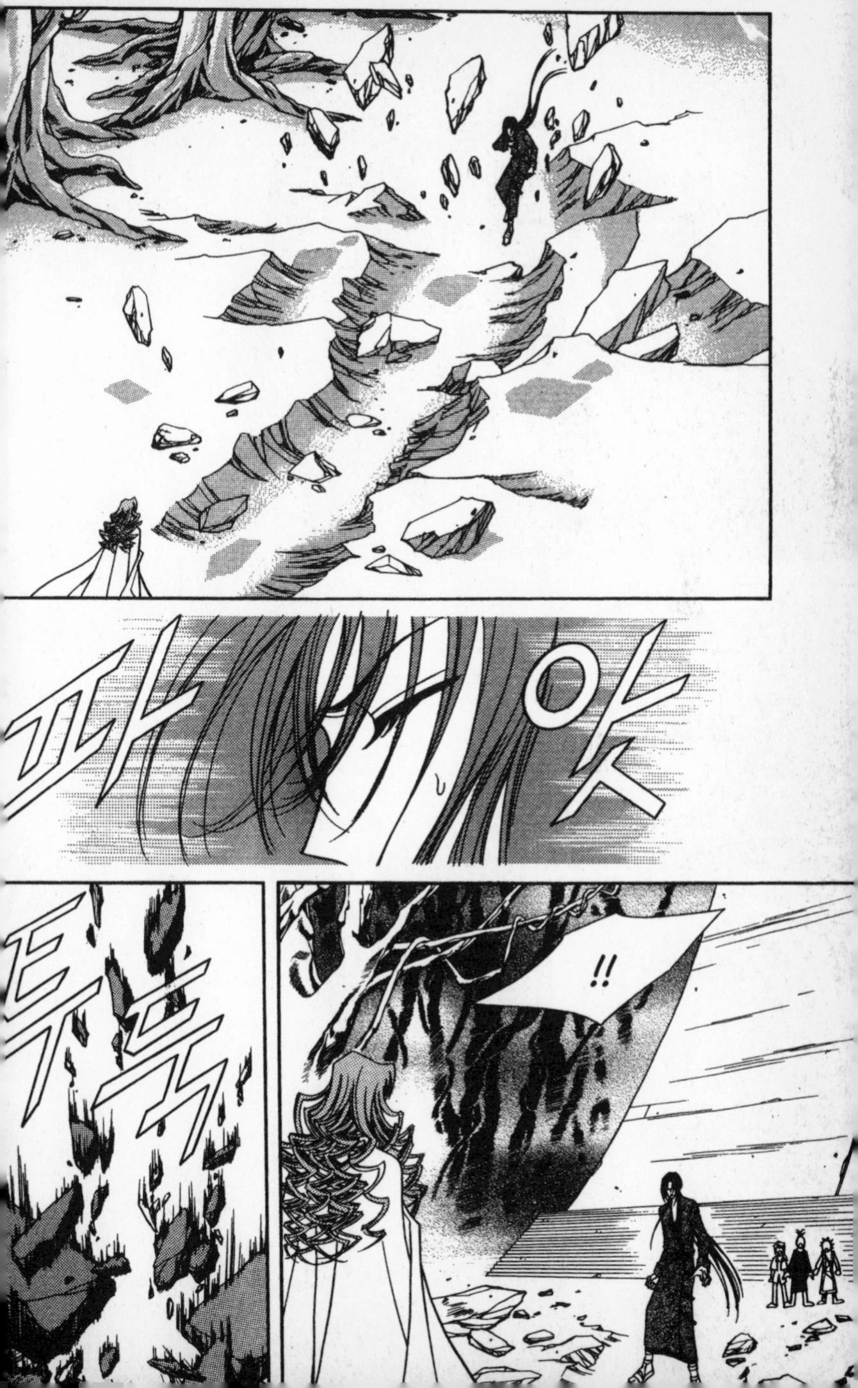
파앗
투득
!!

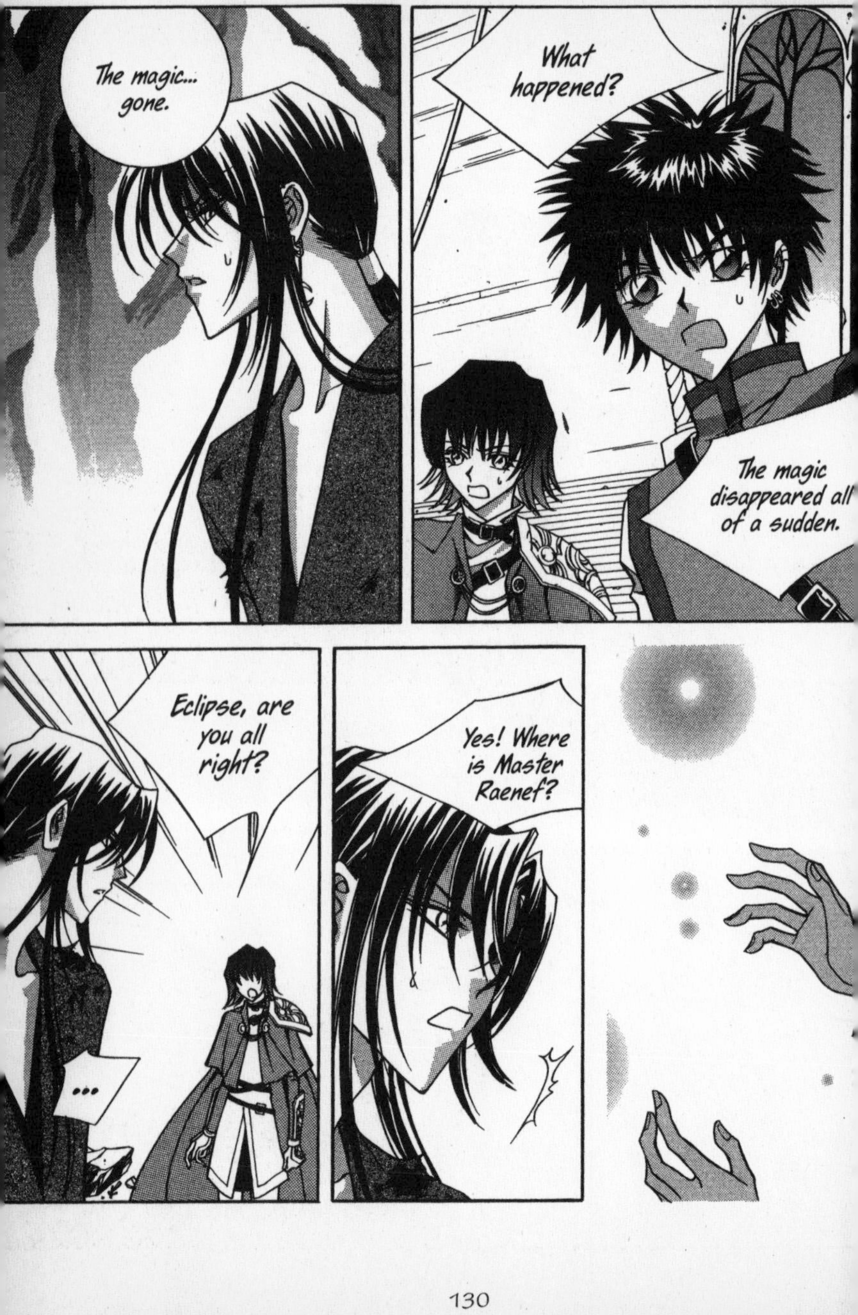
The magic... gone.
What happened?
The magic disappeared all of a sudden.
Eclipse, are you all right?
...
Yes! Where is Master Raenef?

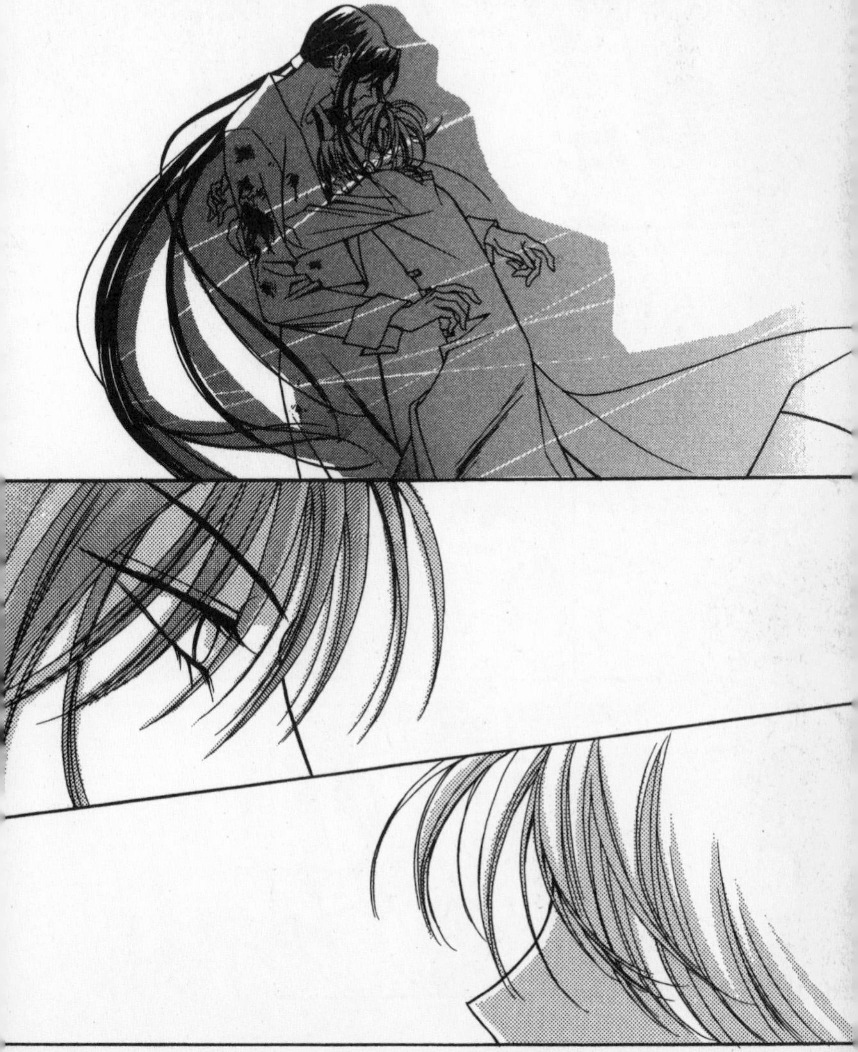

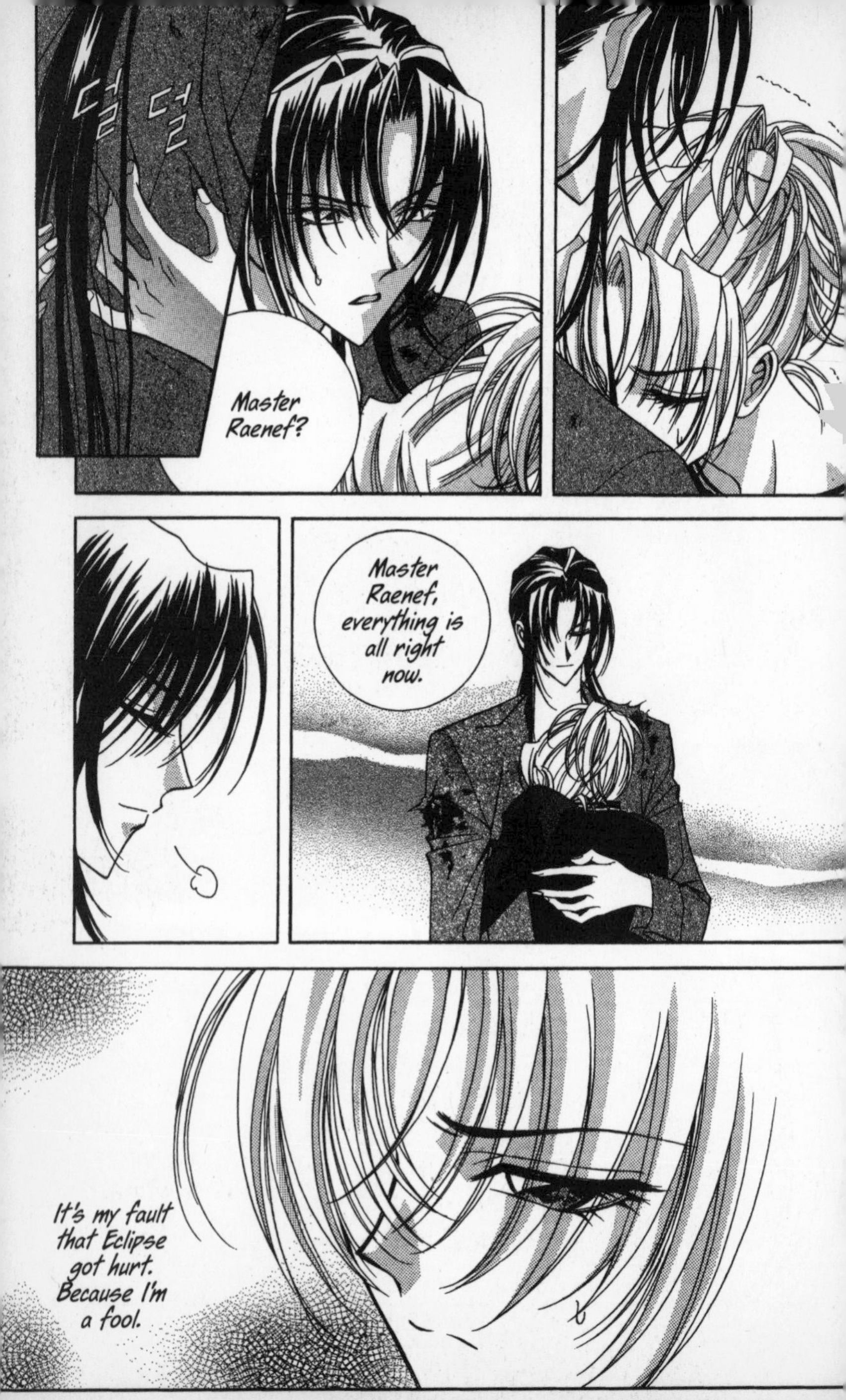
Master Raenef?
Master Raenef, everything is all right now.
It's my fault that Eclipse got hurt. Because I'm a fool.

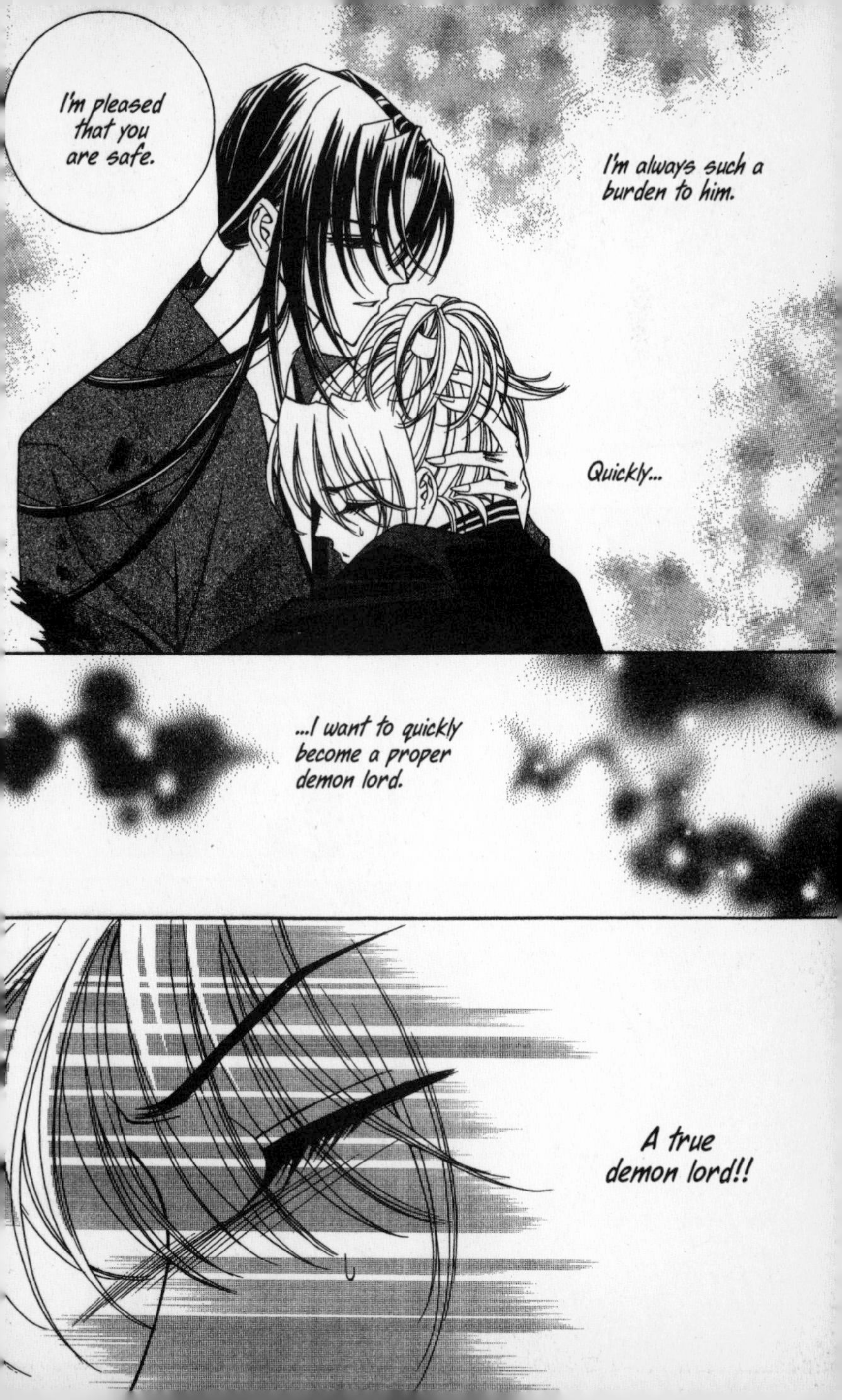
I'm always such a burden to him.
I'm pleased that you are safe.
Quickly...
...I want to quickly become a proper demon lord.
A true demon lord!!

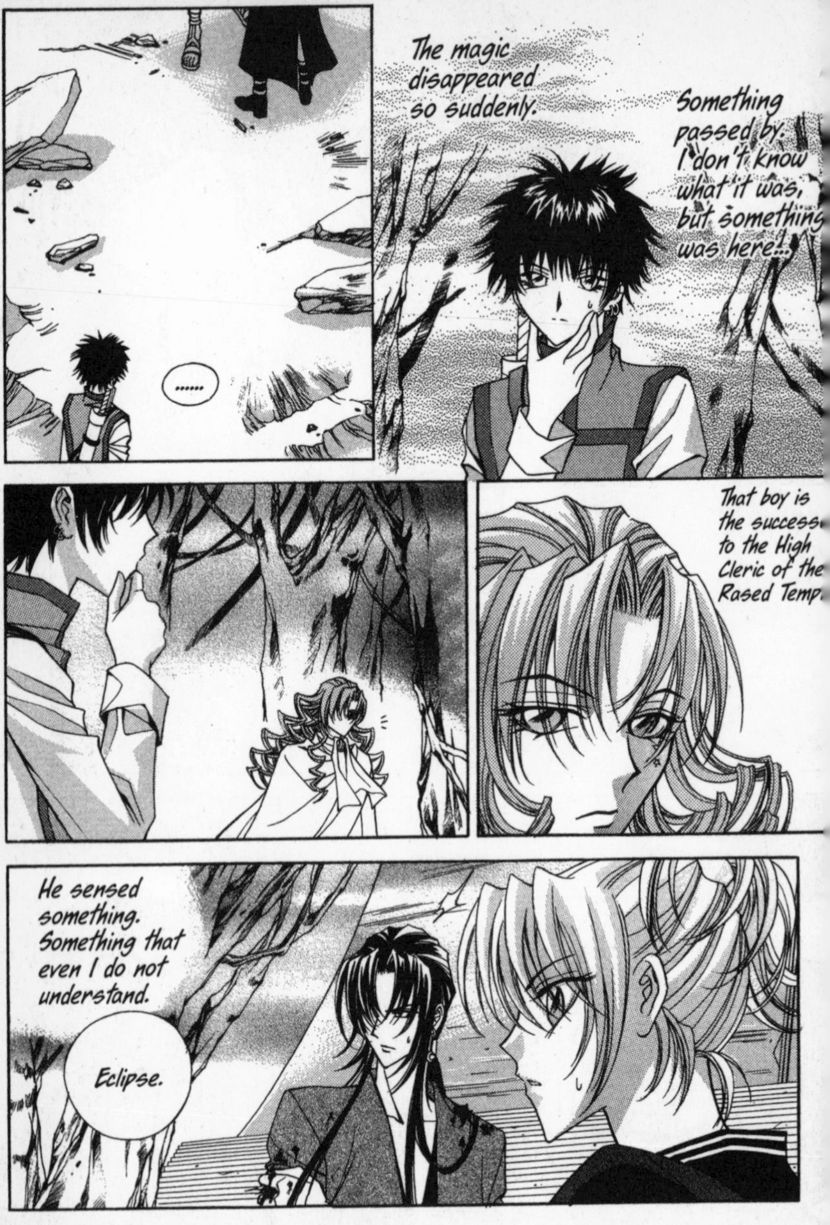
The magic disappeared so suddenly.
Something passed by. I don't know what it was, but something was here...!
......
That boy is the success to the High Cleric of the Rased Temp
He sensed something. Something that even I do not understand.
Eclipse.

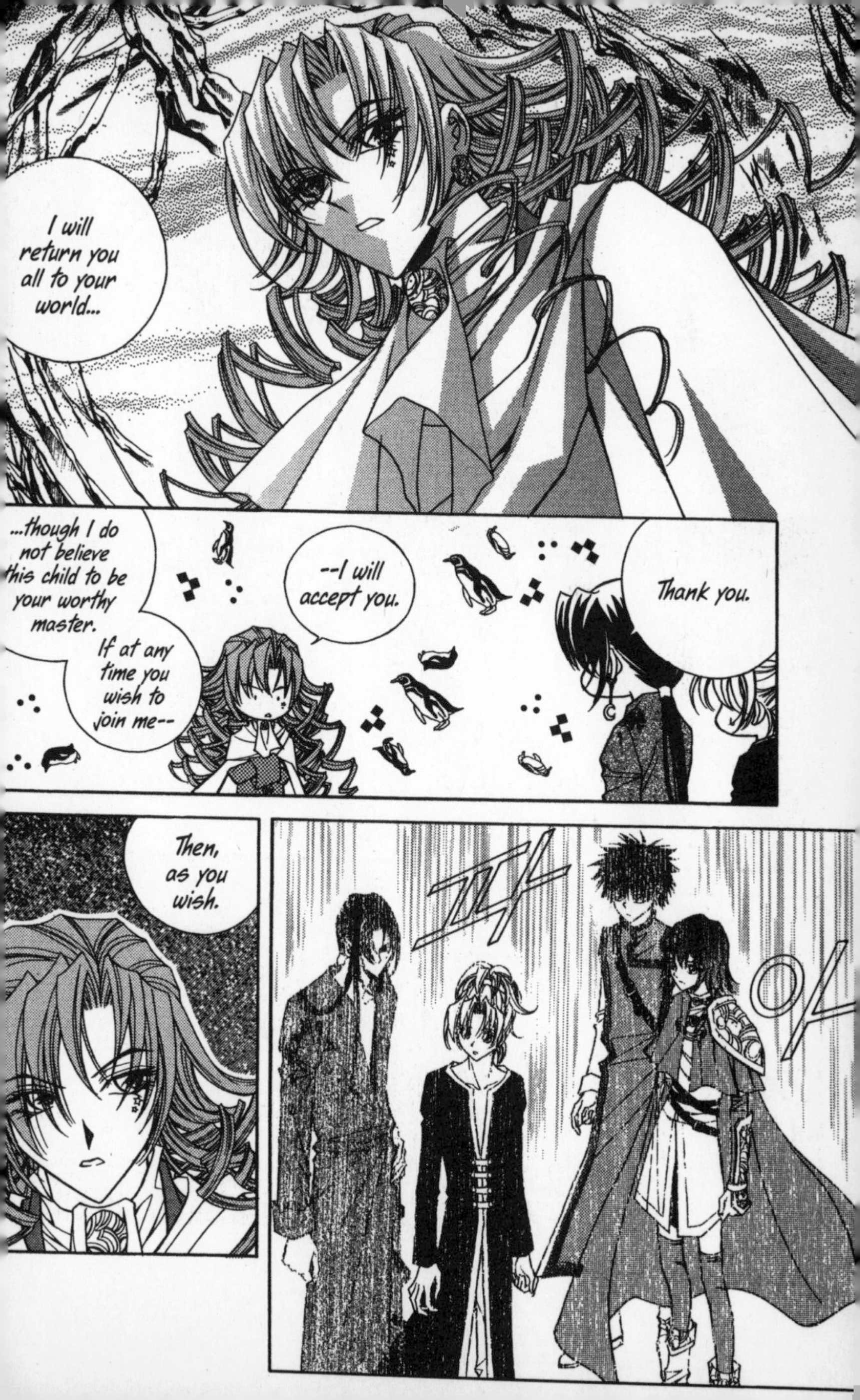
I will return you all to your world...
...though I do not believe this child to be your worthy master.
If at any time you wish to join me--
--I will accept you.
Thank you.
Then, as you wish.

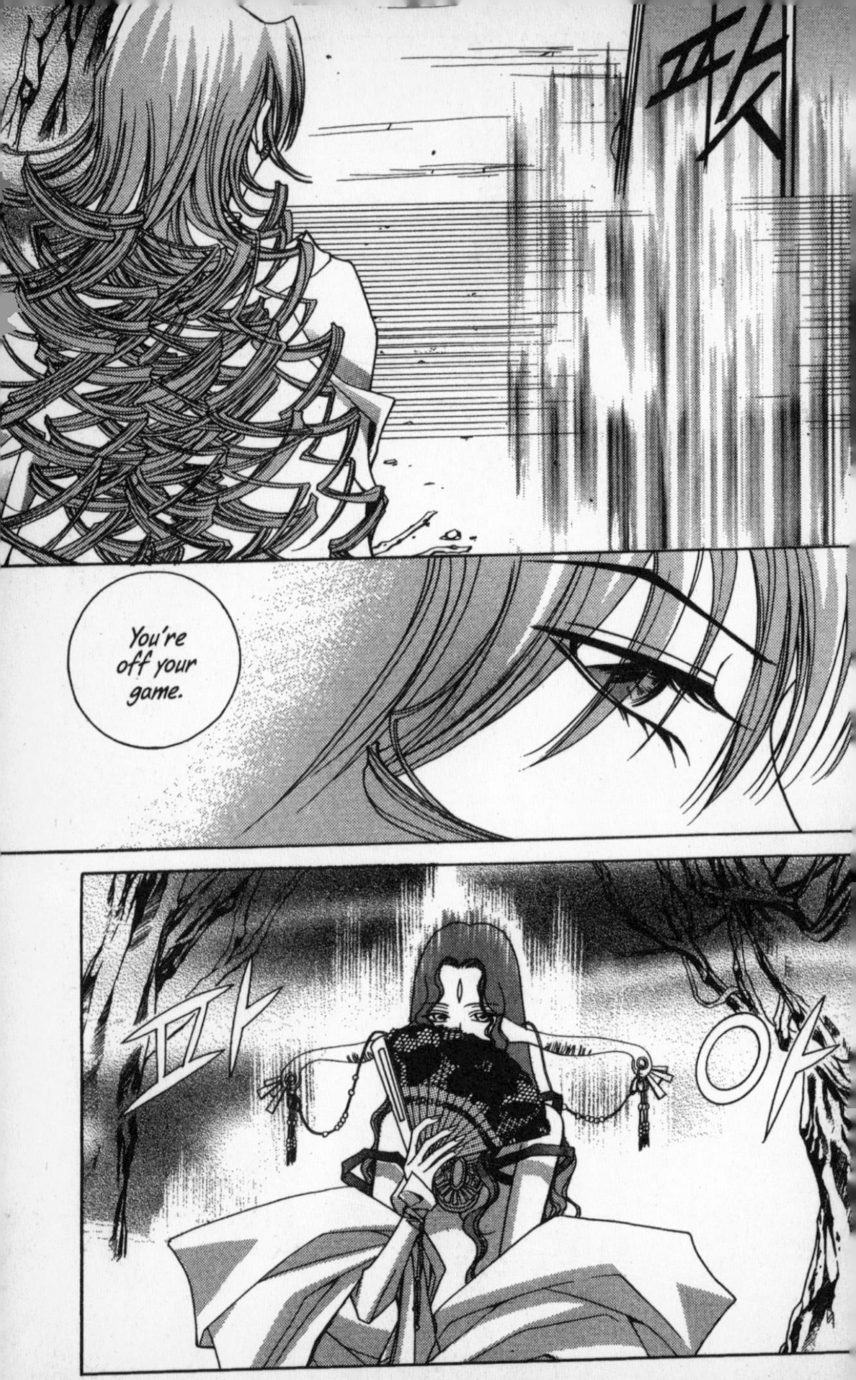
You're off your game.

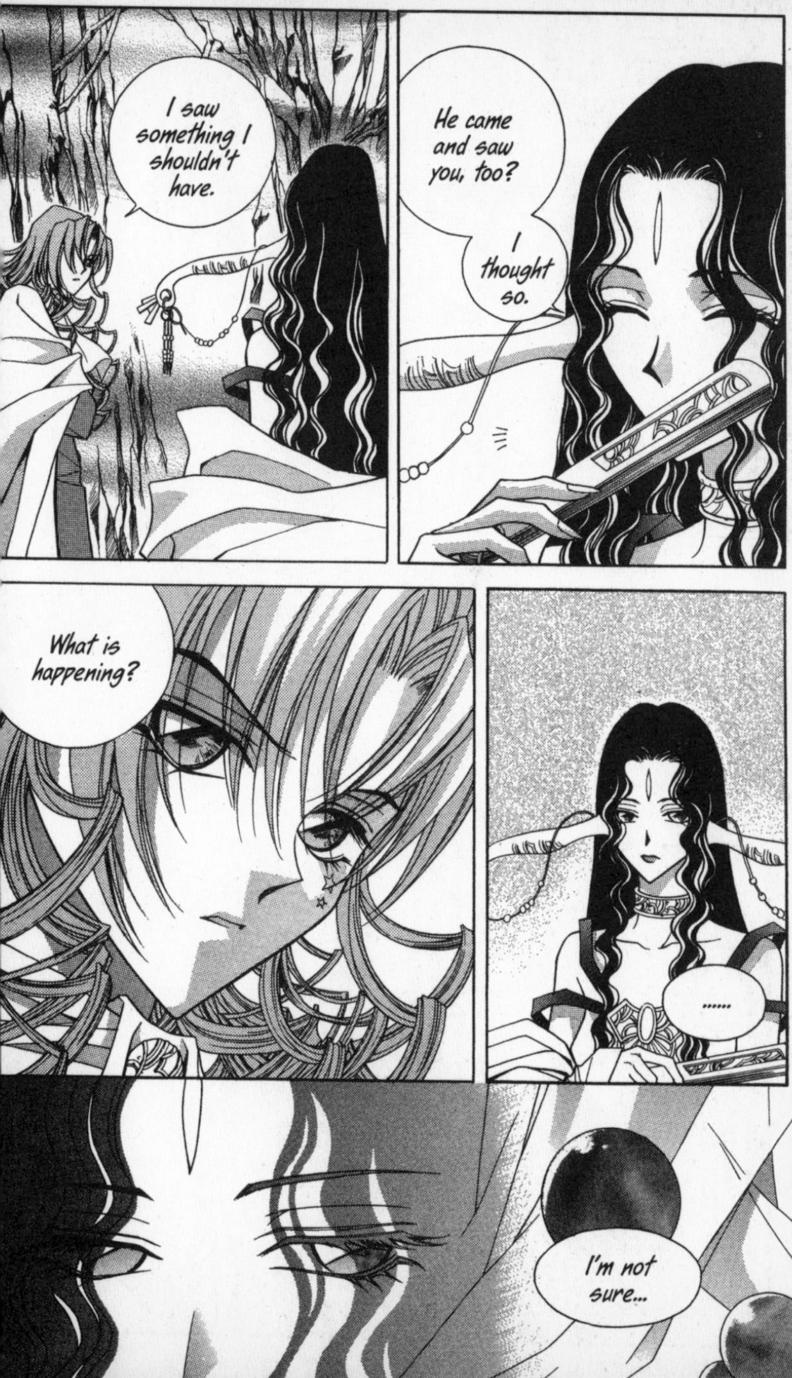
I saw something I shouldn't have.
He came and saw you, too?
I thought so.
What is happening?
......
I'm not sure...

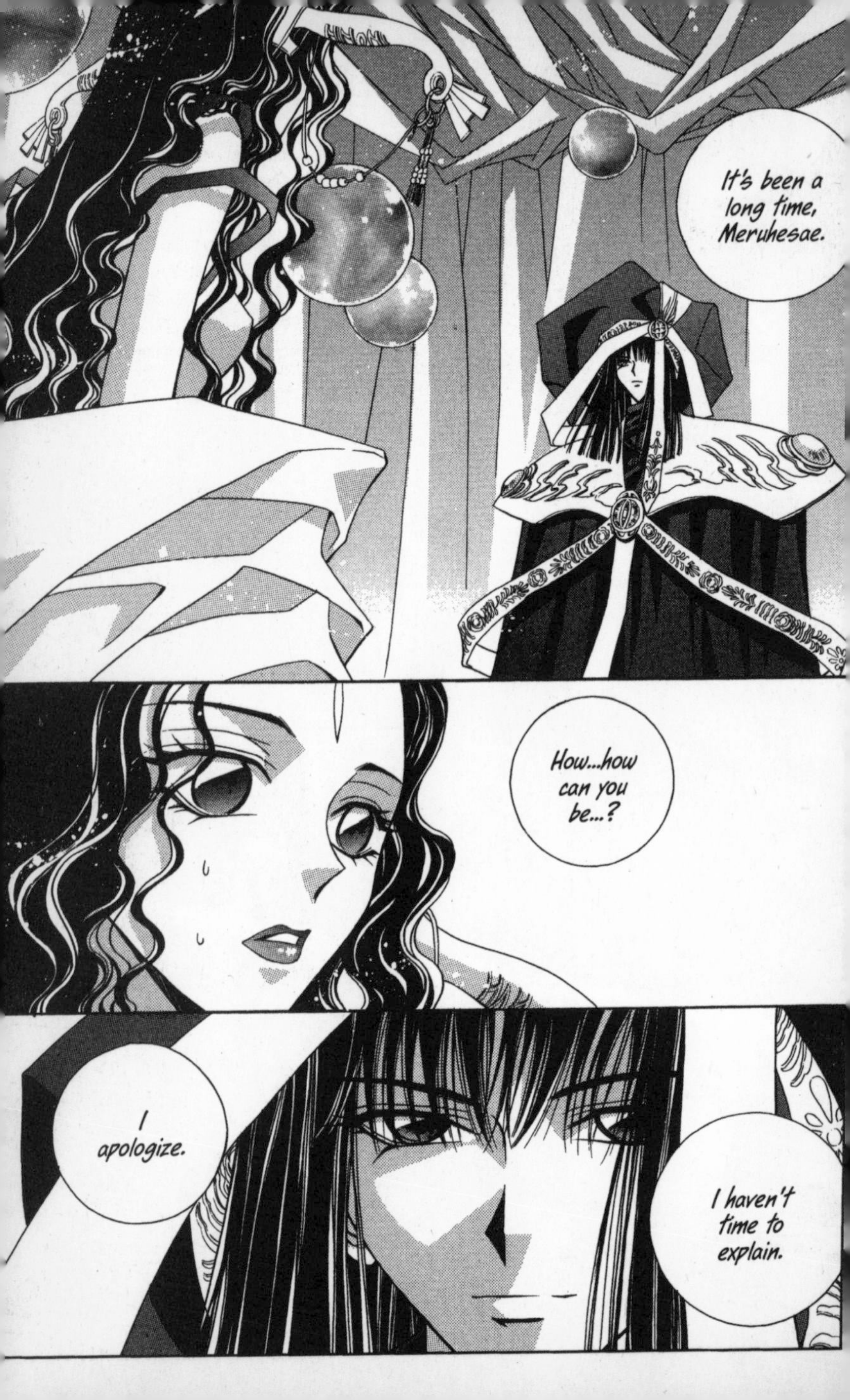
It's been a long time, Meruhesae.
How...how can you be...?
I apologize.
I haven't time to explain.

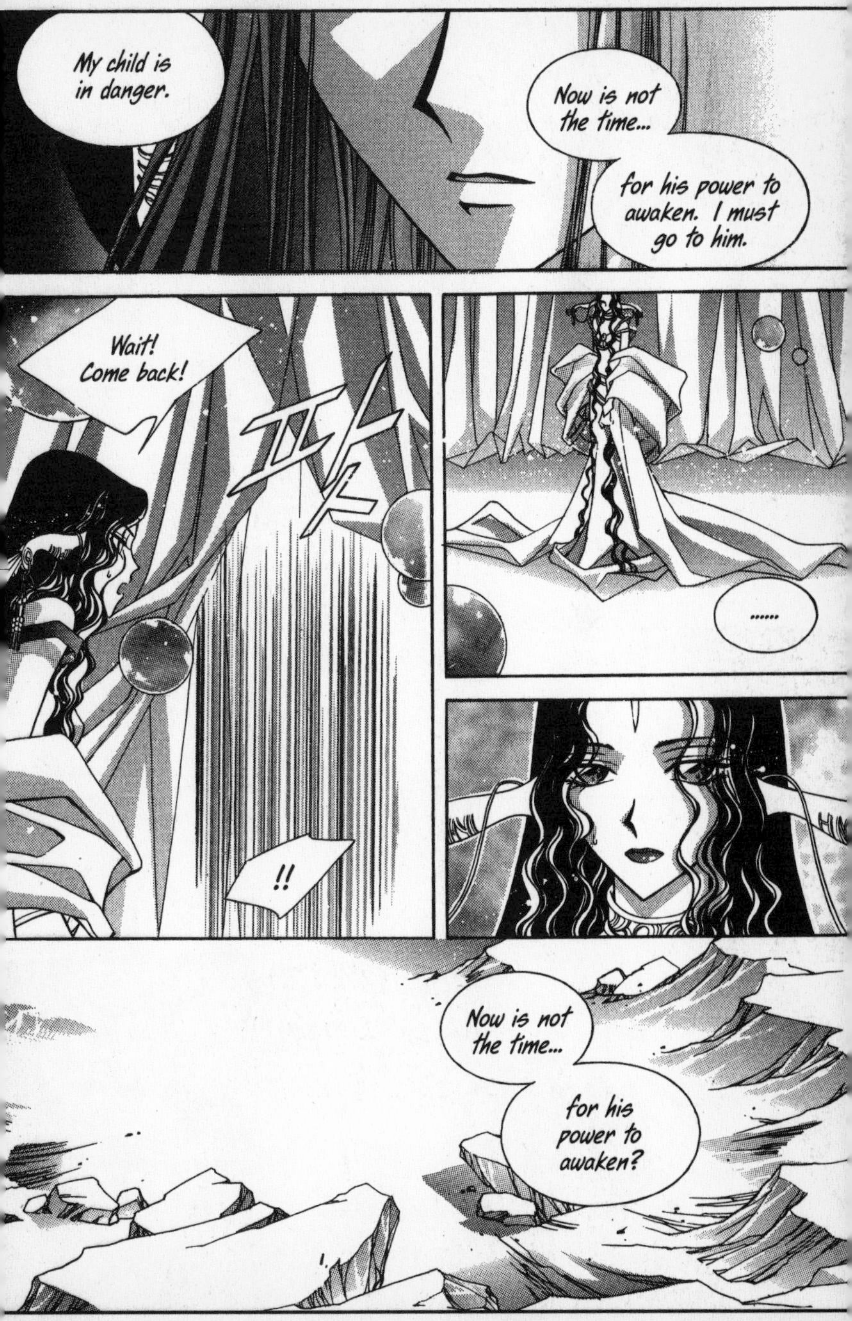
Now is not the time...
for his power to awaken. I must go to him.
My child is in danger.
......
Wait! Come back!
!!
Now is not the time...
for his power to awaken?

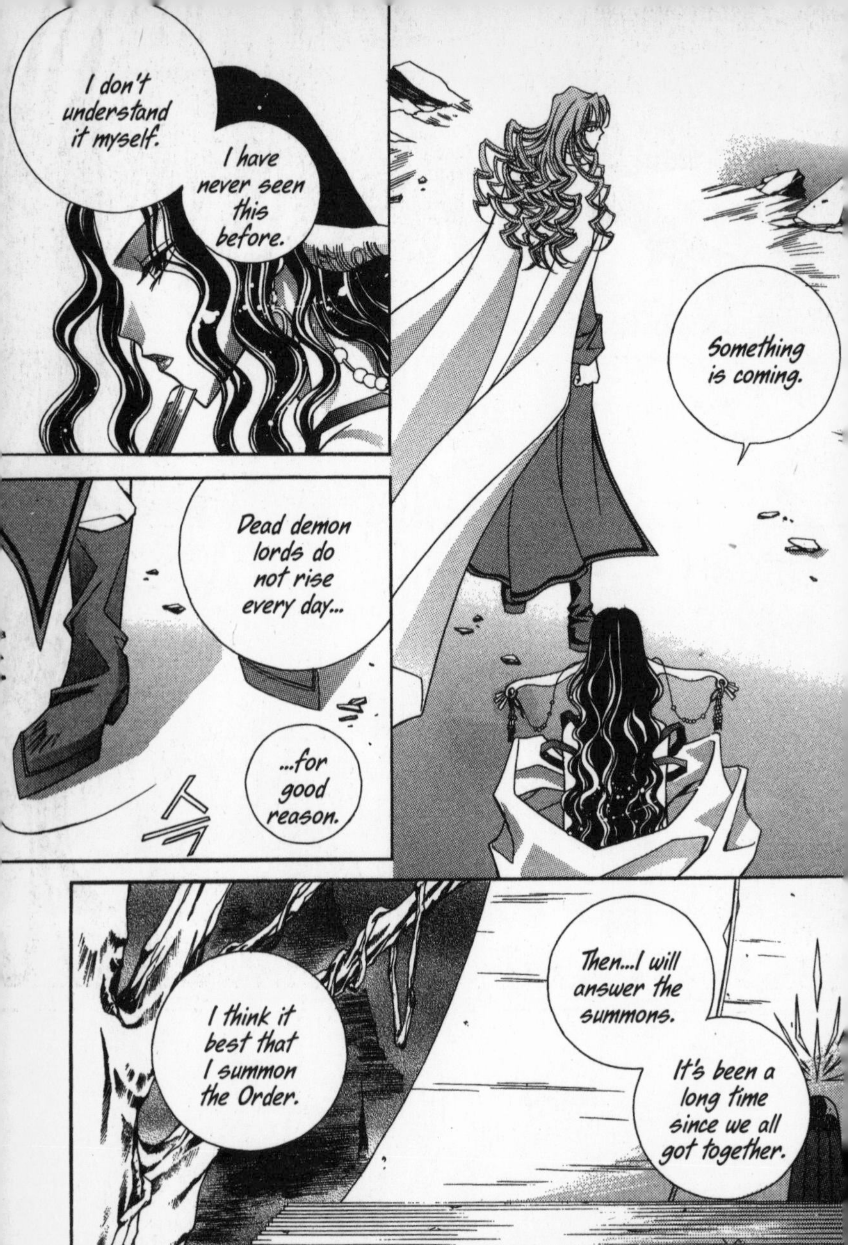
Something is coming.
I don't understand it myself.
I have never seen this before.
Dead demon lords do not rise every day...
...for good reason.
I think it best that I summon the Order.
Then...I will answer the summons.
It's been a long time since we all got together.

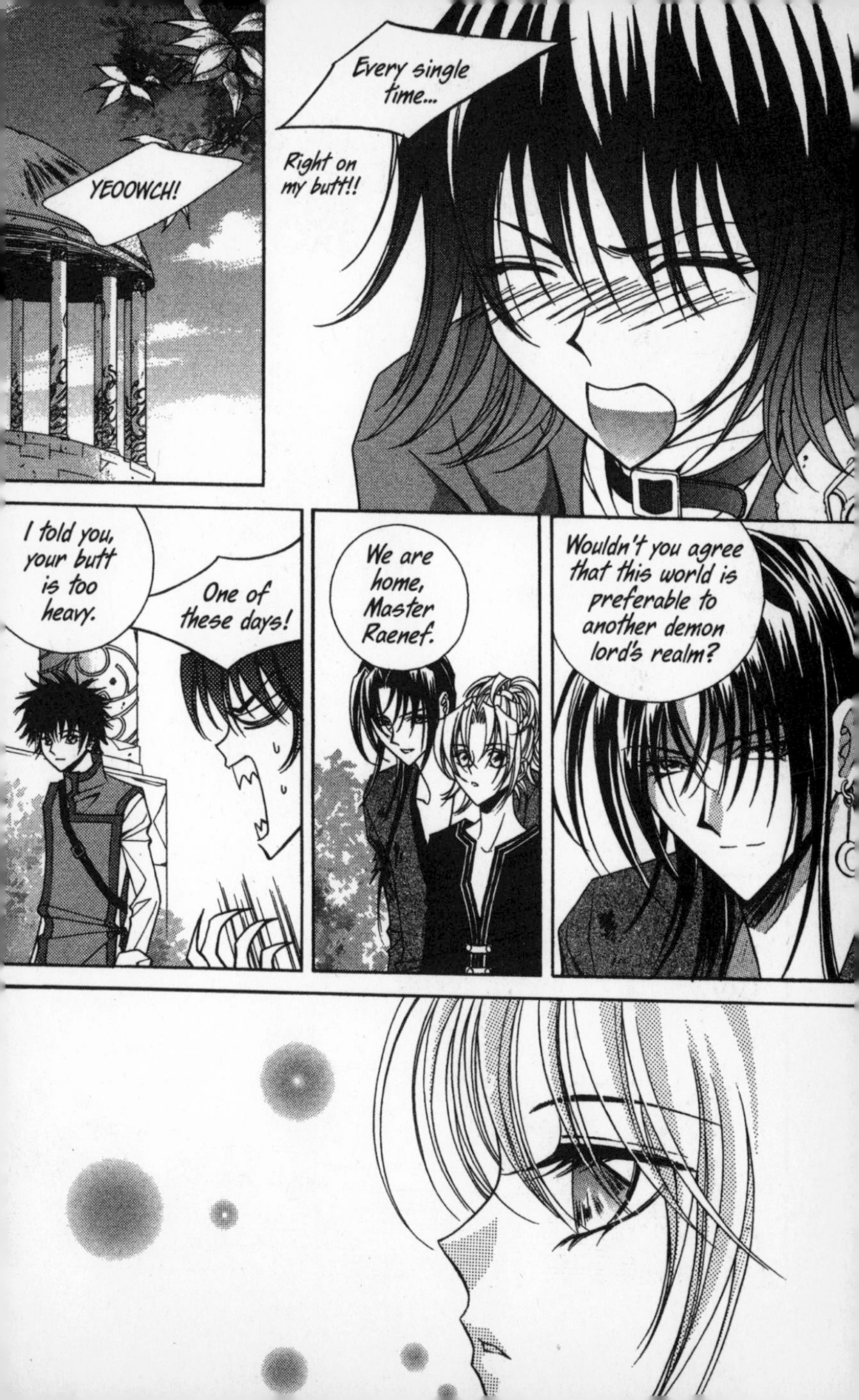

YEOOWCH!
Every single time...
Right on my butt!!
I told you, your butt is too heavy.
One of these days!
We are home, Master Raenef.
Wouldn't you agree that this world is preferable to another demon lord's realm?

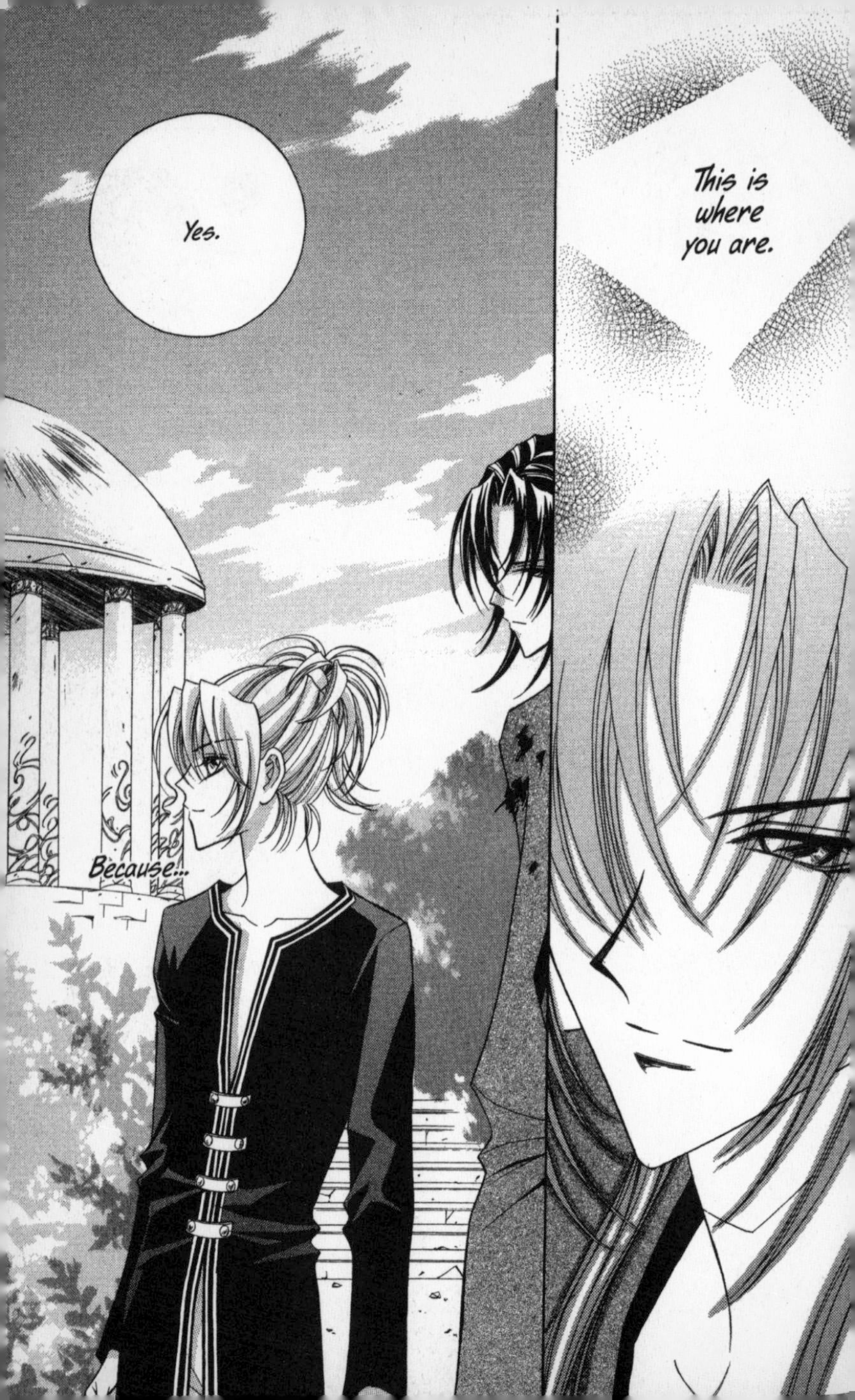
This is where you are.
Yes.
Because...

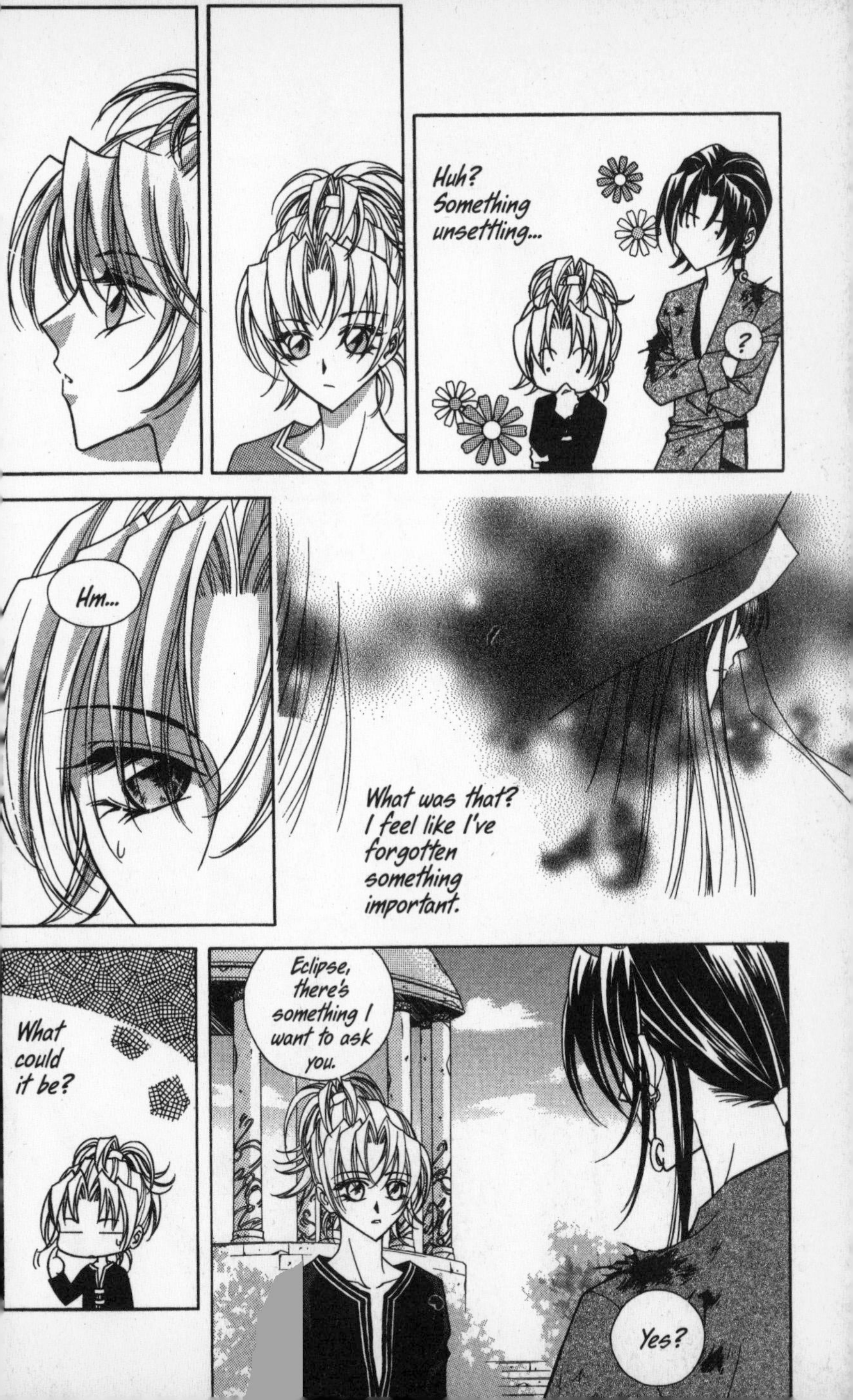
Huh? Something unsettling...
What was that? I feel like I've forgotten something important.
Hm...
Eclipse, there's something I want to ask you.
Yes?
What could it be?

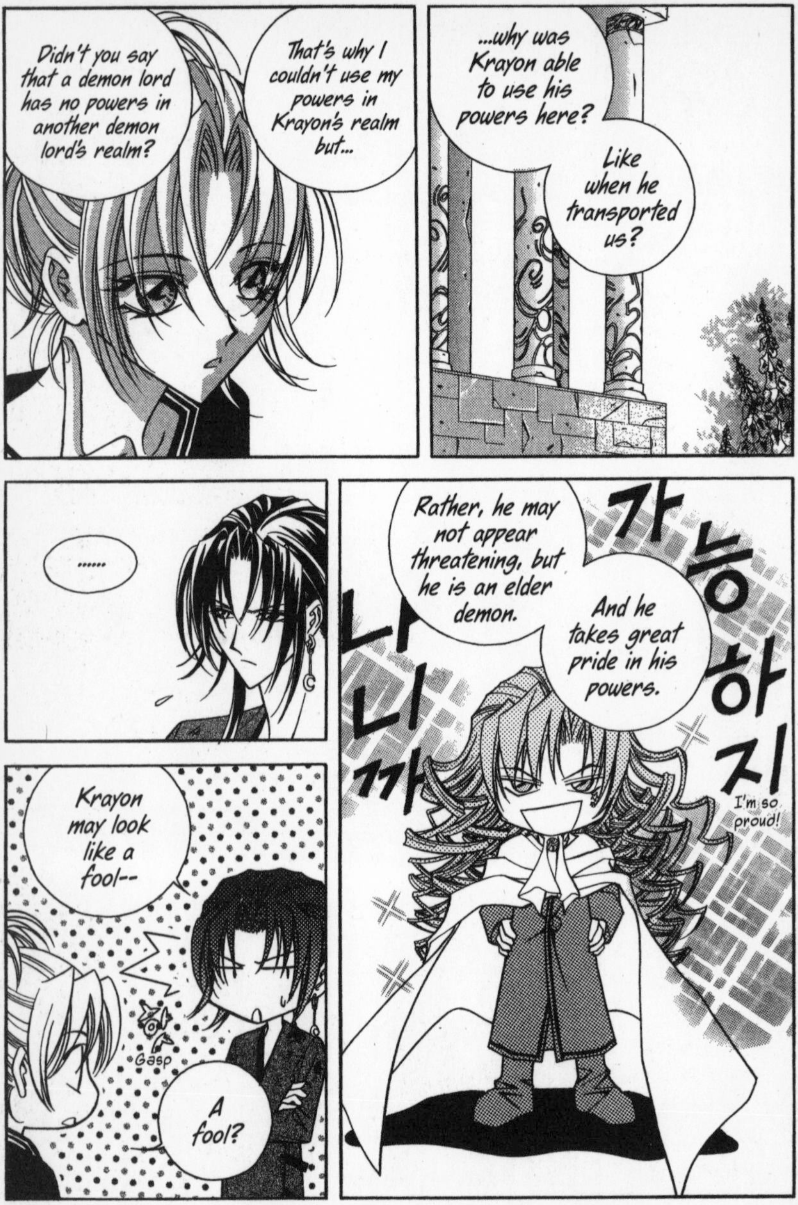
Didn't you say that a demon lord has no powers in another demon lord's realm?
That's why I couldn't use my powers in Krayon's realm but...
...why was Krayon able to use his powers here?
Like when he transported us?
......
Krayon may look like a fool--
Gasp
A fool?
Rather, he may not appear threatening, but he is an elder demon.
And he takes great pride in his powers.
나니까
가능하지
I'm so proud!

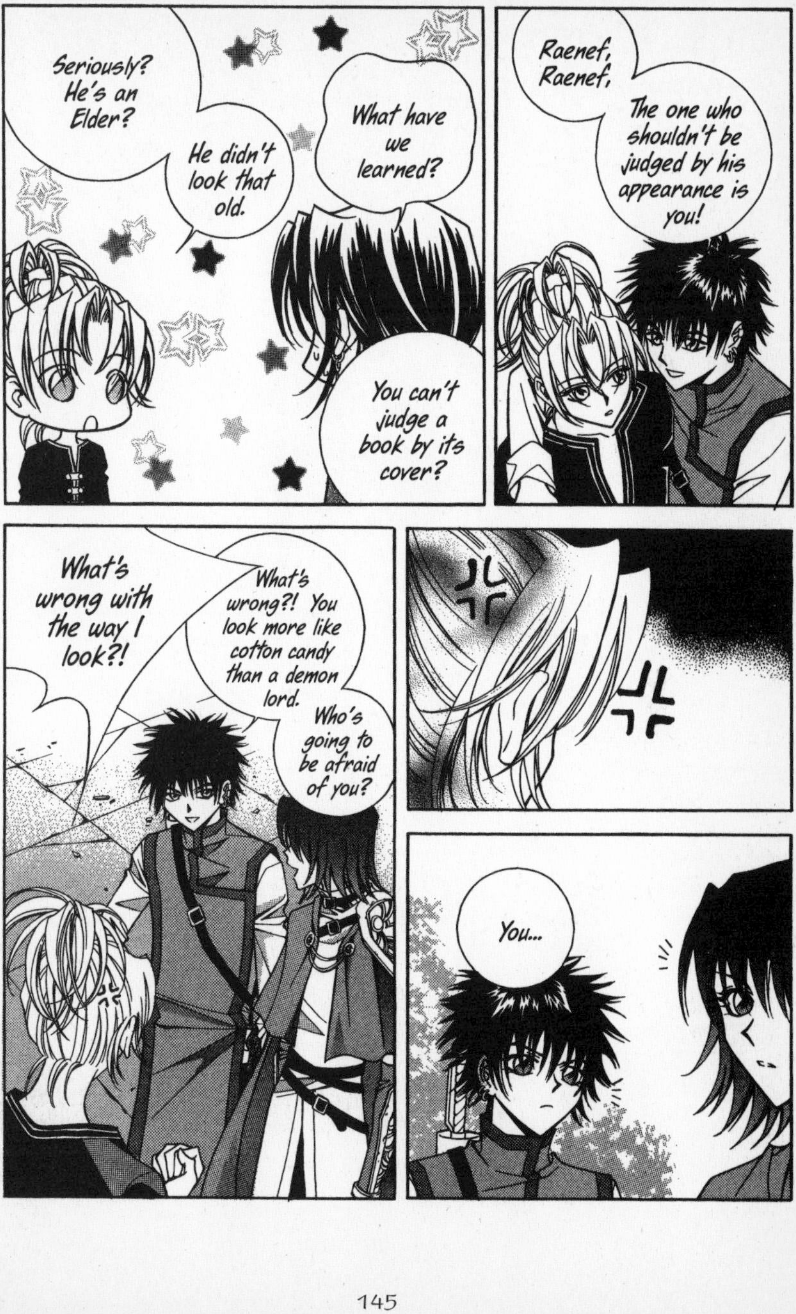
Seriously? He's an Elder?
He didn't look that old.
What have we learned?
You can't judge a book by its cover?
Raenef, Raenef,
The one who shouldn't be judged by his appearance is you!
What's wrong with the way I look?!
What's wrong?! You look more like cotton candy than a demon lord.
Who's going to be afraid of you?
You...

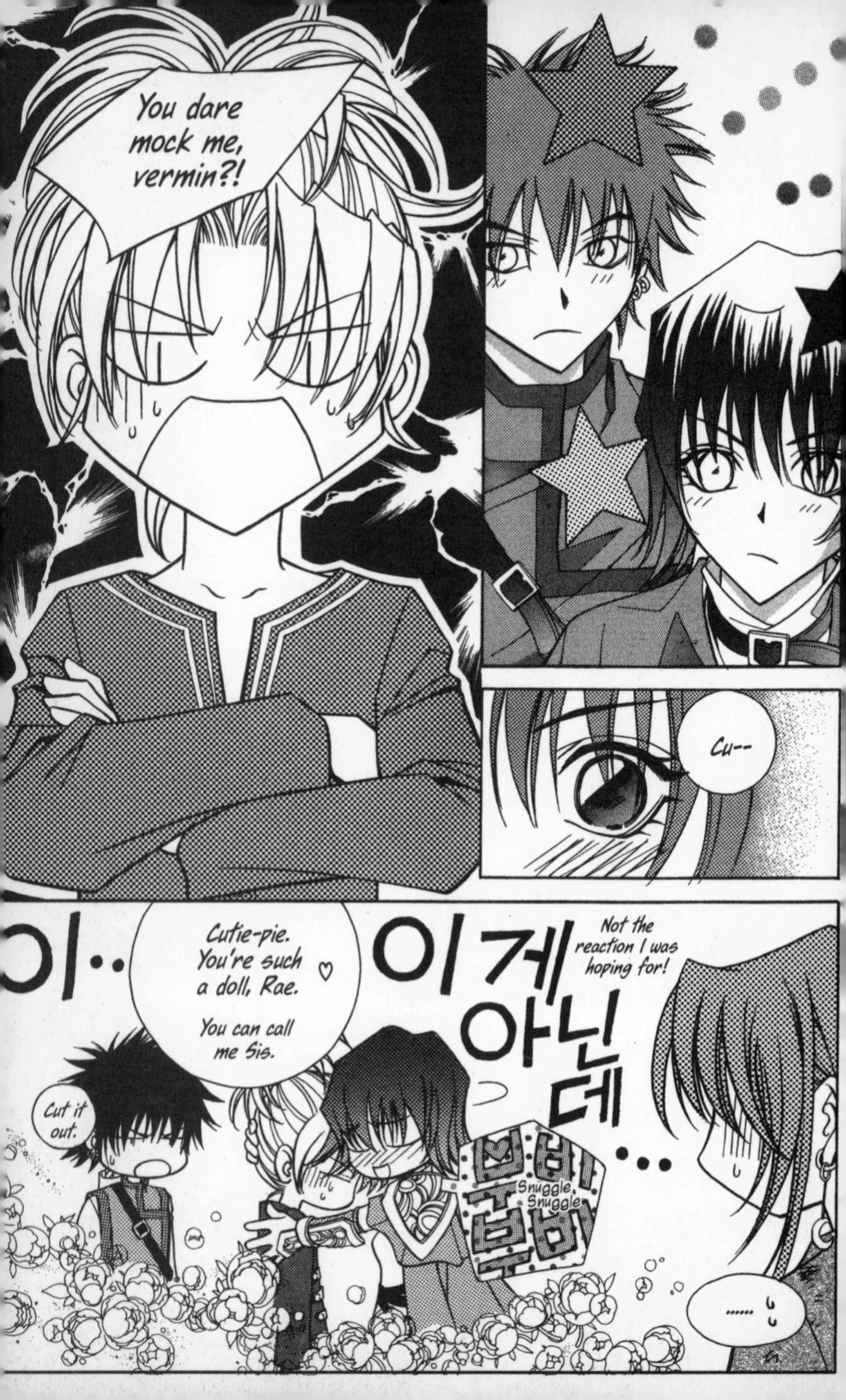
You dare mock me, vermin?!
Cu--
이..
Cutie-pie. You're such a doll, Rae. ♡
You can call me Sis.
이게 아닌데...
Not the reaction I was hoping for!
Cut it out.
부비부비
Snuggle, Snuggle
......

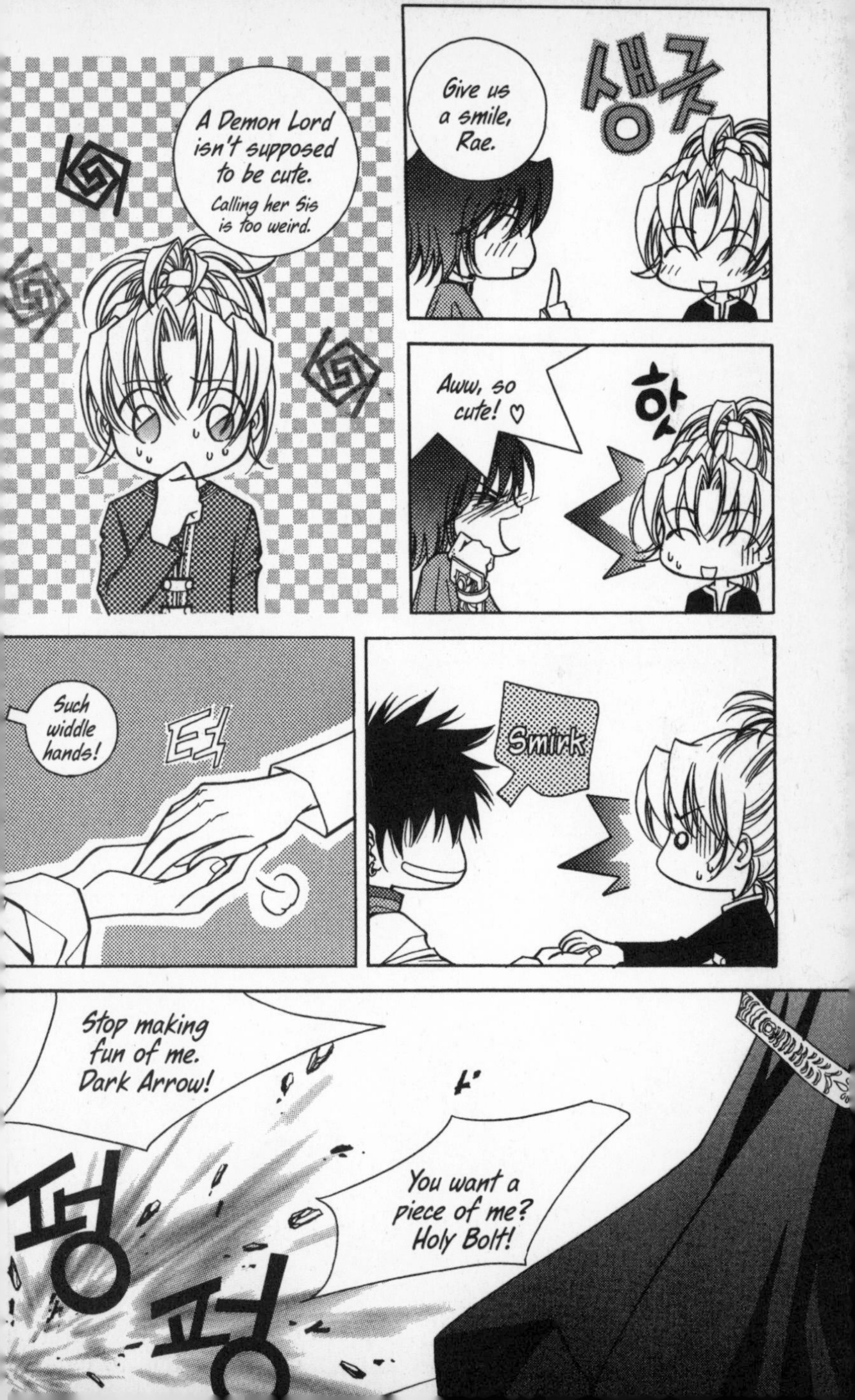
A Demon Lord isn't supposed to be cute.
Calling her Sis is too weird.
Give us a smile, Rae.
생긋
Aww, so cute! ♡
Such widdle hands!
Smirk
Stop making fun of me. Dark Arrow!
You want a piece of me? Holy Bolt!

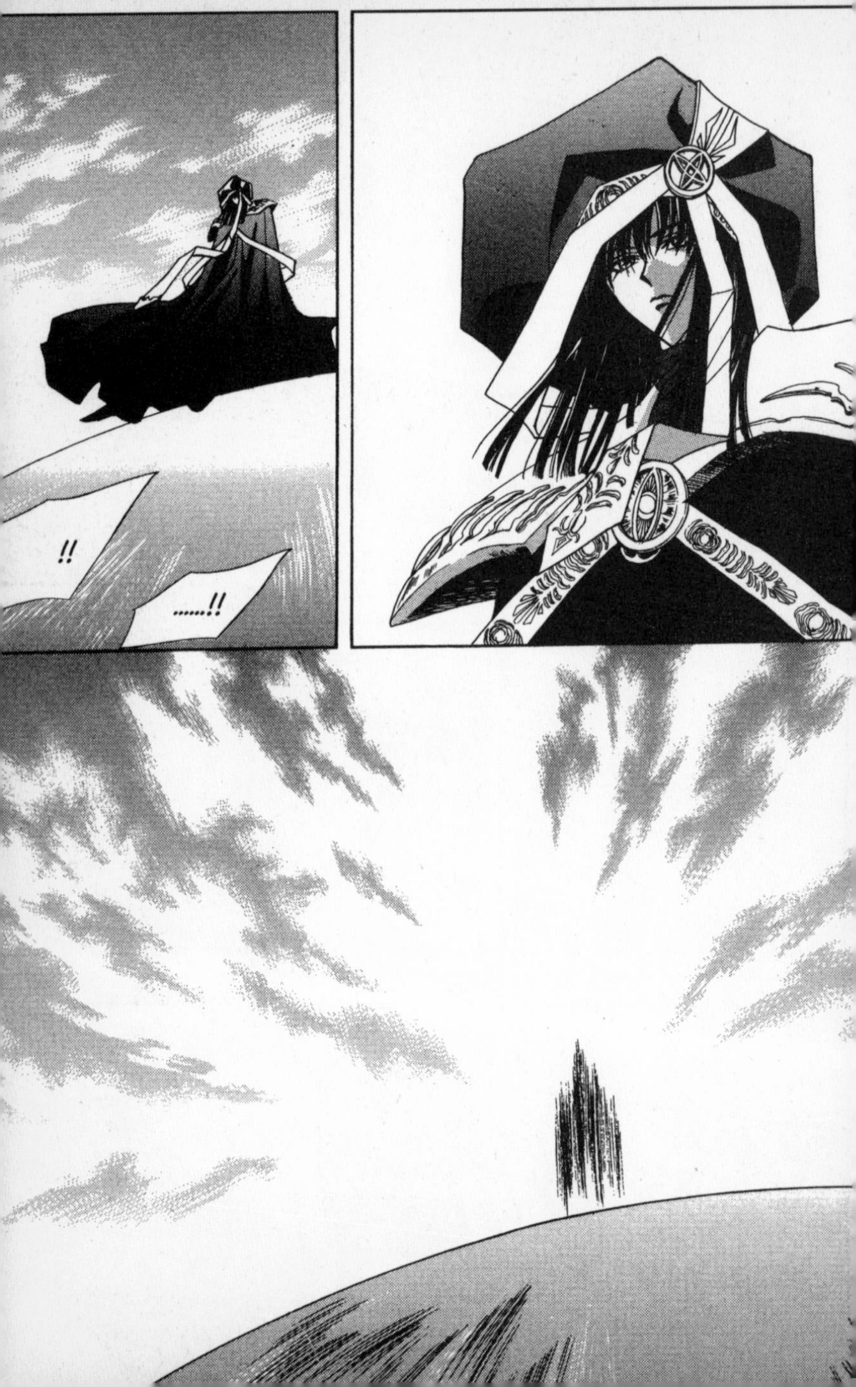
!!
......!!

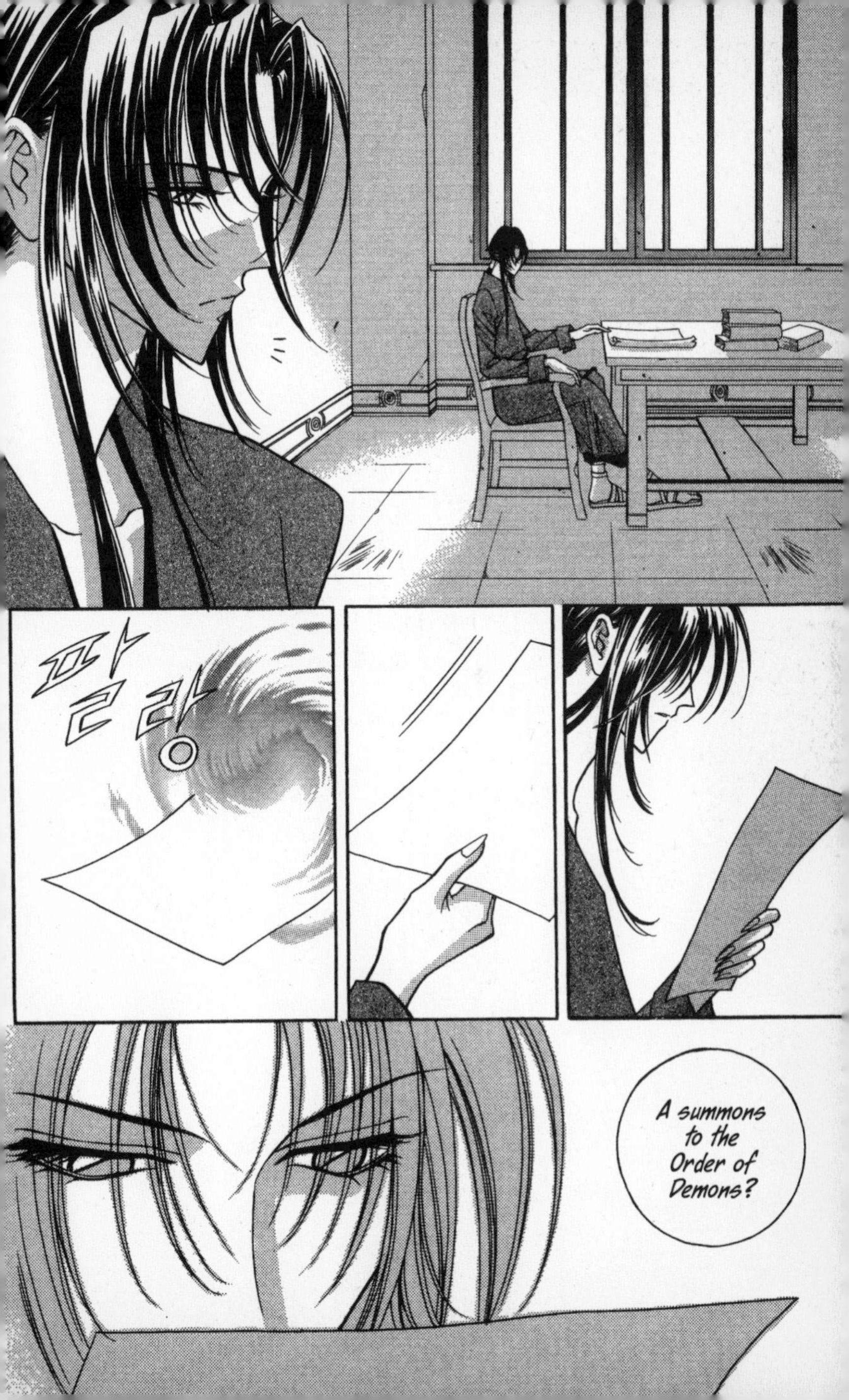
팔랑
A summons to the Order of Demons?

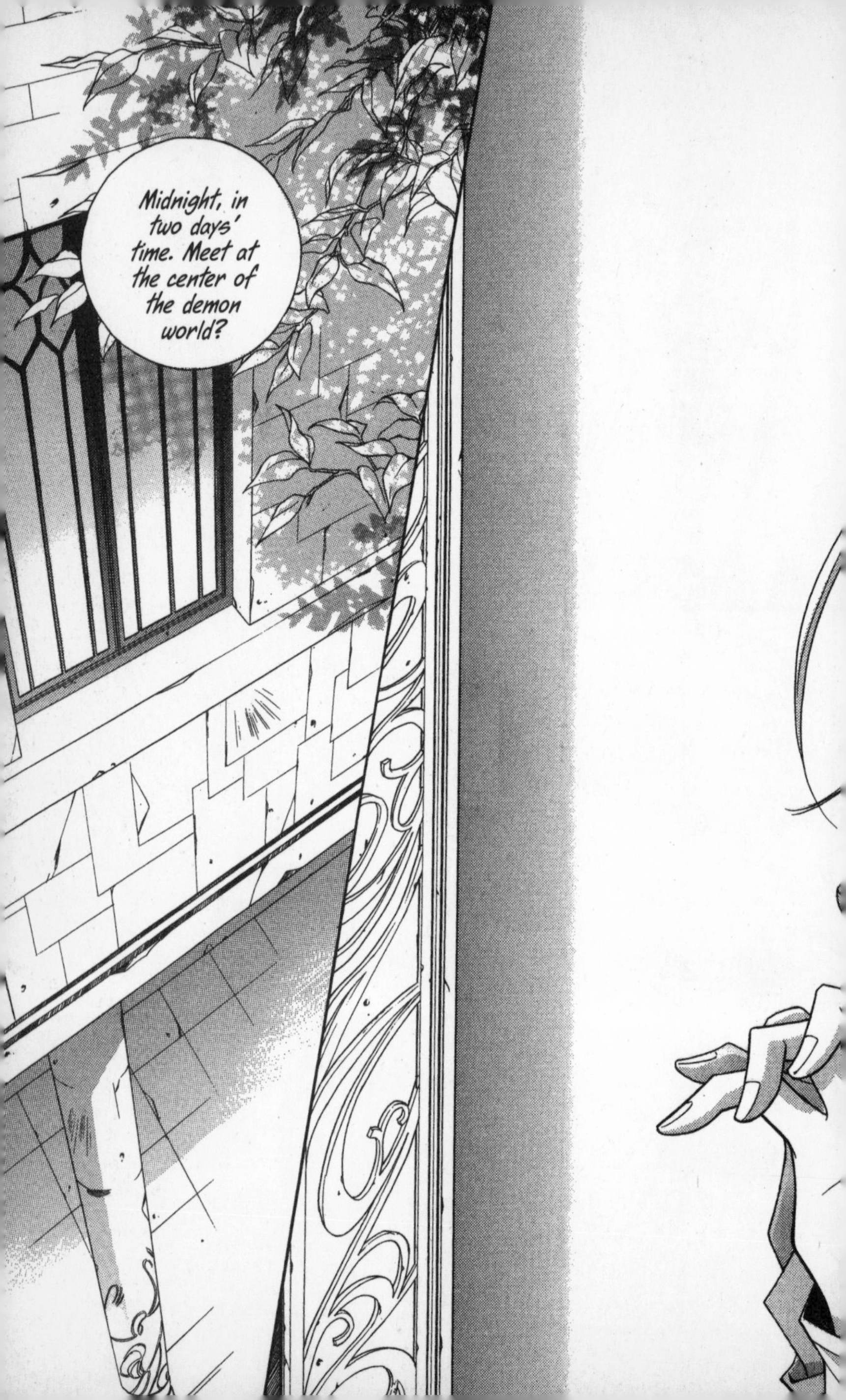
Midnight, in two days' time. Meet at the center of the demon world?

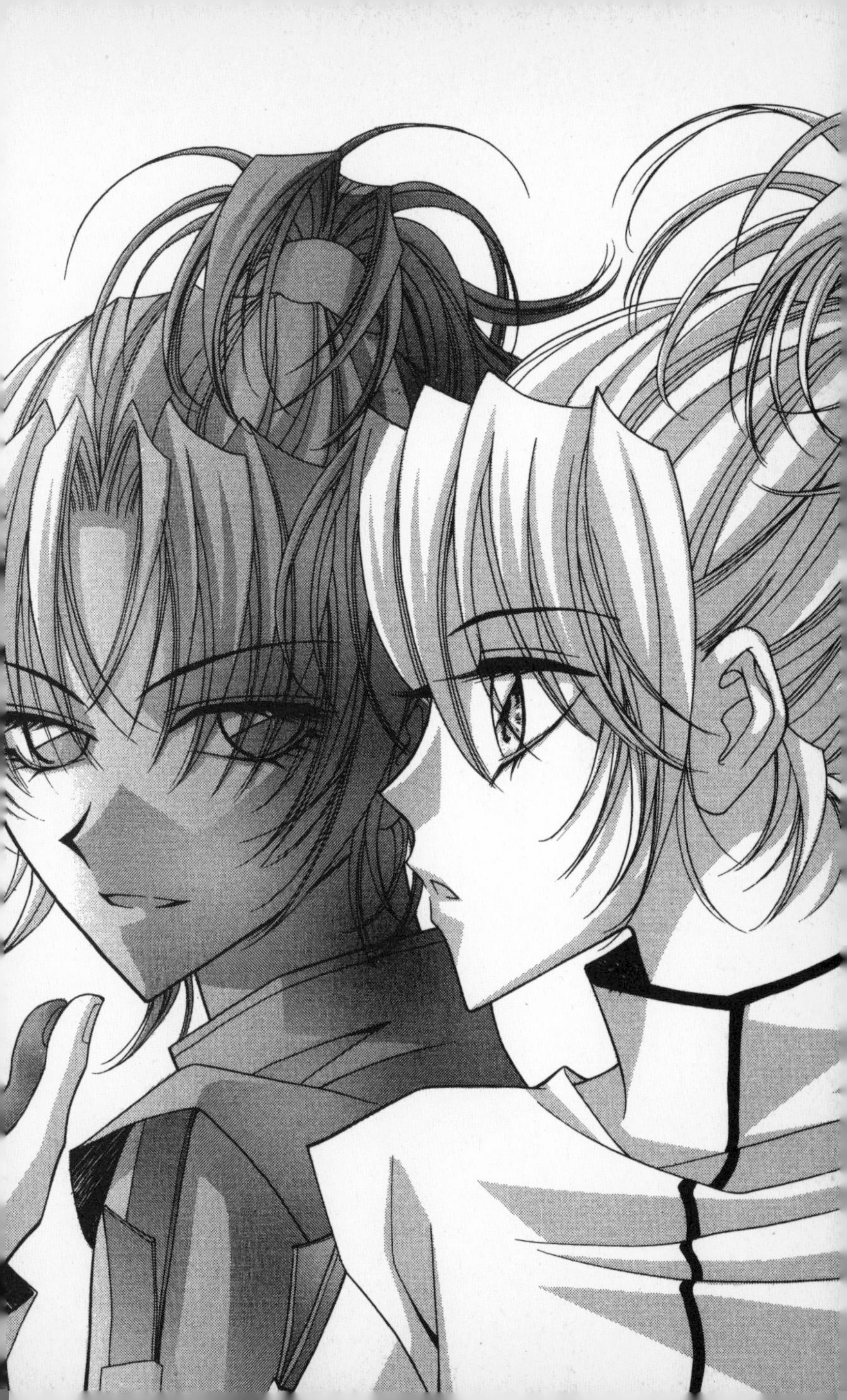

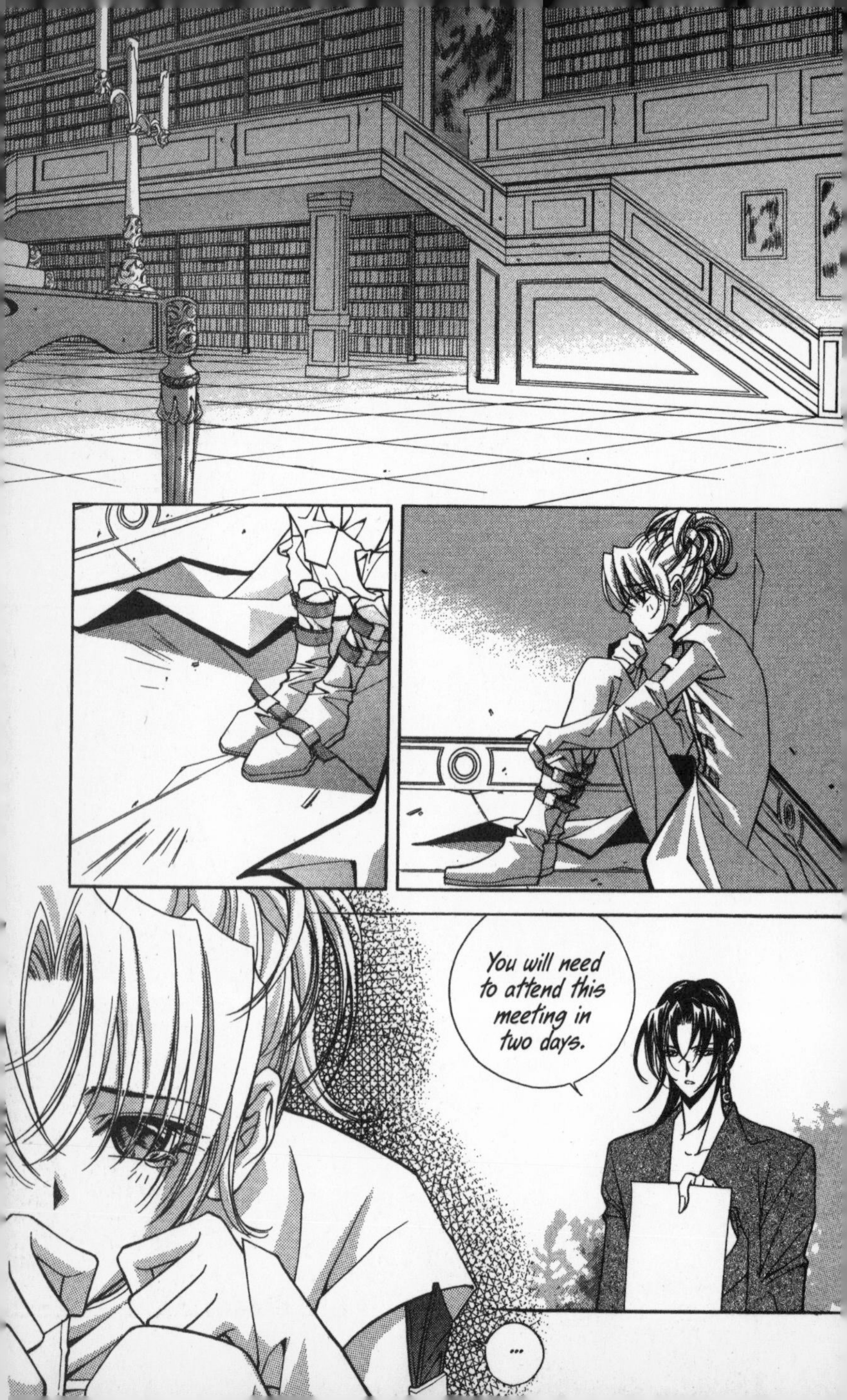
You will need to attend this meeting in two days.
...

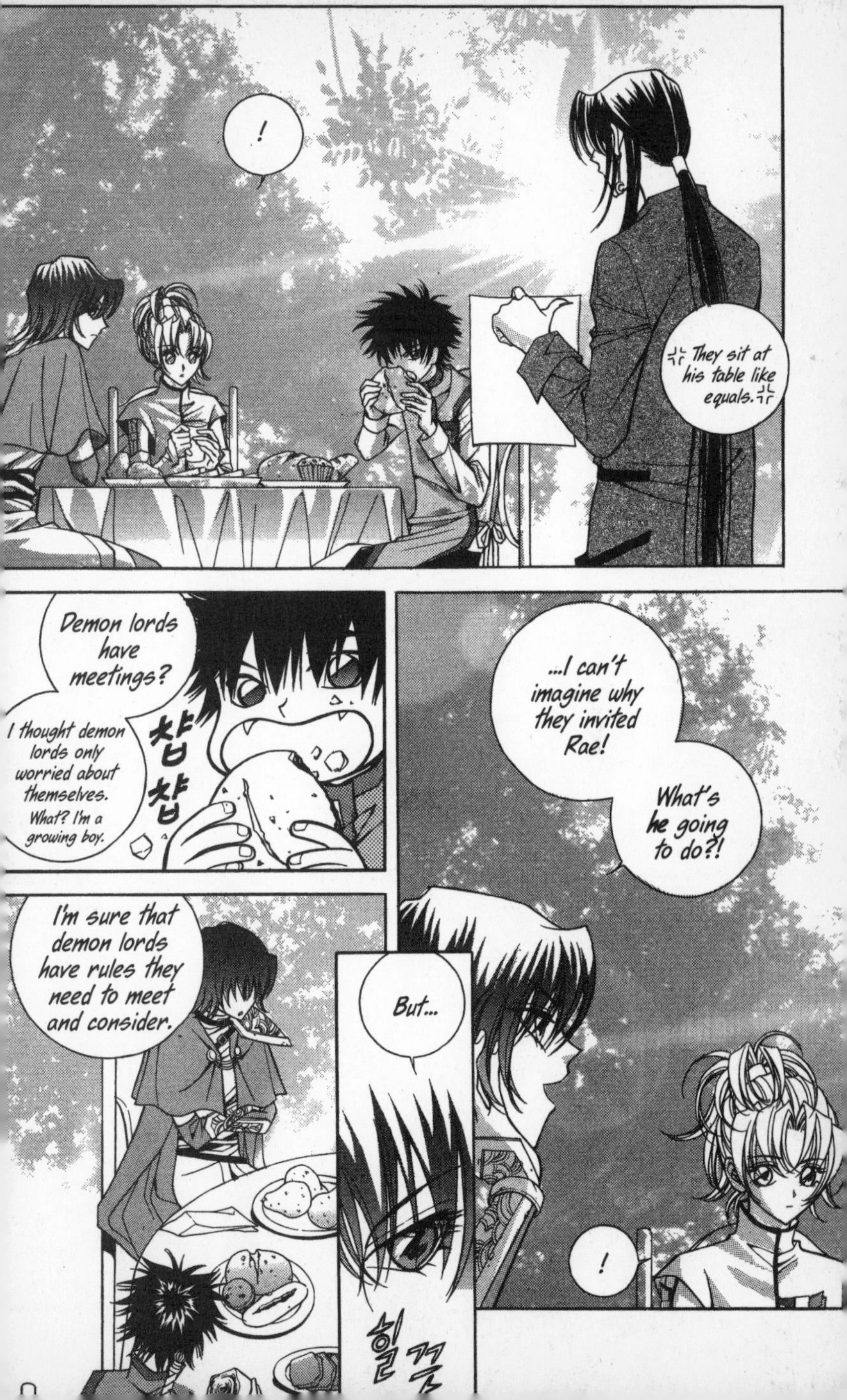
!
They sit at his table like equals.
Demon lords have meetings?
I thought demon lords only worried about themselves.
What? I'm a growing boy.
찹찹
I'm sure that demon lords have rules they need to meet and consider.
But...
...I can't imagine why they invited Rae!
What's he going to do?!
!
힐끔

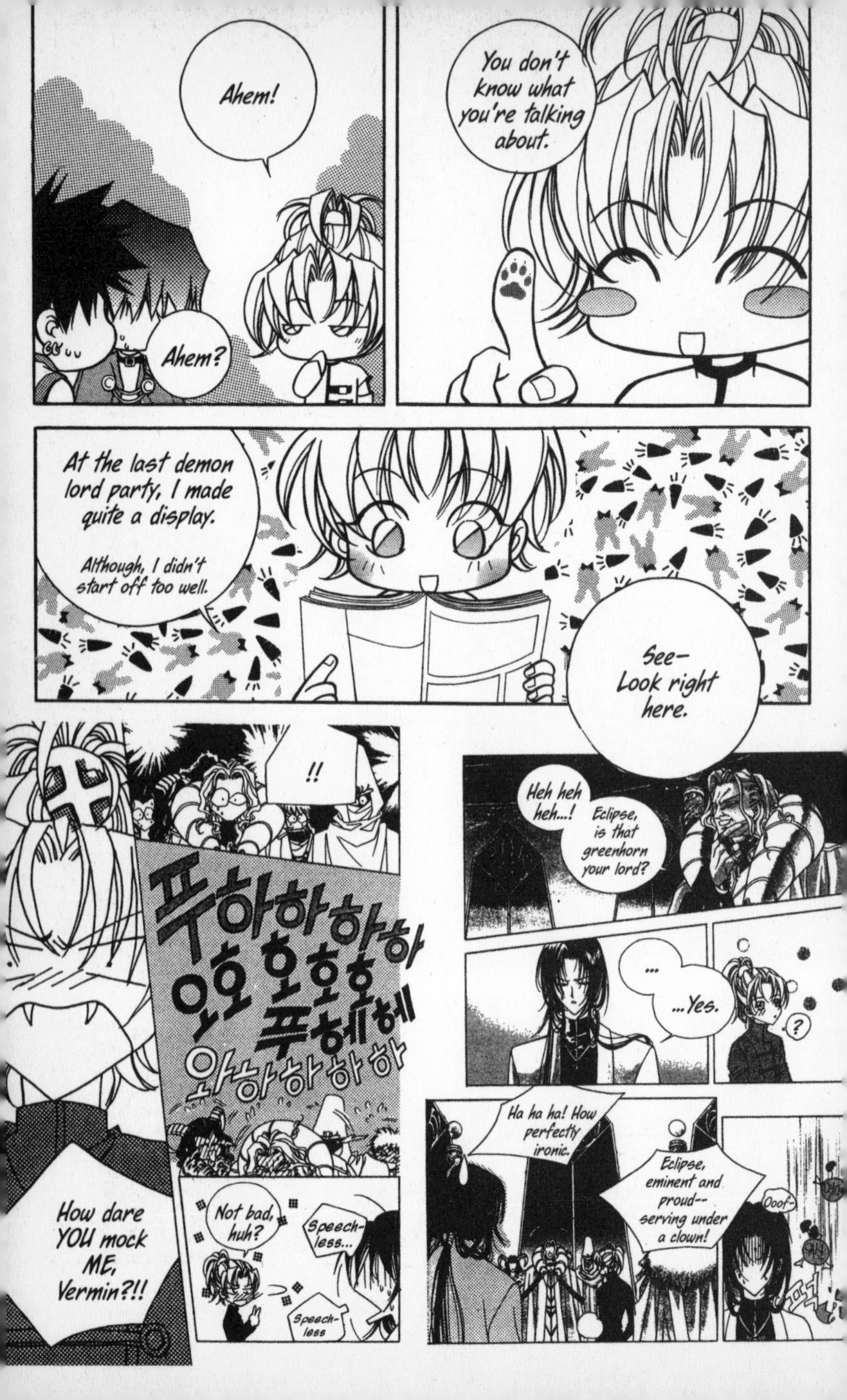
Ahem!
Ahem?
You don't know what you're talking about.
At the last demon lord party, I made quite a display.
Although, I didn't start off too well.
See- Look right here.
!!
푸하하하하
오호호호호
푸헤헤
와하하하하
Heh heh heh...!
Eclipse, is that greenhorn your lord?
...
...Yes.
?
Ha ha ha! How perfectly ironic.
Eclipse, eminent and proud-- serving under a clown!
Ooof-
Not bad, huh?
Speech-less...
Speech-less
How dare YOU mock ME, Vermin?!!

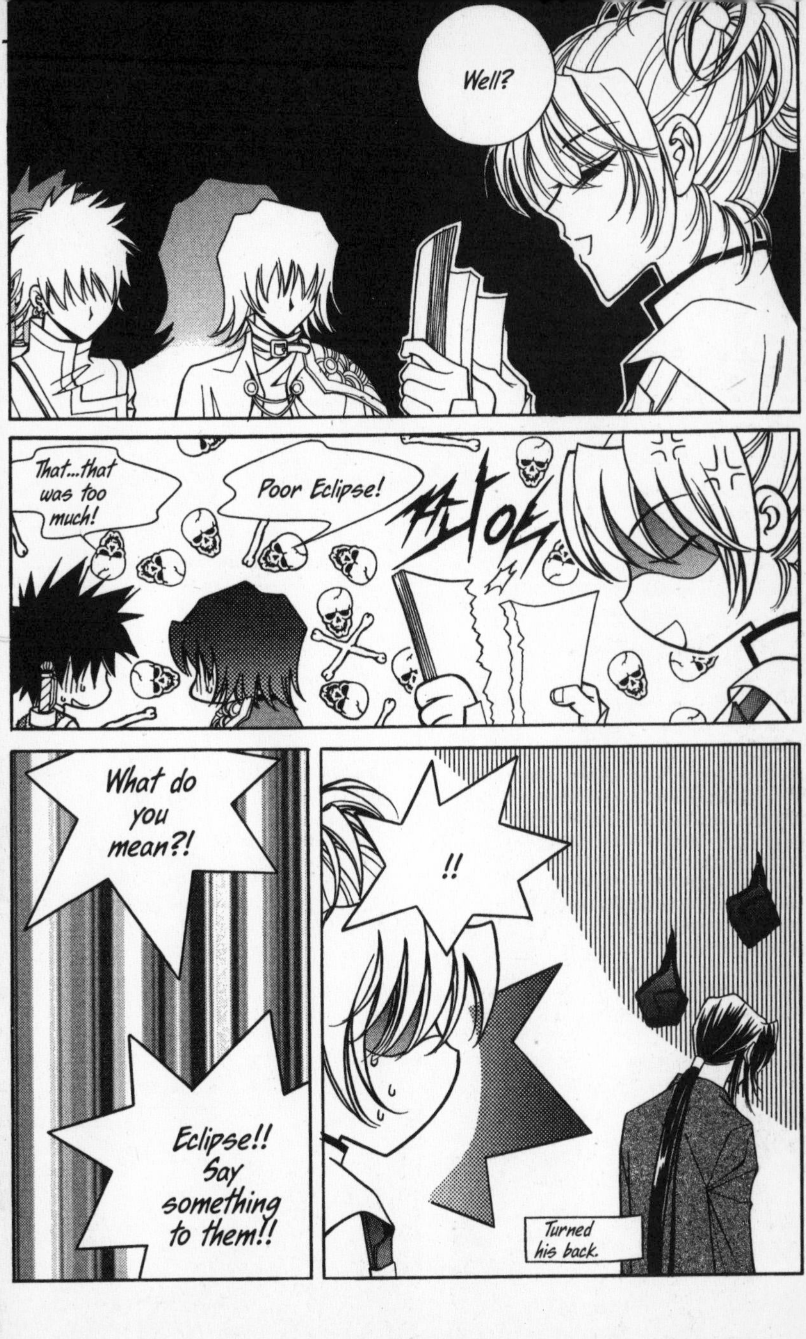
Well?
Poor Eclipse!
That...that was too much!
!!
Turned his back.
What do you mean?!
Eclipse!! Say something to them!!

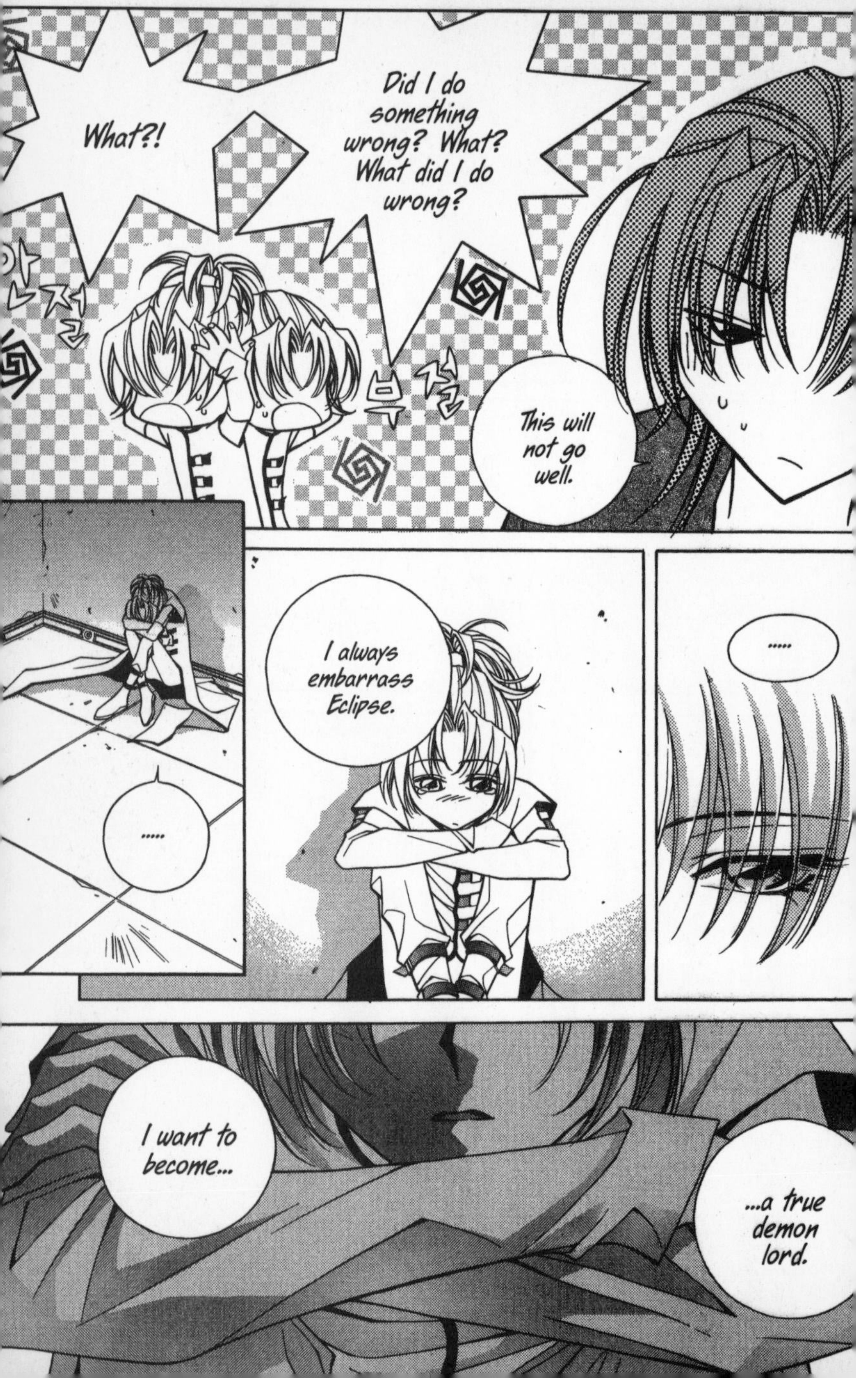
What?!
Did I do something wrong? What? What did I do wrong?
This will not go well.
.....
I always embarrass Eclipse.
.....
I want to become...
...a true demon lord.

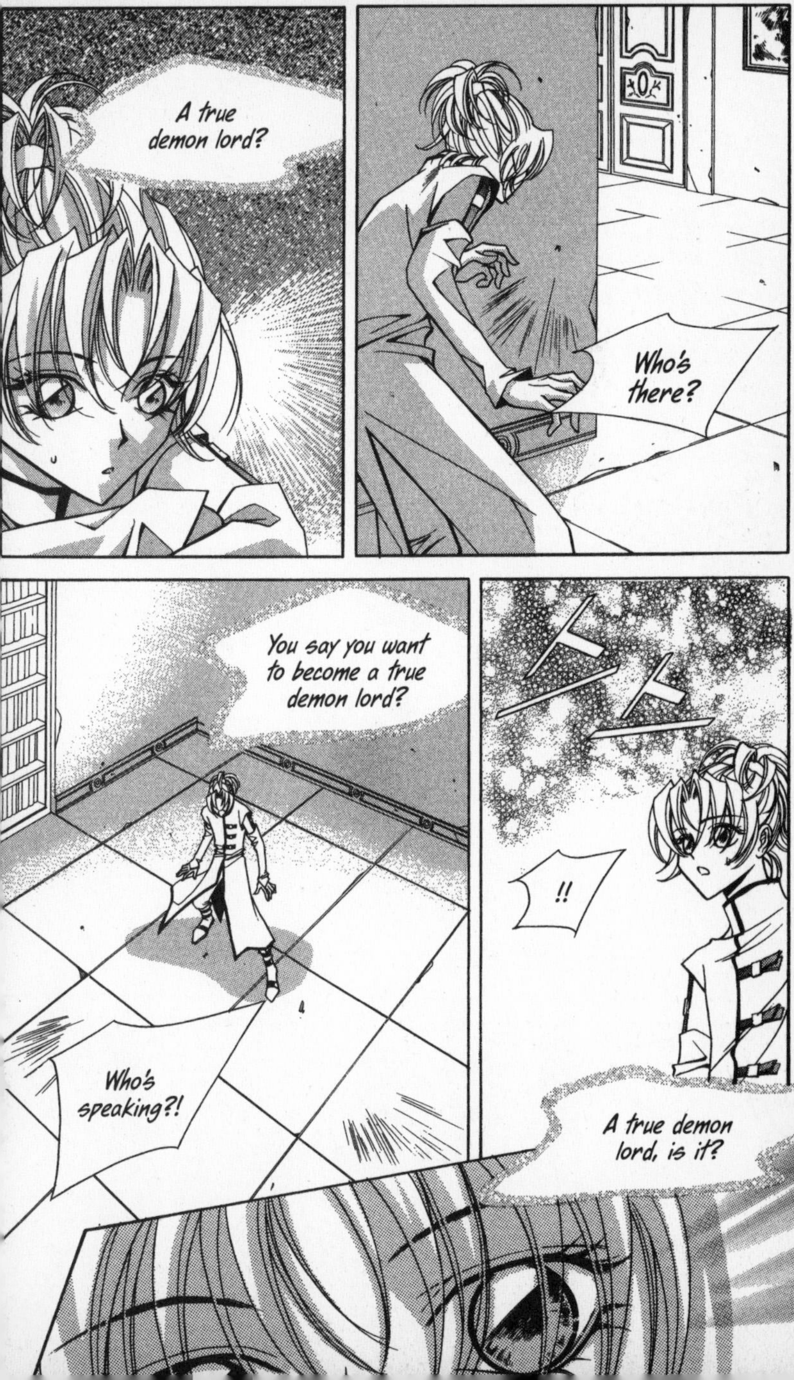
Who's there?
A true demon lord?
!!
You say you want to become a true demon lord?
Who's speaking?!
A true demon lord, is it?

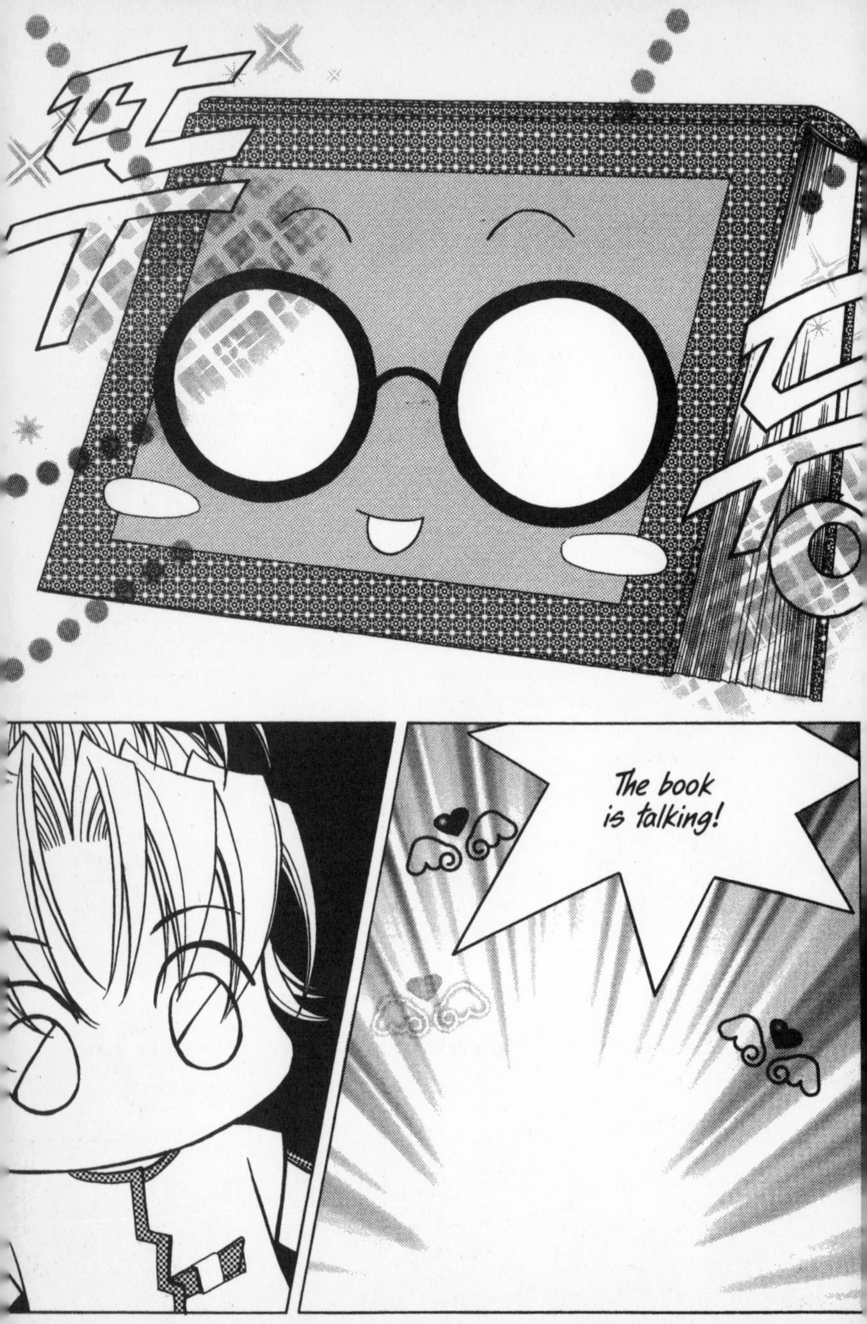
The book is talking!

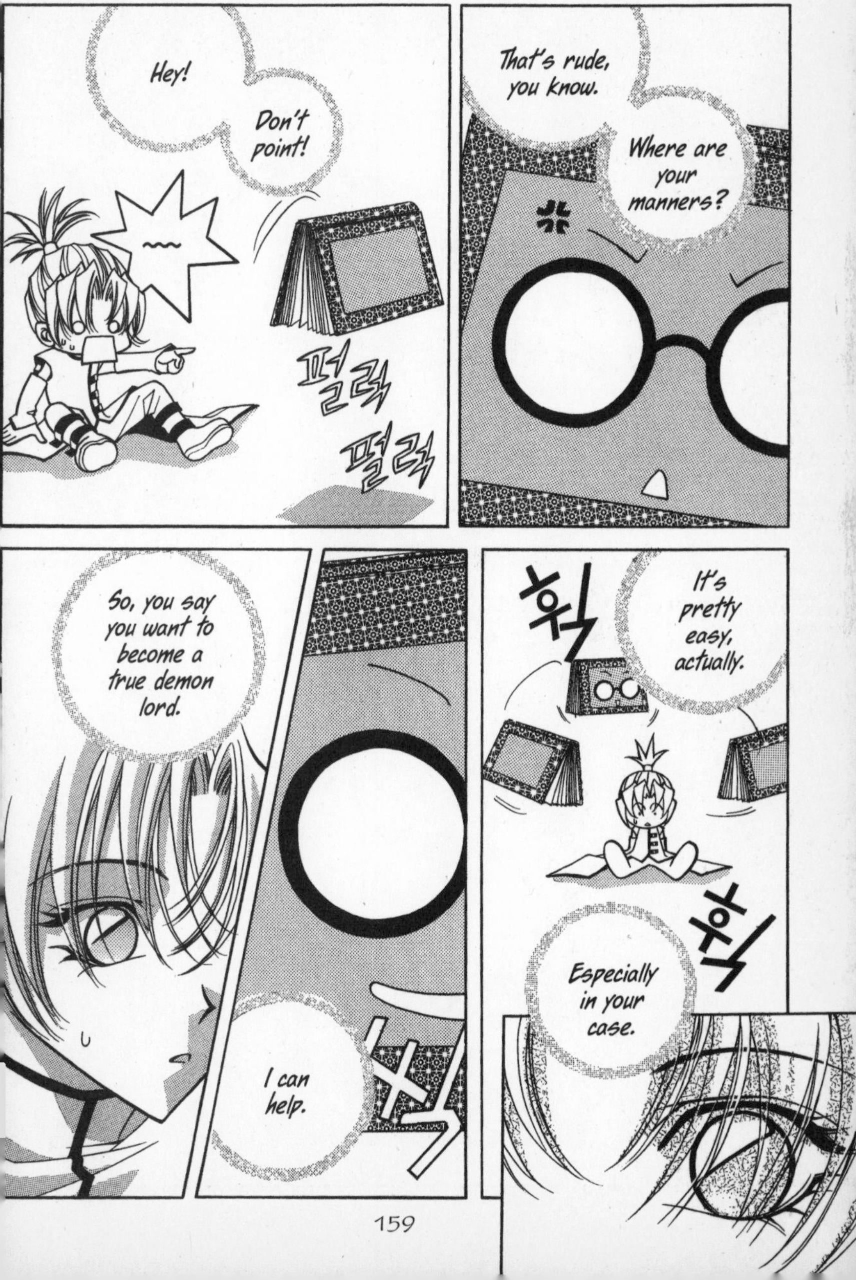

Hey!
Don't point!
펄럭
펄럭
That's rude, you know.
Where are your manners?
So, you say you want to become a true demon lord.
I can help.
휙
It's pretty easy, actually.
휙
Especially in your case.

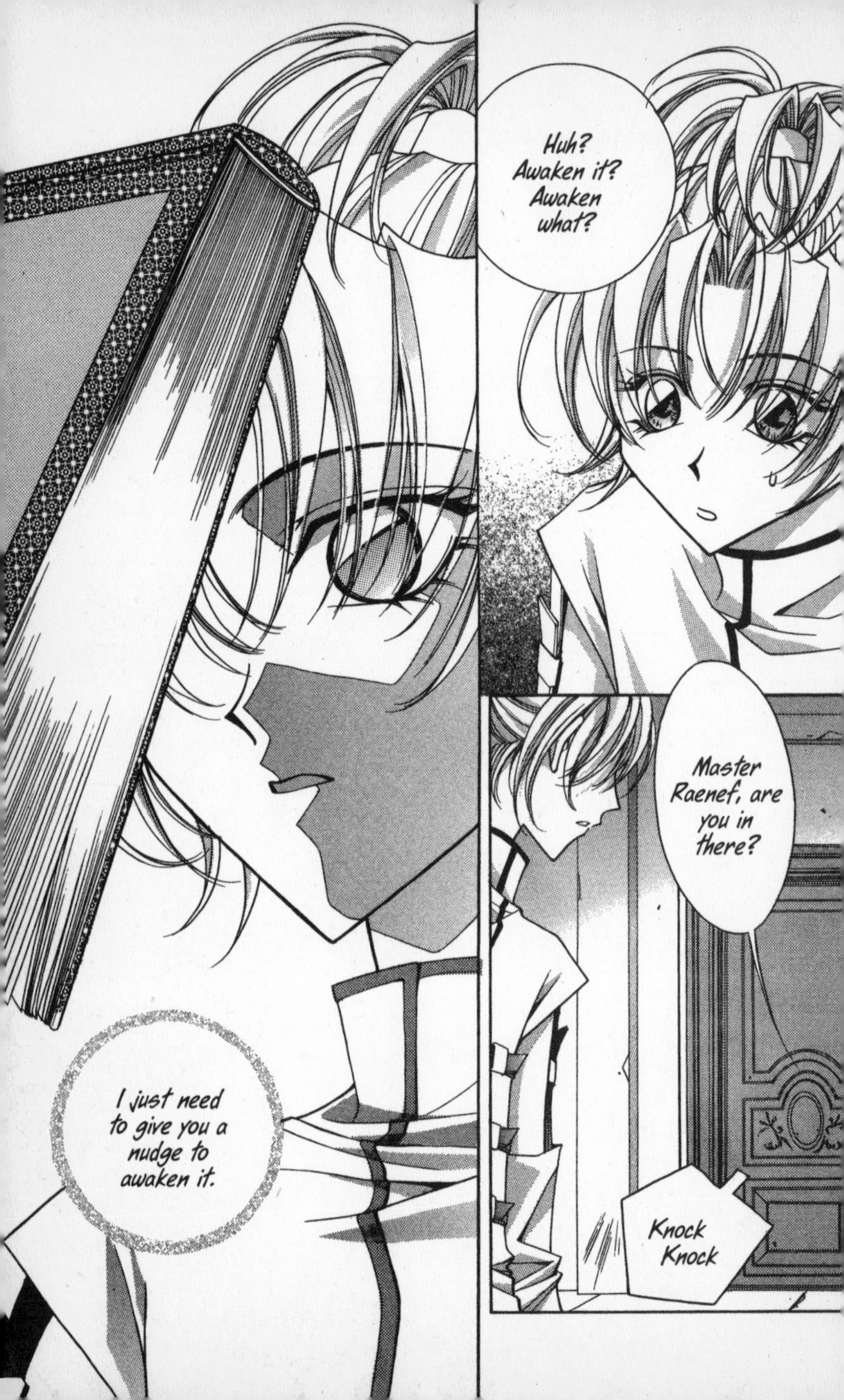
I just need to give you a nudge to awaken it.
Huh? Awaken it? Awaken what?
Master Raenef, are you in there?
Knock Knock

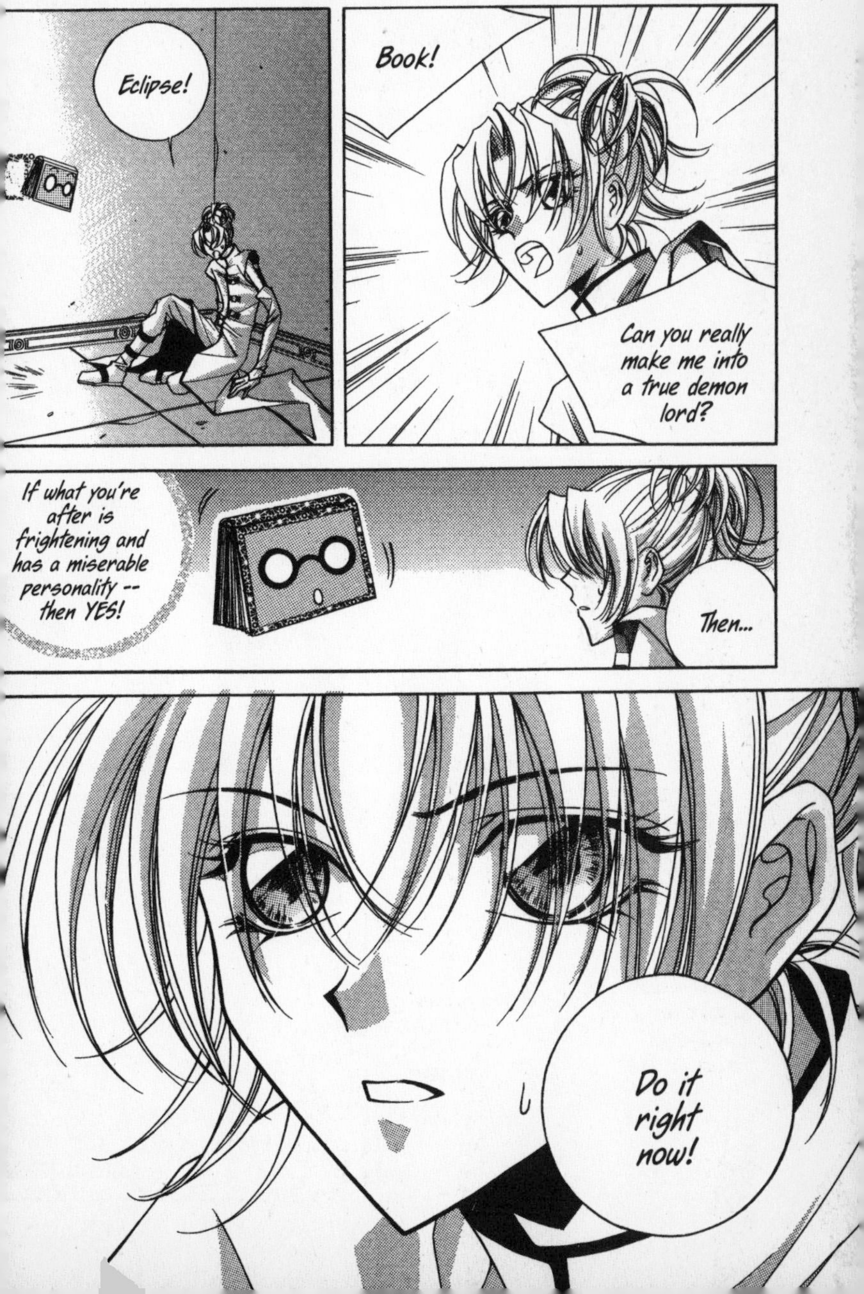
Eclipse!
Book!
Can you really make me into a true demon lord?
If what you're after is frightening and has a miserable personality -- then YES!
Then...
Do it right now!

You can't come back later and tell me you changed your mind, okay?

Nod Nod

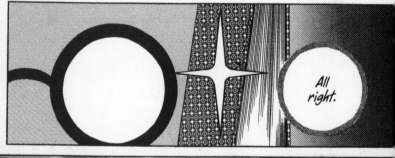

All right.

Flap

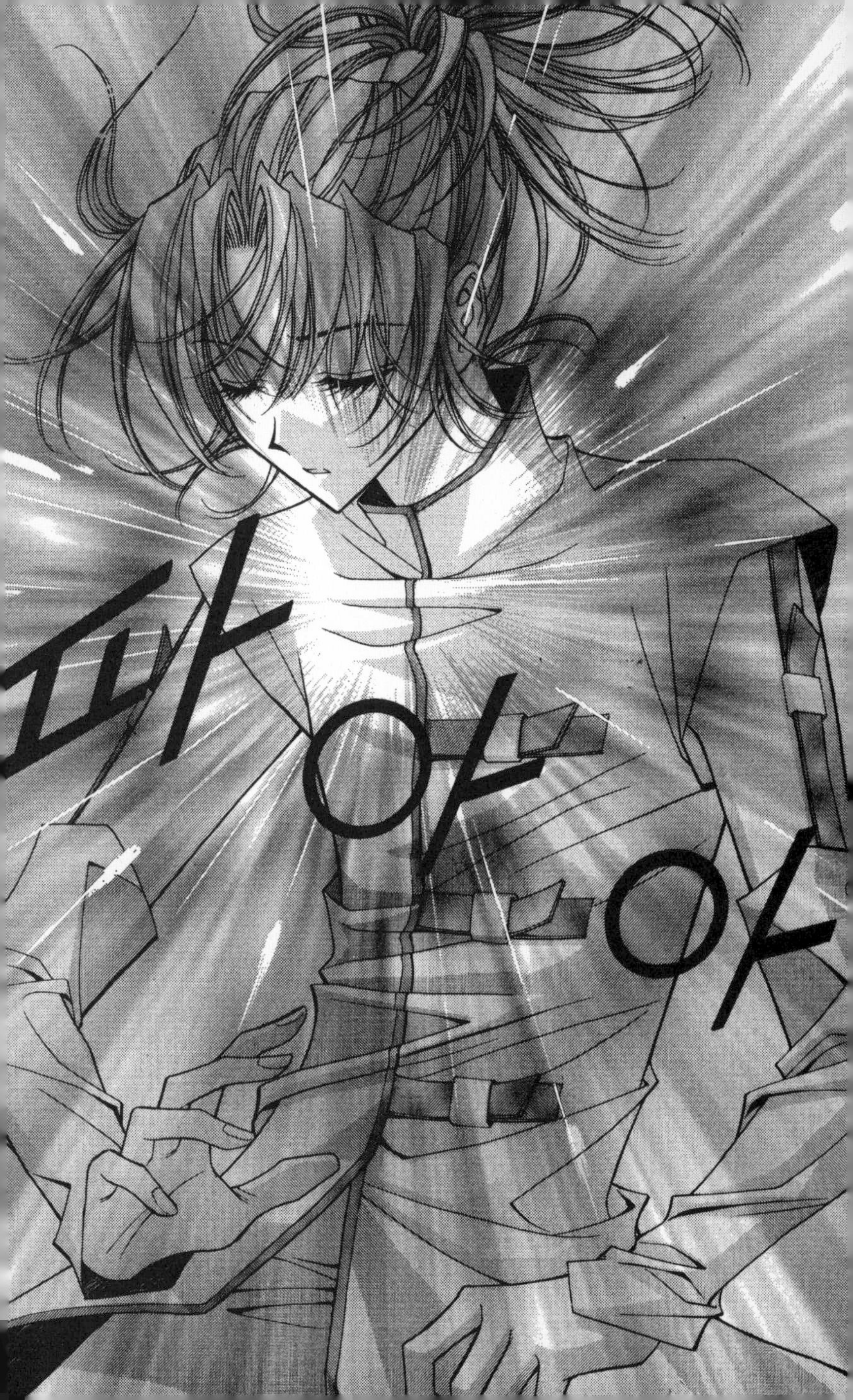
파아아

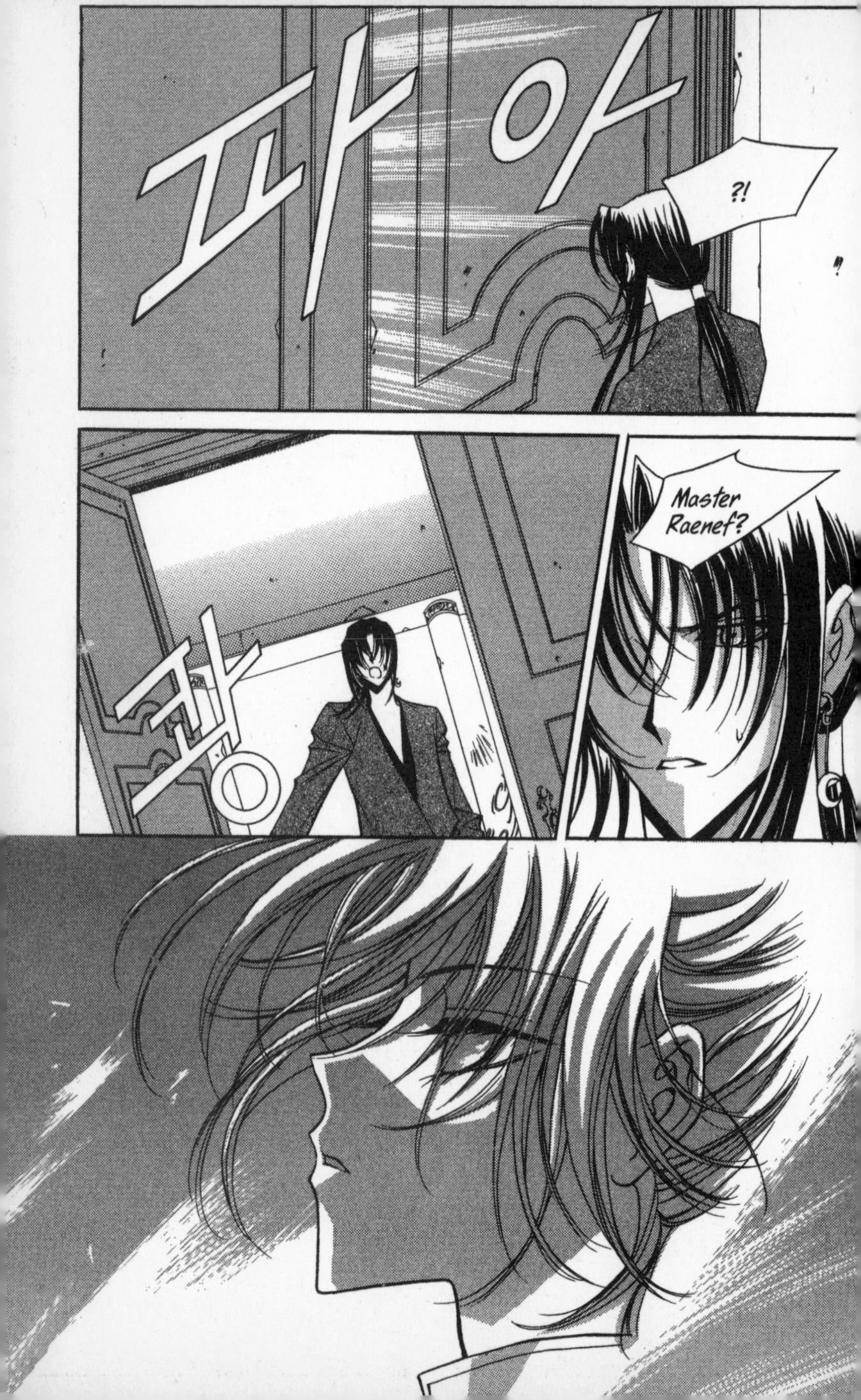
?!
Master Raenef?

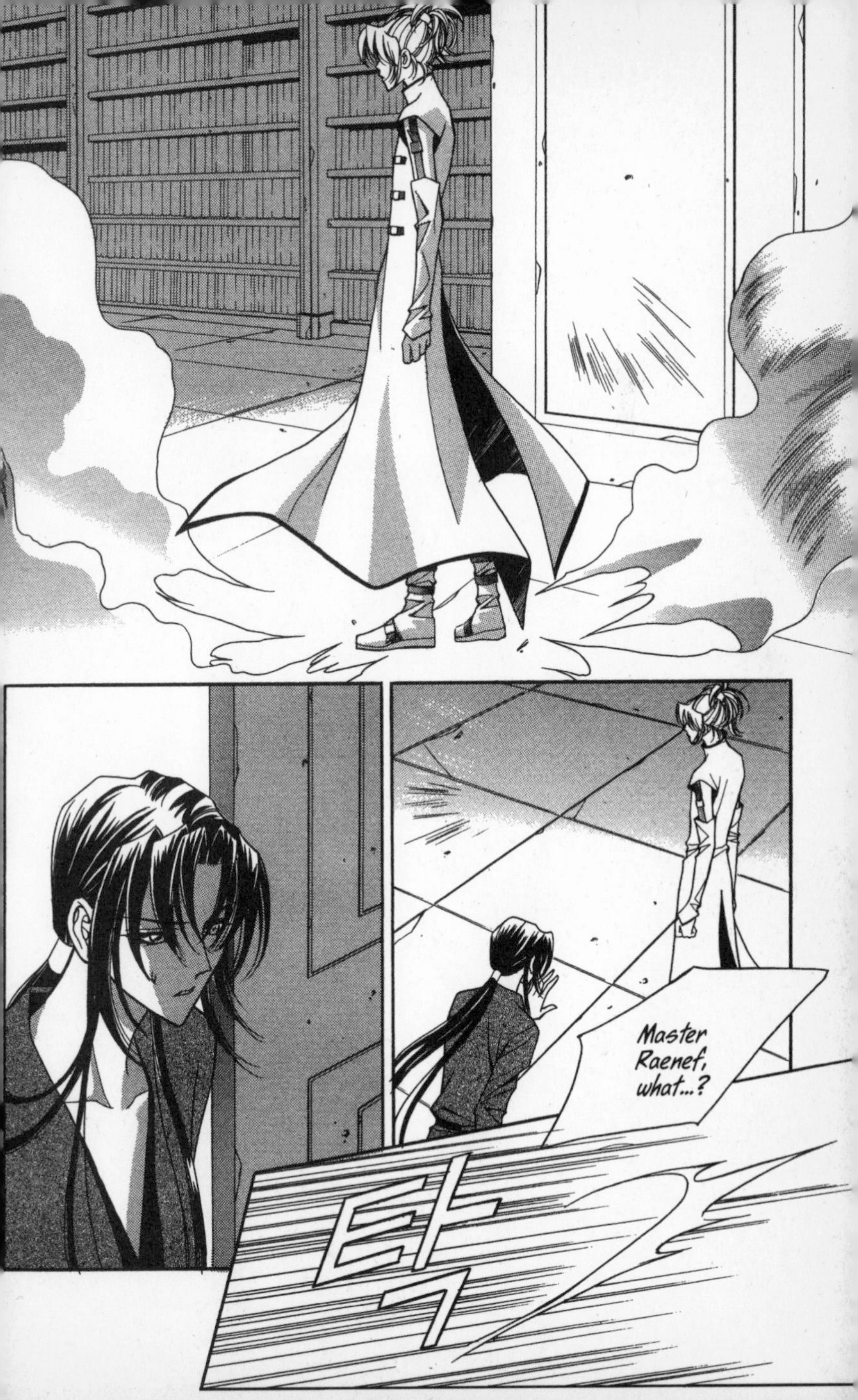
Master Raenef, what...?
탁

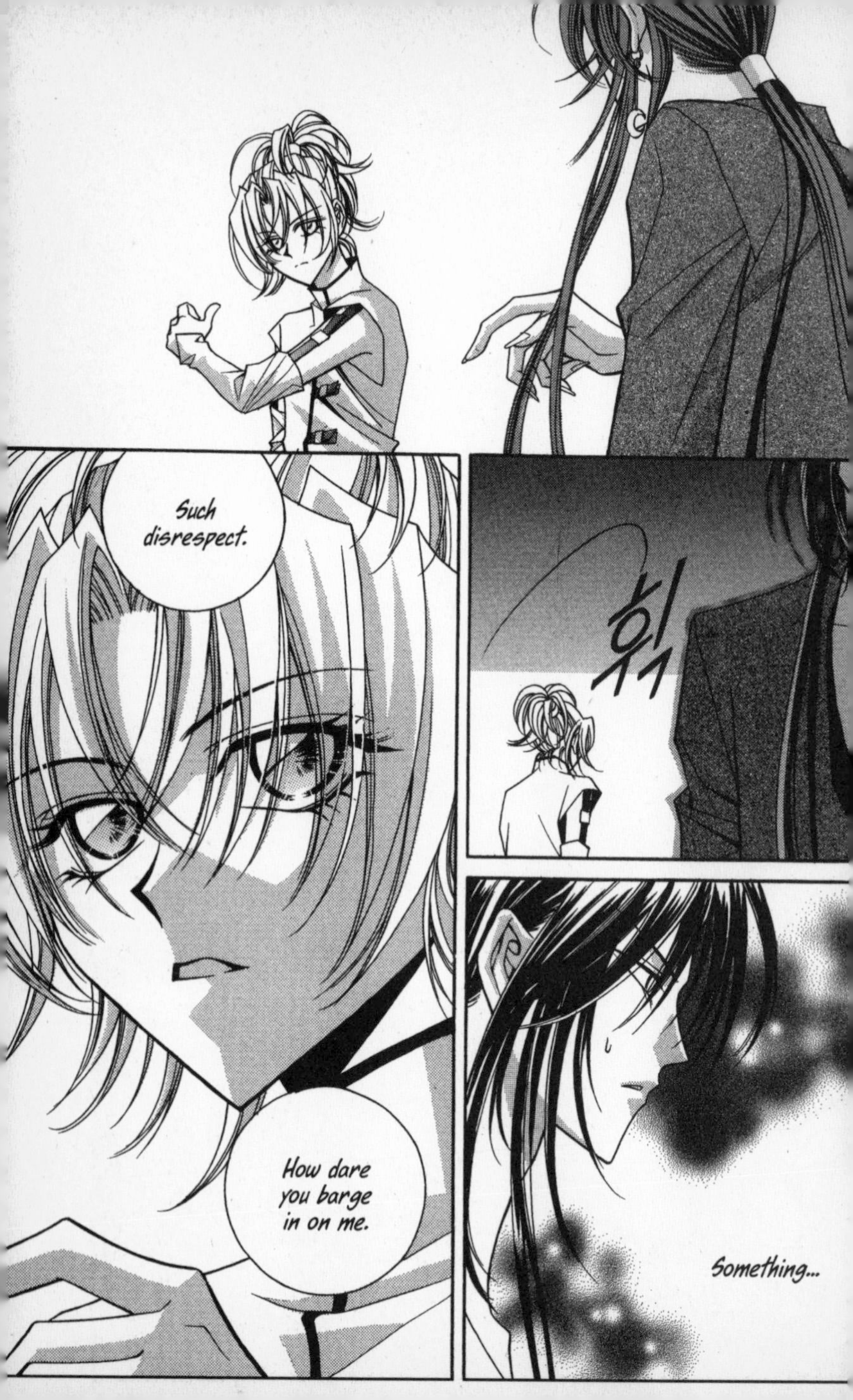
Such disrespect.
How dare you barge in on me.
Something...

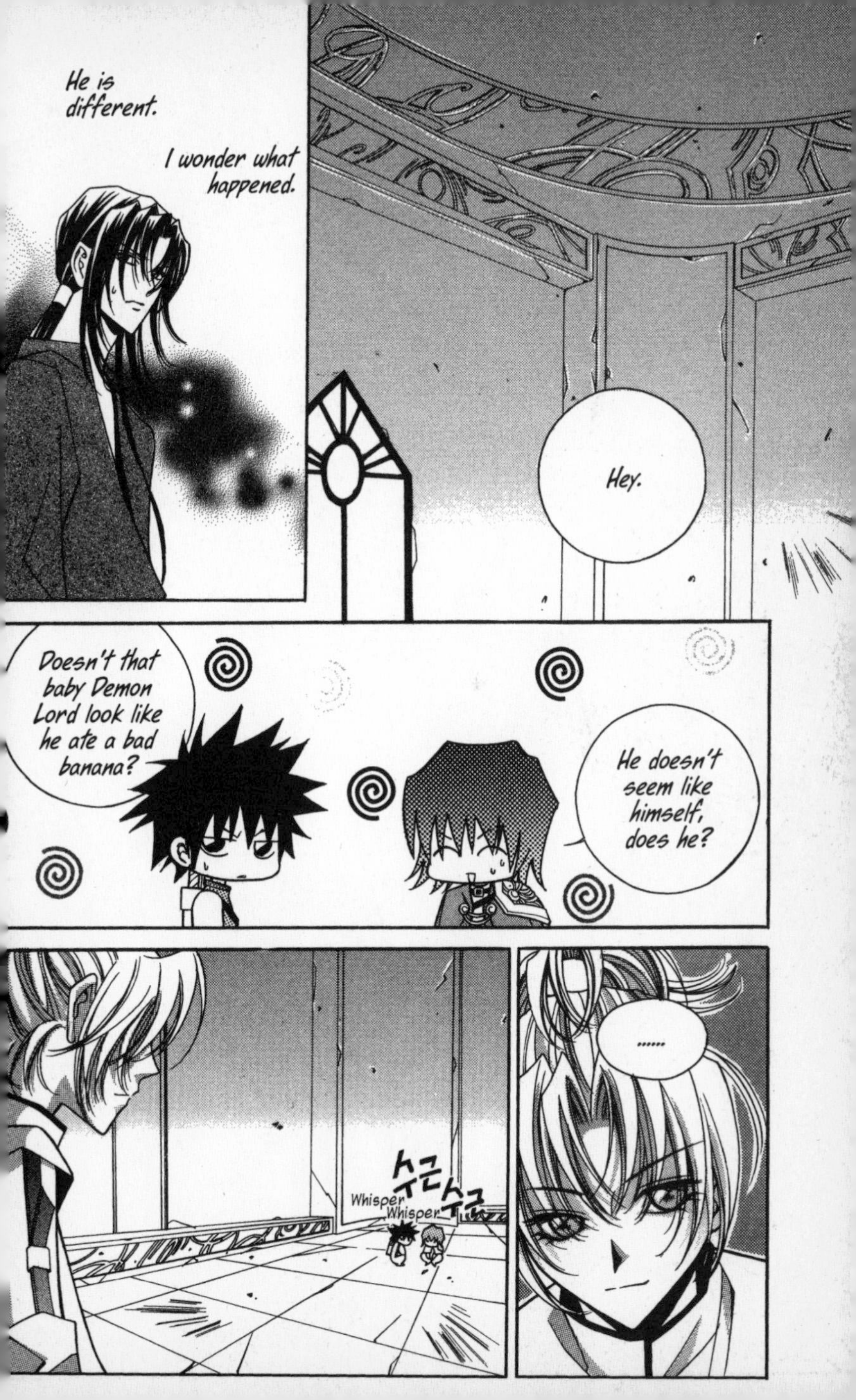
He is different.
I wonder what happened.
Hey.
Doesn't that baby Demon Lord look like he ate a bad banana?
He doesn't seem like himself, does he?
수근수근
Whisper Whisper
......

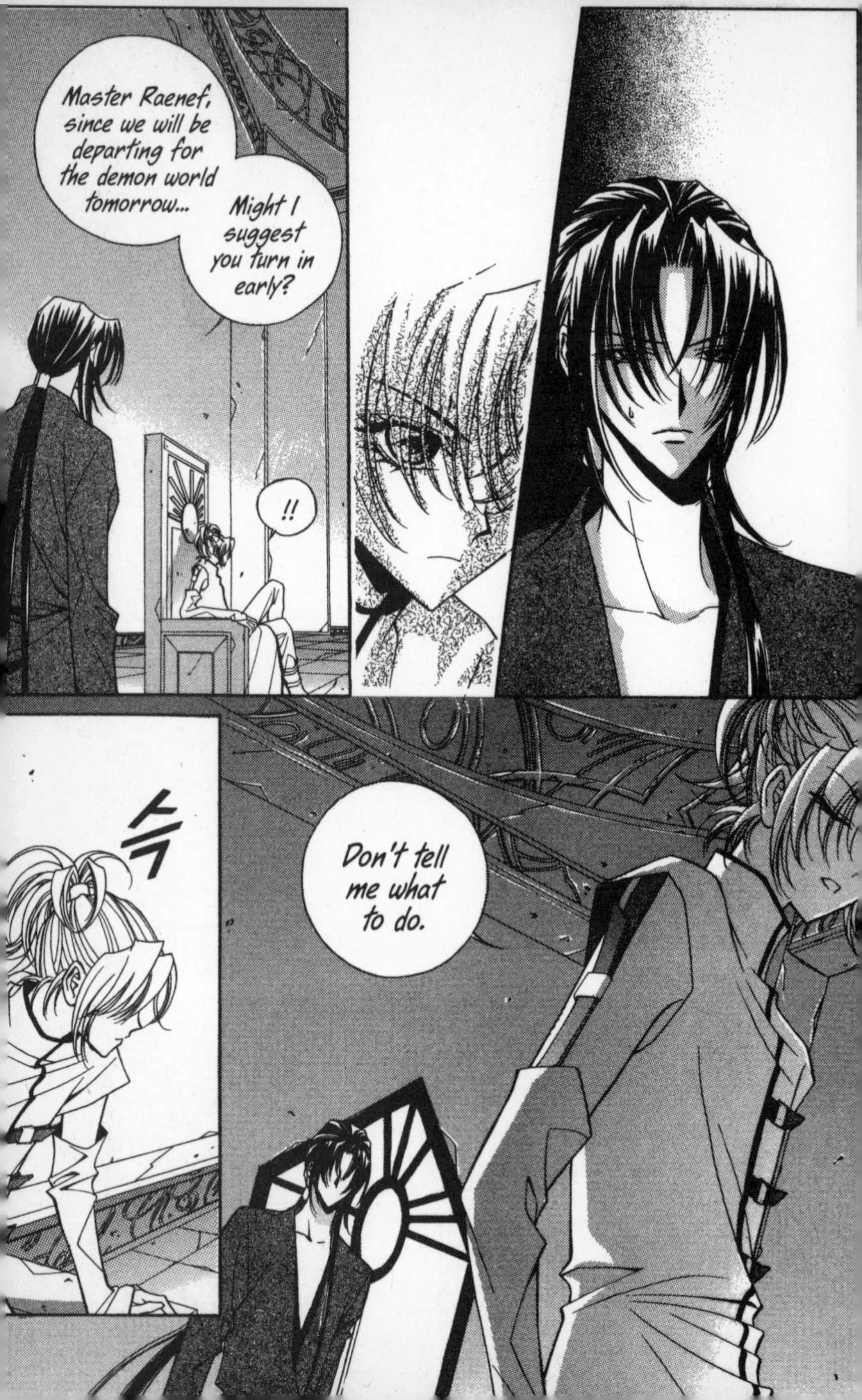
Master Raenef, since we will be departing for the demon world tomorrow...
Might I suggest you turn in early?
!!
Don't tell me what to do.

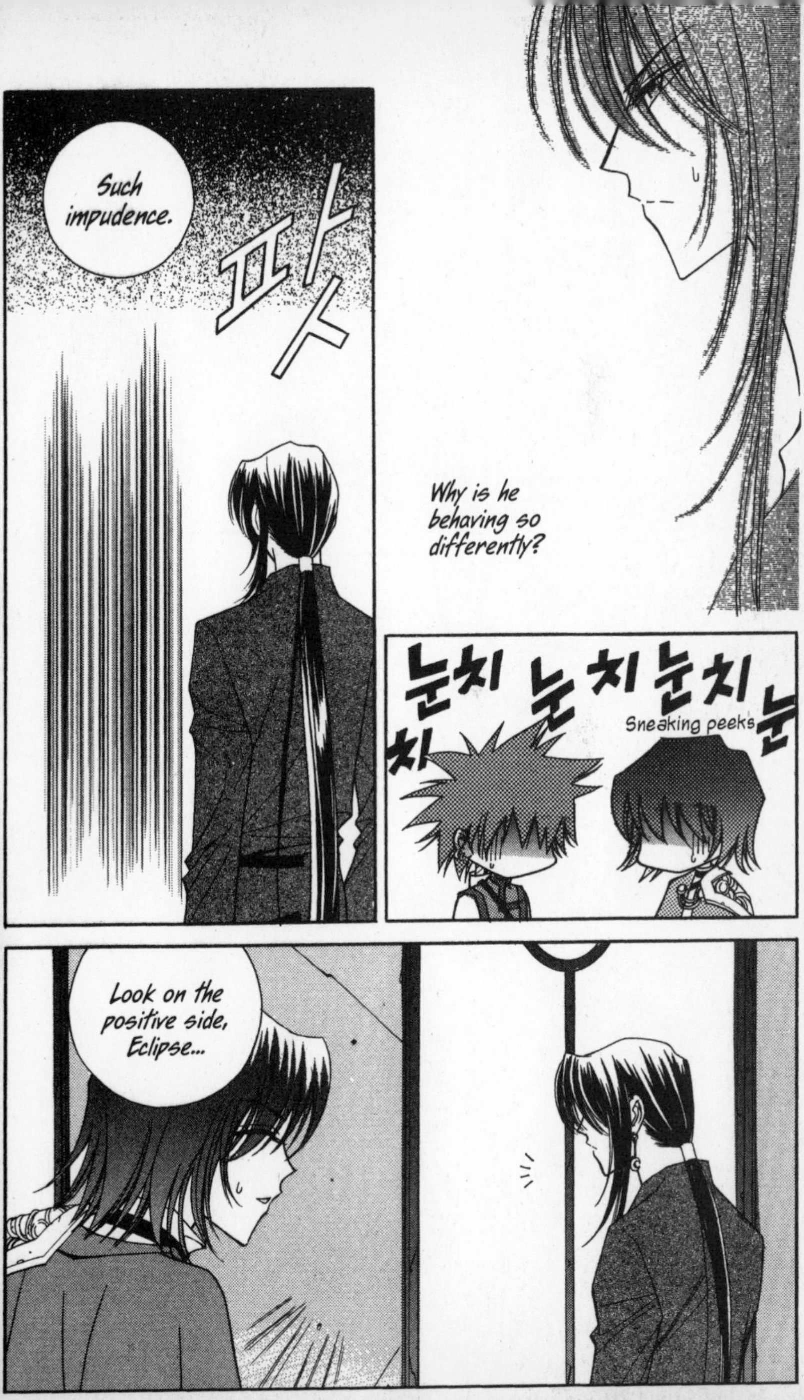
Why is he behaving so differently?
눈치 눈치 눈치 눈치 눈
Sneaking peeks
Such impudence.
팟
Look on the positive side, Eclipse...

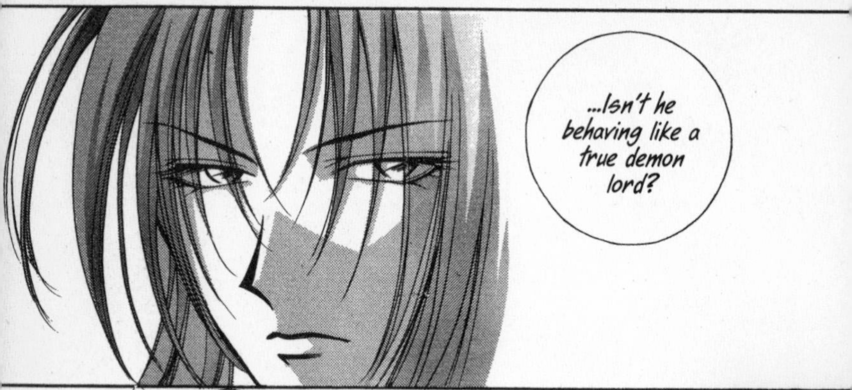
...Isn't he behaving like a true demon lord?

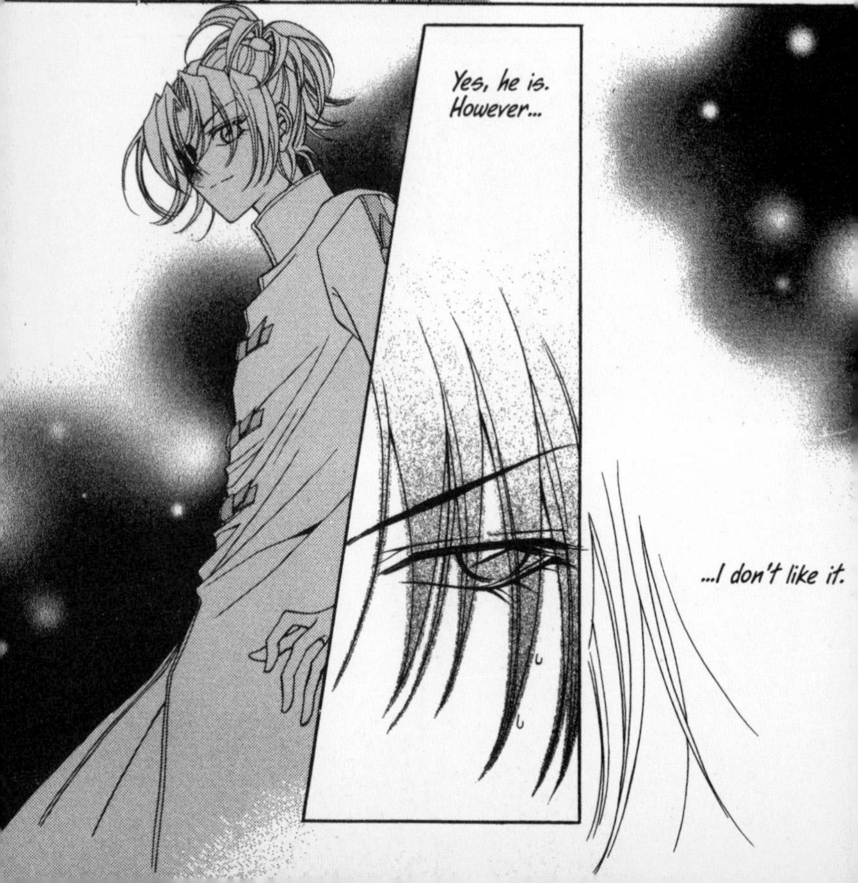
Yes, he is. However...
...I don't like it.

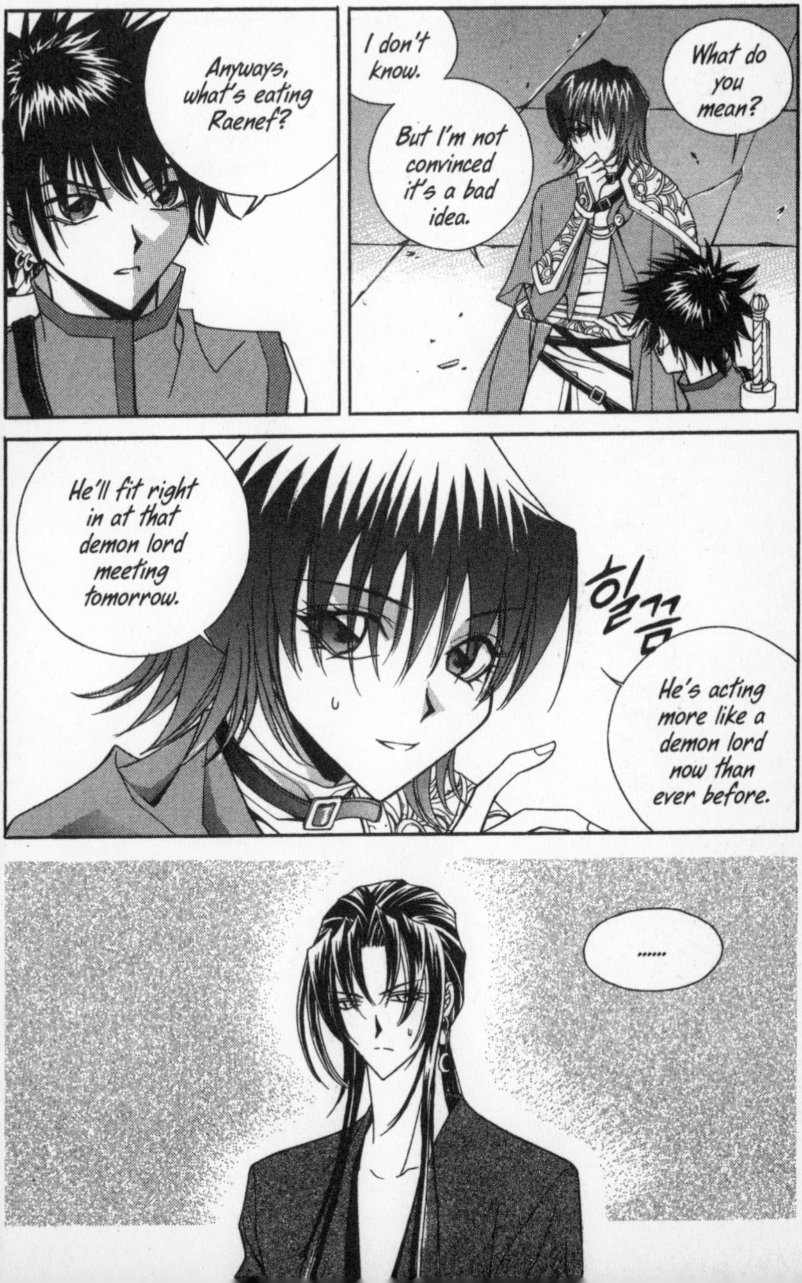
Anyways, what's eating Raenef?
I don't know.
But I'm not convinced it's a bad idea.
What do you mean?
He'll fit right in at that demon lord meeting tomorrow.
힐끔
He's acting more like a demon lord now than ever before.
......

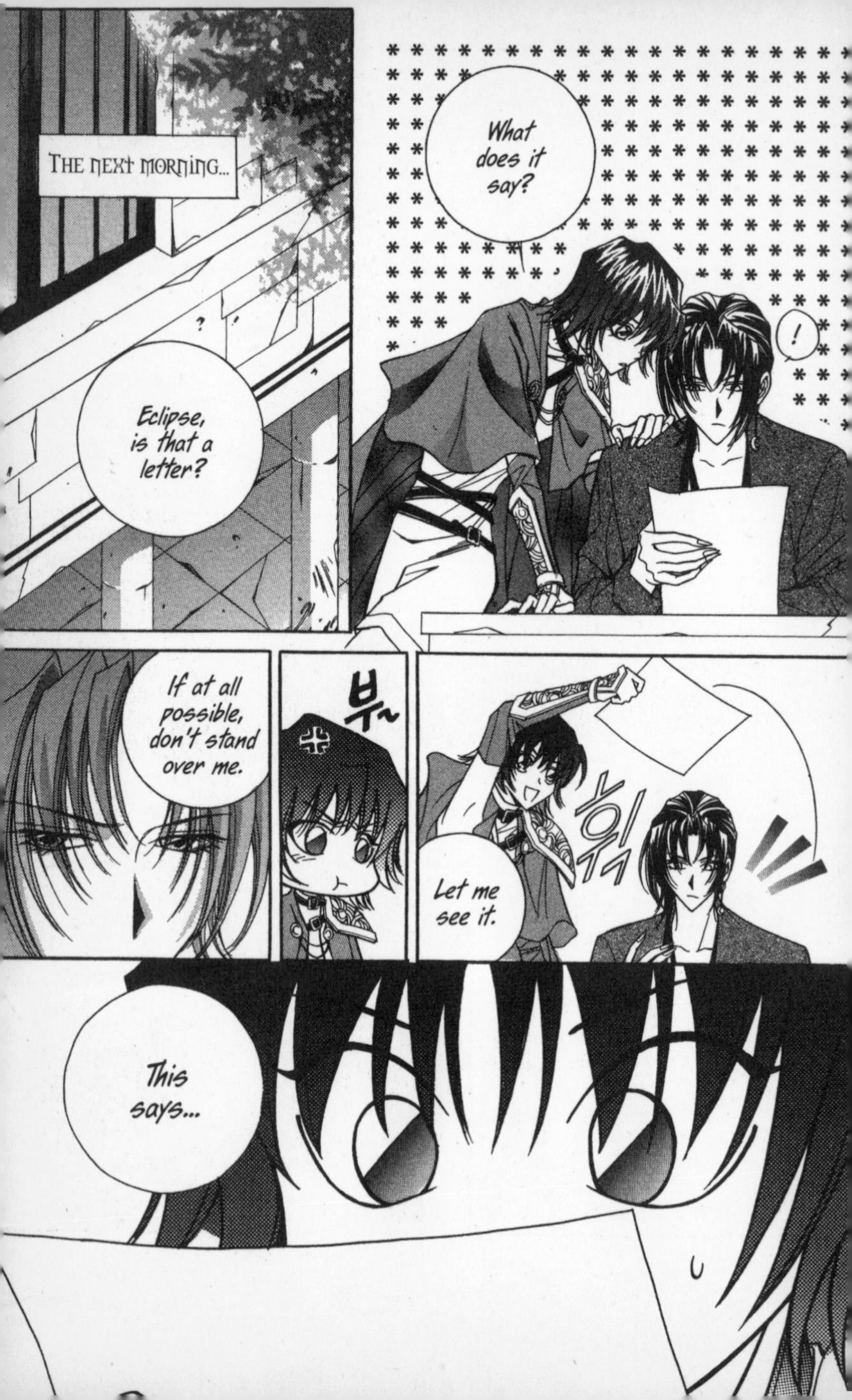
The next morning...
Eclipse, is that a letter?
What does it say?
!
If at all possible, don't stand over me.
부~
Let me see it.
This says...

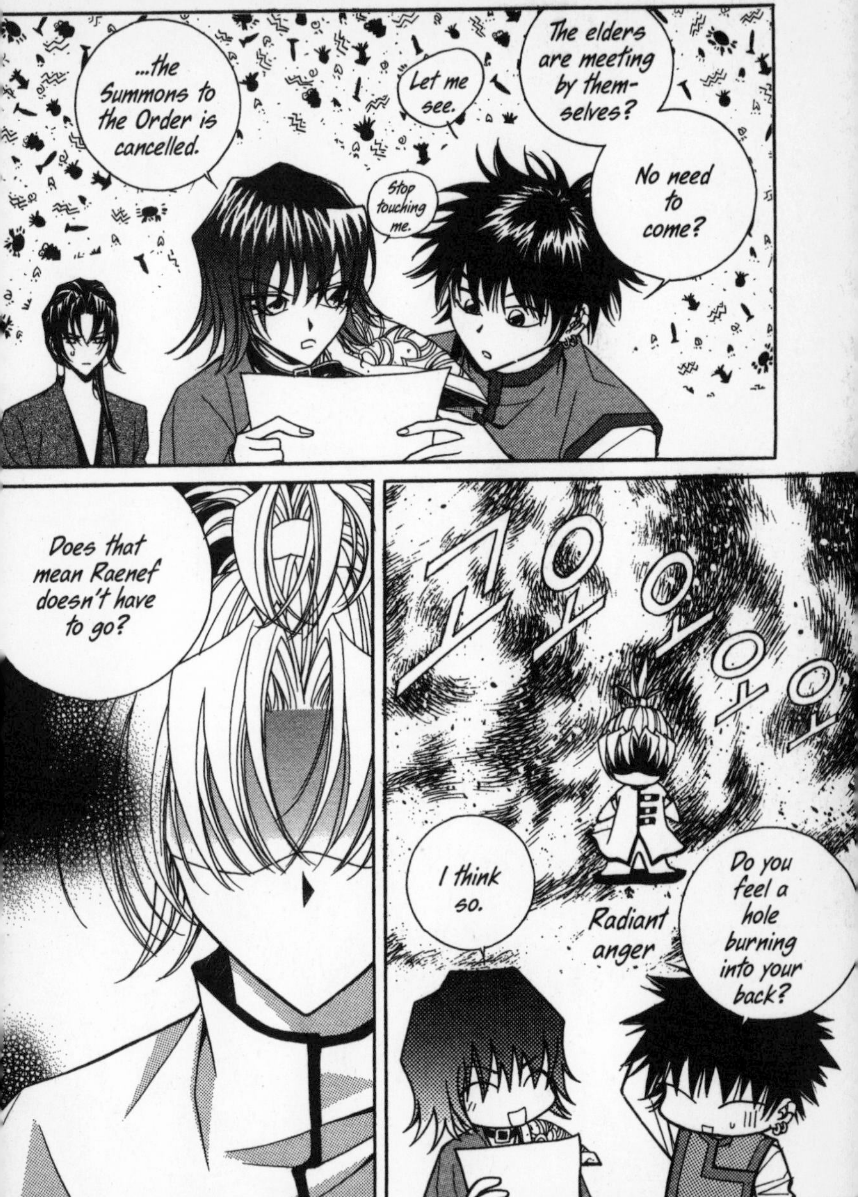
...the Summons to the Order is cancelled.
Let me see.
Stop touching me.
The elders are meeting by themselves?
No need to come?
Does that mean Raenef doesn't have to go?
ZOYOYOYOY
I think so.
Radiant anger
Do you feel a hole burning into your back?

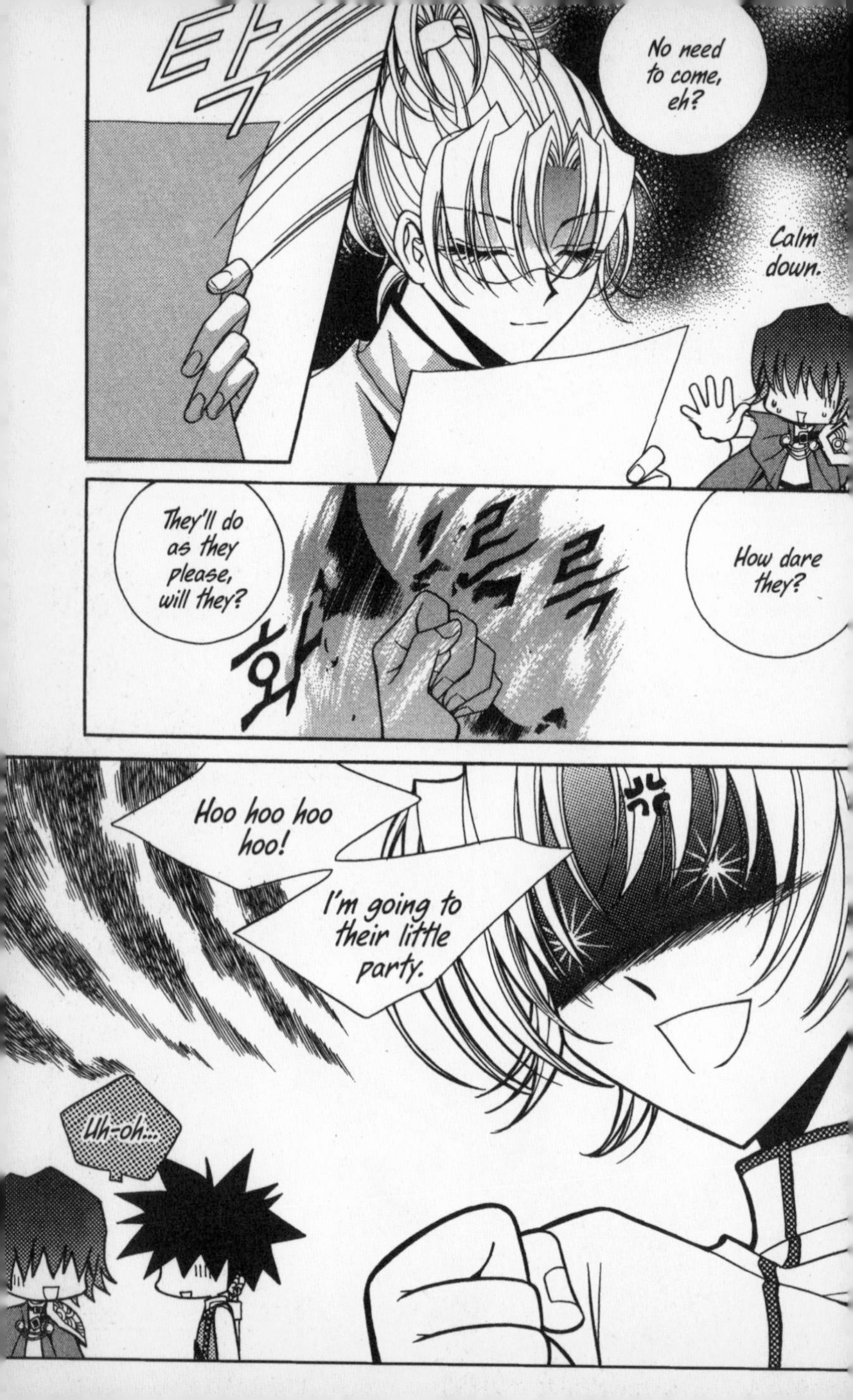
No need to come, eh?
Calm down.
They'll do as they please, will they?
How dare they?
Hoo hoo hoo hoo!
I'm going to their little party.
Uh-oh...

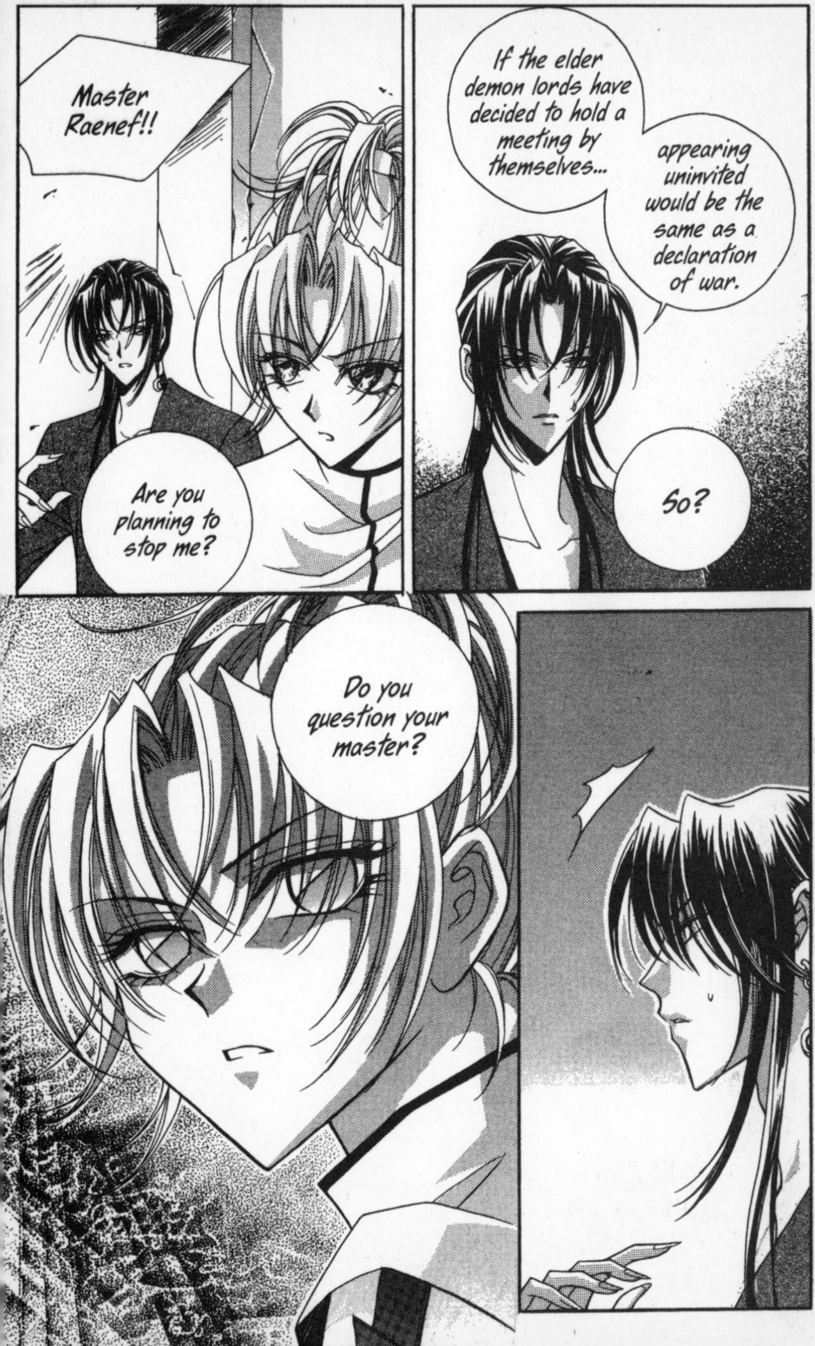
Master Raenef!!
Are you planning to stop me?
If the elder demon lords have decided to hold a meeting by themselves...
appearing uninvited would be the same as a declaration of war.
So?
Do you question your master?

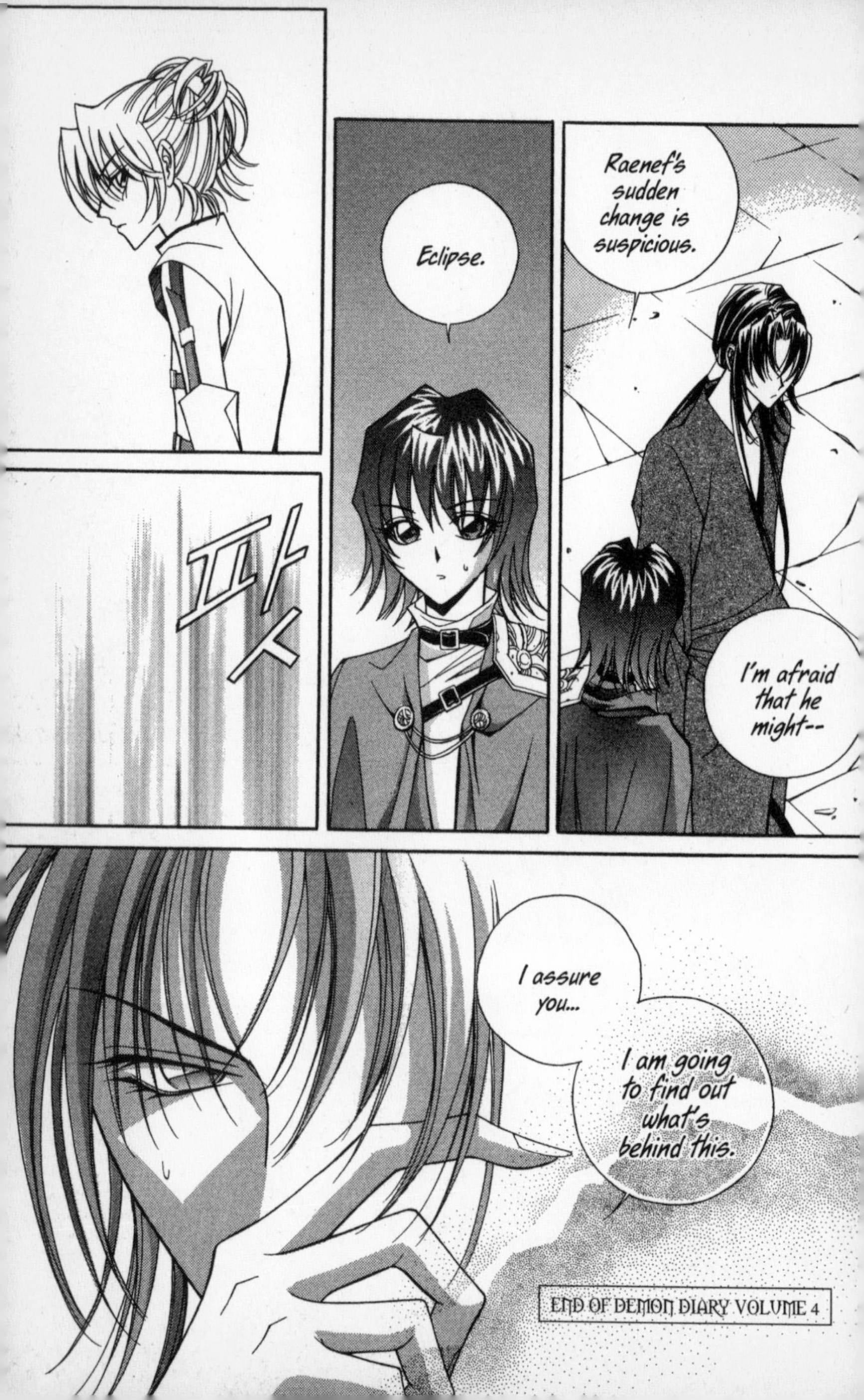
Raenef's sudden change is suspicious.
I'm afraid that he might--
Eclipse.
I assure you...
I am going to find out what's behind this.
END OF DEMON DIARY VOLUME 4

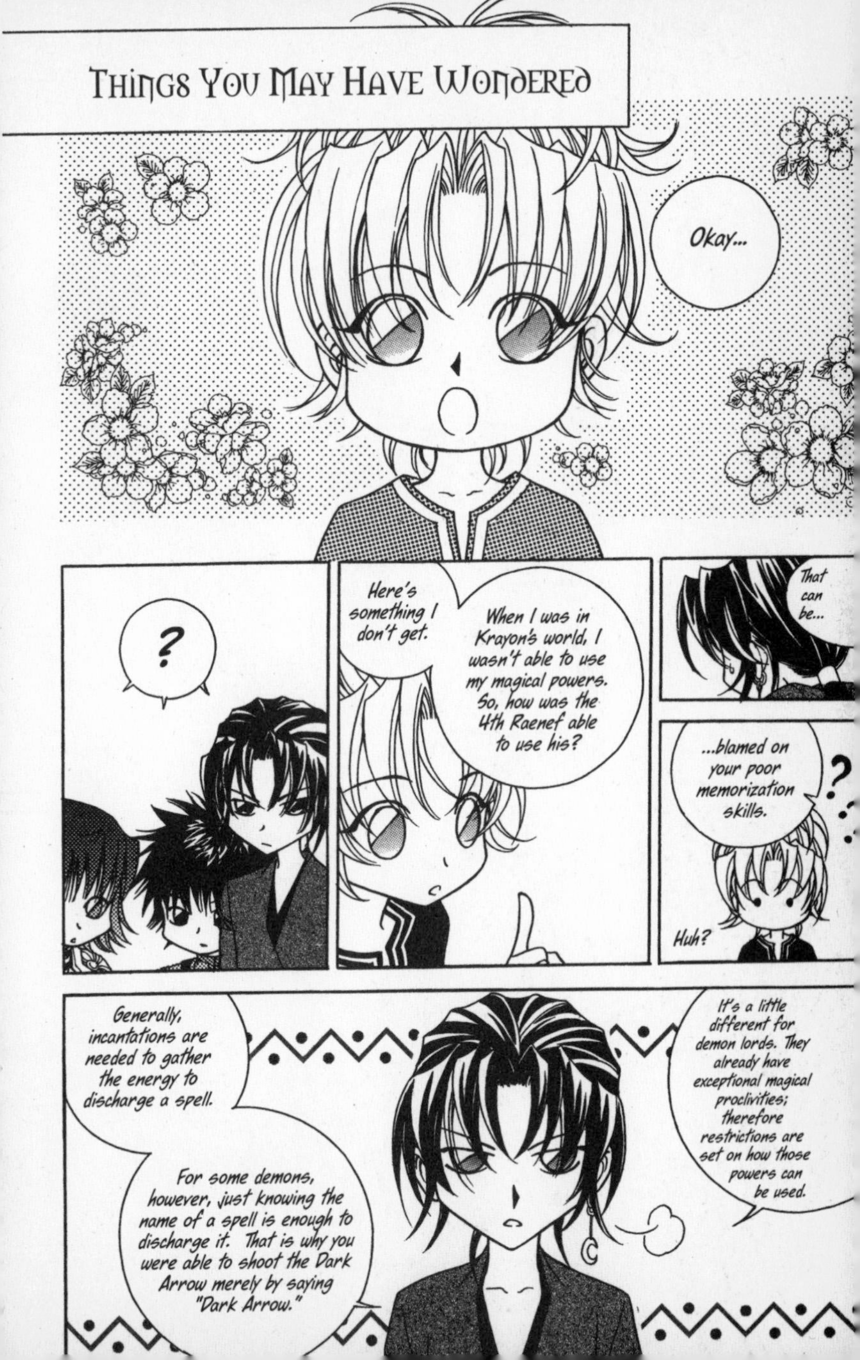

Things You May Have Wondered
Okay...
?
Here's something I don't get.
When I was in Krayon's world, I wasn't able to use my magical powers. So, how was the 4th Raenef able to use his?
That can be...
...blamed on your poor memorization skills.
Huh?
Generally, incantations are needed to gather the energy to discharge a spell.
For some demons, however, just knowing the name of a spell is enough to discharge it. That is why you were able to shoot the Dark Arrow merely by saying "Dark Arrow."
It's a little different for demon lords. They already have exceptional magical proclivities; therefore restrictions are set on how those powers can be used.

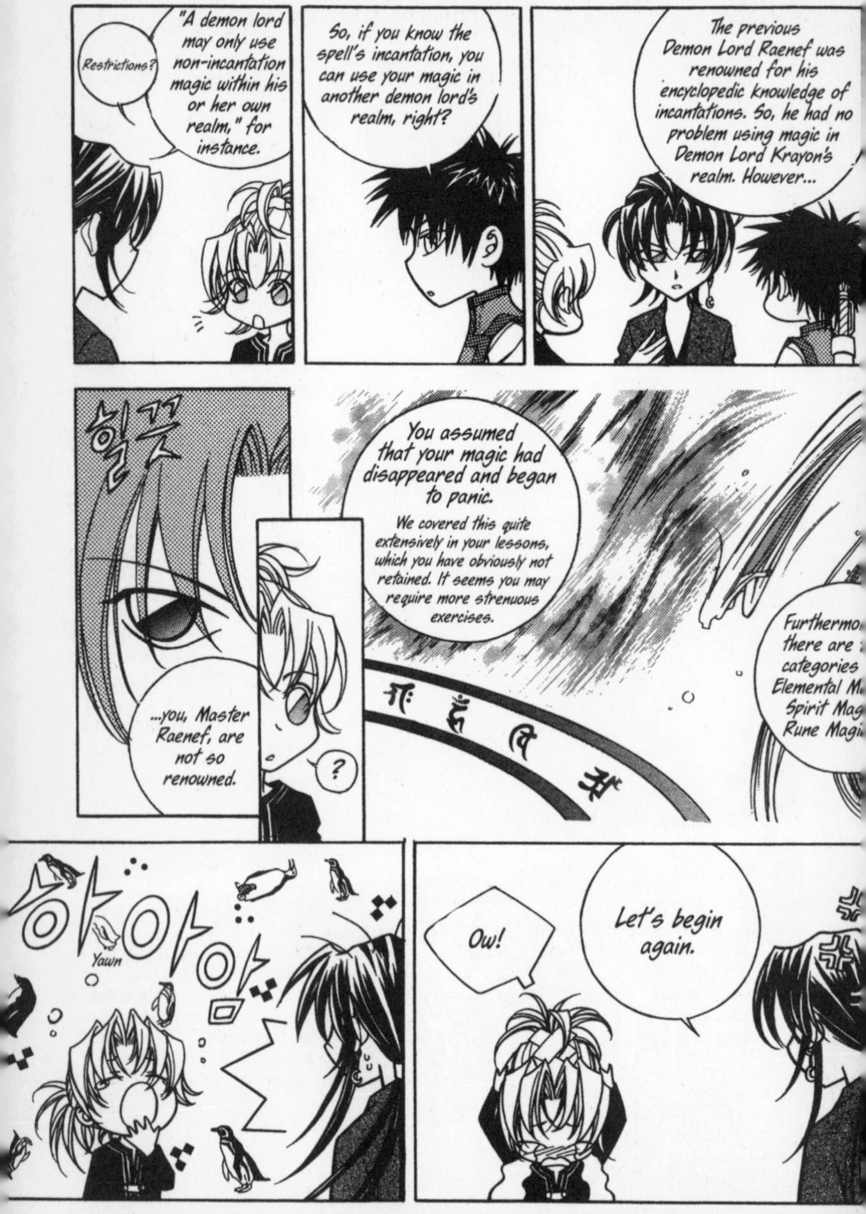
Restrictions?
"A demon lord may only use non-incantation magic within his or her own realm," for instance.
So, if you know the spell's incantation, you can use your magic in another demon lord's realm, right?
The previous Demon Lord Raenef was renowned for his encyclopedic knowledge of incantations. So, he had no problem using magic in Demon Lord Krayon's realm. However...
힐끗
...you, Master Raenef, are not so renowned.
?
You assumed that your magic had disappeared and began to panic.
We covered this quite extensively in your lessons, which you have obviously not retained. It seems you may require more strenuous exercises.
하아아암
Yawn
Ow!
Let's begin again.

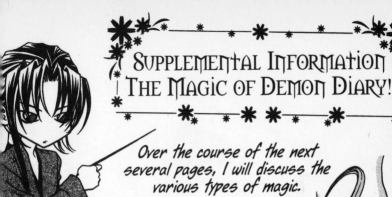

Supplemental Information
The Magic of Demon Diary!

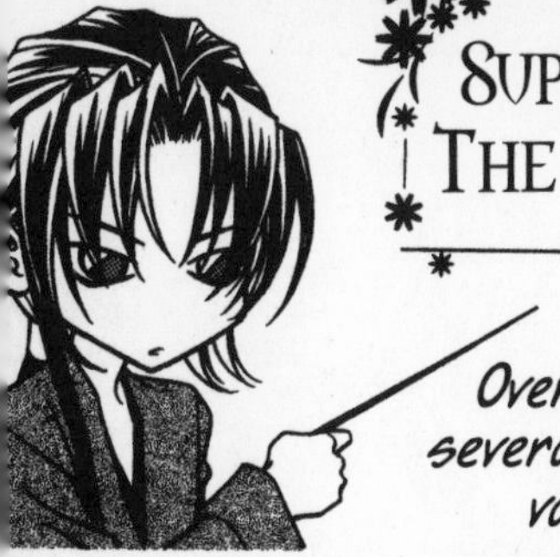

Over the course of the next several pages, I will discuss the various types of magic.

There are several categories at work within the world of Demon Diary.

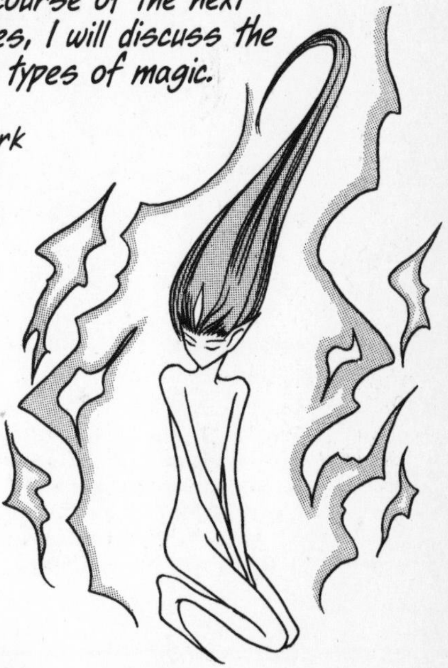

1. Spirit Magic

As the title suggests, Spirit Magic describes any magic that involves the spirit world. Spirits exist in numerous incarnations: fire spirits, wind spirits, terra spirits, etc. There are spirits associated with nature, anger and the mind. Once a spirit is summoned and a contract is sealed, it is indissoluble unless: a) the contract is cancelled, b) the spirit dies or c) the summoner dies.

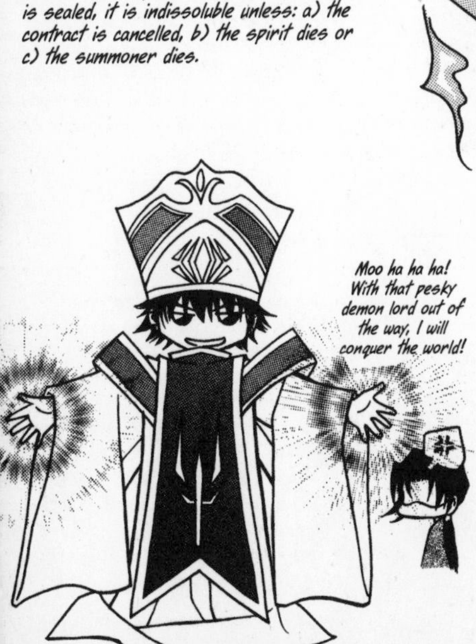
Moo ha ha ha! With that pesky demon lord out of the way, I will conquer the world!

2. Restorative Magic

Generally performed by clerics to heal wounds. There is a Restorative Magic Spell that can cure disease and bring the nearly-dead back from the edge; however it steals some of the lifespan of the user and it is therefore termed "Sacrifice Magic." Demons can use Restorative Magic, but they can only heal themselves and not others.

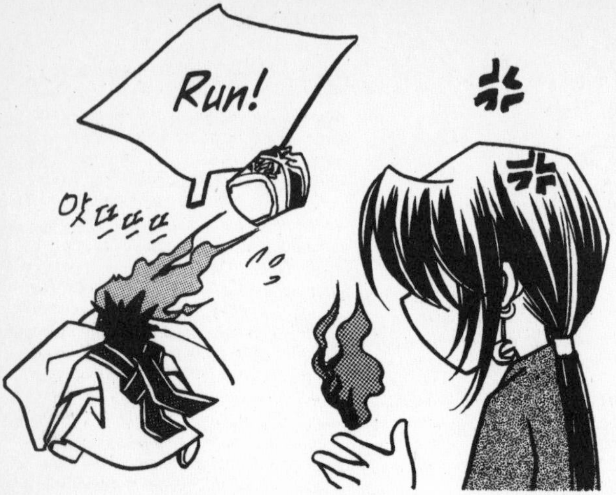
Run!
앗뜨뜨뜨

3. Divine Magic

Divine Magic is, of cours used by clerics, who call upon their respective go for power. A few Divine Magic Spells are effectiv against all manner of lif but Divine Magic is most often used to attack demons. Recall how Chri when he first met Maste Raenef, believed him to b a normal human. Clerics can use either Restorati or Divine Magic but seld both. Rare clerics have strong Divine Magic, and the ability to use both Restorative and Divine Magic, though typically on high clerics fall into this category. Chris has the ability to use both Restorative and Divine Magic.

4. Elemental Magic

A magic that uses the elements to either attack or defend. For example, using fire to create a fireball, freezing water to construct an Ice Arrow, shaping air to form a Magic Shield, etc. It is a category of magic that requires intense concentration and memorization. There are up to 9 levels of Elemental Mag users, with 9 being the highest. A level 9 user must have tremendous strength and discipline in order for the elements to reside within his or her body. Mortals can generally reach level 6 or 7, and a few exceptional individuals have achieved level 8. We have yet to see a mortal at level 9.

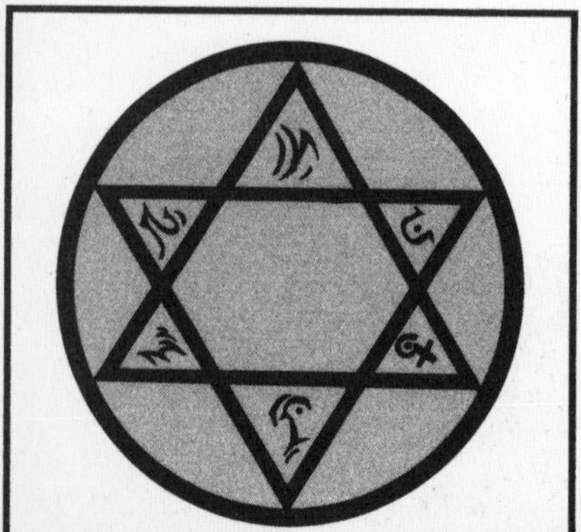

5. Rune Magic

Spells that use diagrams as focal points in ord to attack and defend. Diagrams may be drawn midair with a finger or on the ground with a cane. The more complex the diagram, the more powerful the magic. Of course, only a person with magic powers can perform Rune Magic. If non-magical person were to draw a magical diagram, they would merely find themselves in possession of an attractive doodle. The diagra that Chris used to summon Master Raenef to t Rased Temple was, of course, a Rune used for summoning and teleportation.

6. Dark Magic

Ha ha! It's Dark Arrow!

Users of "pure" magic or users who call forth the powers of the demon are Dark Magic users. Only demons can draw upon their natural magical powers to use Dark Magic. They are also the only beings that can draw upon their magic without using incantations. Mortals must memorize incantations and draw magic into their bodies or "borrow" a demon's powers to use Dark Magic. (Once a demon's powers are "borrowed," the mortal must convert the borrowed powers to Dark Magic, else the borrowed powers will be useless.) The Dark Arrow that Master Raenef so often uses has an incantation that a mortal must recite in order to employ it. As a demon lord, Master Raenef need only say, "Dark Arrow!" and the spell is realized. It is necessary to note that casting a spell without an incantation is only possible in a demon's own realm.

When a demon lord is in another demon lord's realm, he or she must use incantations. For that reason, nothing happened when Master Raenef shouted "Dark Arrow!" in Master Krayon's world. Yet Demon Lord Raenef IV made a practice of learning every incantation before practicing the use of its spell. That is why he could use magic in Master Krayon's world. In Master Krayon's case, he left his corporeal self in his world and sent a shadow self into Master Raenef's world and was able to draw upon his corporeal self for power. It's a little confusing and thus has been omitted from the story.

There are also Time Magic Spells, Air Magic Spells, and other rarely-used Magics. Often these are handed down only within a particular family and cannot be performed by anyone outside of that family.

With that, I conclude the somewhat difficult lesson of Categorical Magic.

Please feel free to consult with me during office hours should you have any additional questions about our subject matter.

Master Raenef!!

Z Z

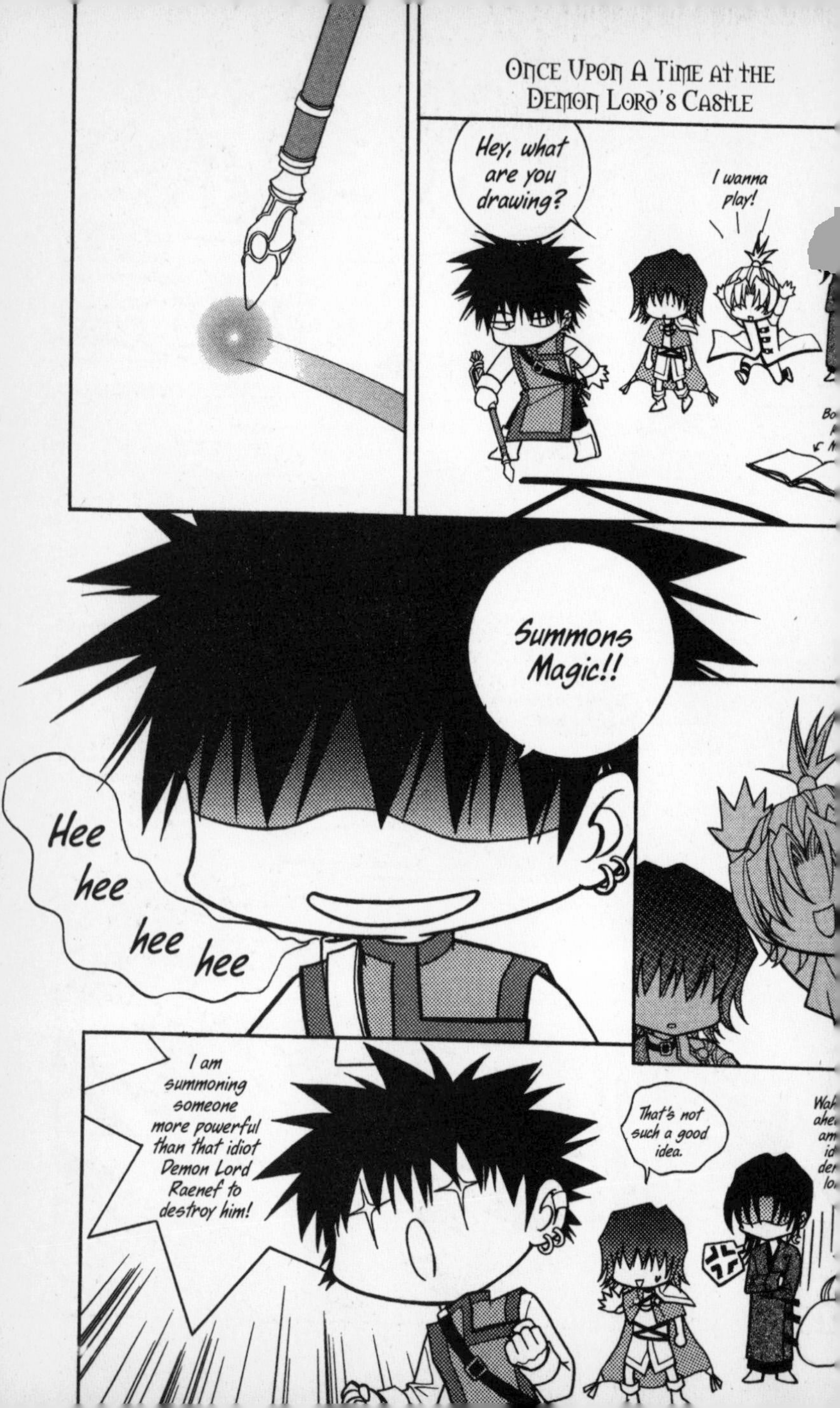
Once Upon A Time at the Demon Lord's Castle
Hey, what are you drawing?
I wanna play!
Summons Magic!!
Hee hee hee hee
I am summoning someone more powerful than that idiot Demon Lord Raenef to destroy him!
That's not such a good idea.

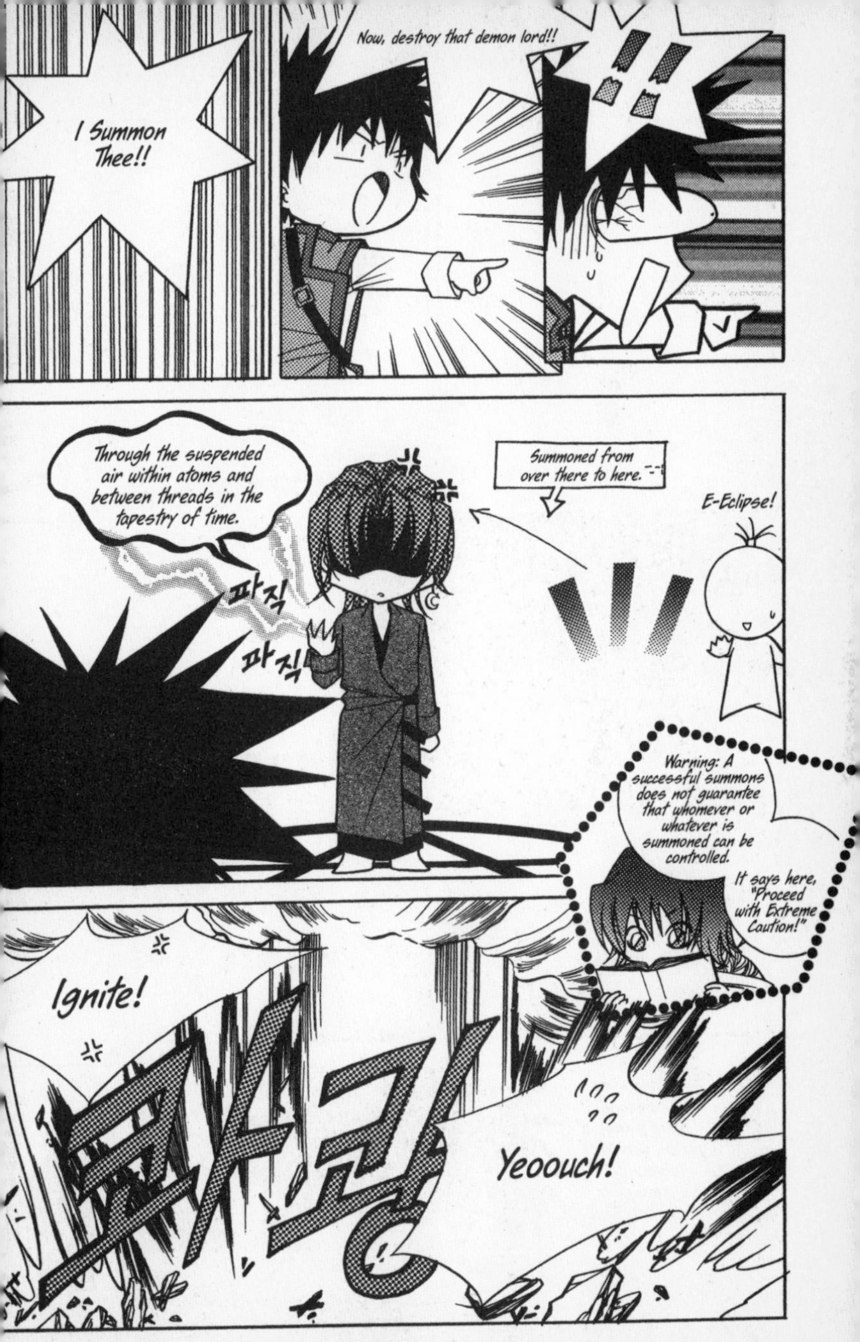
I Summon Thee!!
Now, destroy that demon lord!!
!!
Through the suspended air within atoms and between threads in the tapestry of time.
파직
파직
Summoned from over there to here.
E-Eclipse!
Warning: A successful summons does not guarantee that whomever or whatever is summoned can be controlled.
It says here, "Proceed with Extreme Caution!"
Ignite!
Yeoouch!

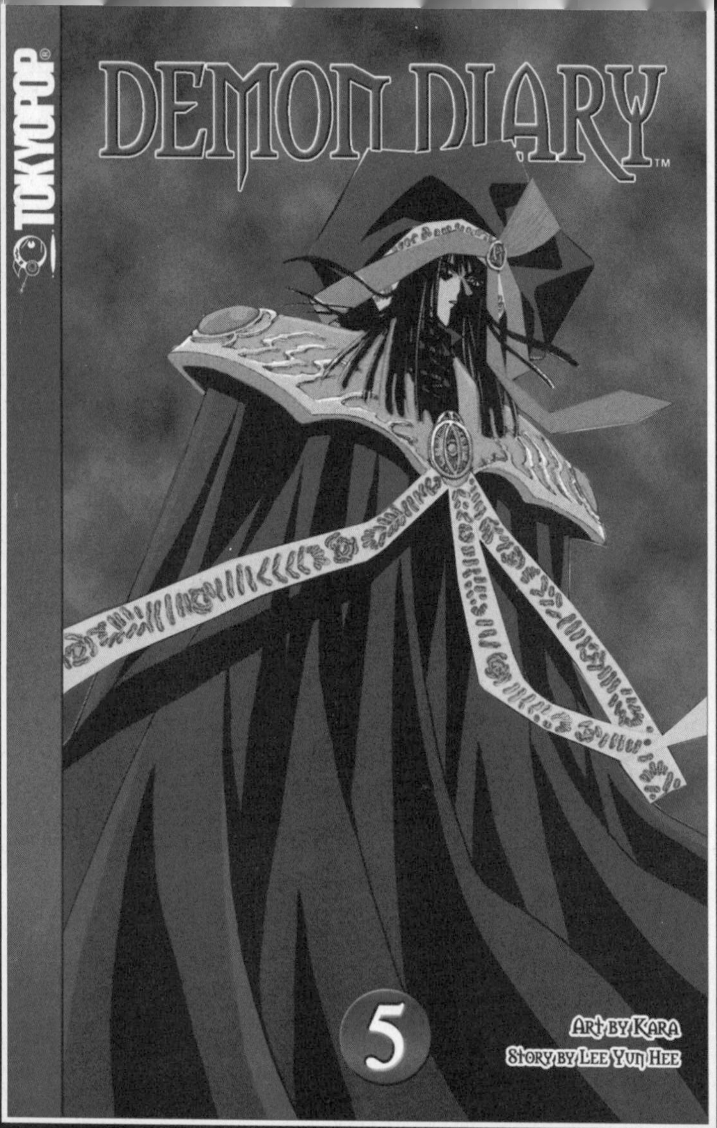
TOKYOPOP®
DEMON DIARY™
5
Art by Kara
Story by Lee Yun Hee

PREVIEW FOR VOLUME 5

At last, Demon Lord Raenef the Fifth is ready to reign in terror...so why isn't anyone happy about it? While Eclipse, Erutis, and Chris try to unravel the mystery of Raenef's new frightening and terrible personality, a very unexpected guest arrives with revelations about Raenef the Fourth's untimely demise. This information could prevent Raenef the Fifth from suffering an early death...if his new headstrong behavior doesn't kill him first!

DEMON DIARY

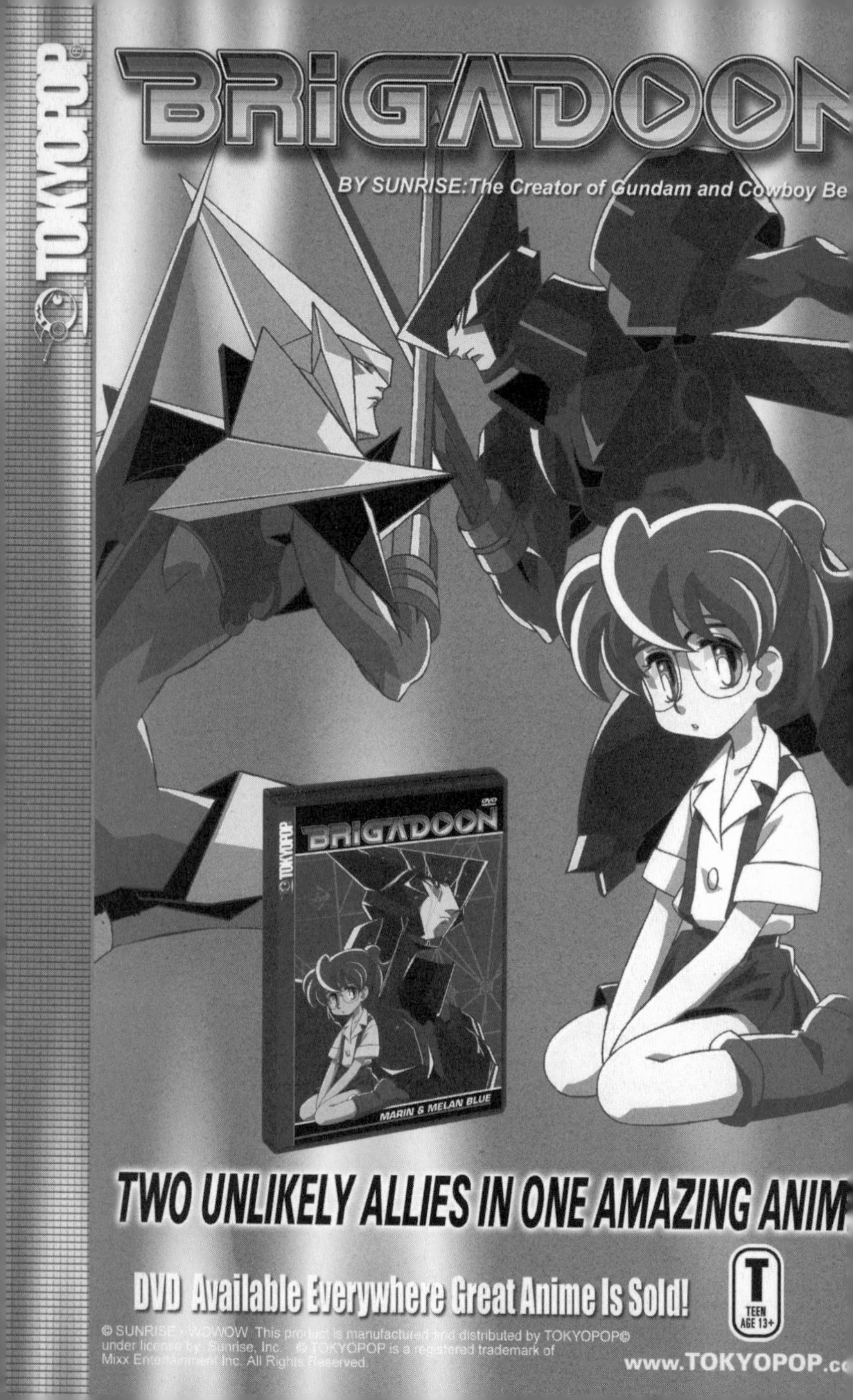
TOKYOPOP
BRIGADOON
BY SUNRISE: The Creator of Gundam and Cowboy Be
DVD
TOKYOPOP
BRIGADOON
MARIN & MELAN BLUE
TWO UNLIKELY ALLIES IN ONE AMAZING ANIM
DVD Available Everywhere Great Anime Is Sold!
T
TEEN AGE 13+
© SUNRISE • WOWOW This product is manufactured and distributed by TOKYOPOP© under license by Sunrise, Inc. © TOKYOPOP is a registered trademark of Mixx Entertainment Inc. All Rights Reserved.
www.TOKYOPOP.co

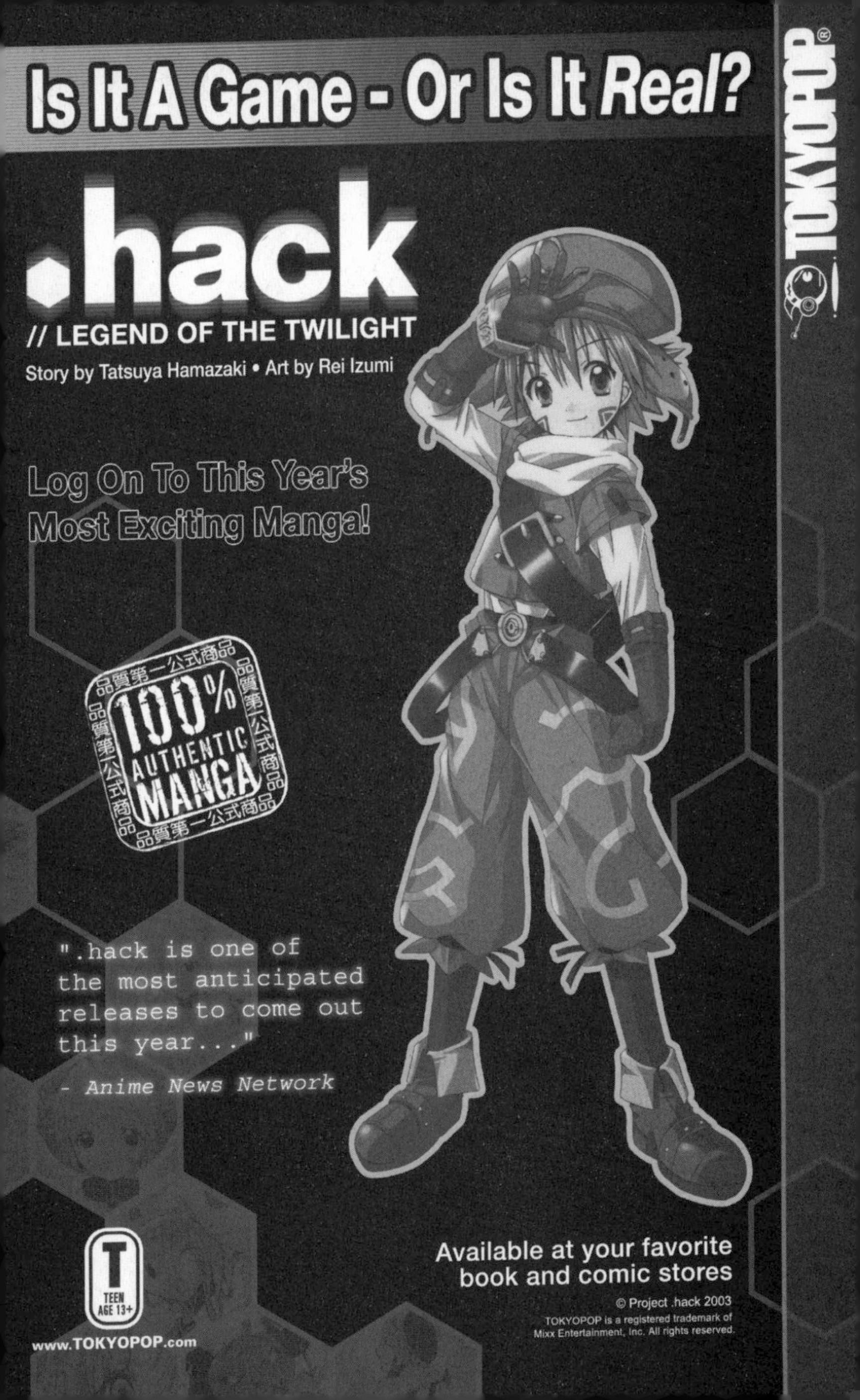
Is It A Game - Or Is It Real?
TOKYOPOP®
.hack
// LEGEND OF THE TWILIGHT
Story by Tatsuya Hamazaki • Art by Rei Izumi
Log On To This Year's Most Exciting Manga!
品質第一公式商品
100% AUTHENTIC MANGA
".hack is one of the most anticipated releases to come out this year..."
- Anime News Network
T TEEN AGE 13+
www.TOKYOPOP.com
Available at your favorite book and comic stores
© Project .hack 2003
TOKYOPOP is a registered trademark of Mixx Entertainment, Inc. All rights reserved.

TODAY'S HOTTEST MANGA COMES TO AMERICA

KING of HELL

BY RA IN-SOO

ONLY ONE MAN CAN BRIDGE THE RIFT BETWEEN HERE & HELL

AVAILABLE NOW AT YOUR FAVORITE
BOOK AND COMIC STORES

www.TOKYOPOP.com

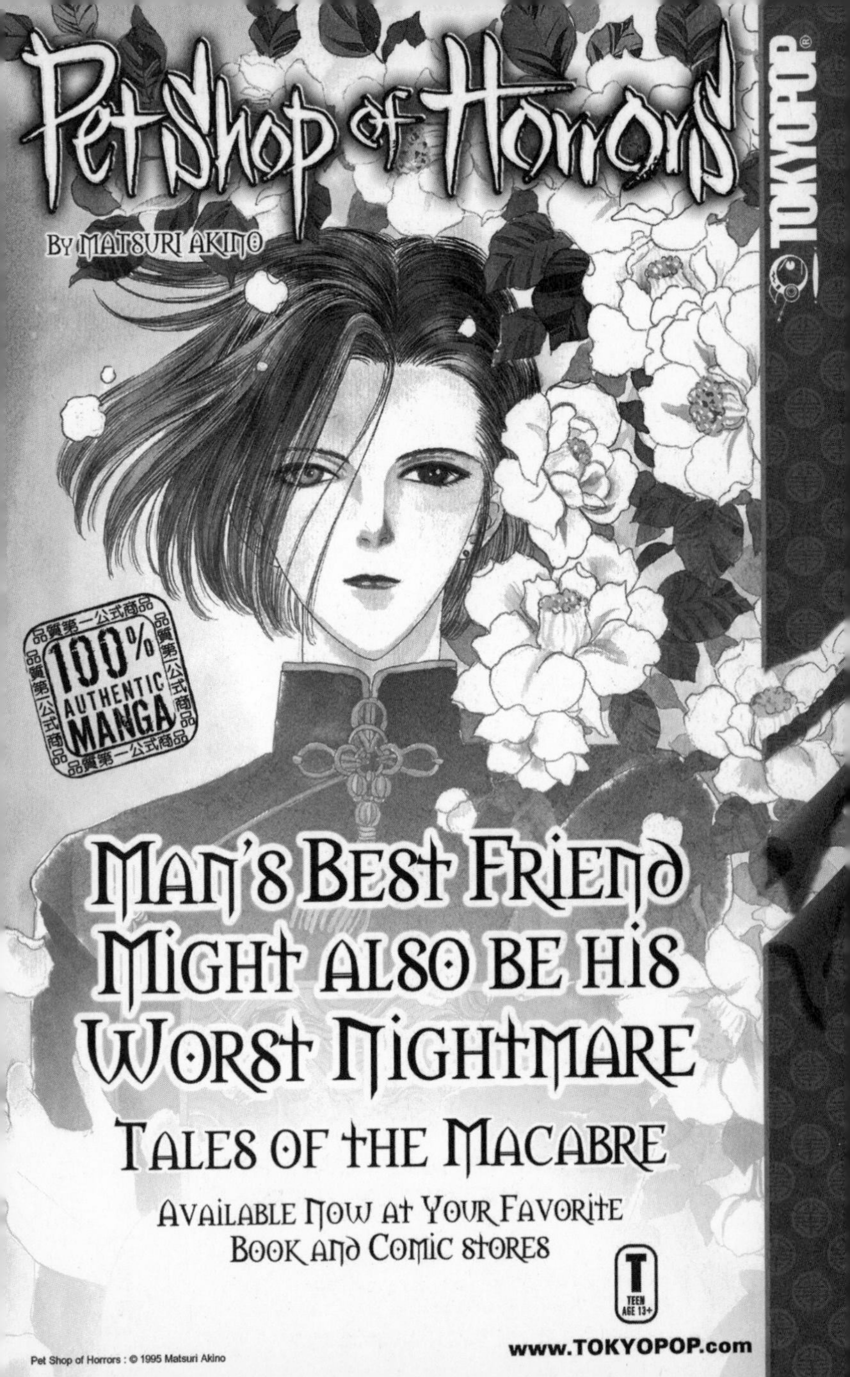
Pet Shop of Horrors
BY MATSURI AKINO
TOKYOPOP®
品質第一公式商品
100% AUTHENTIC MANGA
MAN'S BEST FRIEND
MIGHT ALSO BE HIS
WORST NIGHTMARE
TALES OF THE MACABRE
AVAILABLE NOW AT YOUR FAVORITE
BOOK AND COMIC STORES
T TEEN AGE 13+
www.TOKYOPOP.com

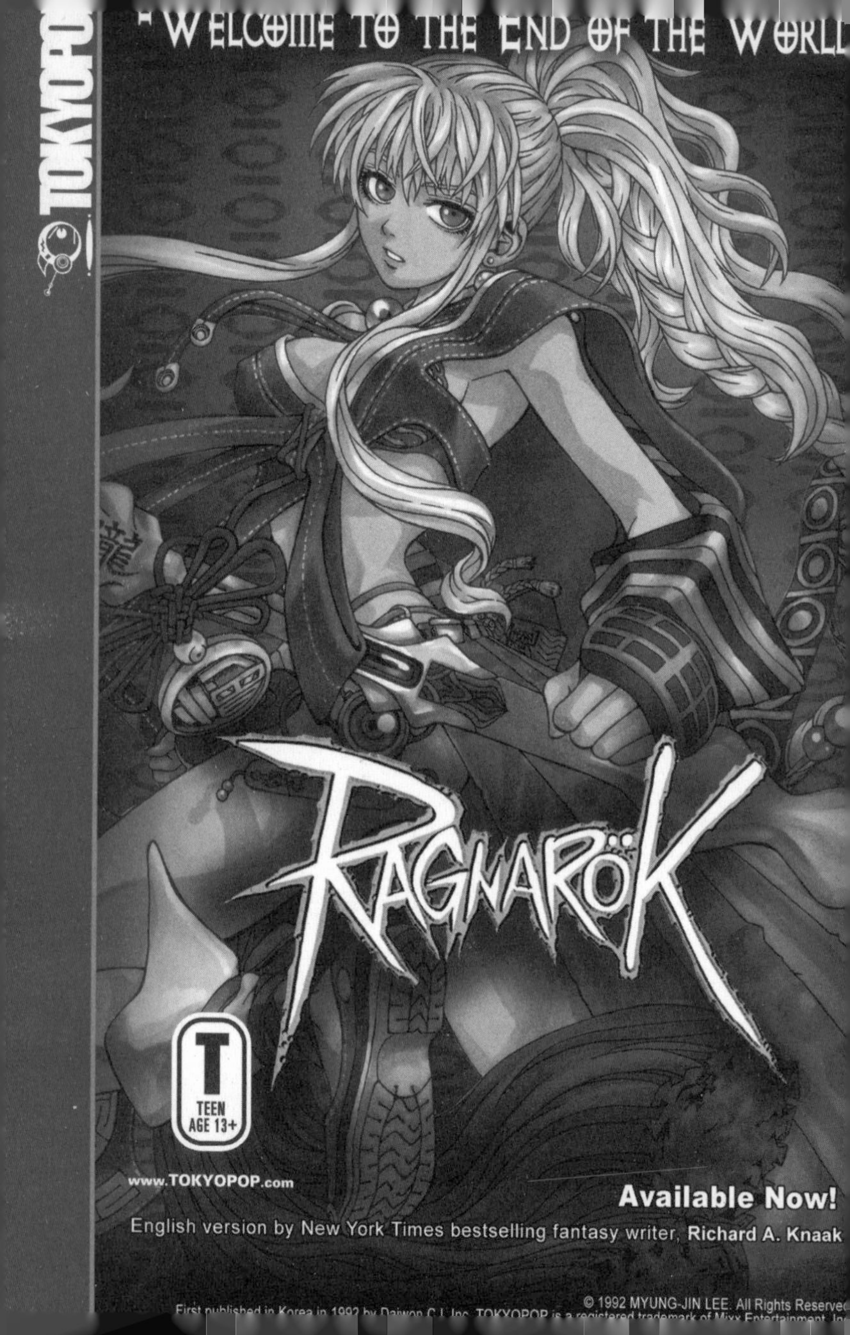